W9-BKR-032

MUSIC AND IDEAS

IN THE SIXTEENTH AND
SEVENTEENTH CENTURIES

The *practice* of music flows—from time to time—with the tide of intellectual history, but the ways in which people *think* about music, as distinct from the musical practice of composing and performing, correspond more closely with general intellectual trends. The sixteenth and seventeenth centuries present a special opportunity to study the relationship between music and ideas because it was a time when the general ferment of ideas and thinking about music often ran parallel, strongly affecting as well the practical composition and performance of music.

Aspects of this period's culture familiar to historians touched music deeply: humanism, religious reform, secularization, the emergence of vernacular literature, documentary historiography, the rise and decline of neo-Platonism, Aristotelian poetics, the scientific movement, the revival of rhetoric, openness to emotional experience, and so on. These intellectual movements and cultural trends are discussed in the following chapters as the author traces the many examples of their penetration in musical thought.

One of the leading scholars of Renaissance and Baroque music and the history of music theory, the late Claude V. Palisca was Henry L. and Lucy G. Moses Professor of Music at Yale University until his retirement in 1992.

STUDIES IN THE HISTORY OF MUSIC THEORY AND LITERATURE

Thomas J. Mathiesen

General Editor

Volume 1

Music and Ideas

in the Sixteenth and Seventeenth Centuries

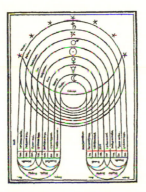

CLAUDE V. PALISCA

UNIVERSITY OF ILLINOIS PRESS

Urbana and Chicago

ISBN-10   0-252-03156-3
ISBN-13   978-0-252-03156-4

⚛ Contents ⚛

ᴈ FOREWORD ᴦ

CLAUDE V. PALISCA'S life as a scholar was dominated to a great extent by his view of music as a branch of knowledge. For him, music was much more than an art, a collection of compositions created across the centuries to serve various purposes, ranging from the enhancement of mundane social functions to the most profound expression of the individual spirit. He was, of course, deeply involved with music as an art and commanded a vast knowledge of repertoire, which was displayed in his many specialized articles, his popular textbook on Baroque music, and above all his multiple editions of Donald J. Grout's famous *History of Western Music* and the anthology he created as its complement, *The Norton Anthology of Western Music*, not to mention his work on the Yale Music Curriculum Project. Like other scholars of his generation, he understood music as representative of the historical and cultural contexts within which it was created, and his writing about music was always informed by a humane perspective.

Palisca's particular perspective was, however, unusual in encompassing the vast intellectual dimension of music represented not only in those technical treatises commonly known as "music theory" but also in the many philosophical, literary, and scientific treatises in which music quite often plays a prominent role. Other scholars recognized selected treatises that addressed particular musical questions in which they were interested, but few if any other scholars could claim much knowledge of Pietro d'Abano, Giorgio Valla, Carlo Valgulio, Antonio Gogava, Francesco Burana, Jacopo Sadoleto, Juan Luis Vives, or Girolamo Mei. In a series of publications extending from his edition of the letters of Girolamo Mei to Vincenzo Galilei and Giovanni Bardi (1960) through his *Humanism in Italian Renaissance Musical Thought* (1985) and *The Florentine Camerata* (1989), coming full circle in his translation of Galilei's *Dialogue on Ancient and Modern Music*, and stopping along the way for specialized studies and comprehensive articles such as his "Theory, Theorists" for the *New Grove Dictionary of Music and Musicians*, Palisca provided a compelling view of the interpenetration of music and the world of ideas.

This was a view that had been only dimly perceived, if at all, by other scholars, and Palisca attempted to make it as clear as possible both through his own work and through his activity as the general editor, beginning with volume 2, of the Music Theory Translation Series published by the Yale University Press. This important series made readily available in English translation, together with extended introductions and—as the series developed—increasingly detailed annotations, treatises written originally in Greek, Latin, Italian, and German by such important authors as Aristides Quintilianus, Boethius, Hucbald, Guido, John, Gaffurio, Zarlino, Burmeister, Kirnberger, and Koch, most of whom will appear in the following chapters.

Palisca's interest in music as an intellectual discipline no doubt both influenced and was influenced by his interest in teaching. He once said that he was really only interested in things that had some pedagogical dimension, and his pedagogical interests were certainly well represented in his work on Grout's textbook, first as a collaborator when Grout was still alive and later as, essentially, author following Grout's death; his development of the *Norton Anthology of Western Music;* his work as director of the seminar on music education, sponsored by the American Office of Education; his service as president of the National Council of the Arts in Education; and of course his long and fruitful tenure as a professor, first at the University of Illinois and then, for the bulk of his career, at Yale University.

The present book reflects this same pedagogical spirit. *Music and Ideas in the Sixteenth and Seventeenth Centuries*, which Palisca intended as much for the general reader as for the specialist, is a kind of *summa* of his life's work. Readers acquainted with his earlier writings will recognize that each of the chapters presents a familiar subject: the relationship between musical style and intellectual history, music as a reflection of universal harmony, the conflict between sense and reason in musical judgment, musical poetics, the influence of humanism on the revival of modal and polyphonic theory, monody and theories of musical expression, the interrelationship of music theory and general science, the development of notions of style, the affections and musical imitation, and musical rhetoric. As the footnotes to the various chapters point out, some of the material is based on Palisca's earlier publications. For the most part, however, these earlier writings were intended for specialists and appeared in academic journals and thematic collective volumes such as *Festschriften* or collections of essays on a particular topic. In *Music and Ideas*, Palisca recasts this material in a series of essays, adding quite a lot that is new. He intended each chapter to be able to stand largely on its own, but he also arranged them to form a sequence leading from the most metaphysical (chapter 2, "Universal Harmony") to the most specific and analytical (chapter 11, "Music and Rhetoric") and, at the end, on to the eighteenth century, beyond the scope of the present book. As a set, these eleven chapters capture for the reader—whether generalist or specialist—the "general ferment of ideas and thinking about music" in the sixteenth and seventeenth centuries that profoundly altered the course of music as it developed in the new "modern" age.

It was Claude Palisca's practice to send me—and others—pre-publication drafts of most of his work for comments and suggestions. When he had received comments from his various readers, he would then do a full revision of his work prior to its release to a copyeditor. Following copyediting, he would often make further changes and improvements. Unfortunately, *Music and Ideas* was not able to benefit from this practice.

In October 2000, I was sent the pre-publication draft of *Music and Ideas*, which Professor Palisca had completed that summer, following revision of an earlier draft written in 1997. On 1 January 2001, I mailed my review, but he never saw it. Claude V. Palisca died on 11 January 2001 at the age of 79 as the result of complications from a stroke, suffered unexpectedly just a few days earlier.

Following his death, Elizabeth Keitel, Professor Palisca's wife, asked me to see through to publication his two final books: the translation, with introduction and annotations, of Galilei's *Dialogue on Ancient and Modern Music*, which was intended for the Music Theory Translation Series; and *Music and Ideas*. On the basis of my long scholarly collaboration with Professor Palisca, extending over twenty-five years, I agreed, well aware of both the responsibility and the difficulties involved in trying to pick up and complete someone else's work. By the end of 2001, I had completed my work on Galilei, and Yale University Press eventually published the book at the end of 2003. I then began to think about *Music and Ideas*.

Inasmuch as Professor Palisca had not seen any of the comments on the pre-publication draft of *Music and Ideas* and had not therefore undertaken any of the revisions he would normally have made, I found myself in a difficult position. Revisions, expansions, and corrections to the manuscript did have to be made in order to complete the work, but I, of course, could not know precisely what he would have done. Professor Palisca normally wrote on a computer but also maintained lots of lists, handwritten notes, photocopies, and so on. In my work on *Music and Ideas*, I employed the most recent versions of his computer files and also reviewed all the paper files containing his notes. I thought long and hard about every revision, and in each case, I tried to be guided by my sense of the decision Professor Palisca would have made, had he been able to do so.

As I stated in my preface to Galilei's *Dialogue*, I should reiterate here: whatever I may have contributed as a kind of amanuensis in the final stages, *Music and Ideas in the Sixteenth and Seventeenth Centuries* is Claude V. Palisca's book, from beginning to end. While there is no doubt in my mind that he would surely have made many additional improvements, I hope this book will draw its readers into his view of the relationships between music and ideas, his view of music as a branch of knowledge, and in this way contribute to the legacy of a distinguished scholar.

Thomas J. Mathiesen
Indiana University
October 2004

≈ I ≈

MUSICAL CHANGE AND INTELLECTUAL HISTORY

CURRENTS IN MUSICAL practice flow—from time to time—with the tide of intellectual history, but the ways in which people *think* about music, as distinct from the musical *practice* of composing and performing, correspond more closely with general intellectual trends. The sixteenth and seventeenth centuries present a special opportunity to study the relationship between music and ideas because it was a time when the general ferment of ideas and thinking about music often ran parallel, strongly affecting as well the practical composition and performance of music.

Aspects of this period's culture familiar to historians touched music deeply: humanism, religious reform, secularization, the emergence of vernacular literature, documentary historiography, the rise and decline of neo-Platonism, Aristotelian poetics, the scientific movement, the revival of rhetoric, openness to emotional experience—the list goes on. These intellectual movements and cultural trends will appear over and over again in the following chapters as we trace the many examples of their penetration in musical thought.[1]

Humanism—the revival of ancient philosophy, literature, and arts— was the most potent engine for change in the early modern period. In the field of music, however, humanism operated indirectly because musicians and critics were inspired by only the *idea* of Greek music as the ancient authors described it, not its sound. A few late Greek hymns or odes written in the standard letter notation of Alypius were known, but no one at that time succeeded in transcribing them effectively. Thus,

---

[1]Bibliographical and other details concerning the authors and works mentioned in this introductory chapter will be provided in subsequent chapters. In addition, the Appendix (see pp. 233–42 *infra*) provides a chronological table of primary sources, and a full bibliography of primary and secondary sources appears at the end of the book.

there was no opportunity to study or hear the music that survived from the ancient world.[2]

Fascination with ancient Greek music began long before a serious study of documents revealed its nature. Anyone who read Plato's *Republic* or Aristotle's *Politics* came away marveling at music's power over human feelings and its influence on moral character. These works of philosophy were translated much earlier than those specifically or technically about music, and they put before thoughtful musicians a new set of goals and the means to reach them.

Plato showed paths through which the harmony of the world could touch the spirit of the musician and by which the musician could influence the moral character and emotional life of the listener. His dialogues, translated into Latin and published by Marsilio Ficino (1433–1499) at the end of the fifteenth century, gave a prominent place to music as a force in the structure of the universe, the control of the emotions, and the education of youth.

In *Timaeus*, Plato conceived the cosmos as a harmony of opposites held together by mathematical ratios. The arithmetic, geometric, and harmonic means, which had concrete functions in earlier music theory, mediated the numerical quantities of these opposites. As they revolved, the planets and stars emitted harmonic musical sounds. The human soul, too, was a system of ratios that could be consonant or dissonant, balanced or unbalanced in its elements, elements music could restore to equilibrium. Of those who adopted Plato's ideas on music and cosmology in the sixteenth century, Franchino Gaffurio (1451–1522) was the most widely read.[3]

---

[2]Today, there are many more examples, though most of them fragmentary, extending back to the time of Euripides, and most have been transcribed into modern notation. See Egert Pöhlmann, *Denkmäler altgriechischer Musik*, Erlanger Beiträge zur Sprach- und Kunstwissenschaft, vol. 31 (Nürnberg: Hans Carl, 1970), which includes three examples first published in the seventeenth and eighteenth centuries (nos. 15–17) now considered to be forgeries. For a new edition including many fragments not known in 1970 but omitting those considered to be forgeries as well as the *koine hormasia*, which was known to the sixteenth century through Gioseffo Zarlino's publication of it in 1558, see Egert Pöhlmann and Martin L. West, *Documents of Ancient Greek Music: The Extant Melodies and Fragments* (Oxford: Clarendon Press, 2001).

[3]See chapter 2.

In the *Republic* and *Laws*, Plato spoke enthusiastically of the power of music and critically of the neglect and abuse of that power. Certain melodic-rhythmic styles—*harmoniai* or modes of song—uplifted human morals, strengthened character, and improved mental health, while others weakened and unsettled the mind and customs. "Leave us these two harmoniai [Dorian and Phrygian]—the enforced and the voluntary—that will most beautifully imitate the utterances of men failing or succeeding, the temperate, the brave—leave us these."[4] Thus speaks Socrates in the dialogue, as he goes on to reject the aulos—an instrument resembling the modern oboe—for its capacity to embrace too many different *harmoniai*, including those he deplored such as the Ionian and Lydian. He would retain only the lyre and kithara, instruments associated with Apollo.

Although people of the Renaissance could think of modern parallels for these moral effects of music, how could factors as elemental as modes, scales, poetic meters, and the choice of instruments affect behavior and well-being? This remained a fascinating mystery. Numerous writers in the fifteenth and sixteenth centuries applied Plato's characterizations of the *harmoniai* to the church modes under the misapprehension that they were one and the same. Even though the link was tenuous, theorists and composers felt encouraged to emulate the ancients and aspire to achieve their moral effects. Heinrich Glarean (1488–1563), convinced that he had reconstructed the modes of the ancients, thought he recognized in motets of Josquin des Prez the acclaimed ethical power.[5]

Plato's maxim that the text must govern the music in a song profoundly infused discussions of texted music. Song, he said, is composed of three things: the text, the melody, and the rhythm; and the melody and rhythm must follow the text. Ficino clearly understood this when he translated the Greek as: "melodiam ex tribus constare, oratione, harmo-

---

[4]Plato *Republic* 3.10 (399c): "ταύτας δύο ἁρμονίας, βίαιον, ἑκούσιον, δυστυχούν-των, εὐτυχούντων, σωφρόνων, ἀνδρείων αἵτινες φθόγγους μιμήσονται κάλλιστα, ταύτας λεῖπε"; trans. in *Strunk's Source Readings in Music History* [hereafter *Strunk's Source Readings*], rev. ed., ed. Leo Treitler (New York: Norton, 1998), 11. Standard translations of the Greek philosophers do not adequately render technical musical terms or names of instruments; the extracts in *Strunk's Source Readings* restore the original terminology, accompanied by explanatory footnotes.

[5]See chapter 6.

nia, rhythmus … atqui harmonia et rhythmus orationem sequi debent."[6] But Ficino's Latin was often misinterpreted. Ficino translated Plato's μέλος (*melos*) as *melodia*, λόγος (*logos*) as *oratio*, ἁρμονία (*harmonía*) as *harmonia*, and ῥυθμός (*rhythmos*) as *rhythmus*. The term *melodia* trapped some into thinking that Ficino simply meant "melody" when he was actually defining the complex of elements that comprise a "song." The Greek ἁρμονία has both a broader and more specific meaning than "harmony," referring sometimes to the agreement of elements in a complex whole, or a kind of mode, but here it refers to the pitch organization or the melodic aspect of song. In 1533, Jacopo Sadoleto (1477–1547), one of the first to draw special attention to the dictum, translated directly from the Greek, rendering μέλος as *chorus*, λόγος as *sententia*, and ἁρμονία as *vox*:

> If you ask what procedure is to be maintained in music, I believe that you should consider all of the following: since a chorus consists of three elements, the sense of the words, the rhythm (this is what the term "numerus" means to us) and pitch, the first and most potent of all is the sense of the words, for it is the base and foundation of the others, and by itself has no little power to persuade and dissuade the mind. But, combined with rhythms and modes, it penetrates more deeply, and if, besides, it is melodized with voice and pitch, it takes possession of the whole inner feeling and person.[7]

Unlike Sadoleto, others who quoted the passage tended to read part-music into Ficino's term *harmonia*: Johannes Ott (Grapheus) in the preface to his collection of thirteen Masses in 1539, Gioseffo Zarlino in his *Istitutioni harmoniche* in 1558 and again in *Sopplimenti musicali*, Giovanni Bardi in his discourse addressed to the singer Giulio Caccini of 1578,

---

[6]*Republic* 3.10 (398c–d): "ὅτι τὸ μέλος ἐκ τριῶν ἐστι συγκείμενον, λόγου τε καὶ ἁρμονίας καὶ ῥυθμοῦ.… Καὶ μὴν τήν γε ἁρμονίαν καὶ ῥυθμὸν ἀκολουθεῖν δεῖ τῷ λόγῳ"; trans. Marsilio Ficino in Plato, *Opera* (Venice: Bernardinus de Choris de Cremona et Simon de Luero, impensis Andree Toresani de Asula, 13 August 1491), f. 201.

[7]Jacopo Sadoleto, *De liberis recte instituendis liber* (Venice: Io. Antonius et fratres de Sabio, sumptu et requisitione D. Melchioris Sessae, 1533), f. 42v: "Quod si quaeratur qui modus sit in musicis tenendus, haec ego omnia attendenda esse puto: cum constet chorus ex tribus, sententia, rhythmo (hic enim numerus nobis est) & uoce, primum quidem omnium potissimum sententiam esse, utpote quae si sedes & fundamentum reliquorum, & per se ipsa ualeat non minimum ad suadendum animo uel dissuadendum: numeris autem modisque contorta penetret multo acrius: si uero etiam cantu & uoce fuerit modulata, iam omnis intus sensus & hominem totum possideat." In the Basle edition of 1538, published by Thomas Platterus, the title changed to *De pueris recte ac liberaliter instituendis*. In this later edition, the passage appears on p. 138.

Caccini in the foreword to his *Le Nuove musiche* in 1602, and Giulio Cesare Monteverdi in the preface to his brother Claudio Monteverdi's *Scherzi musicali* in 1607.[8] All of them emphasized the primacy of the word over the music, but the music they knew was very different from the music Plato had in mind. This was the difficulty in understanding the ancient philosophers without the technical Greek writings, which were unknown before the last quarter of the fifteenth century.

The rediscovery of the specifically musical writings of the ancient Greeks began with the recognition that Boethius's *De institutione musica*, revered throughout the Middle Ages as the foundation of musical studies, was really a compendium of Greek music theory. Although manuscript copies of the treatise, written in Latin around 500 C.E., were widely available and could have answered many questions about Greek music, *De institutione musica* was little read by musicians. Moreover, until the fifteenth century, those who did read it did not realize that it was largely based on two Hellenistic authors, Nicomachus of Gerasa and Claudius Ptolemy, and that it transmitted quite faithfully their accounts of Greek music theory.[9]

That the treatise of Boethius translated Greek sources was first noted by Johannes Gallicus de Namur (ca. 1415–1473) in a manuscript treatise *De ritu canendi vetustissimo et novo* of around 1460.[10] To discover that the system of modes and the theory of consonances described there was an imported tradition was devastating to Gallicus but at the same time enlightening and liberating. He rejoiced in the knowledge that the church fathers had constructed new modes for praising God. He could now describe these church modes, not dependent on those of Boethius, without confusing them as earlier writers had done with the pagan Greek

---

[8]*Missae tredecim quatuor vocum a praestantissimis artificribis compositae* (Nuremberg: H. Grapheus, 1539); Gioseffo Zarlino, *Le Istitutioni harmoniche* (Venice, 1558), bk. 4, ch. 32; idem, *Sopplimenti musicali* (Venice: Francesco de' Franceschi Sanese, 1588), bk. 8, ch. 1; Giovanni Bardi, "Discorso mandato a Giulio Caccini detto romano sopra la musica e 'l cantar bene," in Claude V. Palisca, *The Florentine Camerata: Documentary Studies and Translations*, Music Theory Translation Series (New Haven, CT: Yale University Press, 1989), 92–93; Giulio Caccini, *Le Nuove musiche* (Florence: I Marescotti, 1602; ed. and trans. H. Wiley Hitchcock [Madison, WI: A-R Editions, 1970]), 44; Giulio Cesare Monteverdi, "Explanation of the Letter Printed in the Fifth Book of Madrigals," in *Strunk's Source Readings*, 535–44 (especially 538–40).

[9]Discussed further in chapters 3, 5, and 8.

[10]Discussed further in chapters 3 and 5.

modes, which he understood just barely enough to know they were different.[11]

Franchino Gaffurio, choirmaster of the Duomo of Milan, took the revival of Boethius a step further. Having worked with Gallicus during a period of residence in Mantua, Gaffurio was inspired to undertake a compendium of Boethius, *Theoricum opus musice discipline*, which he completed and published in Naples in 1480 while in exile from Milan. Like Boethius, Gaffurio aspired to a new synthesis of music theory. His *Theorica musice* of 1492, an expansion and revision of the 1480 work, supplemented Boethius with the best authors then available, whether ancient, medieval, or modern, whether translated from the Greek or in their original Latin. He now utilized the encyclopedic works of Boethius's near contemporaries Isidore of Seville and Martianus Capella, a translation of the elementary musical primer by the Greek author Bacchius, Marsilio Ficino's Latin commentaries and translations of Plato, Ermolao Barbaro's translation of Themistius's *Paraphrases* on Aristotle's *On the Soul*, and Pietro d'Abano's commentaries on the Aristotelian *Problems*, as well as other works of Aristotle. Through the *Theorica musice*, Gaffurio placed in the hands of hundreds of musicians and scholars his interpretations of ancient authors the very year Boethius's *De institutione musica* was first printed. Gaffurio's book must have circulated widely: more than fifty copies of the 1492 edition survive, a very large number for an incunabulum. In his last book, *De harmonia musicorum instrumentorum* of 1518, he relied on translations he commissioned from classical scholars of the most comprehensive Greek treatises, those of Ptolemy, Aristides Quintilianus, and Manuel Bryennius.[12]

Meanwhile in 1497, Giorgio Valla (1447–1500) brought out a Latin translation of Cleonides's compendium of the music theory of Aristoxenus, one of Aristotle's most famous pupils. Another classicist, Carlo Valgulio, included in 1497 in a collection of translations from Greek to Latin a dialogue on music by an author then believed to be Plutarch. Gioseffo Zarlino (1517–1590), while preparing *Le Istitutioni harmoniche*, which was to become the most important musical treatise of the sixteenth century, urged Antonio Gogava (d. 1569) to translate the earliest

[11]Johannes Gallicus, *Ritus canendi*, ed. Albert Seay, Critical Texts, no. 13 (Colorado Springs: Colorado College Music Press, 1981), 78 (pt. 1, bk. 3, ch. 12).

[12]Discussed further in chapters 2, 5, and 8.

surviving Greek music treatise, the *Harmonic Elements* of Aristoxenus. In 1562, Gogava published this translation, together with a new translation of Ptolemy's *Harmonics*. They arrived too late for Zarlino to use in his *Istitutioni harmoniche* (1558), but the translations served him well in his *Sopplimenti musicali* of 1588.[13]

While Aristoxenus's anti-mathematical theory remained controversial through much of the sixteenth century, the Plutarchean dialogue aroused lively interest in the Greek chromatic genus, with its scale pattern featuring two consecutive semitones, and the enharmonic, with its two consecutive quarter tones. Soterichus, one of the speakers in the dialogue, lamented that the enharmonic genus, extolled by the ancients as the noblest and treasured for its majesty and severity, had been neglected for centuries.[14] The fabled reputation of the Greek chromatic and enharmonic led Nicola Vicentino (1511–ca. 1576) in his *L'Antica musica ridotta alla moderna prattica* of 1555 to devise new musical scales and instruments to play them. The vogue of chromatic music in the years that followed owed much to his initiative.[15]

The talk in the ancient literature about the power of the modes induced the Swiss humanist Heinrich Glarean to try to construct a system of twelve modern modes in imitation of those attributed to Aristoxenus. Even composers who did not adopt the system promoted in Glarean's *Dodecachordon* of 1547, but held rather to the traditional eight church modes, were swept up by the idea that the modes were a key to musical expression in polyphonic music.[16]

Through the compendia and translations, much of the lore and theory of the ancient Greeks became a common heritage of European scholars and musicians in the sixteenth century. But certain aspects of Greek music and theory remained misunderstood. A classicist who was not a musician set out to learn all he could about Greek musical practice from the original Greek sources without recourse to Boethius or modern musical theory. This was Girolamo Mei (1519–1594), a disciple of the Florentine humanist Piero Vettori who helped Vettori with his commentaries on Aristotle's *Poetics* and with the earliest editions of the

---

[13]Discussed further in chapter 3.

[14]Plutarch *On Music* 38 (1145a).

[15]Discussed further in chapter 5.

[16]Discussed further in chapter 5.

ancient tragedies. In 1573, while working as a cardinal's secretary in Rome, Mei completed his principal work, *De modis musicis*, the first history of Greek music based on written documents rather than a mixture of fact, legend, and mythology. Mei's revelations about the music of the tragedy, some of them disseminated in Vincenzo Galilei's *Dialogo della musica antica, et della moderna* of 1581, inspired a group of Florentine poets and musicians to produce the earliest music dramas around 1600. The same group experimented with a new kind of solo song and speechlike melody accompanied simply with sparse chords in imitation of Mei's findings about the nature of Greek song. Their work stimulated an entirely new approach to musical composition.[17] Thus, without having heard a note of ancient Greek music, the humanists and their followers built on ideas and ideals rediscovered in the ancient writings.

The humanists found more than artistic models and aesthetic goals in ancient culture; they found models for living. To the Christian ideals of divinity, grace, and abstinence, they could oppose those of humanity, beauty, and sensuality. The aspiration to create forms beautiful in themselves, not simply reflective of divine goodness and perfection, now motivated artists and musicians. People enjoyed making music and contemplating it for itself. They valued human feelings and the opportunity to express them through music.

Much sacred polyphonic music left the typical humanist reformer cold. To the literate person uninitiated into the complexities of polyphonic composition, the elaborate settings of sections of the Mass, anthems, or motets performed during the ritual meant little because they obscured the message of the text. Whatever the message, it seemed always to be set in a uniform musical style, insensitive to the feelings expressed. Sometimes a popular tune could be fleetingly recognized in the Masses, which were often based on such songs, or in organ preludes, which resembled common dances. Religious reformers pleaded for a music purged of such secular elements, a music that moved congregations to devout, reverent, and ardent affections.[18]

The quadrivium, the fourfold path to knowledge articulated in the curriculum of Boethius, which made music an equal partner together with arithmetic, geometry, and astronomy, had less appeal to the word-

---

[17]Discussed further in chapter 7.

[18]Discussed further in chapter 6.

bound culture of the Renaissance than to the medieval mind contemplating universal harmony. Instead, partly out of the necessity for political, diplomatic, and commercial communication, the verbal arts of the trivium—grammar, rhetoric, and dialectic—became dominant in the sixteenth century, and music's dependence on poetic or prose texts allied it to these arts. Poetry and music shared the sensible quantities of meter and rhythm. Number operated on the sensuous surface of music and poetry, both of which shared in grammar and rhetoric. Coluccio Salutati (1331–1406) recognized these alliances when he declared that poetry united the quadrivium and trivium:

> Since the proper instrument of the poet is verse, which we measure with and compose out of its parts, that is, feet, and we knit these together not with any rhythms but with established ones from which results and is sought melody, it is clear that poetic narration is composed out of the trivium and quadrivium.[19]

Nevertheless, the influence of Boethius and Pythagorean mathematics remained strong at the beginning of the sixteenth century. The majority opinion still distrusted the sense of hearing as unreliable and depended on reason and numerical ratios to construct musical systems such as scales and to understand the relations of pitches in consonant and dissonant combinations.[20] But a significant group of authors, among them Bartolomé Ramos de Pareja (ca. 1440–after 1491), Carlo Valgulio, Giovanni Spataro (1458–1541), Lodovico Fogliano (before 1500–after 1538), Francisco de Salinas (1513–1590), and Vincenzo Galilei (ca. 1520–1591), partly influenced by Aristoxenus and Ptolemy, defended the sovereignty of the hearing in the domain of musical experience. Aristoxenus had rejected number ratios altogether, declaring that musical knowledge should be based on sensory experience and reasoning upon it, while Ptolemy had acknowledged that both sense experience and numerical rationalization had to be satisfied. Controversies erupted during the sixteenth century between the rationalists and sensualists,

---

[19]Coluccio Salutati, *De laboribus Herculis*, ed. B. L. Ullman (Zurich: Thesaurus mundi, 1951), 18–20 (bk. 1, ch. 3): "Et quoniam versus est poete proprium instrumentum, quem suis partibus, hoc est pedibus, mensuramus atque componimus et non omnibus sed certis numeris alligamus, ex quibus resultat et queritur musica melodia, clarum est poeticam narrationem ex trivio quadruvioque componi ..."; trans. in Claude V. Palisca, *Humanism in Italian Renaissance Musical Thought* (New Haven, CT: Yale University Press, 1985), 333–34.

[20]Discussed further in chapter 3.

pitting Ramos and his pupil Spataro against Gaffurio, Galilei against Zarlino, and Giovanni Maria Artusi (ca. 1540–1613) against Monteverdi.[21] Out of this caldron of ideas emerged new methods of composition free of pseudo-scientific or Pythagorean biases.

In the neo-Platonic view of the universe, a harmony of numbers ruled over the spheres revolving around the earth: the Sun and the Moon, the five known planets, and the fixed dome of the stars.[22] The individual human soul was an analogous harmony, but one that could slip into discord, though music could restore it to concord. Numbers with mystical properties such as 3, 4, and 6 were revered as the foundation of natural phenomena and musical consonance.

A school of scientists trained in the Aristotelian methodology of observation and analysis of cause and effect challenged this harmonic world-view. Girolamo Fracastoro (1483–1553), Giovanni Battista Benedetti (1530–1590), Vincenzo Galilei and his son Galileo, Marin Mersenne (1588–1648), and John Wallis (1616–1703) established simple mathematical principles in a chain of discoveries about the nature of sound, sympathetic resonance, and consonance that laid the basis for a true science of acoustics. This development, liberating the rules of composition from the tyranny of numbers, granted composers broader discretion to follow their own tastes and intuitions.[23]

The idea that a god or other superhuman force takes over the artist's consciousness during the act of creation or conception of a work also attracted many commentators of Platonic and neo-Platonic inclination. Indeed, this explanation prevailed in the fifteenth and early sixteenth centuries. The most stubborn advocate of the theory of poetic furor was the philosopher Francesco Patrizi (1529–1597), who endorsed it in his *Della poetica: La deca disputata* of 1586. Lorenzo Giacomini de' Tebalducci Malespini (1552–1598), a literary critic and amateur musician, rose to refute the theory in the Florentine Accademia degli Alterati around that time. He asked: What is ecstasy, ravishment, furor, and frenzy but a mind concentrating on something while disregarding other objects, as it ardently and furiously operates without hesitation? If art emanates from an external force, it is useless to study its precepts and strive to acquire

---

[21]Discussed further in chapters 3 and 9.

[22]Discussed further in chapter 2.

[23]Discussed further in chapter 8.

the craft. Praise of a poet is misplaced, since it is deserved only for a work that results from independent actions by the individual being praised. One should not look for distant and occult causes, Giacomini counseled, when a phenomenon can be explained more directly. He preferred the common-sense explanation that a poet or artist has the faculty of placing himself in a true affection through concentrated imagination, which enables him to find and express the ideas that are apt to move others. Nor can furor explain music's power to move the affections, which equals or exceeds poetry's.[24]

It was conceivable that a naturally endowed person could make up words and melodies under divine influence in the manner that Ficino improvised his Orphic songs to an accompaniment on the lira or viola da braccio. But the music practiced in the early modern period had to be carefully planned and constructed by musicians highly trained in combining voices and instruments. The concept of *musica poetica* as the making of a work that is complete and polished and passed on to posterity gained recognition in the fifteenth and sixteenth centuries.[25] The concept implied that a musical work, like a poem, sends a message to a reader or listener, one that is unique and original. It is not a spontaneous outpouring: the composer, independent of supernatural forces, elaborates and refines it with great care. Its form is determined by a genre fitting a particular situation. Developing musically a subject defined or not by a verbal text, it is intended to stir the listener's feelings.[26]

Moving and stimulating the affections became the goal of music in the second half of the sixteenth century. By "affection" was meant a relatively stable state of mind or spirit characterized by a certain imbalance of humors, which may have an internal or external cause and which persists as long as the stimulus that caused it is present. The ancients disagreed about the worthiness of the affections. Cicero considered them undesirable perturbations that should be suppressed. For Aristotle, the function of tragedy was to purge certain affections, such as pity and fear, unworthy of citizens who had to defend the state. Yet he trained the orator to move his audience to any affections supporting a cause being argued, and he recognized that music could move people to a variety of affections.

---

[24]Discussed further in chapters 2 and 10.

[25]Discussed further in chapter 4.

[26]Discussed further in chapters 9 and 10.

Music, theater, and poetry could accomplish this by imitating an object or action that in real life awakened a particular affection. Moreover, music, Renaissance philosophers theorized, had the additional capability to stir the affections directly because sound, carried by the air, could penetrate the hearing and reach the animal spirits with its vibrations.[27]

Earlier in the century, writers invoked the formulation of Horace—"docere delectando" (instruct while delighting)—as the poet's mission. Poetry, and by extension music, was thus a recreation in which people took pleasure in learning honest habits. Zarlino identified this as music's task in his *Istitutioni harmoniche* (1558), but many composers aimed higher. Monteverdi's *seconda pratica* was distinguished from Zarlino's *prima pratica* by the striving for expression through musical means that transcended the traditional rules.[28] The new genres of opera—the recitatives, arias, and instrumental numbers—were vehicles for moving the spectators' affections to those felt by the characters. These operatic genres became the models for music generally, both secular and sacred.[29]

When the goal is to capture and move the listener, musical composition and performance become rhetorical acts. Like an oration, a piece of music develops an invention over time, observing a syntax and logic that is not unlike that of a verbal argument. The piece may vary its pace and may be divided into longer and shorter periods, articulated by full or transient resting points. Allusions and graphic images, like the figures of speech, make the expression concrete. Ornament in the form of embellishment adds charm and persuasion. Parallels with verbal rhetoric had ancient roots, but it was only at the end of the sixteenth century that the music-rhetorical devices were recognized, given names—often borrowed from classical rhetoric—, and cast into a pedagogical system in the treatises of Gallus Dressler (1533–1580/89) and Joachim Burmeister (1564–1629), and in the next century by many others, most prominently Athanasius Kircher (1601–1680) and Christoph Bernhard (1628–1692).[30]

---

[27]Discussed further in chapter 10.

[28]These two practices are described in chapter 9.

[29]Discussed further in chapters 4, 7, and 9.

[30]Discussed further in chapter 11.

❧ II ❧

UNIVERSAL HARMONY

HOW MUSIC RELATES to the world at large has perennially fascinated philosophers and musicians. Is music a reflection of a universal harmony ruled by numbers? Is its appreciation a step in the ascent to the ultimate truth, a knowledge of God? Is it a wordless language that speaks the ineffable, a natural medium to express emotion, or an agent for moving the affections? Is it an imitation of nature, as is said of some other arts? Or is it simply a gift to humankind for our delight and to relieve us of boredom and care? Music was each of these things to some author during the period covered by this book.

In the dominant view at the beginning of the sixteenth century, music existed to give pleasure and solace while leading people to moral behavior. This view was handed down by Plato, whose philosophy attracted the most followers among intellectuals at this time. Music pleases us because its form resembles the structure of the human soul. As music harmonizes diverse pitches ordered in time, the soul responds by imitating a harmonious arrangement in its own components. Thus, if the soul's harmony is upset, music can assist in restoring it:

> God gave us a voice and hearing for this purpose, I believe. For speech tends and contributes very much toward this end, and every use of the musical voice was given for the sake of harmony. Harmony, which has motions that are congruent and akin to the wanderings of our soul, was given by the Muses to humankind to deploy with sagacity, not for pleasure devoid of reason, as is now seen to be its use, but so that through it we may calm the dissonant revolutions of the soul and make it a harmony consonant within itself. Rhythm, too, was dedicated to this purpose, so that we might very aptly temper in ourselves an immoderate character lacking grace.[1]

---

[1]Plato *Timaeus* 47c–e: "Φωνῆς τε δὴ καὶ ἀκοῆς πέρι πάλιν ὁ αὐτὸς λόγος, ἐπὶ ταὐτὰ τῶν αὐτῶν ἕνεκα παρὰ θεῶν δεδωρῆσθαι. λόγος τε γὰρ ἐπ᾽ αὐτὰ ταῦτα τέτακται, μεγίστην ξυμβαλλόμενος εἰς αὐτὰ μοῖραν, ὅσον τ᾽ αὖ μουσικῆς φωνῇ χρηστικὸν πρὸς ἀκοὴν ἕνεκα ἁρμονίας ἐστὶ δοθέν· ἡ δὲ ἁρμονία, ξυγγενεῖς ἔχουσα φορὰς ταῖς ἐν ἡμῖν τῆς ψυχῆς περιόδοις, τῷ μετὰ νοῦ προσχρωμένῳ Μούσαις οὐκ ἐφ᾽ ἡδονὴν

13

Harmony's power resides in the numerical ratios discovered by the Pythagoreans for the consonances and other intervals that join in pleasing melody. Although in today's usage, it is a contradiction in terms to say that a melody is a harmony, in ancient times, when simultaneous

Figure 1.

ἄλογον, καθάπερ νῦν, εἶναι δοκεῖ χρήσιμος, ἀλλ' ἐπὶ τὴν γεγονυῖαν ἐν ἡμῖν ἀνάρμοστον ψυχῆς περίοδον εἰς κατακόσμησιν καὶ συμφωνίαν ἑαυτῇ ξύμμαχος ὑπὸ Μουσῶν δέδοται· καὶ ῥυθμὸς αὖ διὰ τὴν ἄμετρον ἐν ἡμῖν καὶ χαρίτων ἐπιδεᾶ γιγνομένην ἐν τοῖς πλείστοις ἕξιν ἐπίκουρος ἐπὶ ταῦτα ὑπὸ τῶν αὐτῶν ἐδόθη"; trans. Marsilio Ficino, in Plato, *Omnia opera* (Basle: H. Frobenius et N. Eplacopius, 1532), 716: "Vocem quoque auditum que eiusdem rei gratia deos dedisse nobis existimo. Nam ad haec ipsa sermo pertinet, plurimumque conducit, omnisque musicae uocis usus harmoniae gratia est tributus. Atque & harmonia, que motiones habet animae nostrae discursionibus congruas atque cognatas, homini prudenter musis utenti non ad uoluptatem rationis expertem, ut nunc uidetur, est utilis: sed a musis ideo data est, ut per eam dissonantem circuitum animae componamus, & ad concentum sibi congruum redigamus. Rhythmus quoque ad hoc uidetur esse tributus, ut habitum in nobis immoderatum gratiaque carentem temperemus." This passage was quoted almost verbatim by Franchino Gaffurio in *Theorica musice* (Milan: Ioannes Petrus de Lomatio, 1492; reprint, New York: Broude Bros., 1967), f. av^r; trans. with introduction and notes by Walter Kurt Kreyszig as *The Theory of Music*, Music Theory Translation Series (New Haven, CT: Yale University Press, 1993), 21–22.

consonances were not cultivated, a melody was indeed a harmony of its consecutive pitches. These pitches belonged to a family called a *harmonia*, similar to a mode.[2] By extension, "harmony" meant an agreeable composite of things in which oppositions were reconciled and tensions resolved: thus, the motto "harmonia est discordia concors" (harmony is concord wrought out of discord), which appears on the title page of Franchino Gaffurio's *De harmonia musicorum instrumentorum* (see figure 1).[3]

Such a state of equilibrium prevailed in the system of the planets and the stars, spheres bound by a harmony of proportionate distances and speeds. Indeed, the Pythagoreans and Plato believed that planetary and stellar rotation, conceived as concentric spheres revolving around the sphere of the earth in the center, produced a harmony of sounds inaudible to humans. Cicero described this "music of the spheres" in his *Dream of Scipio*, which was well known to authors in the sixteenth and seventeenth centuries through Macrobius's commentary, first published in 1472 by Nicolaus Jenson in Venice and then appearing in more than thirty subsequent editions prior to 1600.[4]

"What is this great and pleasing sound that fills my ears?"

"That," replied my grandfather, "is a concord of tones separated by unequal but nevertheless carefully proportioned intervals, caused by the rapid motion of the spheres themselves. The high and low tones blended together produce different harmonies. Of course such swift motions could not be accomplished in silence and, as nature requires, the spheres at one extreme produce low tones and at the other extreme the high tones. Consequently the outermost sphere, the star-bearer, with its swifter motion gives forth a higher-pitched tone, whereas the lunar sphere, the lowest, has the deepest tone. Of course, the earth, the ninth and stationary sphere, always clings to the same position in the middle of the universe. The other eight spheres, two of which move at the same speed [Mercury and Venus],

---

[2]See chapter 5 for further discussion of relationship between the Greek *harmoniai* and the humanistic conception of mode.

[3]Franchino Gaffurio, *De harmonia musicorum instrumentorum opus* (Milan: Gotardus Pontanus, 1518; reprint, New York: Broude Bros., [1979]; Bologna: Forni, 1972).

[4]For a list of early editions, see Macrobius, *Commentary on the Dream of Scipio*, trans., with introduction and notes by William Harris Stahl, Records of Western Civilization (New York: Columbia University Press, 1952), 61–63. The *Dream of Scipio* formed the closing portion of the sixth book of Cicero's *Republic*, most of which has been lost. Some additional portions beyond the *Dream* (amounting to perhaps as much as a third of the entire *Republic*) were discovered in the nineteenth century, but these were not known to earlier scholars.

produce seven different tones, this number being, one might almost say, the key to the universe."[5]

The musical theorist Ugolino of Orvieto (ca. 1380–1457) preferred to think of this celestial harmony as emanating from a hierarchy of angels.[6] For him, all vocal and instrumental music aspired to imitate this divine harmony. Ugolino's successors, however, notably Gaffurio, played down the Christian overlay in favor of the traditional cosmology transmitted by Cicero and his commentator Macrobius, and Marsilio Ficino's annotated Latin translation of Plato's *Timaeus* made accessible the fundamental source on divine harmony and gave renewed impetus to his philosophy.

Plato and his Pythagorean forerunners recognized as consonances pairs of pitches defined by simple numerical ratios limited to the numbers 1, 2, 3, and 4, a set of numbers known to the Pythagoreans as a *tetraktys*. The octave, a pair of pitches that sound practically the same but are eight steps apart, was produced by strings or pipe lengths in the ratio 2:1. The fifth, a pair of pitches five steps apart, sounds like two different pitches but with a pleasing blend between them; its ratio is 3:2. The fourth, four steps apart, exhibits a blend with some tension, but its pair is still highly compatible in the ratio 4:3. Outside the sacred precinct of the first four numbers lie other basic components of melody: the whole tone—adjacent notes in a melody that do not blend well—and a pair

---

[5]Cicero *De re publica* 6.5: "'quid? hic' inquam 'quis est qui conplet aures meas tantus et tam dulcis sonus?' 'hic est' inquit 'ille qui intervallis disiunctus imparibus sed tamen pro rata parte ratione distinctis, impulsu et motu ipsorum orbium efficitur et acuta cum gravibus temperans varios aequabiliter concentus efficit. nec enim silentio tanti motus incitari possunt et natura fert ut extrema ex altera parte graviter, ex altera autem acute sonent. quam ob causam summus ille caeli stellifer cursus cuius conversio est concitatior, acuto et excitato movetur sono, gravissimo autem hic lunaris atque infimus. nam terra, nona, inmobilis manens una sede semper haeret conplexa medium mundi locum. illi autem octo cursus in quibus eadem vis est duorum septem efficiunt distinctos intervallis sonos qui numerus rerum omnium fere nodus est"; trans. in ibid., 73–74. Stahl's translation, which is based on the interpretation offered in Macrobius's *Commentary*, captures the context within which authors of the Middle Ages and the Renaissance would have read the passage. For an alternative translation (of this and all the other surviving passages of the *Republic*), see *Cicero in Twenty-Eight Volumes*, vol. 16, *De re publica, De legibus*, trans. Clinton Walker Keyes, Loeb Classical Library (Cambridge: Harvard University Press, 1928), 271–73.

[6]Ugolino of Orvieto, *Declaratio musicae disciplinae*, 3 vols., ed. Albert Seay, Corpus scriptorum de musica, vol. 7 ([Rome]: American Institute of Musicology, 1959–62), 15–16 (bk. 1, ch. 1).

that blends least well, the semitone. But these small intervals are the glue
that holds together the larger intervals in melody. Their ratios may be calculated from those of the three consonances: the tone, 9:8, results from

removing the interval of the fourth from
the fifth; and the semitone, 256:243,
remains when two whole tones are sub-
tracted a fourth.[7] The system of four steps
forming the interval of the fourth was
called a tetrachord (i.e., "four strings"), as
in figure 2.

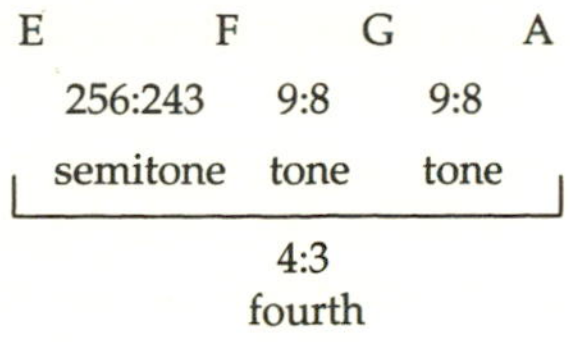

E	F	G	A
	256:243	9:8	9:8
	semitone	tone	tone

4:3
fourth

Figure 2.

Out of these ratios, Plato built the so-called *Timaeus* scale, which was
not really a scale but a collection of ratios that filled out a musical space
delimiting and defining a soul, whether a World Soul or an individual
human soul. A soul, as immaterial, could best be described as a mathematical entity. The World Soul contained the harmony of the universe. A
human soul also constituted a harmony, but one easily thrown into
disharmonious disarray by its interactions with the body. It was thought
that melodies rooted in the simple ratios of the octave, fifth, and fourth,
mediated by the tone and semitone, could restore a soul's primordial
harmony through the sympathetic process of mimesis.[8]

Congruity of ratios in the soul with those in music explains the pleasure we take in artful arrangements of pitches. As Gaffurio (1451–1522)
aptly expressed it in 1492: "when we receive that which is agreeably and
suitably combined in sounds, as it has been mixed and suitably adapted
to us, we are delighted with it, recognizing that we ourselves are composed in its likeness."[9] Christian neo-Platonists, among them Marsilio

---

[7]3:2 − 4:3 = 9:8; 4:3 - (9:8 + 9:8) = 256:243. In order to do the calculations, it is
important to understand that when adding ratios, their intervals must be multiplied; when subtracting intervals, their ratios are divided. Thus 3:2 ÷ 4:3 = 9:8; 4:3
÷ 81:64 (i.e., 9:8 × 9:8 = 81:64) = 256:243. This is because "adding" ratios sets them
in continuous proportion, which is a matter of finding common measures of the
various terms. Subtracting ratios is the reciprocal process.

[8]That is, a kind of elaborate metaphysical process whereby lower things may
be brought into an "imitation" of the higher perfections. For an introduction to
the complex matter of mimesis, see Thomas J. Mathiesen, "Mimesis," in *The New
Grove Dictionary of Music and Musicians*, 2d ed. [hereafter *NGD*], 29 vols., ed. Stanley
Sadie (London: Macmillan, 2001), 16:709.

[9]Gaffurio, *Theorica musice*, f. bi^r (bk. 1, ch. 3): "Quom igitur id quod in sonis
apte conuenienterque coniunctum est excipimus cum nobis immistum atque con-

Ficino (1433–1499), taught that when we enjoy harmonious sounds, we intuit in them divine truth and take a first step toward the ultimate knowledge of God, which we can reach only through a gradual ascent.

Gaffurio, an accomplished composer of a large quantity of sacred polyphonic music and director of the choir of the Duomo of Milan, knew that agreeably combining pitches and temporal durations "suitably adapted to us" could only be achieved by someone with a sensitive ear after long training and hard work. Gaffurio's colleague during a brief exile in Naples, Johannes Tinctoris (ca. 1435–1511) completed in 1477 a highly regarded treatise, *Liber de arte contrapuncti*,[10] that taught how to combine melodic lines, virtually independent voice parts, into such a harmonious fabric. Tinctoris describes a system of composition that better optimizes consonance and more severely controls dissonance than any previous method. He aims at a texture in which the desire for variety, ornament, beauty of line, and tension are subject to a reigning harmony.

Attitudes toward the limits of consonance and dissonance had changed since Plato's time. As polyphony developed in the Middle Ages, the major and minor thirds and the major and minor sixths were accepted as "imperfect" consonances beside the octave, fifth, and fourth, which were called "perfect" consonances. All of these intervals pleased the ear when heard simultaneously among voices and instruments performing together. The fourth, though classified as a "perfect" consonance, sounded stark and hollow unless supported by consonances placed below it. In effect, it had to be treated as a dissonance when it occurred between the lowest and a higher part. All other intervals within the octave, such as the second, augmented fourth, diminished fifth, and sevenths were considered dissonances. Intervals wider than an octave were classified according to what they would be if reduced by one or more octaves.[11]

Respecting this hierarchy of intervals, composers maintained the homogeneous harmonious flow to which Tinctoris and his contempo-

---

uenienter coaptatum sit eo delectamur: nos ipsos eadem similitudine conpactos esse cognoscentes"; trans. *Theory of Music*, 35.

[10]Johannes Tinctoris, "Liber de arte contrapuncti," in *Opera theoretica*, ed. Albert Seay, 3 vols. in 2, Corpus scriptorum de musica, vol. 22 ([Rome]: American Institute of Musicology, 1975–78), 2:11–157.

[11]For example, the consonance of the twelfth results from adding an octave to a fifth ($2{:}1 \times 3{:}2 = 6{:}2 = 3{:}1$); similarly, a ninth is dissonant like a second.

raries aspired. Their method of composition required that the rhythmic moments felt most strongly in basic musical movement must be consonant, with a few very clearly defined exceptions. Tinctoris called the note value determining this movement the "mensurae directio"; later, it came to be called "tactus" in treatises written in Latin and "battuta" (beat) in treatises written in Italian.[12] Dissonances of shorter duration, usually notes of local motion within a single part, could occur between beats, and when coming to a close or cadence at the end of a textual phrase, a dissonance could exceptionally fall on a beat and be resolved or relieved by a consonance on the following beat. But to soften this dissonance, one of the parts must hold its pitch steady while the other part or parts move to cause the dissonance. Since the holding voice displaces the normal motion of the part, it feels syncopated, or "suspended," and this pattern—a syncopated note, a "suspended" dissonance on the beat, a resolution to an imperfect consonance on the next beat, ending with a perfect consonance on the beat after that—made up the most characteristic cadence. The opening phrase of Josquin des Prez's (?) setting of Psalm 129, *De profundis clamavi ad te, Domine* (From the depths I cried to Thee, O Lord), illustrates this technique (figure 3).[13]

---

[12]See, for example, Tinctoris, "Liber de arte contrapuncti," 2:128–35 (bk. 2, chs. 25–27); Adam of Fulda, "Musica," in *Scriptores ecclesiastici de musica sacra potissimum*, 3 vols., ed. Martin Gerbert (St. Blaise: Typis San-Blasianis, 1784; reprint, Hildesheim: Olms, 1963), 3:362 (pt. 3, ch. 7); and Zarlino, *Istitutioni* (1558), 207–9 (bk. 3, ch. 48 "Della battuta"). For a consideration of the relationship during this period between musical pulse and the regular heartbeat of a man with quiet respiration, see Curt Sachs, *Rhythm and Tempo: A Study in Music History* (New York: Norton, 1953), 203 and n. 5.

[13]Josquin Desprez, *Werken*, ed. A. Smijers et al. (Amsterdam: Alsbach 1921–69), *Motetten*, III/35:20–25; also included in *The Norton Anthology of Western Music*, 4th ed., 2 vols., ed. Claude V. Palisca (New York: Norton, 2001), 1:142–48 (and accompanying recording, *Norton Recorded Anthology of Western Music*, vol. 1 [Sony Music Special Products A6 51490]). The attribution to Josquin has recently been considered doubtful, with Champion proposed as a possible alternative (see "Josquin des Prez," in *NGD*, 13:253).

Figure 3. Josquin des Prez (?), *De profundis clamavi ad te, Domine*, mm. 1–10[14]

---

[14]The numbers between the voices identify the intervals (1 = unison, 2 = second, etc.) between each voice.

Figure 3 (cont'd). Josquin des Prez (?), *De profundis clamavi ad te, Domine*, mm. 11–17

The first dissonance occurs in measure 9, brought about by the syncopation of the Altus on the note *a*, the movement of the Superius down to *b*—forming a dissonant second above the *a*—and the entry of the Tenor on *e*, a "dissonant" fourth below the *a*. The prepared dissonance descends to *g#* to form a consonant third against the voices above and below, resolving the dissonance. The Altus now moves back to *a* to sound a unison with the Superius and an octave with the Bassus, completing the cadence. The Tenor, which had entered on *e*, now sounds a fourth below the Superius and the Altus, but this does not offend the ear because it is supported by the Bassus a fifth below as it enters on *A*. An additional instance occurs in measures 11–12. On the fourth beat of measure 11, the Altus's *f* forms the dissonance of a passing seventh with the Bassus, but of greater importance is the consonant preparation of the *d'* in the Superius, which will sound a "dissonant" fourth with the Bassus when it moves to *A* at the beginning of measure 12, as well as a seventh with the Altus. This prepared dissonance then immediately resolves to the consonance of thirds, sixths, and octaves.

In these fourteen measures, the composer maintained a prevailing harmony of consonances, punctuated by dissonances at two cadences and a few short dissonant notes of local motion. He accomplished this while artfully making the lower voices imitate the melody of the Superius as they enter one by one. In all the voices, he matched the word "profundis" (depths) with a descriptive wide downward leap, while the word "clamavi" (cried) is set to a plaintive minor sixth in the top and most prominent voice, imitated later by the Tenor, and in the other voices to the leap of an octave after a rest.

Whether by design, intuition, or happy historical accident, the style of pervading consonance taught by Tinctoris and exemplified in this motet was a perfect analogy for Plato's World Soul or a human soul in a state of healthy and tranquil equilibrium. The composer upset the balance only slightly to express the text through the generally low register of the voices and the anxious pleading minor sixth in the Superius and Tenor.

Although composers such as Tinctoris and Gaffurio read widely and consorted with philosophers, we cannot assume that they set out to realize in sound the divine harmony set forth by the philosophers. In fact, Tinctoris and Gaffurio disagreed about the music of the spheres; Gaffurio defended it, while Tinctoris, citing Aristotle's objections, already denied its existence in his *Liber de arte contrapuncti* of 1477. Although he acknowledged that eminent philosophers such as Plato, Pythagoras, Cicero, Macrobius, Boethius, and Isidore supported celestial music, because they disagreed to such an extent about its workings, it was safer to adopt Aristotle's position that planetary motion produced no sound.[15] Nevertheless, Tinctoris believed that harmony was rooted in nature. "Consonances of sounds and melodies," Tinctoris maintains, "from whose sweetness, as Lactantius says, the pleasure of the ears is derived, are brought about, not by heavenly bodies, but by earthly instruments with the cooperation of nature."[16]

Those who believed in the divine origin of harmony tended to have faith as well in the divine nature of artistic creativity, in the creative force of the "poetic furor." Plato was again the source and Ficino through his translations and commentaries the principal advocate. Plato's *Phaedrus* and *Ion* present the theory that poets create their verses while in a state of frenzy (ἐνθουσιασμός [*enthousiasmos*]) or poetic madness (in later Latin, *furor poeticus*), in which a divine influence guides their thoughts.[17] Cicero, too, held that poets were filled with divine afflatus.[18] Poets and composers immersed in this state become vehicles for higher powers: the Muses, the planets, the World Soul, or the Christian God. Ficino posited four *furores*, those of religious rites, prophecy, love, and poetry. Possessed by any of these, one is not content with ordinary speech but "bursts forth into clamoring and songs and poems. Any madness, therefore, whether the prophetic, hieratic, or amatory, justly seems to be released as poetic furor when it proceeds to songs and poems."[19]

---

[15]Aristotle *On the Heavens* 2.9 (290b–291a). Tinctoris, "Liber de arte contrapuncti," 11–13 (Prologue).

[16]Ibid., 12: "Concordantiae igitur vocum et cantuum quorum suavitate, ut inquit Lactantinus [*sic*], aurium voluptas percipitur, non corporibus caelestibus sed instrumentis terrenis cooperante natura conficiuntur ..."; trans. Albert Seay as *The Art of Counterpoint*, Musicological Studies and Documents, no. 5 ([Rome]: American Institute of Musicology, 1961), 14.

[17]Ficino's translation of Plato's *Ion* was titled *De furore poetico*.

[18]Cicero *In Defense of Archias* 18.

[19]Ficino, *In Phedrum*, ch. 4: "sed in clamorem prorumpit et cantus et carmina. Quamobrem furor quilibet, sive fatidicus sive mysterialis seu amatorius, dum in cantus procedit et carmina, merito in furorem poeticum videtur absolvi"; critical text and trans. in Michael J. B. Allen, *Marsilio Ficino and the Phaedran Charioteer*, Publications of the Center for Medieval and Renaissance Studies, UCLA, vol. 14 (Berkeley: University of California Press, 1981), 84–85. For a somewhat different translation, see D. P. Walker, *Spiritual and Demonic Magic from Ficino to Campanella* (London: The Warburg Institute, 1958), 21. See also Gary Tomlinson, *Music in Renaissance Magic: Toward a Historiography of Others* (Chicago: University of Chicago Press, 1993), 176–83.

Gaffurio discovered another ancient authority for poetic madness, the Greek writer Aristides Quintilianus, whom he read in the Latin translation of Francesco Burana. Aristides Quintilianus benefited from reading both Plato and Cicero, but he also presents a more richly imagined view of the origin of song. As reported by Gaffurio, Aristides Quintilianus posits a soul in a state of ignorance and forgetfulness, not unlike its condition at birth: oppressed with fright and confusion because of the turbulence of the body, the soul, suffused with a divine madness, gives forth melody, which soothes its irrational part.[20]

Francesco Patrizi (1529–1597), who devoted a great deal of attention to music in his *Poetica* of 1586, strongly believed in the presence of an external driving force in the creation of poetry. "Enthusiasm is a natural and forced movement of the spirit by fantasies presented through the light that some deity, genius, or demon infuses into the soul. It operates through the illumined subject receiving that light who does not know what is being done or said."[21] This enthusiasm was the divine furor, the most decisive agent in creating, adorning, and perfecting a work of art. The idea that a poet spun verses while gripped by supernatural forces appealed to many critics, for how else could the human mind conceive the fantastic actions poems relate and do so with such inspired and moving eloquence?

With the publication of Latin translations of Aristotle's *Poetics*, followed by a wealth of commentaries, an opposing point of view made its way in the sixteenth century. It countered the divine furor with a naturalistic explanation of poets' compositional process. Artful language must

---

[20]Gaffurio, *De harmonia musicorum instrumentorum opus*, f. 98r (bk. 4, ch. 17). Cf. Aristides Quintilianus *On Music* 3.25; trans. with introduction and notes by Thomas J. Mathiesen as *On Music in Three Books*, Music Theory Translation Series (New Haven, CT: Yale University Press, 1983), 199–202. Burana's unpublished translation was commissioned by Gaffurio, whose copy is preserved in Verona, Biblioteca Capitolare, CCXL (201) misc. For a full treatment of Burana's importance as an early translator, see Palisca, *Humanism*, 111–17.

[21]Francesco Patrizi, *Della poetica, La deca disputata* (Ferrara: V. Baldini, 1586), 24, quoted in Bernard Weinberg, *A History of Literary Criticism in the Italian Renaissance*, 2 vols. (Chicago: University of Chicago Press, 1961), 2:771, n. 98: "Lo entusiasmo fosse un commouimento d'animo naturale, e sforzato, per le fantasie apprestate dal lume, che nell'anima infonde alcuna Deità, o Genio, ò Demone; e opera secondo il soggetto che quel lume riceue, senza sapere cio che si faccia, o dica l'illuminato."

be learned even by those who possessed great aptitude; poets must be knowledgeable in every liberal art and science and have superior reasoning powers exercised not in a frenzied fit but in cool reflection.

Lorenzo Giacomini de' Tebalducci Malespini (1552–1598), an amateur musician who always included music in his discussion of poetry, set out to refute the idea of poetic furor in his oration *Del furor poetico*, delivered to the Florentine Accademia degli Alterati in 1587 and later published. He insisted on the responsibility of the poet for his work. What others called furor, he said, was "an internal disposition that is often hidden from our knowledge," a gift for conceiving images steeped in associations and affections. The moment of creation may be one in which the spirits are heated and the poet feels an elation and rapture while concentrating his imagination, forgetting everything else. But this heat must be balanced by cool judgment: "To climb to the height of poetry, eloquence, or philosophy, one needs temperate spirits that tend toward coolness to think, investigate, dispute, and judge.... But to execute an idea he has conceived he needs heat to speak effectively, just as a mighty warrior needs ardent rage or impetuosity when he gets ready for courageous deeds, not being able to do great things without great excitement."[22] Although a few stalwart neo-Platonists clung to their belief in poetic furor, the tide turned in the second half of the sixteenth century toward the modern view expressed by Giacomini: the creative artist is independent of astral and supernatural influences, exercising the imagination to imitate real things and actions, though sometimes inventing marvelous and fabulous things that never existed.

Along with the poetic furor, many poetic and musical theorists as well as philosophers abandoned belief in a sounding cosmic harmony. As we have seen, Tinctoris was one of the first to do so in his *Liber de arte contrapuncti* of 1477. A hundred years later, Francisco de Salinas (1513–1590) in his *De musica libri septem* of 1577 went even further,

---

[22]Lorenzo Giacomini, "Del furore poetico," in *Orationi e discorsi* (Florence: Sermartelli, 1597), 59–60: "L'huomo che al altezza de la Poesia o del Eloquenza, o de la Filosofia dee salire, per pensare, inuestigare, discorrere, e giudicare, ha bisogno di spiriti temperati, che inclinino nel freddo ... ma per bene eseguire secondo l'idea in se conceputa, ha bisogno di calore accioche con efficacia esprima, si come fa di mestiero al forte guerriero di feruente ira, o impeto, quando si prepara a valorosi fatti, non si potendo senza gran concitatione cose grande operare." On Giacomini, see also pp. 190–92 *infra*.

discarding altogether the traditional division of music into *musica mundana*, *humana*, and *instrumentalis* established by Boethius and accepted by most subsequent writers. If there is harmony in the cosmos or the human soul, he maintains, it is not audible but something for intellectual contemplation. He accepts the notion that the parts of the soul are united through simple ratios like those of the consonances but would not venture to call this music.[23]

Giovanni Battista Benedetti (1530–1590), an amateur composer and a pioneer in mechanics and acoustic science, undertook one of the most thorough refutations of cosmic harmony in his *Diversarum speculationum mathematicarum & physicarum liber* of 1585, a collection of studies compiled over many years. He adduced arguments from physics, such as the lack of air in distant space and the absence of evidence of rubbing parts or displacement of bodies in the motion of the spheres that could cause sound; moreover, he failed to find harmonic proportions in the sky.[24] Leonardo da Vinci (1452–1519), a century earlier, had expressed similar objections in one of his notebooks, but these were unknown because they were not published until modern times. He held that if planets rubbed against each other to produce sound, the friction created by their great speed and the centuries of constant revolution would have consumed them totally.[25]

Cosmic harmony nevertheless continued to resonate through the seventeenth century. At the end of the century, the Thuringian organist and prolific author Andreas Werckmeister (1645–1706) still believed that the constellations emitted a harmony and that "the entire edifice of harmony consists of certain numbers and proportions, for God set everything into number, measure, and weight, since he himself is a god of

---

[23]Francisco de Salinas, *De musica libri septem, in quibus eius doctrinae veritas tam quae ad harmoniam, quam quae ad rhythmum pertinet, iuxta sensus ac rationis iudicium ostenditur, et demonstratur* (Salamanca: Mathias Gastius, 1577), 1–2 (bk. 1, ch. 1)

[24]Giovanni Battista Benedetti, "Disputationes de quibusdam placidis Aristotelis," ch. 33, "Pytagoreorum opinionem de sonitu corporum coelestium non fuisse ad Aristotele sublatam, " in *Diversarum speculationum mathematicarum et physicarum liber* (Turin: Haeredes Nicolai Bevilaquae, 1585), 190–91. For a fuller treatment, see Palisca, *Humanism*, 186–87 and 257–65.

[25]Paris, Institut de France, MS F, f. 56v; trans. in Edward MacCurdy, *The Notebooks of Leonardo da Vinci*, 2 vols. (New York: Reynal & Hitchcock, 1938), 1:299.

order."[26] For other authors, universal harmony was more a metaphor, prominently displayed in titles such as Johannes Kepler's *Harmonices mundi libri V* of 1619, Marin Mersenne's *Harmonie universelle* of 1636–37, and Athanasius Kircher's *Musurgia universalis* of 1650.[27]

By now scientists and philosophers agreed that sound had no physical reality outside the consciousness of hearing animals. This contradicted both Aristotle, who defined sound as motion, and the Pythagorean tradition, in which musical sound was sonorous number. Galileo maintained that musical pitch was caused by vibrations of a flexible medium such as air to which a sensory organ reacts and that sound had no existence outside the hearing person.[28]

Kepler (1571–1630), an accomplished astronomer, denied that the planets emitted any sound. He opposed the Pythagorean tradition on other grounds as well. It was a mistake to stop at the first four numbers because the major and minor thirds in the ratios of 5:4 and 6:5 were necessary to polyphonic music. He also objected to Plato's construction of the World Soul out of ratios of the Pythagorean scale because numbers were purely abstract quantities, whereas God put archetypal geometric figures in the soul of man, such as polygons, triangles, and squares, which by rotation generated solid figures. He claimed that the relative

---

[26] Andreas Werckmeister, *Hypomnemata musica oder Musicalisches Memorial* (Quedlinburg: T. P. Calvisius, 1697), 1: "der ganze Bau der Harmonie in gewissen Zahlen und Proportionem bestehe, denn Gott hat alles in Zahlen, Maß und Gewichte gesetzet, weil er selber ein Gott der Ordnung ist."

[27] Johannes Kepler, *Harmonices mundi libri V* (Linz: Godefredus Tampachius, 1619); Athanasius Kircher, *Musurgia universalis sive ars magna consoni et dissoni in X libros digesta*, 2 vols. (Rome: Corbelletti [vol. 1] and Grignani [vol. 2], 1650); Marin Mersenne, *Harmonie universelle*, 8 parts (Paris: Cramoisy, 1636–37). On Kircher, see further discussion in chapters 9–11; on Mersenne, in chapters 7–8 and 10. The importance and influence of Kepler was the subject of Arthur Koestler's interesting *The Sleepwalkers: A History of Man's Changing Vision of the Universe* (London: Hutchinson, 1959), but a number of Koestler's views—in particular his assertion that "nobody read" Copernicus's *De revolutionibus*—have recently been effectively refuted by Owen Gingerich's equally fascinating *The Book Nobody Read: Chasing the Revolutions of Nicolaus Copernicus* (New York: Walker, 2004). Likewise, Athanasius Kircher has recently attracted a good deal of attention from historians of science. See, in particular, the collection of articles in Paula Findlen, ed., *Athanasius Kircher: The Last Man Who Knew Everything* (New York: Routledge, 2004).

[28] Galileo Galilei, *Il Saggiatore* (Rome: G. Mascardi, 1623), in *Le opere di Galileo Galilei*, Edizione nazionale sotto gli auspicii di Sua Maestà il re d'Italia, 20 vols. in 21, ed. Antonio Favaro et al. (Florence: Barbèra, 1890–1909), 6:347–48.

speeds of the planets as viewed from the sun manifested figures representing the perfect and imperfect consonances.[29]

The Jesuit Kircher (1601–1680) also set aside the ancient *musica mundana* in favor of a larger concept of harmony embracing all creation, within which God reconciled opposites such as good and evil, consonance and dissonance.[30] Père Mersenne (1588–1648) held a similarly broad concept, but one of a harmonious universe ruled by laws of physics and mechanics that could be discovered through experiment and investigation of natural phenomena, which he believed would ultimately reveal the wonder of the world and sustain religion rather than undermine it.[31]

---

[29]See Rainer Bayreuther, "Johannes Keplers musiktheoretisches Denken," *Musiktheorie* 19 (2004): 3–20; and D. P. Walker, "Kepler's Celestial Music," in *Studies in Musical Science in the Late Renaissance* (London: The Warburg Institute; Leiden: E. J. Brill, 1978), 34–62. For a fuller discussion of Kepler's *Mysterium cosmographicum* (1596) and *Harmonices mundi*, see Koestler, *Sleepwalkers*, pt. 4, chs. 2 and 9 ("The 'Cosmic Mystery'" and "Chaos and Harmony").

[30]See Ulf Scharlau, *Athanasius Kircher (1601–1680) als Musikschriftsteller: Ein Beitrag zur Musikanschauung des Barock*, Studien zur hessischen Musikgeschichte, vol. 2 (Kassel: Bärenreiter, 1969), 84–86; and Joscelyn Godwin, *Athanasius Kircher: A Renaissance Man and the Quest for Lost Knowledge* (London: Thames and Hudson, 1979), 66–71.

[31]For a contextual review of all these figures, see Penelope Gouk, "The Role of Harmonics in the Scientific Revolution," in *The Cambridge History of Western Music Theory*, ed. Thomas Christensen (Cambridge: Cambridge University Press, 2002), 223–45.

➳ III ➥

SENSE OVER REASON:
THE ANTI-THEORETICAL REACTION

Aristoxenus, who depended solely on sense, denied reason,
whereas the Pythagoreans, in contrast, governed themselves solely
by reason, not sense. Ptolemy more sanely embraced both sense
and reason, and his opinion has satisfied many people up to now.[1]

S O WRITES NICOLA VICENTINO (1511–ca. 1576) in the first paragraph of his iconoclastic treatise *L'Antica musica ridotta alla
moderna prattica*, published in 1555. If the ancient Greek writers
disagreed so vehemently, he implies, how could a modern composer
learn anything practical from them? Vicentino thereby excuses the brevity
of his treatise's preliminary "Book on Music Theory" in which he dis-
misses much of Boethius's *De institutione musica*, the source of his
knowledge of the Greek musical debates, as "of no value whatsoever in
our practice."[2] The treatise's following five long "books" are devoted to
that practice.

With this approach, Vicentino broke with the tradition of rehearsing
the standard Boethian topics: human and cosmic music; the theory of
ratios of the consonances and other intervals; arithmetic, geometric, and
harmonic means; and the tetrachords in the three genera. Franchino

---

[1]Nicola Vicentino, *L'Antica musica ridotta alla moderna prattica* (Rome: Antonio
Barre, 1555; reprint in Documenta musicologica, I/17, Kassel: Bärenreiter, 1959), f.
3r: "Aristosseno, accostandosi solo al senso, negaua la ragione, quando per il contrario li Pittagorici si gouernauano solamente con la ragione, e non per il senso.
Ma Tolomeo più sanamente abbracciò il senso, e la ragione insieme, di cui l'oppi-
nione sin' hora è piaciuta à molti"; trans. with introduction and notes by Maria
Rika Maniates as *Ancient Music Adapted to Modern Practice*, Music Theory Translation
Series (New Haven, CT: Yale University Press, 1996), 6 ("Book on Music Theory,"
ch. 1).

[2]Vicentino, *L'Antica musica*, f. 6v: "… non si essere hoggi utile alcuno alla
nostra prattica …"; trans. *Ancient Music*, 20 ("Book on Music Theory," ch. 16).

Gaffurio in his *Theorica musice* (1492) had set the example of traversing the entire Boethian curriculum of five books in his own five books, supplementing the Boethian text with some older sources such as writings of Plato and Aristotle, the late Greek commentaries of Themistius on Aristotle's *On the Soul*, and the Greek musical catechism by Bacchius.[3] Vicentino, for his part, would have little of that.

The Renaissance transformed the historical status of Boethius as a music theorist. For the Middle Ages and extending through the fifteenth century, he was the musical law-giver. In *De institutione musica*, Boethius compiled the best introduction in Latin to the ancient discipline of music, one of the four mathematical sciences—arithmetic, music, geometry, and astronomy—that made up what he called the "quadrivium," the "four paths" to knowledge. His authority rested on solid ground. As author of a textbook on arithmetic, he possessed the method for dealing with every aspect of numerical proportion necessary for defining the relations of pitches, the formation and tuning of scales, and the definition of the consonances and other intervals of music. He had at his command "the division of the monochord" (that is, the *Sectio canonis* sometimes attributed to Euclid) and the major writings on music by Nicomachus and Ptolemy, whose treatises he synthesized and paraphrased.[4]

Studied in the early Renaissance universities as a preparation for theology and philosophy, the teachings of Boethius by the mid-sixteenth century had ceased to be relevant to the training of musicians and composers. But humanists almost concurrently recognized it as the most authoritative source on Greek music available in Latin. In the *Ritus canendi vetustissimus et novus*, an introduction to liturgical music written between 1458 and 1464, Johannes Gallicus de Namur (also known as Johann Legrense, ca. 1415–1473) for the first time treats Boethius not as an original author but as a transmitter and translator of Greek musical thought, describing his treatise as "that *Musica*, which the so often men-

---

[3]See Gaffurio, *Theory of Music*, where Gaffurio's sources are detailed in Kreyszig's introduction and annotations. Further discussion of Gaffurio will be found in chapters 2, 5, and 8.

[4]On Boethius's sources, see A. M. S. Boethius, *Fundamentals of Music*, trans. with introduction and notes by Calvin M. Bower, Music Theory Translation Series (New Haven, CT: Yale University Press, 1989), xxiv–xxix. On Boethius in general and his authority, see Henry Chadwick, *Boethius: The Consolations of Music, Logic, Theology, and Philosophy* (Oxford: Clarendon Press, 1981).

tioned Boethius turned into Latin from the Greek."[5] Gallicus probably learned this from Vittorino da Feltre (1378–1446), who lectured on *De institutione musica* in a school founded at Mantua under the patronage of Marquis Gianfrancesco Gonzaga. Vittorino was particularly well qualified to place Boethius in the context of Greek music and learning because he owned one of the most important codices preserving the principal Greek musical treatises.[6] Thus the bible of music theory that for centuries carried the name of Boethius as its sixth-century Roman author was really a compilation of older Greek writings.

As sophistication grew about Greek music in the hundred years after Gallicus, the philosophical traditions that Boethius represented were identified. Francisco de Salinas, after closely studying the surviving corpus of Greek treatises, could assert in 1577:

> Boethius is entirely Pythagorean, and in his two books concerning arithmetic and in the first four books concerning music he followed Nicomachus and set forth the position of the Pythagoreans; in the fifth, however, he promised opinions of others on matters concerning which the ancient authors disagreed. Here, with subtle judgment, he would have led us to a middle course, but he left it incomplete....[7]

Salinas must have recognized that Boethius's fifth book is almost entirely a translation of Ptolemy's *Harmonics*, Book 1, but he may not have realized that Boethius omitted only a few chapters at the end. With the growing recognition of Boethius as an authority on Greek music and

---

[5]Gallicus, *Ritus canendi*, 11 (pt. 1, bk. 1, ch. 4): "ea namque musica, quam totiens allegatus Boethius de Graeco vertit in latinum."

[6]Venetus Marcianus gr. app. cl. VI/10 (coll. 1300); see Palisca, *Humanism*, 25–27. For a full description of the codex, see Thomas J. Mathiesen, *Ancient Greek Music Theory: A Catalogue raisonné of Manuscripts*, Répertoire International des Sources Musicales, BXI (Munich: Henle, 1988), 716–20. For a study of Vittorino da Feltre's life and work, see William Harrison Woodward, *Vittorino da Feltre and Other Humanist Educators* (Cambridge: Cambridge University Press, 1897; reprint in Renaissance Society of America Reprint texts, no. 5, with a foreword by Eugene F. Rice Jr., Toronto: University of Toronto Press, 1996). For further discussion of Gallicus, see chapter 5.

[7]Salinas, *De musica*, 73 (bk. 2, ch. 18): "Boëtius autem totus Pythagoricus est, et in libris duobus de Arithmetica, et quatuor primis de Musica Nicomachum secutus, Pythagoraeorum tantùm positiones exposuit: quintum autem, in quo promiserat se aliorum opiniones, in quibus veteres autores sententiarum diuersitate discordant, in medium adducturum, & de his subtile iudicium facturum, imperfectum reliquit...."

arithmetic, his *De institutione musica* became a candidate for vernacular translation. Two translations into Italian were in fact completed, but neither one was published: the first, in 1579, was by a literary humanist, Giorgio Bartoli; the second, in 1597, by a musical humanist, Ercole Bottrigari.[8]

The "middle course" Salinas admired in Boethius's last book was of course actually that of Ptolemy, who steered between reason and sensation, a path Salinas himself chose, as he proclaims in the title of his treatise: "Seven Books on Music, in which the truth of its doctrine pertinent to harmony and rhythm is explained and demonstrated with the sanction of both the sense and reason."[9] On the side of reason, the Pythagoreans did not trust the senses and based their science on mathematics. Aristoxenus, according to Vicentino, relied on the senses and opposed the intrusion of mathematics. Neither position entirely excluded the other. The Pythagoreans started with sensory experience to decide which consonances pleased the ear and then looked for the quantitative relationships of the sounding bodies that produced them. Aristoxenus and his followers similarly began with the facts of sensory experience and reasoned about them, but without abstractions such as numerical relationships. Salinas aimed to navigate between these extremes and profit by both the senses and mathematics.

The middle road had appealed also to two earlier theorists, Lodovico Fogliano (before 1500–after 1538) and Gioseffo Zarlino (1517–1590). Fogliano had the advantage of reading Greek and, indeed, once planned to translate the works of Aristotle into Italian.[10] The extent of Fogliano's

---

[8]Giorgio Bartoli, trans., "De la musica di Boethio," Florence, Biblioteca nazionale centrale, Magliabechianus XIX/75; Ercole Bottrigari, trans., "I cinqve libri di mvsica di Anitio Manlio Severino Boetio," Bologna, Civico museo bibliografico musicale, B 43; and a second copy, also in Bottrigari's hand, Bologna, Biblioteca universitaria, 326, Busta I, 1. Concerning these translations, see Claude V. Palisca, "Boethius in the Renaissance," in *Music Theory and Its Sources: Antiquity and the Middle Ages*, ed. André Barbera (Notre Dame, IN: University of Notre Dame Press, 1990), 259–80; reprinted in idem, *Studies in the History of Italian Music and Music Theory* (Oxford: Clarendon Press, 1994), 168–88.

[9]Salinas, *De musica libri septem, in quibus eius doctrinae veritas tam quae ad harmoniam, quam quae ad rhythmum pertinet, iuxta sensus ac rationis iudicium ostenditur, & demonstratur.*

[10]In a letter from Pietro Aretino of 30 November 1537 to Fogliano (quoted by Girolamo Tiraboschi, *Biblioteca modenese*, 6 vols. [Modena: Società tipografica, 1781–

direct knowledge of the body of Greek music theory is a matter of question: in his *Musica theorica* of 1529, Fogliano develops his theory from commonly known facts through Aristotelian logic and in one place with the help of Euclid's *Elements*,[11] but he does not reveal his musical sources. His chapters on sound, consonance, and hearing are based on Aristotle's *On the Soul* and *Physics*.

Fogliano tackled a question that had been debated for half a century. Why had the thirds and sixths come to be regarded as consonances when in the commonly accepted Pythagorean tuning, they had such complex ratios as 81:64 for the major third or ditone (9:8 + 9:8 = 81:64), and 32:27 for the minor third or semiditone (9:8 + 256:243 = 32:27)?[12] Not only did these ratios not belong to the family of small numbers characteristic of the other consonances—2:1, 3:2, and 4:3—but the Pythagorean thirds sounded harsh when played as simultaneous intervals.

The Greeks were not concerned with the sound of simultaneous thirds because their music was largely melodic.[13] In polyphony, however, when thirds were stacked to form three- and four-note chords, both the perfect and imperfect consonances had to form a pleasing sonority. For this reason and disregarding the Pythagorean numbers, musicians tried various tunings of their instruments to sweeten the thirds. To be sure, Walter Odington as early as 1300 had suggested as a practical strategy the simpler ratios of 5:4 and 6:5 for the thirds, and Ramos de Pareja in 1482 had proposed a scale or division of the string that yielded these simpler ratios,[14] a scale fiercely defended by his pupil Giovanni Spataro (1458–

86], 2:307), Pietro encourages him to translate Aristotle's works from Greek into Italian.

[11]Lodovico Fogliano, *Musica theorica* (Venice: Io. Antonius et Fratres de Sabio, 1529; reprint in Bibliotheca musica bononiensis, II/13, Bologna: Forni, 1970), xxxvi.

[12]See chapter 2, n. 7 *supra*.

[13]The nature of accompanying, heterophonic, and polyphonic lines in ancient Greek music seems to have changed over the centuries, and very little precise information is available. See Thomas J. Mathiesen, *Apollo's Lyre: Greek Music and Music Theory in Antiquity and the Middle Ages*, Publications of the Center for the History of Music Theory and Literature, vol. 2 (Lincoln: University of Nebraska Press, 1999), 72–73, 359–62, and 502.

[14]Walter Odington, *Summa de speculatione musicae*, ed. Frederick F. Hammond, Corpus scriptorum de musica, vol. 14 ([Rome]: American Institute of Musicology, 1970), 70 (pt. 2, ch. 10); Bartolomé Ramos de Pareja, *Musica practica* (Bologna:

1541) against Gaffurio's objections.[15] But no one had offered a logical refutation of the Pythagorean ratios or a reasoned defense of the simpler ones. Fogliano accomplished this.[16]

Fogliano began by disposing of the Pythagorean equation of musical sound with number and the idea that the "sonorous number" is the origin and subject of music. Music, he argues, consists of sounds caused by motion, and motion is not a mathematical but a natural phenomenon. Therefore, music is not wholly a mathematical science but partakes equally of natural science.[17] Fogliano deviates from Aristotle, who taught that sound was motion, and defines sound as a passive sensible quality.[18] Sound is thus subject to the judgment of hearing and not to that of reason, which relies on measurement and numbers. Freed from the necessity of determining consonance on numerical grounds, Fogliano proposes a new classification of intervals on the basis of the musical ear's experience. Seven consonances occur within the octave; in order of increasing size they are: minor third, major third, fourth, fifth, minor sixth, major sixth, and octave. The octave and fifth are perfect consonances, the rest, including the fourth, are imperfect.[19] Fogliano devises a tuning of the scale that yields these consonances in their best intonation, which coincidentally manifests the simplest ratios:

Baltasar de Hiriberia, 1482), ed. Johannes Wolf, Publikationen der internationalen Musikgesellschaft, Beihefte, vol. 2 (Leipzig: Breitkopf und Härtel, 1901), 4–12 (pt. 1, tract. 1, chs. 2–4).

[15]Giovanni Spataro, *Errori de Franchino Gafurio da Lodi* (Bologna: Benedetto di Ettore Faelli, 12 January 1521). See especially Errors 22 and 26, ff. 21v–23r.

[16]See further discussion of Fogliano's achievement in chapter 8.

[17]Fogliano, *Musica theorica*, f. 1r–v (bk. 1, ch. 1). Aristotle believed harmonics combined mathematics and physics, *Physics* 2.2 (194a).

[18]Aristotle *On the Soul* 2.8 (420a). Fogliano's source may have been Albertus Magnus, who argued in *De homine*, Part II of his *Summa de creaturis* (Venice: Simon de Luero, impensis Andree Toresani de Asula, 1498), f. 120v, that motion is an object of Aristotle's "common sense," whereas sound is an object of the sense of hearing only.

[19]For a more detailed account of Fogliano's argument, see Palisca, *Humanism*, 235–44.

octave	2:1	major third	5:4
fifth	3:2	minor third	6:5
fourth	4:3	minor sixth	8:5
		major sixth	5:3

Zarlino had a high opinion of Fogliano and probably owed more to his work than he acknowledged. Zarlino embraced Fogliano's classification, with the exception that he and subsequent authors included the fourth among the perfect consonances while limiting its use in polyphonic writing. Zarlino also adopted Fogliano's tuning of the scale and called it by the name that Ptolemy had given to his own favorite tetrachord—"syntonic diatonic." The term "syntonic" refers to the fact that Ptolemy's semitone in the ratio 16:15 (111.7 cents) is wide as compared to the Pythagorean semitone in the ratio 256:243 (90.2 cents) because the upper string defining it is "tight" or "intense" (σύντονος [syntonos]).[20] Ptolemy preferred this tetrachord not only because of its sound but also because its tones and semitone are defined by the class of ratio known as "superparticular," a ratio in which one term is larger than the other by one. When this tetrachord was expanded into an octave by Zarlino, the following scale resulted (figure 4; the numbers above the alphabetical letters are hypothetical string lengths measured from the end of the string represented in the facsimile).

---

[20]The system of cents, developed by Alexander J. Ellis (1814–1890), is a logarithmic scale that permits easier comparison of the size of intervals than ratios do. The Unit is 1/100 of a semitone in equal temperament. Thus Ptolemy's semitone is ca. 12% larger than the equal tempered semitone of our commonly used scale, the Pythagorean semitone is ca. 10% smaller, and the two are 21.5 cents (the so-called syntonic comma) distant from each other.

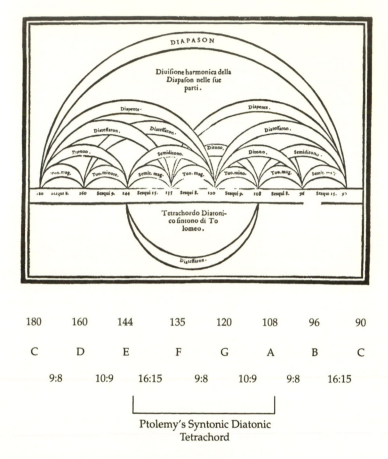

180	160	144	135	120	108	96	90
C	D	E	F	G	A	B	C

9:8   10:9   16:15   9:8   10:9   9:8   16:15

Ptolemy's Syntonic Diatonic
Tetrachord

Figure 4. Zarlino, *Istitutioni harmoniche* (1558), 122.

Here the major thirds (C–E, F–A, G–B) are all in the ratio 5:4 (9:8 + 10:9 = 386.3 cents), judged optimal by the musical ear. The minor thirds (E–G, and A–C) are 6:5 (9:8 + 16:15 = 315.6 cents), but the minor third D–F is 32:27 (10:9 + 16:15 = 294.1 cents), a syntonic comma (21.5 cents) lower than 6:5, and the fifth D–A is 40:27 (680.4 cents), shy of a true fifth of 702 cents by essentially the same amount.[21]

---

[21]Fogliano's tuning is somewhat more complicated, including two possibilities for the notes *D* and *B♭*. He then divides the difference between these to

Unlike Fogliano, Zarlino was reluctant to renounce the wondrous power of number. Attracted to Plato's and Ficino's ideals of universal harmony, he clung to the idea that numerical proportion lay behind the beauty and power of music. Zarlino discerned a significant numerical feature in the modern repertory of consonances. They could all be expressed as ratios with the first six numbers, except for the minor sixth (8:5), which Zarlino rationalized as a minor third joined to a fourth (6:5 + 4:3 = 24:15 = 8:5). He referred to the set of the first six numbers as the *senario*, or *numero senario* (the senary number).[22] This number, like 4 and 10 for the Pythagoreans, had special qualities. It is the sum of the numbers of which it is a multiple ($1 + 2 + 3 = 1 \times 2 \times 3 = 6$), defined by the ancients as the first "perfect" number. There were six planets in the sky (for Zarlino, these were Saturn, Jupiter, Mars, Venus, Mercury, and the Moon). In the *Philebus*, Plato proclaims that hymns may not celebrate more than six generations.[23] There are six species of movement: generation, corruption, increase, diminution, alteration, and change of location. According to Plato's *Timaeus*, there are six differences of position: up, down, ahead, behind, right, left.[24] The world was created in six days. Zarlino lists more such analogies, which altogether consecrated six as the number to contain the sanctum of consonance.

Ratios of the first six numbers, arrayed from the lowest pitches to the highest—2:1, 3:2, 4:3, 5:4, and 6:5—produce the stack of intervals octave–fifth–fourth–major third–minor third. Zarlino recognized that to our ears the resulting chord (for example, C–c–g–c'–e'–g') has the best sounding arrangement of these consonances. Zarlino called the chord formed by this unique series of superparticular ratios within the *senario* the "perfect harmony."[25] Its naturalness was demonstrated in the seventeenth century, when it was discovered that a string at a given tension vibrates at the frequencies of all these pitches and some higher ones at the same time. These frequencies, called partials, comprising the funda-

---

obtain a compromise that deviates from the pure form by a half comma. See Palisca, *Humanism*, 240–43.

[22]Zarlino, *Istitutioni* (1558), 23–24 (bk. 1, ch. 14).

[23]Plato *Philebus* 66.

[24]Plato *Timaeus* 43b.

[25]Zarlino, *Istitutioni* (1558), 28 (bk. 1, ch. 16).

mental pitch and its weaker harmonics, constitute the harmonic series.[26] To Zarlino, the set of six pitches resulted from dividing the string into two, three, four, five, and six parts. If the sound of the full string is compared with that of its half, this is the octave. If the full string is compared with the sound of two-thirds of it, this is the fifth, and so on with the other ratios.

Zarlino wanted a numerological foundation for his theory to give it a solid basis for practical instruction. Counterpoint, as we saw, relied on strict control of consonance and dissonance. The *senario* drew the line between consonance and dissonance, a clear distinction that made the rules for their use in composition necessary and rational.

In seeking a mathematical and physical basis to support his rules of composition, Zarlino emulated the painters who founded their technique on anatomy and perspective and architects who respected the maxims of geometry and proportion. A musician too should have a rational basis for what he does. So *musica practica*, as the art of composition and performance was called, should follow *musica theorica*, the mathematical science of music. Zarlino's *Istitutioni harmoniche* comprised four parts: Parts I and II are theoretical; Part III on counterpoint and Part IV on the modes and on setting texts to music are practical. Rather than separate the two disciplines, as Gaffurio had done, publishing in 1492 a *theorica*, then in 1496 a *practica*,[27] Zarlino believed that the two were inseparable: "music considered in its ultimate perfection contains these two aspects so closely joined that one cannot be separated from the other."[28]

Zarlino realized that musicians did not follow the syntonic diatonic of Ptolemy in tuning instruments, which could not accommodate two different sizes of whole tones (9:8 and 10:9) and two different sizes of minor thirds (6:5 and 32:27). He proposed various strategies, all of them

---

[26]For a brief history of these discoveries, see Burdette Green and David Butler, "From Acoustics to *Tonpsychologie*," in *The Cambridge History of Western Music Theory*, ed. Thomas Christensen (Cambridge: Cambridge University Press, 2002), 246–71.

[27]*Practica musice* (Milan: Ioannes Petrus de Lomatio, 1496; reprint, New York: Broude Bros., 1979); for *Theorica musice*, see chapter 2, n. 1 *supra*.

[28]Zarlino, *Istitutioni* (1558), 26 (bk. 1, ch. 11): "Et per questo nella Musica (considerandola nella sua vltima perfettione) queste due parti sono tanto insieme congiunte, che per le assegnate ragioni non si possono separare l'vna dall'altra."

defined by ratios, for getting the best sounding scales in keyboard instruments, lutes, and viols. But vocal music, being natural, always demanded the ideal tuning of the perfect and imperfect consonances. On this point, he was attacked by Vincenzo Galilei (the father of Galileo), who showed that it was impossible to maintain the syntonic diatonic tuning in performance without hitting some ill-sounding consonances, and by the scientist Giovanni Battista Benedetti, who pointed out that Zarlino's tuning, if actually applied, would cause the vocal pitch of a composition to go flat or sharp. The controversy between Zarlino and Galilei, begun in 1578, lasted until Zarlino died in 1590, though the debate about reason and sensation continued.

Several practical problems arise in the syntonic diatonic tuning. First, if a voice part moves up a 9:8 whole tone and then back down a smaller 10:9 whole tone, the pitch of the melody rises by the difference between them, 81:80, the syntonic comma. Moreover, when a voice part, as at a cadence, changes a whole tone to a semitone for a smoother ending, for example altering a *G* to *G♯* before *A*, the *G♯–A* semitone (16:15) leaves a smaller semitone, 25:24, for *G–G♯* because the tone between *G* and *A* is the smaller 10:9 whole tone. But if such a cadence is made on *G*, because *F–G* is the larger 9:8 tone, the semitone *F♯–G* (16:15), leaves a larger semitone (135:128) for *F–F♯*. There are now two sizes of tones and three sizes of semitones. Not only does the pitch of a voice part waver, but the consonances between the voice parts vary in size, and some become intolerable to the ear.

While Galilei supported his objections by arithmetical arguments such as these,[29] Benedetti very cleverly introduced excerpts from actual musical compositions. He showed how a choir's pitch would ascend or descend almost a semitone in performing a short passage if it held to the intervals of Ptolemy's syntonic tuning and to the consonances in the ratios of the *senario*.[30] The remedies Galilei and Benedetti proposed

---

[29]Vincenzo Galilei, *Dialogo della musica antica, et della moderna* (Florence: G. Marescotti, 1581), 4–10; trans. with introduction and notes by Claude V. Palisca as *Dialogue on Ancient and Modern Music*, Music Theory Translation Series (New Haven, CT: Yale University Press, 2003), 16–33.

[30]Giovanni Battista Benedetti, two undated letters to Cipriano de Rore of around 1563, in *Diversarum speculationum mathematicarum et physicarum liber*, 277–83. For a full account of Benedetti's proof, see Claude V. Palisca, "Scientific Empiricism in Musical Thought," in *Seventeenth Century Science and the Arts*, ed. H. H. Rhys

required "tempering" or altering the natural or just tuning of the consonances. Benedetti's solution approached equal temperament, in which each tone is divided into two equal semitones and twelve equal semitones fill the octave. Galilei went all the way and advocated equal temperament for instrumental music, which the Western world gradually adopted during the next two centuries.

Vincenzo Galilei (ca. 1520–1591) had been Zarlino's pupil for a short time in Venice in the mid-1560s and remained faithful to his teachings until he began to correspond with Girolamo Mei (1519–1594) in May 1572. As they exchanged more than thirty letters during the next six years, Mei pointed out misconceptions in Zarlino's *Istitutioni* about Greek music and about the relation between musical practice and mathematics. Mei cautioned Galilei about rooting musical practice in science.

> The true end of the sciences is altogether different from that of the arts, since the end and proper aim of science is to consider every contingency of its subject and the causes and properties of these purely for the sake of knowing truth from falsehood, without caring further how the arts will use this knowledge, whether as an instrument, as material, or otherwise for the pursuit of their ends.[31]

Mei also urged Galilei to try an experiment on his lute to determine which tuning singers used in performing polyphony.[32] He suggested that Galilei stretch out on his lute two strings, equal in length and thickness; tune them to a unison; and then mark under one string the frets according to the syntonic diatonic tuning, under the other according to the Pythagorean tuning, which Mei assumed was still being used. Then Mei suggested Galilei compare the pitch of corresponding frets to see

---

(Princeton, N.J.: Princeton University Press, 1961), 91–137; reprinted with a prefatory discussion of more recent research in idem, *Studies*, 200–235. For Benedetti's examples, see chapter 8 *infra*.

[31]Mei, letter to Vincenzo Galilei, 8 May 1572, trans. Palisca, *Florentine Camerata*, 65, from idem, *Girolamo Mei (1519–1594), Letters on Ancient and Modern Music to Vincenzo Galilei and Giovanni Bardi: A Study with Annotated Texts*, 2d ed., Musicological Studies and Documents, no. 3 (Stuttgart: Hänssler-Verlag, American Institute of Musicology, 1977), 103: "... agevolmente puo rispondere l'essere il real fine delle scienzie in tutto differente da quel de le arti conciosiache fine e mira propria de la scienza è considerare ogni accidente del suo subbietto et le cagioni et le proprietà di quelli per la sola cognizione del vero e del falso senza altro piu rispetto de l'uso a che sene servino le arti le quali sene vaglino ò per instrumento ò per materia, ò altramente nel condurre il fine loro."

[32]Mei, letter to Galilei, 17 January 1578, in Palisca, *Mei*, 140.

which of the strings yielded the intonation that was normally sung. Since we lack Galilei's side of the correspondence, we cannot say whether Galilei performed the experiment and what he found. But four months later on 7 June 1578, Galilei sent Zarlino a discourse that challenged his former teacher's position on the syntonic tuning.[33]

From the mid-1560s, Galilei was supported by Giovanni Bardi (1534–1612), count of Vernio, scion of one of the Florentine banking families. In the 1570s and early 1580s, a group of noblemen interested in the arts, letters, and sciences met regularly as an informal academy at Bardi's palace in Florence for discussions and musical performances. One of Bardi's protégés, the singer and composer Giulio Caccini (1551–1618), later called this group Bardi's "Camerata," that is, a circle of comrades or a salon. Music was a frequent topic, and Mei's letters, which dealt mainly with Greek music and its importance for modern practice, were read and discussed. Inspired by these conversations, Galilei wrote an imaginary dialogue in which he represented Bardi as the principal interlocutor conversing with an amateur musician and composer Piero Strozzi (ca. 1550–1609). He later stated that the purpose of the book was to instruct Bardi's circle in the foundations of music theory and the history of Greek and modern music. This is the *Dialogo della musica antica, et della moderna* of 1581.[34]

The first eighty pages of the *Dialogo*, the longest section, are devoted to a critique of Zarlino's theories on tuning and on the modes. Galilei had learned from Mei how the Greek modes differed from those of the medieval church. By abandoning the ancient modes, Mei believed, musicians lost the power of song to move listeners to various affections. They also forfeited this emotional effect by adopting the practice of polyphony, which was unknown to the Greeks and Romans, who always sang a single melody even if many were singing. This was the secret of its efficacy. Moreover, they accompanied their songs in unison or something near unison. Galilei, in the section of the *Dialogo* best known today, developed Mei's ideas into a scathing critique of modern contrapuntal music.[35] He urged composers to return to simple melody accompanied

---

[33]The date is given in Zarlino, *Sopplimenti*, 5 (Proemio).

[34]See n. 29 *supra*.

[35]A portion of this section is translated in Vincenzo Galilei, "From *Dialogue on Ancient and Modern Music*," in *Strunk's Source Readings*, 462–67; extended excerpts

by unobtrusive chords. Galilei's *Dialogo* was a manifesto for what would later be called "monody," music for a single voice accompanied lightly by chords rather than by contrasting melodic lines or counterpoints.

In the *Dialogo*, Galilei began to demolish the philosophical basis of Zarlino's theoretical system. He continued this project in his next publication, *Discorso intorno all'opere di Messer Gioseffo Zarlino* (1589), and in several treatises and discourses he left in manuscript that have recently been published.[36] In these writings, he renewed his attack not only on Zarlino's *Istitutioni* but also on his *Sopplimenti musicali*, in which Zarlino had replied to Galilei's *Dialogo*.

Galilei disagreed with Zarlino on the relationship of art to nature. Zarlino maintained that the true forms of the consonances—those within the *senario*—were products of nature and not of art or human invention.[37] Galilei replied that all musical intervals are natural, whether within or outside the *senario*. The major thirds in the ratios 5:4 and 81:64 are equally natural. It is also natural for the seventh to be dissonant in the 9:5 ratio. The production of sound by plucked strings is natural, but manipulating the strings to make consonances and dissonances is artificial:

> It is natural that a stretched string when struck makes a sound. It is also natural that stretching it more tightly makes the pitch higher than before, as it is natural that loosening it causes the sound to become lower. But stretching the string more or less, and forming this or that interval with it is altogether artificial. It is as natural to be pleased with the consonance of the octave as to be displeased with the dissonance of the seventh, the former because it accords with the formation of our sense [of hearing], and the latter because it disagrees with it.[38]

---

from Mei's letter of 1572 to Galilei appear in ibid., 485–95. For the full "Critique of Counterpoint," see Galilei, *Dialogue*, 197–227.

[36]*Discorso intorno all'opere di Messer Gioseffo Zarlino da Chioggia, et altri importanti particolari attenenti alla musica* (Florence: G. Marescotti, 1589; reprint in Collezione di trattati e musiche antiche edite in fac-simile, Milan: Bollettino bibliografico musicale, 1933); Frieder Rempp, *Die Kontrapunkttraktate Vincenzo Galileis* (Cologne: A. Volk, 1980); and Palisca, *Florentine Camerata*, 152–207 ("Three Scientific Essays by Vincenzo Galilei").

[37]Zarlino, *Sopplimenti*, 8 (bk. 1, ch. 1).

[38]Galilei, "Il primo libro della prattica del contrapunto intorno all'uso delle consonanze," ed. in Rempp, *Kontrapunkttraktate*, 15: "è naturale che la corda tesa et percossa faccia il suono. è naturale ancora che tirandola di nuovo il suono di lei si faccia piu acuto di quello che prima era; si come ancora è naturale che allentan-

There is an infinite number of intervals, Galilei insists, although the quantity of dissonances is greater than that of consonances. Of these, musicians use only the small number best known to the hearing. Limiting the free use of intervals that lie outside the *senario* is an unnecessary restriction. The augmented fourth and diminished fifth (approximately in the ratio 7:5), for example, are very useful and sound almost consonant in certain contexts.[39] As for the intervals of Ptolemy's syntonic diatonic tuning, Galilei did not believe that the consonances sung by a choir could be defined in terms of simple ratios. They vary in size according to the harmonic context. Only the octave is heard in its true tuning.[40] As for instruments, they used a variety of tuning systems. Players of lutes and viols spaced the frets on their fingerboards according to geometric proportions that resulted in something close to equal temperament. Keyboard instruments generally were tempered to provide good sounding imperfect consonances in the most frequently used keys while deviating slightly from the true tuning of the perfect consonances. Stringed instruments of the violin family could freely bend their tuning. Skilled wind players adjusted within limits to the tuning of others performing around them.[41]

The controversies surrounding tuning methods, although they involved mathematical and theoretical considerations, arose from practical necessities. Ensembles in which instruments played different sizes of tones and semitones were notoriously disagreeable to hear.[42] Mixing instruments tuned to different systems demanded compromises. A single standard of tuning was the obvious remedy, but most musicians

---

dola, il suono s'ingravisca, ma tirandola piu et meno, et formando questo o quello intervallo con il suono di essa, è tutto artifiziale, tanto è naturale il dilettarci l'Ottava con il consonare, quanto è naturale il dispiacerci della Settima con il dissonare: quella come conforme, et come disforme questa con il nostro senso."

[39]Galilei, *Dialogo*, 88; trans. *Dialogue*, 219.

[40]Galilei, *Dialogo*, 31; trans. *Dialogue*, 81–82.

[41]Galilei, *Dialogo*, 30, 42–48; trans. *Dialogue*, 78, 106–15.

[42]This problem is the main subject of the dialogue Ercole Bottrigari first published under the pseudonym Alemanno Benelli, *Il Desiderio overo de' concerti di varii strumenti musicali* (Venice: R. Amadino, 1594; reprint in Bibliotheca musica bononiensis, II/28, Bologna: Forni, 1969), and later under his own name (Bologna: G. Bellagamba, 1599); trans. by Carol MacClintock as *Il desiderio; or, Concerning the Playing together of Various Musical Instruments*, Musicological Studies and Documents, no. 9 ([Rome]: American Institute of Musicology, 1962).

were unwilling to give up their familiar methods. Toward the end of the sixteenth century, the weight of opinion began to shift toward the obvious solution, equal temperament. The discovery of an ancient authority, Aristoxenus, whose testimony could be cited in its favor, encouraged the movement. His *Harmonic Elements* of the mid-fourth-century, B.C.E., or at least the part that survived, was first translated into Latin by Antonio Gogava in 1562. Some of its contents were known earlier through disapproving summaries in Ptolemy's *Harmonics* and Boethius's *De institutione musica* and through Daniele Barbaro's Italian translation of the architecture treatise of Vitruvius.[43] But until Vincenzo Galilei called him "truly one of the greatest, most judicious, and learned musicians the world has ever had,"[44] Aristoxenus continued to be ignored.

The opponents of Aristoxenus never failed to evoke his heretical assertion that the whole tone could be divided into two equal semitones. According to Pythagorean mathematics, no superparticular ratio such as the tone's 9:8 or 10:9 can be divided into equal parts because there is no ratio of whole numbers that multiplied by itself yields a superparticular ratio. In other words, the square root of a superparticular ratio is a surd, an irrational number. Aristoxenus, who was a mathematician, knew this. But it did not prevent him from dividing the tone into equal semitones because he could accomplish this entirely by ear.[45] Galilei insists that Aristoxenus was consciously dividing a quality, not a quantity:

> Aristoxenus knew very well (as I showed you) that the quality of sound had to be distributed in equal parts, not the quantity of a line, string, or space. He was operating as a musician on a sonorous body, not as a pure mathematician on a continuous quantity.[46]

---

[43]Daniele Barbaro, *I dieci libri dell'architettura di M. Vitruvio tradotti e commentati* (Venice: Francesco de' Franceschi Senese e Giovanni Chrieger Alemanno, 1567).

[44]Galilei, *Dialogo*, 54: "per esser egli stato veramente vno de maggiori giuditiosi e dotti musici, che mai habbia hauuto il mondo"; trans. *Dialogue*, 131. See also Claude V. Palisca, "Aristoxenus Redeemed in the Renaissance," in *Studies*, 189–99.

[45]For an explanation of this passage in Aristoxenus's *Harmonic Elements*, see Mathiesen, *Apollo's Lyre*, 327–29.

[46]Galilei, *Dialogo*, 53: "sapeua Aristosseno, d'hauere à distribuire in parti vguali la qualità del suono, & non la quantità della linea, corda, & spatio: operando allhora come Musico intorno al corpo sonoro, & non come semplice Matematico intorno la continua quantità"; trans. *Dialogue*, 127.

Aristoxenus assigns to the whole tone twelve equal units and to the fourth thirty such units. He divides the fourth in his "syntonic" or "intense" diatonic into two equal tones each of twelve units, leaving a semitone of six.[47] By extension, this could result in an octave of twelve semitones, each of six units, although Aristoxenus does not actually propose this. Ptolemy, Aristides Quintilianus, and all subsequent commentators, including Galilei, double the number of units in the fourth to sixty so that it is divisible by 4 as well as 5 and 3.[48] Galilei observes that Aristoxenus's approach requires a fourth somewhat larger than that in the ratio 4:3, but he adds that this is not a problem inasmuch as assuming a fourth as 4:3 or the fifth as 3:2 would be contrary to Aristoxenus's principle that magnitudes are qualitative rather than measured in numbers.[49]

Modern authors have objected to calling the division of Aristoxenus "equal temperament" because he failed to define it mathematically and left no practical instruction on how to achieve it.[50] Galilei, however, devised a method for placing frets on a fingerboard that approximates equal temperament. He locates a semitone 18:17 from the lowest note and then calculates each succeeding semitone in the same way, that is, each half step is 18:17 in relation to the previous one.[51] This yields a semitone that is 99% of the mathematically correct size for equal temperament. In his last published work, the *Discorso* of 1589, Galilei unequivocally urged the adoption of equal temperament:

> No demonstrable distribution besides this one can be found among stable steps that is simpler and more perfect and more powerful, whether played or sung, or in which the part of the whole that each interval comprises can

---

[47]The best description of this tuning is in Cleonides *Harmonic Introduction* 7; the entire treatise trans. *Strunk's Source Readings*, 35–46.

[48]Ptolemy *Harmonics* 1.12 (trans. in Ptolemy, *Harmonics*, trans. and commentary by Jon Solomon, Mnemosyne supplementa, no. 203 [Leiden: Brill, 2000], 41); Aristides Quintilianus *On Music* 1.9 (trans. *On Music*, 83–86; reprinted in *Strunk's Source Readings*, 56–59); Galilei, *Dialogo*, 42 (trans. *Dialogue*, 105–6).

[49]Galilei, *Dialogo*, 52–55; trans. *Dialogue*, 125–34.

[50]In modern times, the equal-tempered semitone was determined to be the twelfth root of 2.

[51]Galilei, *Dialogo*, 53; trans. *Dialogue*, 128. For a survey of practical methods of temperament, see Mark Lindley, *Lutes, Viols and Temperaments* (Cambridge: Cambridge University Press, 1984).

be comprehended exactly by the sense with as great facility and clarity as could be desired.[52]

Giovanni Maria Artusi (ca. 1540–1613), who earned a reputation as an arch-conservative by criticizing Claudio Monteverdi's free use of dissonance in his madrigals, was surprisingly forward-looking in his enthusiasm for equal temperament. To those who faulted Aristoxenus for saying that six tones constituted an octave because six 9:8 tones add up to 531441:262144 or more than the octave 524288:262144, Artusi replied that since the tones of Aristoxenus resulted from dividing the octave into twelve equal parts, six such tones were therefore precisely an octave.[53] Artusi's interlocutor Vario expresses his disdain for Ptolemy's syntonic diatonic—Zarlino's favored tuning: "according to the nature of the syntonic species described by Ptolemy and called natural by many, there are so many absurdities thereby arising that it is a stupor; imperfections are not lacking—they rain by sevens."[54] Luca, who usually reflects Artusi's views, agrees that "to avoid them and to believe that the syntonic of Aristoxenus was sung and played on instruments would be well, as you have told me many times. For then, every cantilena could be transposed to where it is most comfortable for the composer."[55] In the music of the late sixteenth century, which became increasingly chromatic, an Aristoxenian temperament caused the chromaticism to sound equally well whether or not the sharps and flats belonged to the key.

---

[52]Galilei, *Discorso intorno all'opere di Gioseffo Zarlino da Chioggia*, 113: "ne altra Distributione dimostrabile fuor' di questa può trouarsi tra corde stabili, più semplice e' più perfetta, & più capace tanto sonata quanto cantata: doue viene esattamente compreso dal senso che parte sia del tutto ciascun' interuallo, con quella facilità & chiarezza maggiore che desiderar si possa ...."

[53]Giovanni Maria Artusi, *L'Artusi ouero delle imperfettioni della moderna mvsica* (Venice: Giacomo Vincenti, 1600), Ragionamento 1, ff. 35v–36r.

[54]Ibid., f. 33v: "secondo la natura della spetie Syntona da Tolomeo descritta, & da molti detta, Naturale; sono tanti gli assurdi che ne nascono, che è vn stupore; non ci mancano imperfettioni; ci piouono à sette à sette"; trans. with introduction and commentary by Malcolm Litchfield in "Giovanni Maria Artusi's *L'Artusi overo delle imprefettioni della moderna musica* (1600): A Translation and Commentary" (M.A. thesis, Brigham Young University, 1987), 253.

[55]Ibid., f. 34r: "à vietarli sarebbe bene come molte volte hauete detto voi, credere che la Syntona d'Aristosseno, fosse quella, che si Cantasse, e Sonasse ne gl'Instrumenti; che all'hora si potrebbe trasportare ogni Cantilena verso doue più al Compositore fosse di comodo"; trans. Litchfield, "Artusi," 257.

Thus Artusi, Zarlino's most faithful pupil, like his least faithful pupil, Galilei, turned against his teacher's excessive rationalism. Sensory experience was the best judge of matters musical. But an important part was also played by the intellect:

> which then considers what proportions the sounds have among themselves and the parts of the cantilena, the intervals, the invention, the subject, the order, the form given to that material, and if the style is faultless—all things which belong to the intellect: discerning, understanding, and judging them; this is the part that belongs to the intellect.[56]

Artusi's credo echoes that of Aristoxenus, who put it succinctly: "Through hearing we assess the magnitudes of intervals, and through reason we apprehend their functions."[57] Aristoxenus followed the principle of his teacher, Aristotle, who believed that the intellect cannot know anything that is not first received by the senses. After the sense has experienced something, it presents it to the intellect. Both Artusi and Galilei followed Aristoxenus in recognizing that sense and reason must be partners.

---

[56]Ibid., f. 11r: "che poi và considerando quali proportioni habbino fra di loro quei suoni, & quelle parti di quella Cantilena, e quelli interualli, l'inuentione, e'l soggietto, l'ordine, la forma data à quella materia; se il stile è purgato: cose tutte, che allo intelletto s'appartengono, il discernere, intenderle & giudicarle; & questa è quella parte, che allo intelletto s'appartiene"; trans. Litchfield, "Artusi," 121.

[57]Aristoxenus *Harmonic Elements* 33 (da Rios 42): "τῇ μὲν γὰρ ἀκοῇ κρίνομεν τὰ τῶν διαστημάτων μεγέθη, τῇ δὲ διανοίᾳ θεωροῦμεν τὰς τούτων δυνάμεις"; trans. Andrew Barker, *Greek Musical Writings*, vol. 2, *Harmonic and Acoustic Theory* (Cambridge: Cambridge University Press, 1989), 150.

❧ IV ❧

The Poetics of Musical Composition

M USICA PRACTICA was a broad category in the education of a Renaissance musician. It usually began with instruction in singing, reading musical notation, and playing an instrument. Technical matters such as intervals, scales, modes, and organization of musical time were taught from a practical standpoint. These were applied to instruction in improvisation, which might be impromptu embellishment of written music, invention of counterpoints to a written melody, making up melodies and harmonies on a keyboard or lute over a given bass, devising spontaneous variations on a tune or air, creating an accompaniment to a song, or improvising a prelude or exercise before beginning to perform a written piece—all skills of mental composition performers were expected to possess and employ.

Written composition was the most demanding part of *musica practica*. German authors set this discipline apart as a special branch and called it *musica poetica*. Nicolaus Listenius (b. ca. 1510) defined it in his *Musica* of 1537:

> *Poetica* is that which strives neither for knowledge of things nor for mere practice, but leaves behind some work after the labor. For example, when someone writes a musical song, the goal of this action is the consummated and completed work. For it consists in making or fabricating something, that is, a kind of labor that leaves behind itself, even after the artist dies, a perfect and completed work. Therefore the musical poet is someone engaged in the occupation of leaving something behind.[1]

---

[1] Nicolaus Listenius, *Musica* (Wittenberg: Georg Rhau, 1537), f. Aiiij[V]: "Poetica quae neque rei cognitione, neque solo exercitio contenta, sed aliquid post laborem relinquit operis, veluti cum a quopiam Musica, aut musicum carmen conscribitur, cuius finis est opus consummatum et effectum. Consistit enim in faciendo sive fabricando, hoc est, in labore tali, qui post se etiam, artifice mortuo, opus perfectum et absolutum relinquat, Vnde Poeticus musicus, qui in negotio aliquid relinquendo versatur." Listenius also employed the term earlier in his *Rudimenta musicae* (Wittenberg: Georg Rhau, 1533).

49

Listenius respected here the meaning of the Greek verb ποιέω (*poieo*: to make or create), but he added a further distinction: it is a creative act that leaves behind a finished object. This normally means setting something down in writing, which Johannes Tinctoris called *res facta* (a thing made), distinguished from *cantare super librum*, improvising a counterpoint on a chant read from a chantbook.[2]

To identify a finished composition with a particular "musical poet" or composer was a relatively new development. Before the fourteenth century, most music was anonymous, and even thereafter music was frequently copied and transmitted without attribution. Moreover, it was often intentionally altered in transmission, with the result that the composer's authentic work was not preserved. Listenius suggests that a composer should polish a work to the point where it is fixed and remains so for posterity. Performers are then expected to respect such a text as a particular composer's final work.

The term "poetics" soon began to appear in titles of treatises on musical composition. Heinrich Faber (1500–1552) called his unpublished treatise of 1548 *Musica poetica* and emphasized the superiority of composed over improvised music.[3] Likewise, Gallus Dressler (1533–1580/89) titled his series of lectures *Praecepta musicae poeticae*, which he delivered between 21 October 1563 and 29 February 1564 as Cantor at the *Lateinschule* in Magdeburg.[4] Seth Calvisius (1556–1615) regarded the expression as poor Latin and corrected it to *melopoiia* in his title ΜΕΛΟ-ΠΟΙΙΑ *sive melodiae condendae ratio, quam vulgo Musicam poeticam vocant* (Erfurt: Georg Baumann, 1592). Joachim Burmeister (1564–1629), however, still preferred *Musica poetica* for the title of his important text on

---

[2]Tinctoris, "Liber de arte contrapuncti," 107–10 (bk. 2, ch. 20); trans. *Art of Counterpoint*, 103.

[3]Manuscript in Zwickau, Ratsschulbibliothek.

[4]The treatise was first edited by Bernhard Engelke ("Gallus Dressler, Praecepta musicae poëticae," *Geschichtsblätter für Stadt und Land Magdeburg* 49/50 [1914–1915]: 213–50) and subsequently re-edited and translated into French as Gallus Dressler, *Præcepta musicæ poëticæ*, ed. O. Trachier and S. Chevalier, Centre d'Études Supérieures de la Renaissance, Collection "Épitome musical" (Paris–Tours: Minerve, 2001). A new edition with English translation by Robert Forgács is forthcoming as volume 3 in Studies in the History of Music Theory and Literature, published by the University of Illinois Press.

composition published in 1606.[5] In it, he directed attention to the composer's duty to express the words being set, whether a secular poem or a liturgical prose text.

Musica poetica implied that composing is more than making counterpoint, that the composer addresses a message, like the author of a poem or an oration, to a reader or listener. The music amplifies, enhances, and interprets the message conveyed by the verbal text. Bishop Jacopo Sadoleto (1477–1547) was perhaps the first sixteenth-century writer to draw attention to Plato's definition of a song (*Republic* 3.10 [398c-d]) as comprised of text, rhythm, and melody—with text the most important and the other two subservient to it—when he condemned modern music as negligent of the message and too much addicted to mere play of sound. Later, Gioseffo Zarlino and other authors quoted or paraphrased the definition in their own writings.[6] Plato's definition would become a motto of Claudio Monteverdi's *seconda pratica*.[7]

Zarlino also demanded that a composition be more than a well-executed counterpoint: it must serve its proper end, to benefit and please, as Horace said of poets—"aut prodesse volunt, aut delectare poetae."[8] Like a poem, a piece of music should turn around some subject, which the composer "adorns with various movements and harmonies to bring maximum pleasure to the audience."[9] The composer may invent the

---

[5]Joachim Burmeister, *Musica poetica: Definitionibus et divisionibus breviter delineata, quibus in singulis capitibus sunt hypomnemata praeceptionum instar συνοπτικῶς addita* (Rostock: S. Myliander, 1606); trans. with introduction and notes by Benito V. Rivera as *Musical Poetics*, Music Theory Translation Series (New Haven, CT: Yale University Press, 1993).

[6]Sadoleto, *De liberis recte instituendis*, f. 42v; Zarlino, *Sopplimenti*, 277 (bk. 8, ch. 1): "... Melodia: laquale si compone (come altroue dichiarai) di Oratione, di Rhythmo, & d'Harmonia: dellequali essendo l'Oratione la parte principale, l'altre due sono come sue serue...." Zarlino had cited Plato's definition in *Istitutioni* (1558), 81 (bk. 2, ch. 14), but not the priority of the text. See also chapter 1, pp. 3–4 and nn. 6–7 *supra*.

[7]See *infra* and chapters 7 and 9.

[8]Horace *Ars poetica* 333–34, quoted in Zarlino, *Istitutioni* (1558), 172 (bk. 3, ch. 26); book 3 translated and annotated by Guy Marco and Claude V. Palisca as *The Art of Counterpoint: Part Three of* Le istitutioni harmoniche, *1558*, Music Theory Translation Series (New Haven, CT: Yale University Press, 1968; reprint, New York: Norton, 1976; reprint, New York: Da Capo, 1983), 51–53.

[9]Ibid.: "... adorna con varie modulationi, et varie harmonie, di modo che porge grato piacere a gli ascoltanti."

subject or take it from an existing composition such as a plainchant melody, a tenor part, or several parts from a polyphonic work. If it is an original subject, it should be suited to the words and to their meaning. After one voice announces the subject, the others should be derived from it. This process is called "making counterpoint."[10]

Zarlino assumes that the composer, as often as not, starts with ideas of other known or anonymous composers, but this does not confer a license to plagiarize; rather, it is a challenge to embellish familiar music with new treatments and elaborations. Far from suffering from Harold Bloom's "anxiety of influence,"[11] the Renaissance composer enjoys paying tribute and reverence to music that has already earned recognition. The process resembles a scholastic gloss upon an authoritative work of philosophy or literature. Thus, many of the polyphonic chansons of the fifteenth century are reworkings of other versions of the same song.[12] Likewise, the preferred method of composing a Mass, described in detail by Pietro Pontio, was to compose it around the motives of a favorite motet or madrigal.[13] This unifies the Mass in a way different from the earlier practice of basing all movements on the same plainchant or tune placed in the tenor part or paraphrased in all the parts. The borrowings are now more audible to the listener than was a melody buried in an

[10]Ibid.: "... Far contrapunto."

[11]Harold Bloom, *The Anxiety of Influence: A Theory of Poetry* (New York: Oxford University Press, 1973).

[12]For a discussion of many examples, see Howard Mayer Brown, "Emulation, Competition, and Homage: Imitation and Theories of Imitation in the Renaissance," *Journal of the American Musicological Society* 35 (1982): 1–48.

[13]Pietro Pontio, *Ragionamento di musica* (Parma: Erasmo Viotto, 1588; reprint in Documenta musicologica, I/XVI, Kassel: Bärenreiter, 1959), 156–58 (Rag. 4). See also Lewis Lockwood, "A View of the Early Sixteenth-Century Parody Mass," in *Queen's College Department of Music Twenty-Fifth Anniversary Festschrift (1937–1962)*, ed. Albert Mell (New York: Queen's College Press, 1964), 53–77; idem, "On 'Parody' as a Term and Concept," in *Aspects of Medieval and Renaissance Music: A Birthday Offering to Gustave Reese*, ed. Jan LaRue (New York: Norton, 1966), 560–75; and Quentin W. Quereau, "Sixteenth-Century Parody: An Approach to Analysis," *Journal of the American Musicological Society* 31 (Fall 1978): 407–41.

inner voice, and this method gives the composer more freedom to wander from the musical subject and respond to the text.[14]

By convention, the beginning of the existing composition serves as a polyphonic subject for the opening of the Kyrie, Gloria, Credo, Sanctus, and Agnus Dei, while internal subjects of the model are reworked elsewhere in these and other movements. Composers of such "imitation" or "parody" Masses tended also to replicate the closing gestures of the model in a number of the Mass movements. The models imitated in this way are usually themselves "imitative" in another sense, since the voice-parts of the model enter one after another singing essentially the same music at a different pitch level. Depending on the strictness of the imitation, Zarlino called this technique *fuga* or *imitazione*. *Fuga* was stricter in its duplication of the subject and was similar to the practice now called "canon." *Imitazione* was a less exact presentation of the original melody.

Such a complex of imitative statements making up a "point of imitation" was carefully worked out by the original composer with an ear to harmony and balance. A composer who borrowed the model's opening point of imitation embedded it like a gem in a new setting at the beginning of the Mass. When the borrowed material was brought back later, the composer devised for variety's sake equally satisfying solutions because it was considered inept to copy the model exactly more than once. Thus, the imitating composer entered into a friendly rivalry with the original inventor of the passage.

When Zarlino instructed the composer to find a "subject" and adorn it, he could not have meant that a single subject would pervade a lengthy composition such as a motet or madrigal. The opening subject was often varied slightly in subsequent statements on different words, and this gave the listener the feeling that the work was all about one musical idea. Many of the verbal phrases, however, had their own subjects contrasting with the first, and not all the subjects were developed through fugue or imitation, a procedure more pervasive in Masses than in motets or secular vocal music. The imitative texture is often relieved by passages in which all or most of the voices pronounce the words together in chordal or block harmonies. In the Mass, this was a way to emphasize

---

[14]Numerous critical treatments pertaining to the subject can be retrieved from *Musical Borrowing: An Annotated Bibliography*, ed. J. Peter Burkholder, Andreas Giger, and David C. Birchler (http://www.music.indiana.edu/borrowing/).

particularly important phrases (such as "Et incarnatus est") in the Credo. In motets, chansons, and madrigals, such "note-against-note" declamatory passages are more frequent and serve many different expressive purposes.

Zarlino belonged to a school of Venetian composers founded by his teacher Adrian Willaert (ca. 1490–1562), choirmaster at St. Mark's, who was celebrated for his fidelity to the accents, meanings, and feelings of the texts he set. Born in Flanders, Willaert had studied with Jean Mouton (before 1459–1522) in France and settled in Italy at an early age, where the humanist movement deeply influenced him to pay close attention to the syntax and interpretation of the Latin and Italian languages. Zarlino's *Istitutioni* is assumed to be transmitting the teachings of Willaert. Zarlino, for instance, rules that a voice should not come to a cadence unless it has completed a period of prose or verse, something often disregarded by contemporary Flemish and French composers but characteristic of Willaert's music. He assigns cadence formulas different weights or degrees of finality, according to their suitability to commas, colons, or periods.[15]

In one important passage of his instruction in counterpoint, Zarlino introduces a discourse on how to adapt the consonances and dissonances to the sentiments of a text:

> When a composer wishes to express harshness, bitterness, and similar things, he will do best to arrange the parts of the composition so that they proceed with movements that are without the semitone, such as those of the whole tone and ditone. He should allow the major sixth and major thirteenth, which by nature are somewhat harsh, to be heard above the lowest note of the texture, and he should use the suspension [*sincopa*] of the fourth or the eleventh above the lowest part, along with somewhat slow movements, among which the suspension of the seventh may also be utilized. But when a composer wishes to express effects of grief and sorrow, he should (observing the rules given) choose melodies that proceed through the semitone, the semiditone, and similar intervals, often using minor sixths or minor thirteenths above the lowest note of the composition, these being by nature sweet and soft, especially when combined in the right way and with discretion and judgment.[16]

---

[15]On this, see p. 64–68 *infra*.

[16]Zarlino, *Istitutioni* (1558), 339 (bk. 4, ch. 32): "volendo esprimere li primi effetti, quando vsarà di porre le parti della cantilena, che procedino per alcuni mouimenti senza il Semituono, come sono quelli del Tuono, et quelli del Ditono,

Zarlino also advises composers that departing from the steps of a mode by means of accidentals makes music less virile and more languid and sweeter. He urges composers to proceed with powerful and fast movements for a cheerful text, with lingering and slow movements for tearful subjects. He cautions them to avoid linguistic "barbarisms," such as making long syllables short or short syllables long, but neither the Latin pronunciation of that time nor the Italian language observed quantity. He probably meant that composers should accent the proper syllables, since it was Willaert's practice to place accented syllables on the stronger rhythmic points or longer notes in a composition.[17]

As choirmaster for St. Mark's in Venice—the position Willaert had also held—Zarlino led and composed mainly sacred music. Nevertheless, he also referred to madrigals in his *Istitutioni*, including some of his own, and he did not recognize separate sets of rules for sacred and secular genres or for instrumental music. Although music theorists who succeeded him accepted most of his precepts, they tended to loosen their application in secular and instrumental music. This was one of the signs that distinct genres of composition began to evolve toward the end of the sixteenth century.

Among these later theorists, Pietro Pontio (1532–1595) of Parma stood out for his sensitivity to the demands of various genres. His teacher was probably Cipriano de Rore (1516–1565), a Flemish composer who worked in Italy from an early age. Pontio held important positions in churches in Bergamo, Parma, and Milan. His *Ragionamento di musica* (1588), a dialogue between a teacher and a disciple, treats problems of musical composition in an informal conversational manner, illustrating

---

facendo vdire la Sesta, ouero la Terzadecima maggiore, che per loro natura sono alquanto aspre, sopra la chorda più graue del concento; accompagnandole anco con la sincopa di Quarta, o con quella della Vndecima sopra tal parte, con moui-menti alquanto tardi, tra i quali si potrà vsare etiandio la sincopa della Settima. Ma quando vorrà esprimere li secondi effetti, allora vsarà (secondo l'osseruanza delle Regole date) li mouimenti, che procedeno per il Semituono: et per quelli del Semiditono, et gli altri simili; vsando spesso le Seste, ouero le Terzedecime minori sopra la chorda più graue della cantilena, che sono per natura loro dolci, et soaui; massimamente quando sono accompagnate con i debiti modi, et con dis-crettione, et giuditio"; trans. by Vered Cohen, with an introduction by Claude V. Palisca, as *On the Modes*, Music Theory Translation Series (New Haven, CT: Yale University Press, 1983), 95.

[17]Ibid., 340–41 (bk. 4, chs. 32–33).

them with short musical examples. The fourth *ragionamento*, or dialogue, addresses the important but previously neglected topic of genre. Out of the practice of counterpoint, Pontio says, "come various compositions, such as Masses, motets, Psalms, ricercari, lamentations, and madrigals, all of which use the same consonances and dissonances that are found in counterpoint but not in the same manner or style, as we might call it."[18] Although Pontio does not have a term for genre, he recognizes that for each type of composition, such as a Mass or motet, a distinct "manner or style" is fitting.

The motet, an anthem on a sacred text, demanded that the parts move "with gravity." Such a part tends to enter with relatively long notes and slowly gathers speed, but never exceeds four notes to a beat.[19] The standard measure Pontio had in mind was *alla breve*, in which the breve was divided into two beats, each worth a semibreve (see figure 5). When there are four or five voices, two or three of them may have longer notes while the others move more quickly.

Figure 5. Pietro Pontio, *Ragionamento di musica*, 155 (Rag. 4)

---

[18]Pontio, *Ragionamento*, 123 (Rag. 4): "... vengano variate compositioni, come Messe, Motetti, Salmi, Recercari, Lamentationi, & Madrigali; quali tutti si seruino delle medesime consonantie, & dissonantie, che nel contrapunto si truouano; ma non già nell'[i]stesso modo, ò stille, che dir vogliamo." A later section of *ragionamento* 4 is translated in *Strunk's Source Readings*, 471–78.

[19]On the sense of "beat" during this period, see chapter 2, p. 19 and n. 12 *supra*.

Figure 5 (cont'd). Pietro Pontio, *Ragionamento di musica*, 155 (Rag. 4), transcription

A Mass employs a style similar to the motet but requires more repetition of subjects or inventions from one movement to another. The Kyrie, Gloria, Credo, Sanctus, and Agnus begin with similar material, but each varies the order of entries. In one section, the Tenor may begin, while in another, the Superius or Bassus starts the point of imitation.

Because a Psalm has many verses and each verse many words, the method of fugue and imitation is less well suited to this genre because it would unduly prolong the performance of the Psalm. Most often, all the voices declaim the words at the same time in chordal fashion, with the final verse more elaborate. The Magnificat, though like a Psalm, may be composed in a more learned style because of its solemnity, with the parts making imitations upon the traditional plainsong recitation formulas. The lessons of Holy Week belong to the same genre, but the composer should pepper the harmony generously with dissonances to make them more tearful for the days remembering the Passion and crucifixion of Jesus.[20]

---

[20]Pontio, *Ragionamento*, 155–59 (Rag. 4).

A ricercare, originally a prelude a lutenist improvised before beginning a song, had developed in the course of the sixteenth century into a kind of instrumental motet, a piece for keyboard or instrumental ensemble consisting of a series of points of imitation. Pontio teaches that it should have longer inventions than a motet and that the entry of the "parts" may be more distant from each other. It is customary, he adds, to repeat the same invention two, three, or more times and even continue to the end with the same subject, as was sometimes the custom of Jaches Buus, Annibale Padovano, Claudio Merulo, and Luzzasco Luzzaschi.[21]

In a madrigal, Pontio allows the parts to have faster motion than in a motet and to proceed in tandem, with syncopations or suspensions occurring on shorter notes. The composer makes the music reflect the words, choosing harsh and bitter harmonies for harsh and bitter thoughts, fast music for running or fighting, conjunct or disjunct ascending and descending passages for references to rising up or falling down, and the like.[22]

This technique was called "imitating the words." The text had always been the starting point for vocal music, but the features emphasized by the composer changed over time. In some cases, the form of a poem would guide the structure of the composition, as in the fourteenth-century French rondeaux, virelais, and ballades. In other cases, the liturgical function of a text would dominate, whether an antiphon, hymn, Mass, Psalm, and so on. Beginning in the mid-sixteenth century, composers focused on the expressive qualities of a text, its rhythms, sounds, images, meanings, and the affections it was intended to move. The composer became more like a poet, an imitator of nature, a mimetic artist in the Aristotelian sense.

Whether music was an imitative art became a matter for debate shortly after Giorgio Valla's Latin translation of Aristotle's *Poetics*

---

[21]Ibid., 159–60 (Rag. 4).

[22]Ibid., 160 (Rag. 4). Pietro Cerone (1566–1625), a native of Bergamo who worked for a long time in Spain and the Spanish-dominated Kingdom of Naples, elaborated on Pontio's characterization of these and other genres in his colossal treatise *El melopeo y maestro: Tractado de música theorica y pratica* (Naples: Juan Bautista Gargano y Lucrecio Nucci, 1613). Convinced that Spanish musicians were behind in their knowledge and methods, he aimed to communicate to them all that he had learned from Italian practitioners and theorists, borrowing liberally from their writings. Its date belies the vintage of its precepts, which are from the late sixteenth century.

appeared in 1498.[23] His own commentary on it in his encyclopedic *De expetendis et fugiendis rebus opus* of 1501 was followed by numerous other translations and commentaries.[24] Aristotle included music in his assertion that the musical and literary arts were diverse species of imitation: "Epic poetry and tragedy, also comedy and dithyrambic poetry, and the music of the aulos and the kithara in most of their forms, are all generally speaking modes of imitation."[25] In these arts, he said, the imitation is made through rhythm, language, or harmony, either singly or combined. Book 8 of Aristotle's *Politics* includes a substantial portion devoted to music; here, speaking of the songs of the legendary Olympus, Aristotle states that "everybody when listening to imitations is thrown into a corresponding state of feeling, even apart from the rhythms and mele themselves."[26] Melodies "contain imitations of character," and "rhythms and mele contain representations of anger and mildness, and also of courage and temperance and all their opposites and the other ethical qualities, that most closely correspond to the true natures of these qualities (and this is clear from the facts of what occurs—when we listen to such representations we change in our soul)."[27]

---

[23] Ἐπιτομὴ λογικῆς. *G. Valla Placentino Interprete. Hoc in volumine hec continentur: Nicephori [Blemmidae] logica. G. Valla libellus de argumentis. Euclidis quartus decimus elementorum. Hypsiclis interpretatio eiusdem libri euclidis. Nicephorus [Gregoras] de astrolabo. Proclus de astrolabo. Aristarchi samii de magnitudinibus distantiis solis lune. Timeus de mundo. Cleonidis musica. Eusebii pamphili de quibusdam theologicis ambiguitatibus. Cleomedes de mundo. Athenagore philosophi de resurrectione. Aristotelis de celo. Aristotelis magna ethica. Aristotelis ars poetica. Rhazes de pestilentia. Galenus de inequali distemperantia. Galenus de bono corporis habitu. Galenus de confirmatione corporis humani. Galenus de presagitura. Galenus de presagio. Galeni introductorium. Galenus de succidaneis. Alexander aphrodiseus de causis febrium. Pselus de victu humano* (Venice: Simon Bevilaqua, 1498).

[24] *De expetendis et fugiendis rebus opus* (Venice: Aldus Romanus, 1501). On Giorgio Valla, see Palisca, *Humanism*, 67–87.

[25] Aristotle *Poetics* (1447a): "Ἐποποιία δὴ καὶ ἡ τῆς τραγῳδίας ποίησις ἔτι δὲ κωμῳδία καὶ ἡ διθυραμβοποιητικὴ καὶ τῆς αὐλητικῆς ἡ πλείστη καὶ κιθαριστικῆς, πᾶσαι τυγχάνουσιν οὖσαι μιμήσεις τὸ σύνολον ...."

[26] Aristotle *Politics* 8 (1340a12–13): "ἔτι δὲ ἀκροώμενοι τῶν μιμήσεων γίγνονται πάντες συμπαθεῖς, καὶ χωρὶς τῶν ῥυθμῶν καὶ τῶν μελῶν αὐτῶν ...."

[27] Ibid. (1340a39–40): "ἐν δὲ τοῖς μέλεσιν αὐτοῖς ἐστι μιμήματα τῶν ἠθῶν·"; (1340a18–23): "ἔστι δ' ὁμοιώματα μάλιστα παρὰ τὰς ἀληθινὰς φύσεις ἐν τοῖς ῥυθμοῖς καὶ τοῖς μέλεσιν ὀργῆς καὶ πραότητος, ἔτι δ' ἀνδρίας καὶ σωφροσύνης καὶ πάντων τῶν ἐναντίων τούτοις καὶ τῶν ἄλλων ἠθικῶν (δῆλον δὲ ἐκ τῶν ἔργων, μεταβάλλομεν γὰρ τὴν ψυχὴν ἀκροώμενοι τοιούτων)· ...."; trans. *Strunk's Source Readings*, 28–29.

Sixteenth-century commentators elaborated on the function of music in this scheme. Before turning to poetry, Giovanni Giorgio Trissino (1478–1550) gives examples of imitation in painting, dance, and music in his *La quinta e la sesta divisione della poetica* (1549) because it is easier to recognize action in these arts than in poetry. He attributes this to the condition that dance and music are actions that imitate other actions, whereas poetry, unless recited or sung, is not an action.[28] Benedetto Varchi (1503–1565), in *L'Hercolano* (1570), interprets Aristotle's "rhythm, language, or harmony" as either separable or joined in imitation:

> We can imitate and counterfeit customs, affections or passions, and actions of men with rhythm alone, as in dancing, or with rhythm and harmony, as in dancing and playing, or with rhythm, harmony, and language, that is, words, as in dancing, playing, and singing.[29]

Girolamo Mei constructed a scheme of the various imitative arts in his commentary on chapter 6 of the *Poetics* (1449b–1450a). Never published, it occurs in a letter of 10 January 1560 to Piero Vettori (1499–1585), who was preparing a commentary on the *Poetics* (published in 1560).[30] Mei diagrammed the "constructive" arts (*arte fattive*), dividing them into those that imitate solid bodies—through *chiaroscuro*, colors, relief, sculpture, and gesture—and those that imitate actions—with rhythm alone, as in dance; with words only, as in prose; with melody alone; with rhythm and melody, as in kithara music; with rhythm, words, and melody, as in the tragedy and dithyramb; and with rhythm, words, and verse, as in poetry.[31]

---

[28]"La quinta e la sesta divisione della poetica [ca. 1549]," in *Trattati di poetica e retorica del cinquecento*, 3 vols., ed. Bernard Weinberg (Bari: G. Laterza e Figli, 1970–74), 2:7–90. See also *La quinta e la sesta divisione della poetica* (Venice: Andrea Arrivabene, 1562; reprint in Poetiken des Cinquecento, vol. 25, Munich: Fink, 1969).

[29]Benedetto Varchi, *L'Hercolano* (Florence: Giunti, 1570), 272: "perche potemo imitare, e contraffare i costumi, gl'affetti, o vero passioni, e l'azzioni degli huomini, o col numero solo, come ballando, o col numero, e coll'harmonia, come ballando, e sonando, o col numero, e coll'harmonia, e col sermone, cioè colle parole, come ballando, sonando, e cantando." On the poetics of imitation, see also Palisca, *Humanism*, 396–401.

[30]Piero Vettori, *Commentarii in primum librum Aristotelis de arte poetarum* (Florence: Haeredes B. Iuntae, 1560; 2d ed., Florence: officina Iuntarum, Bernardi filiorum, 1573).

[31]The diagram is transcribed in Palisca, *Humanism*, 336 from London, British Library, Add. 10268, f. 209. For a text and commentary, see Donatella Restani, *L'Itinerario di Girolamo Mei dalla «poetica» alla musica con un'appendice di testi*, Studi e testi

As later in France, the theorists of imitation were not unopposed. The Platonic philosopher Francesco Patrizi spent most of his *Della poetica, La deca disputata* of 1586 refuting the proposition stated at the head of Book 9 that "the ancient poems imitated with harmony and rhythm."[32] He objected in general to the idea of imitation or resemblance, although he conceded that song, having words, could express the affections and that instrumental music could resemble or imitate song.[33] Patrizi proposed a classification of the arts inspired by ancient authors in which music embraced poetry and all the performing arts, attributing this encyclopedic scheme to Michael Psellus.[34] The classification divides music into four parts. The first, the material aspect, included metric, harmonic, and rhythmic material. The second, the "apergastic" or productive aspect consisted of four parts: (1) metrics, which considered syllables, feet, and quantities of verse; (2) harmonics, which defined high and low pitches, intervals, ratios, and consonances and dissonances; (3) rhythmics, which took up durations of movement, figure, and gesture; and (4) "odics," the art of perfect melos. The third part was the "exangeltic" or instrumental, concerned with the arts of singing to the kithara, lyre, and aulos, through which the previously named parts were made audible. The

---

per la storia della musica, vol. 7 (Florence: Olschki, 1990), 28–34 and 176–78. For a translation, see Palisca, *Mei*, 45. Paul O. Kristeller considers similar schemes in "The Modern System of the Arts: A Study in the History of Aesthetics (I)," *Journal of the History of Ideas* 12 (1951): 506.

[32]Francesco Patrizi, *Della Poetica, La deca disputata* (Ferrara: V. Baldini, 1586), in *Della poetica*, 3 vols., ed. Danilo Aguzzi Barbagli (Florence: Palazzo Strozzi, 1969–71), 2:165: "Se l'antiche poesie imitarono con armonia e con ritmo."

[33]Ibid., 2:165–77 (*La deca disputata*, bk. 9). See also Palisca, *Humanism*, 402–5.

[34]Psellus was an eleventh-century Byzantine scholar and philosopher. Danilo Barbagli, the editor of Patrizi's *Della poetica*, thinks the scheme is actually derived from Aristides Quintilianus's *On Music*, but in fact it follows quite closely the description in one of Michael Psellus's "letters" (see Charles-Émile Ruelle, "Rapports sur une mission littéraire et philologique en Espagne," *Archives des missions scientifiques et littéraires* III/2 [1875]: 616–19; the letter appears in a number of manuscripts), which may be based in turn on the description in Martianus Capella's *De nuptiis Philologiae et Mercurii* 9.936, where it is attributed to Lasus of Hermione. It has been commonly assumed that Patrizi must have derived this classification from the little quadrivial introduction attributed to Psellus and published as *Opus dilucidum in quatuor mathematicas disciplinas* (Venice: S. Sabio, 1532), but the definitions do not appear in this work. Since Patrizi was quite familiar with the writings of Martianus Capella and Psellus, he may have known the "letter" and certainly knew the passage in *De nuptiis*.

fourth and final part, the "hypocritical," dealt with putting into operation the other three parts by means of song, dance, and mime.[35]

Imitating and expressing or moving the affections may seem like two sides of the same coin, but the theory of imitation as applied to music had greater breadth. Although "imitation" was not the best word for a composer's effort to embody, represent, or express emotion, it had the advantage of including music's ability to represent or express human actions and ideas, as well as sounds and motion in nature. Music had always done all of these things, but the imitative urge certainly intensified during the Renaissance. In France, chansons such as Janequin's *Le chant des oiseaux*, imitating bird calls, or *La battaille*, simulating the sounds of battle, and in Italy madrigals such as Monteverdi's *Hor ch'el ciel e la terra e'l vento tace* (from the *Madrigali guerrieri, et amorosi ... Libro ottavo*, published in 1638) unabashedly evoke natural sounds (or the lack of them). Other compositions imitate popular music, street cries, or the chattering of women doing their laundry. The principal kind of imitation, however, is the "imitation of the words" of a text—*imitare le parole*, which may be anything from "painting" a musical image of a word to capturing the mood of a line or stanza of poetry.[36] The best contemporary description of this technique is a critique of the practice by Vincenzo Galilei in his *Dialogo della musica antica, et della moderna*:

> ... if a text introduces ideas of fleeing or flying, they [modern contrapuntists] call it imitating the words when they make the music move with such speed and so little grace that just imagining it is enough. When the words say "disappear," "swoon," "die," or indeed "exhausted," they make the parts suddenly fall silent so abruptly that instead of inducing in listeners corresponding affections, they provoke laughter and contempt and make them think they are almost being made fun of. When the words say "alone," "two," or "together," they make one sing alone, or two, or all together with unaccustomed gallantry. Other composers set this specific line from one of the *sestine* of Petrarch, "Et col bue zoppo | Andrem cacciando l'aura" (And with the lame ox we will go chasing the breeze), to jerking, undulating, and syncopating notes that make the singers sound as if they had the hiccups.

---

[35]Patrizi, *Della poetica*, 1:311–12 (*La deca istoriale*, bk. 6). On Patrizi's classification, see Palisca, *Humanism*, 412–18.

[36]For a survey of the practical and theoretical significance of the idea of imitating nature and words in Renaissance music, see Armen Carapetyan, "The Concept of *Imitazione della natura* in the Sixteenth Century," *Journal of Renaissance and Baroque Music* (= *Musica disciplina*) 1 (1946): 47–67.

When the idea of a drum roll or the sound of trumpets or such an instrument comes up, as it sometimes does, they try to represent to our ears this very sound with voices without caring at all that the words are pronounced in a totally outlandish manner.

When they find words denoting a variety of colors, as in dark or white hair and such, they set them to black or white notes to express this idea cleverly and stylishly, expecting the hearing to sense superficial shape or color, objects specifically of the sight and the touch of solid bodies. There has been no lack of even more corrupt composers who sought to paint the words "azzurra" (blue) and "pavonazza" (peacock-blue) with notes that sound like the words, not unlike the way present-day stringmakers color gut strings.

In another instance, when the poem says "Nell'inferno discese in grembo à Pluto" (He descended into Hell into the lap of Pluto), they make some of the voice parts reach so low that the singer, endeavoring to represent someone lamenting, sounds like he wants to frighten and terrorize children rather than speaking in song. On the other hand, when a text says "Questo aspirò alle stelle" (This one aspired to the stars), they ascend to a height that someone who shrieks from extreme internal or external pain could never approach. When a word says, as sometimes occurs, "weep," "laugh," "sing," "shout," "scream," or expressions like "false deceits," "harsh chains," "tough laces," "tall mountain," "hard reef," "cruel woman," or the like—not to mention their sighs, old-fashioned manners, and the rest—to adorn their impertinent and vain designs they pronounce the words in the very unaccustomed way of some exotic barbarian.[37]

---

[37]Galilei, *Dialogo*, 88–89: "Altra volta diranno imitar le parole, quando tra quei lor concetti vene siano alcune che dichino fuggire, ò volare; le quali profferiranno con velocità tale et con sì poca gratia, quanto basti ad alcuno imaginarsi; & intorno à quelle, che haueranno detto, sparire, venir meno, morire, ò veramente spento; hanno fatto in vn'instante tacere le parti con violenza tale, che in vece d'indurre alcuno di quelli affetti, hanno mosso gli vditori à riso, & altra volta à sdegno; tenendosi per ciò d'esser quasi che burlati. quando poi haueranno detto, solo, due, ò insieme; hanno fatto cantare vn solo, due, e tut'insieme con galanteria inusitata. hanno altri nel cantare questo particolar verso d'vna delle Sestine del Petrarca. Et col bue zoppo andrà cacciando Laura, profferitolo sotto le note à scosse, à onde, & sincopando, non altramente che se eglino hauessero hauuto il singhiozzo: & facendo mentione il concetto che egli hanno tra mano (come alle volte occorre) del romore del Tamburo, ò del suono delle Trombe, ò d'altro strumento tale, hanno cercato di rappresentare all'vdito col canto loro il suono di esso, senza fare stima alcuna, d'hauer pronunciate tali parole in qual si voglia maniera inusitata. quando ne hanno trouate che dinotino diuersità di colori, come brune, ò bianche chiome, & simili; hanno fatto sotto ad esse, note bianche & nere, per esprimere à detto loro quel si fatto concetto astutamente & con garbo: sotto-

This, of course, reflects the critic's view of the practice of "imitating the words." Actually, many of the best composers indulged in these imitations, which added to the charm and variety of their madrigals and motets and brought the texts to life. Among them were Willaert, Rore, Luca Marenzio, Orlando di Lasso, Carlo Gesualdo, and Monteverdi.

Galilei envisioned a different kind of imitation of nature: a composer should imitate the speech of actors in tragedies and comedies: their pitch, accents, gestures, and rate of speaking when they act the part of a gentleman commanding a servant, a prince speaking to a vassal, a lover to his beloved, a supplicant, an angry person, a married woman or a girl, a wily prostitute, and so on.[38]

The recitative style of the stage, which issued partly from the critique of the *imitazione delle parole*, was itself an imitation, a musical imitation of speech, from everyday to impassioned speech. The aria of seventeenth-century opera took over the expression of generalized feelings or affections, trying to capture the mood and content of an entire soliloquy without, however, sacrificing the "imitation" of certain key words.

None of the creators of systems of the arts spoke of an important and rather obvious way in which music was inevitably linked with the first art of the trivium, grammar. In both music and grammar, temporally organized statements have beginnings, middles, and ends; they are made up of small units that combine to form meaningful phrases

---

ponendo in quel mentre il senso dell'vdito, à gli accidenti delle forme, & de colori; i quali oggetti sono particolari della vista, & del tatto nel corpo solido, non sono mancati di quelli, che hanno come piu vitiati, cercato di dipignere con le note, la voce azzurra & pauonazza secondo il suono delle parole, non altramente che colorischino hoggi le corde d'intestini, gli artefici di esse. & altra volta che vn verso hauerà detto cosi. Nell'inferno discese in grembo à Pluto, haueranno per ciò fatto discendere talmente alcuna delle parti della Cantilena, che il cantore di essa ha piu tosto rappresentato all'vdito in quel mentre, vno che lamentandosi voglia impaurire i fanciulli & spauentargli, che vno il quale cantando ragioni: doue per il contrario dicendo. Questi aspirò alle stelle, sono ascesi nel profferire talemente in alto, che ciascuno che strida per qual sivoglia eccessiuo dolore interno, ò esterno, non vi aggiunse giamai. Sotto vna parole che dirà, come alle volte occorre; Piangere, Ridere, Cantare, Gridare, Stridere; oueramente falsi inganni, aspre catene, duri lacci, monte alpestro, rigido scoglio, cruda donna, ò altre sì fatte cose; lasciando da parte quei loro sospiri, le disusate forme, & altro; le profferiscono per colorire gli impertinenti & vani disegni loro, ne piu in soliti modi di alcuno remoto barbaro"; trans. *Dialogue*, 222–23.

[38]Galilei, *Dialogo*, 89; trans. *Dialogue*, 224.

and sentences or periods of various lengths with closures of varying degrees of finality. This analogy of music with grammar was already recognized in the early Middle Ages. The ninth-century anonymous treatise *Musica enchiriadis* begins with the analogy,[39] and Guido of Arezzo in his *Micrologus* of 1026–28 compared the elements of a melody with those of speech or verse. As there are letters, syllables, parts, feet, and lines in verse, so too there are tones, groups of tones or "syllables," groups of syllables called neumes, and phrases called "distinctions" in music.[40] The "distinctions" are marked by pauses. The early twelfth-century commentator Johannes compared these to the *distinctiones* of the fourth-century grammarian Aelius Donatus: the colon, comma, and period.[41]

These bonds between grammar and music were sometimes obscured in medieval polyphony, which depended so much on purely musical and rhythmic means of organization; in the Renaissance, on the other hand, the junctures between grammar and music were given high priority in the art of composition because composers increasingly saw their art as imitative and expressive of the texts they set for vocal performance. From around 1540, instructions in composition emphasized the importance of respecting the grammatical structure of texts set to music. Clarity in articulation of segments of text became the norm, and composers learned to avoid excessive overlapping, as when voices imitate the

---

[39]*Musica et scolica enchiriadis una cum aliquibus tractatulis adiunctis*, ed. Hans Schmid, Bayerische Akademie der Wissenschaften, Veröffentlichungen der Musikhistorischen Kommission, vol. 3 (Munich: Bayerische Akademie der Wissenschaften; C. H. Beck, 1981), 3; trans. with introduction and annotations by Raymond Erickson as *Musica Enchiriadis and Scolica Enchiriadis*, Music Theory Translation Series (New Haven, CT: Yale University Press, 1995), 1. See also the commentaries to this passage in "Inchiriadon Uchubaldi Francigenae," *Musica et scolica enchiriadis una cum aliquibus tractatulis adiunctis*, 187–88; and in the "Anonymus codicis Pragensis (*olim* Tetschensis R. 273)," ibid., 224.

[40]*Guidonis Aretini Micrologus*, ed. Jos. Smits van Waesberghe, Corpus scriptorum de musica, vol. 4 ([Rome]: American Institute of Musicology, 1955), 162–63 (ch. 15); trans. by Warren Babb as *Hucbald, Guido, and John On Music: Three Medieval Treatises*, ed. and ann. by Claude V. Palisca, Music Theory Translation Series (New Haven, CT: Yale University Press, 1978), 70.

[41]Johannes Affligemensis, *De musica cum tonario*, ed. Jos. Smits van Waesberghe, Corpus scriptorum de musica, vol. 1 ([Rome]: American Institute of Musicology, 1950), 76–81; trans. *Hucbald, Guido, and John*, 115–17. This figure is also known as Johannes Cotto and John Cotton.

melody of the first voice that enters, obscuring the diction and preventing the discrete mood of a phrase from being communicated.

An important consideration often voiced in the mid-sixteenth century is the accentuation of the text, whether Latin, Italian, or French. The typical polyphonic motet of around 1500 contained many "barbarisms," as the humanists called them: misplaced stresses and indifference to length of syllables. Willaert gained the reputation in the 1540s of being faultless in this regard, and he taught his many pupils to respect the stresses and grammatical form of texts that they set to music. In Paris, a group of poets around Jean-Antoine de Baïf (1532–1589) aimed to revive the ancient meters, and similar experiments in Italy and Germany explored the application of metric quantity rather than stress to determine the note values of the music.[42]

Several music theorists gave rules for achieving close rapport between word and musical sound. On a basic level, they aimed to make the text intelligible by communicating the units of thought and punctuation through different levels of musical closure, by not interrupting the flow of a thought through importune cadences, by preserving the accents and lengths of syllables, and by capturing the general mood of a text. Giovanni del Lago (ca. 1490–1544) in his *Breve introduttione di musica misurata* (1540) sums up these rules, most collected from other authors. To identify the units of a "sentence" (*sententia*) in prose texts, del Lago follows the categories of Donatus, who defined these as *distinctio, subdistinctio,* and *media distinctio,* which corresponded respectively to a period, colon, and comma. As del Lago notes, the English scholar Bede (672–735) renamed them *clausula, membrum,* and *incisio.* del Lago allows a cadence for a period and colon but otherwise counsels the composer to evade the cadence by building up to one and then turning away from the expected resolution:

---

[42]See Edward E. Lowinsky, "Humanism in the Music of the Renaissance," in *Proceedings of the Southeastern Institute of Medieval and Renaissance Studies, Summer, 1978,* ed. Frank Tirro, Medieval and Renaissance Studies, vol. 9 (Durham, NC: Duke University Press, 1982), 87–220; reprinted in Edward E. Lowinsky, *Music in the Culture of the Renaissance and Other Essays,* 2 vols., ed. Bonnie J. Blackburn (Chicago: University of Chicago Press, 1989), 1:154–218; and D. P. Walker, "The Aims of Baïf's Académie de poésie et de musique," *Journal of Renaissance and Baroque Music* (= *Musica disciplina*) 1 (1946): 91–100.

Sometimes to feign making a cadence, then at its conclusion assume a consonance not nearest to this cadence as a refuge, is praiseworthy.... This is done so that the thought of the text sung may be heard.[43]

Zarlino takes pains to justify the evaded cadence. Speaking of writing in two voices, which may be interpreted as two structural voices that are supplemented with others, he says:

... cadences were devised to mark off full sections of a larger composition and to punctuate the complete sentences of the text. Such a termination rightly concludes with the most perfect consonances—octave or unison—so that what is completed comes to a perfect conclusion. But to make the intermediate divisions in the harmony and text, when the words have not reached a final conclusion of their thought, we may write those cadences that terminate on the third, fifth, sixth, or similar consonances. Such an ending does not result in a perfect cadence; rather this is now called "evading the cadence" (*fuggir la cadenza*). It is fortunate that we have such evaded cadences. They are useful when a composer in the midst of a beautiful passage feels the need for a cadence but cannot write one because the period of the text does not coincide, and it would not be honest to insert one.[44]

del Lago also advises composers to lighten the weight of cadences by pausing on a step of a mode other than the final. The final, naturally, is the most conclusive. But one may locate cadences on other steps to break the musical flow, some regular, such as the cofinal (usually the fifth

---

[43]Giovanni del Lago, *Breve introduttione di musica misurata* (Venice: Ottaviano Scotto, 1540; reprint in Bibliotheca musica bononiensis, II/17, Bologna: Forni, 1969), [39]: "Alcuna uolta fingere di far cadentia, & poi nella conclusione di essa cadentia pigliare una consonantia non propinqua ad essa cadentia per accommodarsi e cosa laudabile.... Accio che sia intesa la sententia delle parole cantate."

[44]Zarlino, *Istitutioni* (1558), 225 (bk. 3, ch. 53): "le Cadenze furono ritrouate, si per la perfettione delle parti di tutto il concento; come anco, accioche per il suo mezo si hauesse a finire la sentenza perfetta delle parole; è honesto, che volendola terminare per esse, che si finisca per vna delle consonanze perfettissime, cioè per la Ottaua, o almeno per l' Vnisono; accioche il Perfetto proportionatamente si venga a finire col Perfetto. Ma quando si vorrà fare alcuna distintione mezana dell' harmonia, et delle parole insieme, le quali non habbiano finita perfettamente la loro sentenza; potremo vsar quelle Cadenze, che finiscono per Terza, per Quinta, per Sesta, o per altre simili consonanze: perche il finire a cotesto modo, non è fine di Cadenza perfetta: ma si chiama fuggir la Cadenza; si come hora la chiamano i Musici. Et fu buono il ritrouare, che le Cadenze finissero anco in tal maniera: conciosia che alle volte accasca al Compositore, che venendoli alle mani vn bel passaggio, nel quale si accommodarebbe ottimamente la Cadenza, et non hauendo fatto fine al Periodo nelle parole; non essendo honesto, che habbiano a finire in essa"; trans. *Art of Counterpoint*, 150–51.

degree) and sometimes the third degree, and even steps considered irregular within a given mode.[45]

While Zarlino directs his precepts mainly toward musical setting of sacred prose, del Lago offers instruction applicable as well to poetry, particularly secular poetry. The composer must scan the lines and locate the caesuras and elisions, observing the accents in the standard lines, such as *settenari*, *ottonari*, and *endecasillabi*. The accented syllables should be emphasized in the music by sustaining them. del Lago urges the composer to observe syllable length by setting short syllables to short notes and long syllables to longer note values. This advice is problematic because most modern languages, including much post-classical Latin, lacked consistently definable syllable length. Stress, rather, is the basis of poetic meter in modern French, Italian, Spanish, and German, as it is in English.[46]

Partly in response to the demands of humanists and patrons, composers around the middle of the sixteenth century began to express the sentiments in texts with heightened intensity and sensitivity. They felt freer to do this in secular music because liturgical practice and tradition and a dependence on plainsong subjects held them back when dealing with sacred texts. Nicola Vicentino encouraged this trend, even challenging the customary unity of mode:

> ... composers must always sustain the mode carefully whenever they write sacred works that anticipate the response of choir or organ, such as Masses, Psalms, hymns, or other responses expecting a reply. There are, moreover, a few other Latin compositions that seek to maintain the design of the mode, whereas other vernacular compositions enjoy great latitude in treating many and diverse passions; for example, sonnets, madrigals, and chansons, which begin cheerfully and then at the end may be full of sadness and death, or vice versa. On such words, a composer may forsake the modal order in favor of another mode, for no choir needs to respond to the mode. On the contrary, the composer's sole obligation is to animate the words and, with harmony, to represent their passions—now harsh, now sweet, now cheerful, now sad—in accordance with their subject matter. This is why every bad

---

[45]del Lago, *Breve introduttione*, [41]. See also Palisca, *Humanism*, 338–44.

[46]del Lago, *Breve introduttione*, [40–41]. For a detailed discussion of del Lago's rules for text-setting, see Don Harrán, "The Theorist Giovanni del Lago: A New View of the Man and His Writings," *Musica disciplina* 27 (1973): 107–51. For Mei's and Pietro Bembo's views on accent, see Palisca, *Humanism*, 348–56.

leap and every poor consonance, depending on their effects, may be used to set the words.[47]

Perhaps in response to Vicentino and as something of an afterthought, Zarlino added toward the end of the final Part of his *Istitutioni* the chapter "How Harmonies Are Accommodated to Given Words."[48] Not only should the harmonies be adapted to the words, he counseled, but also the movements of the parts, for going outside the scale of the chosen mode by means of sharps and flats—"accidental" as opposed to "natural" notes—creates a languid and sweet effect, whereas natural melodic successions are more sonorous, virile, and able to express harshness and bitterness. Cheerful words should be accompanied by powerful and fast movements, while tearful subjects should proceed with slow and lingering notes. Zarlino's focus on individual words was perhaps naive or careless, though his references to "each word" (*ogni parola*) and "any of the words" (*alcuna delle parole*), which he left unchanged in the 1573 edition, represented an attitude typical of this time. This early tactic toward greater text-music correspondence, a kind of word-painting called "madrigalism" by modern critics, invited, as we saw, Galilei's ridicule.

---

[47]Vicentino, *L'Antica musica*, f. 48r (bk. 3, ch. 15): "Quando comporrà cose Ecclesiastiche, & che quelle aspetteranno le risposte dal Choro, ò dall' Organo, come saranno le Messe, Psalmi, Hymni, ò altri responsi che aspetteranno la risposta. Anchora saranno alcune altre compositioni Latine che ricercheranno mantenere il proposito del tono, & altre volgari lequali hauranno molte diuersità di trattare molte & diuerse passioni, come saranno sonetti. Madrigali, ò Canzoni, che nel principio, intraranno con allegrezza nel dire le sue passioni, & poi nel fine saranno piene di mestitia, & di morte, & poi il medesimo uerrà per il contrarió; all'hora sopra tali, il Compositore potrà uscire fuore dell' ordine del Modo, & intrerà in un' altro, perche non haurà obligo di rispondere al tono, di nissun Choro, ma sarà solamente obligato à dar l'anima, à quelle parole, & con l'Armonia di mostrare le sue passioni, quando aspre, & quando dolci, & quando allegre, & quando meste, & secondo il loro suggietto; & da qui si cauerà la ragione, che ogni mal grado, con cattiua consonanza, sopra le parole si potrà usare, secondo i loro effetti"; trans. *Ancient Music*, 150.

[48]Zarlino, *Istitutioni* (1558), 339–40 (bk. 4, ch. 32): "In qual maniera le Harmonie si accommodino alle soggette Parole."

☙ V ❧

HUMANIST REVIVAL OF THE MODES AND GENERA

IT REMAINS A QUESTION whether the church modes functioned in secular polyphonic music as they did in the sacred sphere. In the late Middle Ages, composers began to write sacred motets for three and more voices on plainchant melodies assigned to the tenor part, which was the backbone of the composition. Mass movements and eventually entire Masses were similarly tied to plainsong. Since these plainsong melodies were identified with particular modes, the modality of the chant lent some of its characteristics to the polyphonic composition. There was less reason for composers to observe the conventions of the modes in secular pieces independent of any chant, though they may have done so by habit.

The system of church modes served in the early Middle Ages to order and classify the plainchant repertory; later, it guided composers in creating new chants. This system, generally arranged in eight modes, grew partly out of an analogous Byzantine system, but in the ninth century, its theoretical exposition was influenced by Boethius's account of the Greek system of *tonoi* and octave species.[1]

The modal system of the church recognized four finals on which a chant might end: *D*, *E*, *F*, and *G*. Around each of these finals, two scales were arranged, a higher one called "authentic" and a lower one called "plagal." An authentic scale ranged approximately from the final to its upper octave; the limits of a plagal scale were around a fourth below these. These eight scales, each spanning more or less an octave, set descriptive limits (often overstepped) on the melodies in each of the modes. Because a particular form of the octave comprising five tones and

---

[1]For a useful overview of modal theory during this period, see David E. Cohen, "Notes, Scales, and Modes in the Earlier Middle Ages," in *The Cambridge History of Western Music Theory*, ed. Thomas Christensen (Cambridge: Cambridge University Press, 2002), 307–63.

two semitones—with at least two tones separating the semitones—had come to be accepted by the time of late antiquity, these elements may be arranged in only seven ways, and each of seven modes therefore has a certain species or arrangement of tones (T) and semitones (S). An eighth species would duplicate the first. For example, the octave of the authentic Mode 1 (also sometimes called Dorian), starting on its final *D* has the species T-S-T-T-T-S-T. Its associated plagal, Mode 2 (Hypodorian), has the same final, but its octave starts on *A*. Thus, its species is T-S-T-T-S-T-T. Similarly, the modes on the final *E* were numbered 3 and 4 (Phrygian and Hypophrygian), on *F* (rarely used) 5 and 6 (Lydian and Hypolydian), and on *G* 7 and 8 (Mixolydian and Hypomixolydian).[2]

Certain pitches and melodic patterns characterize the individual modes, such as the step employed for reciting a psalm or psalm verse and the path through which that step was approached; the steps on which internal phrases of a chant came to rest; and typical runs, turns, and leaps. Medieval theorists also pointed out that each authentic octave was comprised of a fifth topped by a fourth, each of which exhibited a characteristic species, and each plagal octave reversed the pattern, placing the fourth under that of a fifth. These species contributed to the distinct sound of a melody in a particular mode.

Because simultaneous singing of several parts obscures some of these melodic qualities, polyphonic music expresses modality by other means as well. Those who wrote on the modes had almost nothing to say on this point until the fifteenth century. Then, inspired by reading about the moral and emotional power of the Dorian, Phrygian, Lydian, and other modes in ancient times, musicians fancied that this power could be regained by paying attention to modal qualities. In the eleventh century, Guido of Arezzo had already attributed particular emotional effects to melodies in the different modes as he experienced them, but now people began to expect that the plainchant modes to which the Greek names were sometimes applied should be capable of the effects reported in the ancient literature: Dorian melodies should be steadfast (as Plato held), Phrygian angry and warlike, Mixolydian lamenting, and so on.

---

[2]For a time, the eighth mode was called "Hypermixolydian" (see pp. 74–75 *infra*). On the use and development of the octave species and their relationship to the modes in the Middle Ages, see ibid., 334–38.

The Greek philosophers professed a belief in the power of music to affect moral character, to move listeners to various affections, and to calm them. This capacity of music was called its *ethos*, which can be ascribed not only to modes having certain octave species but also to the range of the voice, the pitch-level of a melody, its genus—whether diatonic, chromatic, or enharmonic—, and its rhythms and meters. When Franchino Gaffurio read Plato's *Republic* and *Laws* in Marsilio Ficino's translation as well as Aristotle's *Politics*, works virtually unknown at that time, he assumed that the modes they described were more or less the same as the correspondingly named church modes and that the emotional, moral, and ethical powers the philosophers discussed could also be attributed to the church modes.

In his *Practica musice* of 1496, Gaffurio urged composers to choose the mode according to the mood they wished to establish:

> Let the composer of a vocal piece strive to make the music agree in sweetness with its words, so that when these are about love or a plea for death or some lament let him set and dispose mournful sounds so far as he can, as the Venetians do. What I believe will most contribute to this is to order the piece in the fourth, sixth, or even second mode, since these modes are more relaxed and are known to produce this kind of effect easily. But when the words speak of indignation and rebuke, it is fitting to utter harsh and harder sounds, which are ascribed most often to the third and seventh modes. To be sure, words of praise and modesty seek somehow intermediate sounds, which are properly ascribed to the First and Eighth Modes.[3]

For further information on the modes, Gaffurio refers the reader to the fourth book of his *De harmonia musicorum instrumentorum*, which he expected to publish in the near future. It was delayed until 1518, but when it did finally appear, Gaffurio fulfilled his promise and devoted Book 5 to the Greek modes and their affective qualities.[4]

---

[3]Gaffurio, *Practica musice*, ff. eeiiij^v–eev^r (bk. 3, ch. 15): "Studeat insuper cantilenae compositor cantus suauitate cantilenae verbis congruere: vt quum de amore vel mortis petitione aut quauis lamentatione fuerint verba flebiles pro posse sonos (vt Veneti solent) pronuntiet et disponat. huic enim plurimum conferre existimo: cantilenam in quarto aut sexto tono seu etiam in secundo dispositam: qui quidem toni cum remissiores sint: noscuntur huiusmodi effectum facile parturire. Quum vero verba indignationem et increpationem dicunt: asperos decet sonos et duriores emittere: quod tertio ac septimo tono plerumque solitum est ascribi. Verum laudis et modestiae verba medios quodammodo sonos expetunt primo atque octauo tono quamdecenter inscripta."

[4]See chapter 2, n. 3 *supra*.

Despite the importance ascribed to the choice of mode, the instruction books of the period show little consistency in characterizing the emotional associations of the eight church modes.[5] Whereas much of the technical information about modality was derived from an analysis either of plainchant or of polyphonic practice, the statements on ethos show a mixed pedigree. Some characterizations were clearly transferred from the classical Greek system. Other characterizations had independent medieval origins within the plainchant tradition, deriving partly from Guido of Arezzo[6] and Johannes[7] and partly from patristic literature, particularly Clement of Alexandria, St. Ambrose, and St. Augustine. Finally, a number of moral-ethical-emotional associations appear to be founded on experience with polyphonic music.

To Western musicians—until the discoveries of humanists in the last third of the sixteenth century—the Greek modes were those described by Boethius in Book 4 of his *De institutione musica*.[8] They are eight—Hypodorian, Hypophrygian, Hypolydian, Dorian, Phrygian, Lydian, Mixolydian, and Hypermixolydian. These names were given to eight intervallically identical transpositions of the double-octave system (the so-called Greater Perfect System) to higher or lower pitches. Boethius also enumerated octave species. These, his charts show, ensued in the middle octave when the modes or *tonoi* were projected over a three-octave system (conventionally represented as *A–a''*), but he did not apply the ethnic names to these species. Nor did Boethius speak of modal ethos in relation either to the transpositions of the double-octave system or to the species. In the ninth century, the names Hypodorian, Hypophrygian, and so on, were mistakenly applied to the set of octave species beginning on

---

[5]The next section of this chapter, through the discussion of Rore's madrigals, is based on my essay, "Mode Ethos in the Renaissance," in *Essays in Musicology: A Tribute to Alvin Johnson*, ed. Lewis Lockwood and Edward Roesner ([Philadelphia, PA]: American Musicological Society, 1990), 126–39.

[6]*Guidonis Aretini Micrologus*, 158–61 (ch. 14); trans. in *Hucbald, Guido, and John*, 68–69.

[7]Johannes Afflighemensis, *De musica*, 109–13 (ch. 16); trans. in *Hucbald, Guido, and John*, 133–35.

[8]A. M. S. Boethius, *De institutione arithmetica libri duo: De institutione musica libri quinque. Accedit geometria quae fertur Boetii. E libris manu scriptis*, ed. Godofredus Friedlein (Leipzig: B. G. Teubner, 1867), 341–48 (bk. 4, chs. 15–17); trans. *Fundamentals of Music*, 153–60.

A.[9] In ascending order, the starting notes of these species were separated by tone, semitone, tone, tone, semitone, tone, tone, like the natural *A*-scale. The last mode, Hypermixolydian, was later demoted down a fifth to become the Hypomixolydian, the plagal of the Mixolydian.[10] Henceforth, with few exceptions, musicians and theorists assumed that the plainchant modes were identical to the similarly named Greek modes and that the ethical characters attributed by ancient writers to the Greek modes could be transferred to those of plainchant.

How was it possible for the Greek modes to move listeners to various passions, virtues, or moral attitudes? We should keep in mind the many ways in which the true Greek modes differed in their musical essence from the modern. First, height of pitch was considered a factor in ethos; though the Greek literature is ambiguous, some general correspondences can be outlined. For this purpose, pitch-keys, or *tonoi*, must be distinguished from octave species, sometimes also called *harmoniai*. Of the *tonoi*, or keys, some are *hypatoid*, or low; some *mesoid*, or intermediate; and others *netoid*, or high. Aristides Quintilianus associated the low with music for tragedies, the middle with the dithyramb—a choral ode originally in honor of Dionysus—, and the high with the *nomos*, which was a formula for singing epic poetry or a tune for instrumental improvisation (see table 1). Aristides Quintilianus also distinguished song composition with respect to ethos, of which there were three classes: the *diastaltic*, which awakened the spirit; the *medial*, which quieted the soul; and the *systaltic*, which moved it to painful passions.[11]

Somewhat earlier, Cleonides associated these three ethical categories with the regions of the voice and the genres of composition. The *diastaltic* ethos, through the lower region of the voice, represented a majestic

---

[9]Jacques Chailley, ed., *Alia musica (Traité de musique du IXe siècle): Edition critique commentée avec une introduction sur l'origine de la nomenclature modale pseudo-grecque au Moyen-Age* (Paris: Centre de documentation universitaire et Société d'édition d'enseignement supérieur réunis, 1965), 198–99 (§§137–38).

[10]*Musica Hermanni Contracti*, ed. and trans. Leonard Ellinwood, Eastman School of Music Studies, no. 2 (Rochester, New York: Eastman School of Music, 1936), 32, 37, 41–42, 51, 63, and 65.

[11]Aristides Quintilianus *De musica* 1.12; trans. *On Music*, 92–93. For diverse views of ethos among the Greek writers, see Mathiesen, *Apollo's Lyre*, 388–89, 482–84, 537–38, 545–48, 550–52; and Brenno Boccadoro, *Ethos e varietas: Trasformazione qualitativa e metabole nella teoria armonica dell'antichità greca*, Historiae musicae cultores, vol. 93 (Florence: Olschki, 2002).

spirit and a manly state of the soul; it was suitable for narrating heroic deeds and for tragic poetry. The *hesychastic* ethos, employing the middle of the range, led to a calm and peaceful disposition and fitted hymns, paeans, eulogies, and didactic poetry. The *systaltic* ethos, which exploited the highest region of the voice, drew the mind down into a humble and feminine state; it was suited to the expression of erotic affections as well as to dirges and lamentations.[12] The associations may be summarized in table 1, which, it should be remembered, is a composite of disparate sources.

Region of the voice/ Modes	Ethos	Genres	Affections
low (hypatoid) [B–e] Hypophrygian Hypolydian Hypodorian	diastaltic	heroic poetry, tragedy	majestic, peaceful, tranquil, manly
median (mesoid) [f–c'] Dorian Phrygian Lydian	hesychastic	hymns, paeans, eulogies, didactic dithyrambic poetry	calm, peaceful
high (netoid) [c'–g'] Mixolydian Hypermixolydian	systaltic	dirges, laments, *nomoi*	humble, erotic, painful, feminine

Table 1. Classical Categories of Ethos Associated with Pitch

Some of the expressive powers of the individual modes seem also to have been based on pitch. Plato and Aristotle contrasted tense and relaxed, that is, high-pitched and low-pitched modes. Indeed, Plato rejected two classes of modes, the threnodic—"the Mixolydian, Syntono-Lydian and those of that sort"—and the soft or convivial modes—the "slack" Lydian and Iastian.[13] He admitted only the Dorian and Phrygian, which best imitated expressions of temperate and brave men.[14] There was evidently a "syntonic," intense, or high Lydian, and a slack or low Lydian, and the Dorian and Phrygian were between them in a more

---

[12]Cleonides *Harmonic Introduction* 13; trans. in *Strunk's Source Readings*, 45–46.

[13]Plato *Republic* 3.10 (398e): "Μιξολυδιστί, ἔφη, καὶ συντονολυδιστὶ καὶ τοιαῦταί τινες."

[14]Plato *Republic* 3.10 (399a).

central pitch range.[15] At least some of the ethical force of the Greek modes, then, depended on pitch level, whereas octave species rather than pitch level distinguished the plainchant modes. This difference made it improbable that there could be any transfer of the ancient ethical effects to the modern modes.

Another aspect of ancient ethos, however, associated with the system of *harmoniai* made the two systems somewhat analogous. According to some modern commentators, the *harmoniai* were octave scales similar to the plainchant modes. These scales could be related to the octave species but undoubtedly were more complex collections of melodic formulae. Many of the associations that became attached to the entities called Dorian, Phrygian, and so on, probably referred to the qualities of the *harmoniai*. Thus, when Heracleides Ponticus praised the Dorian as manly and majestic and the dialogue *On Music* (1136e–f) attributed to Plutarch called it the steadiest and foremost in masculine ethos, they probably meant its potential melodic content. Heracleides considered the Hypo-dorian pretentious, bold, and ostentatious. Aristotle described the Phrygian as violently exciting, affective, and capable of arousing religious ecstasy. There was also some agreement among the ancients concerning the Mixolydian, which Plato called mournful, Aristotle plaintive and restrained, and the Plutarchean dialogue passionate.[16]

How the *harmoniai* achieved such differentiated effects remains a mystery. Mere octave species seems inadequate for this end. As far as we know, the *harmoniai* had no finals, dominants, or internal relationships that would establish a hierarchy of tensions and points of rest, although the *mese* ("middle note") may have had a gravitational function, if we can believe one of the Aristotelian *Problems*, where we read that the melody returns again and again to the *mese*.[17] Still, the term might have more than one meaning in this text. Ptolemy, in his *Harmonics*, employs a

---

[15]For an annotated translation of this section of the *Republic*, see *Strunk's Source Readings*, 9–19.

[16]Heracleides on the authority of Athenaeus *Deipnosophistae* 14 (624d); Aristotle *Politics* 8.5–6 (1340b and 1342b); Plato *Republic* 3.10 (398d); and Plutarch *On Music* 16 (1136d). The passages from Athenaeus, Aristotle, and Plato are translated in *Strunk's Source Readings*, 10–12, 26–34, and 87–88.

[17]*Problems* 19.20 (919a). It is generally accepted that the *Problems* were not actually authored by Aristotle but were compiled over the following centuries, assuming their final form perhaps as late as the fifth century C.E.

system of naming notes both "by function" and "by position." If this system would apply to the Aristotelian *Problems*, which is by no means certain, a piece of music might have two notes that would qualify as the *mese*. For example, the Mixolydian's functional *mese* is next to the top of its central octave, the Dorian's is in the middle, and the Hypodorian's is the bottom note of the central octave. If a melody tended to concentrate on this central octave, regularly returning within it to the functional mese, the upward tendency of the Mixolydian, the centrality of the Dorian, and the downward tendency of the Hypodorian might well have influenced the emotional character of the melody. On the other hand, in the Epitaph of Seikilos, the best example of a melody clearly structured around a single octave and approximately contemporary with Ptolemy, the melody emphasizes the *mese* by position (three of the Epitaph's four lines begin with this note) rather than the *mese* by function, which never appears in a structurally important position.[18]

The arrangement of tones, semitones, and microtones in a *harmonia*'s scale may very well have affected its ethical character. Both the tradition of ancient Greek music theory and the Western medieval systems recognized only seven diatonic octave species. But the medieval tradition rejected one of these and applied the ethnic names to individual octave species different from those of the Greeks. If we place the species and their nomenclature according to Cleonides in a parallel arrangement with the ecclesiastical tradition, we find that only one species has a common name, the Hypodorian (see table 2).[19]

---

[18]For a full discussion of Ptolemy's nomenclature, see Mathiesen, *Apollo's Lyre*, 459–66; for the Epitaph of Seikilos, see ibid., 148–51.

[19]Cleonides *Harmonic Introduction* 9; trans. in *Strunk's Source Readings*, 41–43.

Greek nomenclature	Species of octave	Medieval/Renaissance nomenclature
Mixolydian	S T T S T T T [B–b]	none; later Locrian
Lydian	T T S T T T S [c–c']	none; Glarean: Ionian
Phrygian	T S T T T S T [d–d']	Dorian
Dorian	S T T T S T T [e–e']	Phrygian
Hypolydian	T T T S T T S [f–f']	Lydian
Hypophrygian	T T S T T S T [g–g']	Mixolydian
Hypodorian	T S T T S T T [a–a']	Hypodorian; Glarean: Aeolian

Table 2. Classical and Medieval Names of the Octave Species

The disparity between the Greek and medieval systems may be obvious to us, but it was not to the composers and theorists of the medieval modes. As a consequence, the ethical characteristics of the Greek modes were often unwittingly assigned to the similarly named medieval modes. This particularly affected the four authentics, Dorian, Phrygian, Lydian, and Mixolydian. Accordingly, Gaffurio speaks of the Dorian's modesty and constancy, while Heinrich Glarean (1488–1563) in his *Dodecachordon* qualifies it as majestic and grave and adds that it is well suited to heroic poetry (see table 3).[20] Hypodorian is thought by Gaffurio to be full of inertia and sluggishness but by Pietro Aron (ca. 1480–ca. 1550) as suitable for tears and lamentations.[21] Glarean, on the other hand, deems it serious, forbidding, and submissive.[22] These characterizations of the Hypodorian extend through the treatises of Juan Bermudo (ca. 1510–after 1559), Nicola Vicentino, Hermann Finck (1527–1558), and Gioseffo Zarlino.[23]

[20]Gaffurio, *De harmonia musicorum instrumentorum opus*, ff. 83v–84r (bk. 4, ch. 2); Heinrich Glarean, *ΔΩΔΕΚΑΧΟΡΔΟΝ [Dodecachordon]* (Basle: Henrichus Petri, 1547; reprint, New York: Broude Bros., 1967), 118 (bk. 2, ch. 21).

[21]Gaffurio, *De harmonia musicorum instrumentorum opus*, f. 86r–v (bk. 4, ch. 6); Pietro Aron, *Trattato della natura et cognitione di tutti gli tuoni di canto figurato* (Venice: Bernardino de Vitali, 1525; reprint in Bibliotheca musica bononiensis, II/9, Bologna: Forni, 1971), ff. eiv^r–fi^r (ch. 25).

[22]Glarean, *Dodecachordon*, 102–3 (bk. 2, ch. 16).

[23]Juan Bermudo, *Declaración de instrumentos musicales* (Ossuna: Juan de Léon, 1555), f. Qi^v (bk. 5, ch. 33); Vicentino, *L'Antica musica*, ff. 44v–45r (bk. 3, ch. 6); Hermann Finck, *Practica musica, exempla variorum signorum, proportionum et canonum, iudicium de tonis, ac quaedam de arte suaviter et artificiose cantandi continens* (Wittenberg:

There is a persistent tendency in the Renaissance to lean on the classical legends and regard the Phrygian as inciting to anger and war.[24] Characterizations of the Hypophrygian are less consistent, perhaps because classical literature provided little guidance: for Gaffurio, it was grave and quiet; for Aron, restful and tranquil; for Glarean, melancholic and plaintive; and for Finck, suitable to serious, witty, and lamenting texts.[25]

Of the Lydian, qualified by Plato as soft, convivial, and slack, Gaffurio reports that it is jovial and pleasing according to some but that in ancient times it was used for funerals and lamentations. Aron deemed it capable of relieving melancholy, anxiety, and troubles. Glarean, citing ancient authorities, said that it was convivial, and Bacchic, while to Bermudo it was lascivious and sensual, and to Vicentino haughty and cheerful.[26] The Hypolydian was seen as the opposite: tearful and lamenting. The Mixolydian, which in the classical literature had a reputation of being mournful, plaintive, and at once passionate and restrained, preserved its general character in the minds of some authors (Bartolomé Ramos de Pareja [ca. 1440–after 1491] and Gaffurio), whereas others regarded it as lascivious (Aron and Zarlino) and still others as haughty and proud (Bermudo and Vicentino).[27] There was no classical tradition for the

---

haeredes Georgii Rhaw, 1556), f. Rriij^v (bk. 4); Zarlino, *Istitutioni* (1558), 302 (bk. 4, ch. 5). For a useful overview of modal theory during the Renaissance, see Cristle Collins Judd, "Renaissance Modal Theory," in *The Cambridge History of Western Music Theory*, ed. Thomas Christensen (Cambridge: Cambridge University Press, 2002), 364–406.

[24]For example, Gaffurio, *De harmonia musicorum instrumentorum opus*, ff. 85v–86r (bk. 4, ch. 5); Aron, *Trattato della natura*, ff. eiv^r–fi^r (ch. 25); Glarean, *Dodecachordon*, 123 (bk. 2, ch. 23); Finck, *Practica musica*, f. Rriiij^r (bk. 4).

[25]Gaffurio, *De harmonia musicorum instrumentorum opus*, f. 87r–v (bk. 4, ch. 8); Aron, *Trattato della natura*, ff. eiv^r–fi^r (ch. 25); Glarean, *Dodecachordon*, 110–13 (bk. 2, ch. 18); Finck, *Practica musica*, f. Rriiij^r (bk. 4).

[26]Plato *Republic* 3.10 (398e); Gaffurio, *De harmonia musicorum instrumentorum opus*, ff. 85v–86r (bk. 4, ch. 5); Aron, *Trattato della natura*, ff. eiv^r–fi^r (ch. 25); Glarean, *Dodecachordon*, 127–33 (bk. 2, ch. 25); Bermudo, *Declaración de instrumentos musicales*, f. Q1v (bk. 5, ch. 3); Vicentino, *L'Antica musica*, f. 45v (bk. 3, ch. 9).

[27]Ramos de Pareja, *Musica practica*, 57 (pt. 1, tract. 3, ch. 3); Gaffurio, *De harmonia musicorum instrumentorum opus*, ff. 85v–86r (bk. 4, ch. 5); Aron, *Trattato della natura*, ff. eiv^r–fi^r (ch. 25); Zarlino, *Istitutioni* (1558), 327–28 (bk. 4, ch. 24); Bermudo, *Declaración de instrumentos musicales*, f. Q2v (bk. 5, ch. 3); Vicentino, *L'Antica musica*, ff. 45v–46r (bk. 3, ch. 11).

Hypomixolydian. Some of these characteristics may be summarized in table 3.

Mode	Classical	Gaffurio, *De harmonia*	Aron, *Trattato della natura*	Glarean, *Dodecachordon*
I Dorian	majestic, masculine, steadfast	constant, severe, moves phlegm	happy, joyful, excites all affections	grave, prudent, dignified, modest
II Hypodorian	haughty, pompous, confident	slow, slothful, sluggish	tearful, grave	severe, forbidding, submissive
III Phrygian	exciting, martial	incites to anger, war	pugnacious, angry	mournful, incites to battle, rage
IV Hypophrygian	austere, appeases anger	quiet, grave, calms excitement	restful, tranquil	melancholic, plaintive
V Lydian	funereal, sad, convivial	weeping, lamenting	relieves melancholy, burdens	convivial, Bacchic
VI Hypolydian	Bacchic, intoxicating	tearful, lamenting	induces tears, compassion	pleasing, not elegant
VII Mixolydian	threnodic, lamenting	exciting, withdrawn	mixture of modesty, joviality	suitable for praises
VIII Hypomixolydian		sublime, free of corruption	merry, happy	natural charm, sweetness

Table 3. Ethos of the Modes: Classical and Renaissance Compared

Besides the tradition of ethos that relied on the coincidence of the classical and modern names, there was another that appears to have been based on the plainchant experience. It is represented by the authors Johannes Aegidius de Zamora (fl. 1260–80), Ramos de Pareja, Aron, and German theorists such as Finck.[28] It should be noted that this

---

[28]Johannes Aegidius de Zamora, *Ars musica*, ed. Michel Robert-Tissot, Corpus scriptorum de musica, vol. 20 ([Rome]: American Institute of Musicology, 1974),

medieval tradition was not unadulterated with classical associations, nor was it immune to later mutations inspired by the polyphonic experience (see table 4).

A more practical approach to modal ethos in the Renaissance recognized a mode's distinctive melodic and harmonic combinations—both successive and simultaneous—and the moods they awakened. This pragmatic stance, taken by Zarlino and Vicentino, corrected some of the most inappropriate classical and patristic characterizations. Zarlino, who cited most of the classical associations in the *Istitutioni*'s historical chapter 5 of Book 4, closed that discussion with a cynical commentary in which he attributed the variety and contradictions concerning the modes to changing customs and usages, a lack of understanding by writers, and errors of transmission. In the practical chapters of Book 4—on the modes in plainchant and polyphony—as well as in Book 3 on counterpoint, Zarlino, recognizing the twelve modes defined by Glarean in the *Dodecachordon* (although later renumbering them in his *Dimostrationi harmoniche* [1571]),[29] sought out musical properties that had expressive potential. His comments on Mode 1 are typical. It had an effect "midway between sad and cheerful" because of the minor third heard in the harmony formed on the first and fifth degrees (*D* and *A*), which made it "religious and devout and somewhat sad; hence we can best use it with words that are full of gravity and that deal with lofty and edifying things."[30]

100–105 (ch. 15); Ramos de Pareja, *Musica practica*, 57 (pt. 1, tract. 3, ch. 3); Finck, *Practica musica*, f. Rriij^v–Riiij^v (bk. 4).

[29]See pp. 87–88 *infra*.

[30]Zarlino, *Istitutioni* (1558), 322 (bk. 4, ch. 18): "Et perche il Primo modo hà vn certo mezano effetto tra il mesto, & lo allegro; per cagione del Semiditono, che si ode nel concento sopra le chorde estreme della Diapente, & della Diatessaron; non hauendo altramente il Ditono dalla parte graue; per sua natura è alquanto mesto. Però potremo ad esso accommodare ottimamente quelle parole, le quali saranno piene di grauità, & che trattaranno di cose alte, & sententiosetrans"; trans. *On the Modes*, 58.

Mode	Aegidius de Zamora, *Ars musica* (ca. 1270)	Ramos de Pareja, *Musica practica*	Finck, *Practica musica*
I Dorian	flexible, suited to all affections	flexible, suited to all affections; moves phlegm and arouses from sleep, alleviates laziness, sadness	arouses the somnolent, relieves cares, arouses mourning, purges phlegm
II Hypodorian	severe, mournful	severe, mournful	mournful, heavy, serious, humble
III Phrygian	severe, inciting, restores health	severe, inciting, suits proud, irritable, wild men	moves choler and bile, suits battles, lofty deeds
IV Hypophrygian	caressing, chatty, flattering	caressing, chatty, adulating, lascivious, without charm	represents servant who serves the pleasures of a lord
V Lydian	modest, delightful, sweetens, relieves despair	delightful, modest, merry, cheers the sad, despairing	gentler affections, calms the disturbed, modest, delightful, merry, solace for the afflicted and desperate
VI Hypolydian	induces tears, piety	induces tears, piety	opposite of Lydian
VII Mixolydian	erotic and happy, represents adolescence	erotic and happy, represents adolescence	used in invectives, terrifying, not serious to elders
VIII Hypomixolydian	sweet and gloomy, in manner of solitary people	sweet and gloomy, in manner of solitary people	appeasing, soothes anger with gentleness

Table 4. Ethos of the Modes: The Medieval Ecclesiastical Tradition

Of the third mode (on *E*), setting aside all that is told of it as a martial mode, Zarlino said: "If the third mode were not mixed with the ninth mode [the Aeolian on *A*], and were heard by itself, its harmony would be somewhat hard," but because of the way it is conventionally mixed with the ninth mode, this effect is tempered, and "some have been of the opinion that the third mode moves one to weeping. Hence they have accommodated to it words which are tearful and full of laments."[31]

Equally significant are Zarlino's comments on the affections of the twelve modes in his book on counterpoint. He noted that among the imperfect consonances, the major thirds and sixths and their compounds are lively and cheerful, while the minor thirds and sixths, though sweet and smooth, are sad and languid. Consequently, when major thirds and sixths prevail in the harmony formed on the final or the fifth degree in the authentic modes or on the final and first degree in the plagal modes, these modes are "gay and lively," as in the G and C modes. This is partly because in four- or five-part harmony, the major third lies below the minor, which is the most natural arrangement. Other modes are sad or languid because the minor third dominates the harmony on these degrees, as in the modes on D and A. Here the minor third is below the major third, which strikes the hearing as less natural.[32]

Vicentino, writing at about the same time as Zarlino, was more gullible. He eclectically and pragmatically adapted the classical traits to practical experience. The object of his *L'Antica musica ridotta alla moderna prattica* was, after all, to adapt ancient music to modern practice. Thus he found Mode 1 (Dorian) agreeable and devout and more virtuous than wanton; yet he could not resist adding that the Dorian people sang their songs of praise and of great deeds in this mode. Of the second mode (Hypodorian), he declared that its nature was akin to the first, but more cheerful and modest because the species of fourth was now below that of the fifth. The third mode (Phrygian) he found to have little cheer unless accompanied by a mixture of the chromatic and enharmonic, in which case it could be cheerful in four voices. Any reference to the irate nature of its Greek namesake is missing. The fourth mode (Hypo-

---

[31]Ibid., 324 (bk. 4, ch. 20): "Se questo Modo non si mescolasse col Nono, & si vdisse semplice, hauerebbe la sua harmonia alquanto dura: ma perche è temperata dalla Diapente del Nono, & dalla Cadenza, che si fa in a, che in esso grandemente si vsa; però alcuni hanno hauuto parere, che habbia natura di commouere al pianto; la onde gli accommodarono volentieri quelle parole, che sono lagrimeuoli, & piene di lamenti"; trans. *On the Modes*, 64.

[32]Ibid., 156–57 (bk. 3, ch. 10); trans. in *Art of Counterpoint*, 21–22.

phrygian) he deemed funereal, and the fifth (Lydian) proud and haughty, yet cheerful, which he found held as well for the sixth (Mixolydian).[33]

What has this theorizing about ethos to do with how music was composed and heard? We know that a number of composers were conscientious about observing the limits and musical identity of the modes they chose for compositions.[34] They include Adrian Willaert, Cipriano de Rore, Orlando di Lasso, and Giovanni Pierluigi da Palestrina. Rore, for example, published two collections of madrigals that are arranged by mode and therefore give evidence of the composer's deliberate modal choices.[35] In the *Primo libro a 5 voci* (1542), the order of texts is arbitrary, unlike Lasso's *Penitential Psalms*, for example, which are also arranged by mode but in a predetermined order of texts. We may hypothesize, therefore, that in the 1542 collection, Rore's choice of mode for a particular text was guided by the nature of the text. Some of the madrigals strongly support the conventional pairing of mode and affection, others only weakly or not at all.

Of the three madrigals in Mode 1 (Dorian), *Poggian'al ciel* best fits the reputed character of this mode. In it, an anonymous poet praises a lady who is virtuous despite her seductiveness and Cupid's persistent temp-

---

[33]Vicentino, *L'Antica musica*, ff. 44v–45v (bk. 3, chs. 5–10). For a recent study of musical ethos, see Brenno Boccadoro, "Éléments de grammaire mélancolique," *Acta musicologica* 76 (2004): 25–65.

[34]Some of these composers have been identified, thanks to the work of a number of scholars: Bernhard Meier, *Die Tonarten des klassischen Vokalpolyphonie* (Utrecht: Oosthoek, Scheltema & Holkema, 1974); trans. by Ellen S. Beebe as *The Modes of Classical Vocal Polyphony: Described According to the Sources, with Revisions by the Author* (New York: Broude Bros., 1988); and Meier, Foreword to Cipriano de Rore, *Opera omnia*, 8 vols., Corpus mensurabilis musicae, vol. 14 ([n.p.]: American Institute of Musicology, 1956–97), pp. III–IV; Harold S. Powers, "Tonal Types and Modal Categories in Renaissance Polyphony," *Journal of the American Musicological Society* 34 (1981): 428–70; Jessie Ann Owens, "Mode in the Madrigals of Cipriano de Rore," in *Altro Polo: Essays on Italian Music in the Cinquecento*, ed. Richard Charteris (Sydney: Frederick May Foundation for Italian Studies, 1990), 1–16; Frans Wiering, "The Language of the Modes: Studies in the History of Polyphonic Modality" (Ph.D. dissertation, University of Amsterdam, 1995); and Cristle Collins Judd, *Reading Renaissance Music Theory: Hearing with the Eyes*, Cambridge Studies in Music Theory and Analysis (Cambridge: Cambridge University Press, 2000).

[35]These two collections, the *Primo libro a 5 voci* (Venice: H. Scotus, 1542) and the *Primo libro a 4 voci* (Ferrara: G. de Buglhat et A. Huches, 1550), are analyzed with respect to system, clef, final, and mode by Owens, "Mode in the Madrigals of Cipriano de Rore."

tations. *Quand'io son tutto volto* in Mode 2 (Hypodorian) begins by stating that Laura is the poet's light, which he fears may be extinguished. Presently, he loses that light and wanders blindly—and silently, for his words can convey little—, fleeing the thought of death, weeping in solitude. The subject is consistent with the classical description of the mode as threnodic, Gaffurio's conception of it as mournful, and Zarlino's as apt to represent weeping, sadness, loneliness, captivity, and calamity. Aside from frequently flattening the sixth degree above the final, Rore keeps within the limits of the mode throughout the composition.

The classical martial association of the Phrygian may have prompted Mode 3 (Phrygian) for Francesco Maria Molza's poem, *Altiero sasso*, which mentions the "great ancient people's honors to Mars." Likewise, Petrarch's *La vita fugge*, the poet's complaint of being at war with everything, is set in this mode. The third madrigal in this mode, Nicolo Amanio's *Strane ruppi, aspri monti*, is a better fit with Zarlino's characterization of the mode as harsh and apt for moving a listener to tears. Here Rore intensifies these feelings by utilizing at the opening a stepwise descending fourth motive, *A-G-F-E*, which in the next century would become a figure of lament. Inconclusive-sounding progressions of a major sixth to a fifth and chains of suspensions contribute to the aching mood.

In these and other examples, a significant correlation between the contemporary concepts of modal ethos and Rore's settings leads us to conclude that he chose certain modes partly on the basis of conventional lore about the ethos of the ancient, medieval, and modern modes and partly on their inherent polyphonic resources, including distinctive species of fifths and fourths, regular and irregular cadences, ambitus, the types of vertical sonorities, and the final.

The polyphonic medium, as composers and theorists discovered in the course of the sixteenth century, offered a wealth of resources for endowing a work with a modal identity and for exploiting music's expressive potential. The humanist movement stimulated the search for these resources because it convinced people that mode was the key to music's power and because patrons and cultivated listeners wanted, beyond entertainment, music that conveyed something to them.

Pietro Aron took on the task of analyzing in his *Trattato della natura et cognitione di tutti gli tuoni di canto figurato* (1525) a representative repertory of chansons, motets, and Masses to determine their modes.[36] In the course of this investigation, he showed that the most revealing criteria were the finals and cofinals, the species of fifths and fourths outlined in the ascents and descents of a melody, the presence of the reciting tone, the use or absence of accidentals, and cadences. Other writers, particularly Zarlino and Pietro Pontio, emphasized the importance of placing cadences on appropriate degrees of a mode according to a structural plan that supported the syntactic divisions and punctuation of a text, particularly in a longer piece. Theorists also called attention to the range of the individual voices, for this was the best indication whether a composition should be classified as authentic or plagal in mode. The tenor part of compositions in the authentic mode exhibited the characteristic range of the octave of the final; the tenor part of plagal compositions had a range about a fourth below the final. The Superius usually had a range similar to the Tenor's, while the Bassus and Altus behaved as if in the complementary mode: plagal if the Tenor was authentic and the converse. Thus, polyphonic practice gave a new meaning to authentic and plagal.

Although the Renaissance inherited from the Middle Ages a system of eight modes arrayed around the four finals on *D*, *E*, *F*, and *G*, musicians recognized for a long time that some plainchant melodies and polyphonic compositions ended on *A* or on *F* (with a *B♭*). Many polyphonic compositions ended on *C*. Those ending on *A* sounded as if written in the modern minor mode, while those ending on *F* or *C* sounded like pieces in major. Glarean, disturbed by the failure of theorists to recognize these two modes, proposed an expansion of the system to twelve modes, the ninth and tenth on *A*, which he called Aeolian and Hypoaeolian, and the eleventh and twelfth on *C*, which he named Ionian and Hypoionian. He borrowed these names from Aristoxenus and boasted that he had rediscovered long-lost ancient modes.[37] Glarean's innovation was welcomed, particularly by Zarlino, who, with-

---

[36]A partial translation of the treatise appears in *Strunk's Source Readings*, 415–28. For an exhaustive study of mode in the sixteenth century and later, see Meier, *The Modes of Classical Vocal Polyphony*, and Wiering, "The Language of the Modes." See also Judd, "Renaissance Modal Theory."

[37]Glarean's motivation for his expansion of the system of modes from eight to twelve is detailed in Sarah Fuller, "Defending the *Dodecachordon*: Ideological Currents in Glarean's Modal Theory," *Journal of the American Musicological Society* 49 (1996): 191–224. See also Judd, "Renaissance Modal Theory," 383–89.

out acknowledgment, assimilated the new modes into his own version of the twelve-mode system.

While modal theory was achieving this consolidation, humanist scholars began to undermine its authority and relevance by resurrecting the authentic ancient Greek modes. That the church modes were not the same as the similarly named Greek modes seems to have been first realized in the circle of Vittorino da Feltre, founder of a school for patrician youth in Mantua and a collector of Greek manuscripts. He owned the now-famous manuscript containing some of the best texts for the treatises on music by Ptolemy, Porphyry, Aristides Quintilianus, and Bacchius, as well as the Plutarchean dialogue *On Music*, a few important anonymous treatises (the so-called Bellermann's Anonymous), and three anonymous Greek hymns now attributed to Mesomedes.[38] Vittorino lectured on the music treatise of Boethius not simply as a manual on one of the mathematical arts of the quadrivium but as a document in the history of Greek music and music theory. His pupil and associate Johannes Gallicus de Namur testified that in spite of all his musical training in the north, he never understood music until his studies in Mantua, where he heard Vittorino lecture on "that *Musica*, which the so often mentioned Boethius turned into Latin from Greek."[39] This important acknowledgment of Boethius's *De institutione musica* as a prime resource for investigating the nature and history of the Greek modes placed it in an entirely different light. Studying Boethius in this new light persuaded Gallicus that he described a system totally different from the church modes. The Greek "tropes and modes," Gallicus said, "differ only in location, and in the whole appear alike."[40] They were "artificial" transpositions to lower and higher pitches of a single double-octave system, unlike the church modes, which were all naturally different and destined to praise God.

Gaffurio, influenced by Gallicus, had some inkling of the difference between the two systems but never defined it clearly. For his part, Zarlino shunned the Greek system as having little relevance to modern

---

[38]See chapter 3, n. 6 *supra*.

[39]Gallicus, *Ritus canendi*, 11 (pt. 1, bk. 1, ch. 4): "ea namque musica, quam totiens allegatus Boethius de Graeco vertit in latinum."

[40]Ibid., 73 (pt. 1, bk. 3, ch. 10): "Hi tropi modique Graeci, Quos et vocavere tonos, Expressi Graecis litteris Ac declarati Latinis Arte magis compositi, Quam natura conditi, Solis locis hic differunt Totique parent similes."

practice, though he gave it some attention in his book on the modes (Part 4 of the *Istitutioni*), deploring that the ancient sources, in disagreement among themselves, left the matter in a confused state. Two scholars working in Rome in the mid-sixteenth century searched for an answer to the riddle of the modes in whatever treatises on music they could find among the Greek manuscripts. One of them, Francisco de Salinas, was a blind Spanish organist schooled in Greek and Latin; the other, Girolamo Mei, was a classicist trained in Florence by the noted humanist Piero Vettori. Mei finished his *De modis* in 1573, parts of which attained limited circulation in manuscript copies but remained unpublished until the end of the twentieth century.[41] Salinas published his conclusions in 1577.[42]

Mei became interested in the Greek modes while helping Vettori edit some of the Greek tragedies and prepare his commentaries on the *Poetics* of Aristotle. Mei's *De modis* was an exhaustive, purely historical study of the ancient and modern modes, based on primary documents. In the early 1570s, however, Mei realized that his discoveries about ancient music could be the basis of a reform of modern music, and he began a treatise in Italian that laid the groundwork for such a movement. Meanwhile, he circulated the fourth of four books of *De modis* to a circle of learned academicians in 1573 and imparted much of his knowledge to Vincenzo Galilei and Giovanni Bardi. Galilei used the information in his *Dialogo della musica antica et della moderna* (1581), as did Bardi in an unpublished academic discourse.[43]

Mei, faced with the same confusion of accounts that frustrated Zarlino, realized that the authors did not describe a single system but different ones. The oldest, Aristoxenus (b. ca. 360 B.C.E.) is said to have known thirteen *tonoi*, in which a double-octave system could be located on any of thirteen pitch levels, a semitone apart. His followers added two more to form a symmetrical array, resulting in five principal *tonoi*, five below these (similarly named with the prefix hypo-), and five above (named with the prefix hyper-).[44] Claudius Ptolemy (d. after 160 C.E.) described a system of eight *tonoi*, but he did not approve of it because

[41]Girolamo Mei, *De modis*, ed. Eisuke Tsugami (Tokyo: Keiso Shobo, 1991).

[42]See chapter 2, n. 23 *supra*.

[43]Bardi, "Discorso mandato a Giulio Caccini," 90–131 (see chapter 1, n. 8 *supra*).

[44]On Aristoxenus's thirteen *tonoi*, see Mathiesen, *Apollo's Lyre*, 385–87.

only seven were necessary to produce seven octave species, the maximum number possible.[45] Mei believed that the emotional effect of the *tonoi* depended largely on the location of the *mese*, or middle note, of a *tonos* and therefore on the height of the melody within a singer's range. He realized that each *tonos* was associated with a particular octave species, but he did not theorize about ways in which the species affected the emotions. Although he correctly identified the species that belonged to each *tonos*, his explanation of their interaction in practice has not been adopted by present-day opinion.[46]

Salinas devoted three chapters to the Greek modes in his monumental *De musica libri septem* (chapters 11–13 of Book 4), in which he relied mainly on Ptolemy. To his credit, Salinas was the first to distinguish in a printed book between the *tonoi* and *harmoniai* in Ptolemy's system. By a change of *tonos*, Salinas explains, paraphrasing Ptolemy, a melody is moved higher or lower in pitch but maintains the same character. By a mutation of *harmonia*, the melody is transformed because the interval scheme or octave species has changed. This was an important distinction because it attributed melodic identity and ethos to the *harmoniai* rather than the *tonoi*. Salinas did not show how the *tonoi* were related to the *harmoniai*, but perhaps he thought this was obvious.[47]

The Chromatic and Enharmonic Genera

The expressive potential of another resource of ancient Greek music—the chromatic and enharmonic genera—waited longer to be acknowledged by Western musicians. Boethius and those who copied him described three genera of tetrachord: diatonic, chromatic, and enharmonic. The diatonic tetrachord, in descending order, consists of two tones and a semitone, the chromatic of a semiditone (minor third) and two semitones, and the enharmonic of a ditone (major third) and two dieses (more or less quarter-tones) that fill up the remainder of the fourth. The actual size of these units varies in the different "shades" or tunings.[48] Only the diatonic was used in plainchant and early polyphony.

---

[45]Ibid., 463–66.

[46]For a full discussion of Mei's interpretation of the *tonoi*, see Palisca, *Humanism*, 303–14.

[47]Ibid., 301–3.

[48]See Mathiesen, *Apollo's Lyre*, 311–13.

Most modern musicians—and even some of the Greek theorists—
dismissed the chromatic and enharmonic as unwieldy and difficult to
sing. But curiosity about these two genera was aroused by reading the
dialogue *On Music* then attributed to Plutarch. Carlo Valgulio's translation of this late Greek dialogue, together with his introduction to it, cast
a positive light on the enharmonic.[49]

Salinas quotes in the original Greek the passage in which Soterichus,
one of the speakers in the dialogue, laments the loss of the enharmonic
genus and then provides a Latin translation derived—without acknowledgment—from Valgulio:[50]

> The musicians of our time have repudiated altogether the most beautiful and
> charming genus, which the ancients cultivated, because of its majesty and
> severity ...; the majority of them have no knowledge or concern at all about
> the enharmonic's intervals. So much laziness and sloth overcomes them that
> they believe that of all things presented to the sense the enharmonic diesis is
> least perceptible, and they banish it from songs and melodic compositions.[51]

It was one thing to bemoan the enharmonic's neglect, another to
adapt it to modern music. Nicola Vicentino set out to do this for both
the enharmonic and the chromatic. In a famous formal debate in Rome
in 1551 between Vicentino and the Portuguese Papal singer Vicente
Lusitano (d. after 1561), Vicentino contended that the chromatic and
enharmonic were never abandoned, that musicians unconsciously still
used them and did so in ignorance of their real potential. Whenever they
sang consecutive semitones, this was chromatic; when they leaped a

---

[49]The introduction is translated and presented in facsimile in Carlo Valgulio,
"The Proem on Plutarch's *Musica* to Titus Pyrrhinus," in Palisca, *Florentine Camerata*, 13–44.

[50]*Charoli valgulii Prooemium in Musicam Plutarchi ad Titum Pyrrhinum* (Brescia:
Angelus Britannicus, 1507), ff. biij[r]–dv[v]; and "Plutarchi Chaeronci philosophi
clarissimi, Musica. Carlo Valgulio Brixiano interprete," in *Plutarchi Caeronei,
philosophi, historicique clarissimi opuscula (quae quidem extant) omnia* (Basle: And. Cratandrus, 1530), ff. 25v–32v.

[51]Salinas, *De musica*, 217 (bk. 4, ch. 25): "At vero Musici nostri temporis pul-
cherrimum omnium, maximeque decorum genus, quod veteres propter maiestatem, grauitatemque ipsius colebant, penitus repudiarunt, adeo vt ne qualiscunque
perceptio curaque sit plerisque Enharmoniorum interuallorum. Et tanquam
ignauia, atque secordia inuasit eos, vt Diesim Enharmonion, ne speciem quidem
omnino cadentium sub sensum praebere putent, eamque de canticis, atque modu-
laminibus exterminent." The passage is Plutarch *On Music* 38 (1145a), as it appears
on f. 31v in the 1530 Basle edition.

major third, they took this from the enharmonic genus, while leaping a minor third was borrowed from the chromatic. Vicentino lost the debate, but he persisted in his campaign to prove that a deliberate exploitation of the two genera could unleash the power that ancient music reputedly had on listeners. He went around demonstrating this— first in Ferrara, later in Rome—with an experimental group of singers, whom he swore to secrecy until 1555, when he published his theories in *L'Antica musica ridotta alla moderna prattica*.[52]

Vicentino's chromatic and enharmonic turned out to be different from the ancient forms in that he divided the entire gamut into semitones in the chromatic and into dieses in the enharmonic. Because no modern instrument could play music written in these systems, Vicentino designed a harpsichord he called the *archicembalo* with two manuals, each with three banks of keys that permitted playing the unusual intervals while combining them in well-tuned consonances, both melodic and simultaneous. He also devised and had built an *arciorgano*.[53]

According to Pietro Cerone (1566–1625), the Ferrarese composer Luzzasco Luzzaschi (1545[?]–1607) played this organ fluently and wrote compositions for it.[54] Enharmonic instruments in imitation of Vicentino's were built in Rome, Venice, Florence, and elsewhere. A vogue of chromatic composition spread in Rome and Ferrara, where Vicentino performed his first experimental works. Vicentino himself published a number of compositions in the idiom, among the most artful being the madrigal *Laura che 'l verde lauro* on a sonnet of Petrarch.[55] Other notable chromatic *tours de force* by composers in Vicentino's musical circle are Luzzaschi's *Quivi sospiri* on a text from Dante's *Inferno*,[56] Orlando di

---

[52]See chapter 3, n. 1 *supra*. The debate is described by Vicentino in bk. 4, ch. 43. See also Maniates, *Ancient Music*, xiv–xxii and 448–50 (appendix IV).

[53]Bk. 5 of *L'Antica musica* is devoted to a description of the *archicembalo*; see also Maniates, *Ancient Music*, xlviii–li.

[54]Cerone, *El Melopeo*, f. 1041.

[55]Nicola Vicentino, *Madrigali a cinque voci, Libro quinto* (Milan: Paolo Gottardo Pontio, 1572); ed. in *Opera omnia*, ed. Henry W. Kaufmann, Corpus mensurabilis musicae, vol. 26 ([n.p.]: American Institute of Musicology, 1963), 96–101.

[56]Luzzasco Luzzaschi, *Secondo libro de madrigali* (Venice: Gardano, 1576); ed. in Alfred Einstein, *The Golden Age of the Madrigal* (New York: Schirmer, [1942]), 53.

Lasso's *Prophetiae Sibyllarum*,[57] and Luca Marenzio's *Solo e pensoso*, also on a Petrarch sonnet.[58] In the latter, the Superius sings the chromatic scale in long held notes as a background for the imitative counterpoint of the other four parts, a vivid portrayal of the solitary poet wandering in a deserted landscape. The most famous master of the chromatic idiom was Carlo Gesualdo (ca. 1561–1613), almost all of whose later madrigals take advantage of the melodic and harmonic riches of the chromatic genus.

Giovanni Battista Doni (1595–1647), inspired by the work of Mei and Salinas, undertook a renewed investigation of the modes and genera in the early 1630s, culminating in his "Trattato de' generi e de' modi della musica."[59] He left this scholarly treatise unfinished in manuscript but published a popularization of it, *Compendio del Trattato de' generi e de' modi della musica* (1635), in which he promoted a revival of the ancient system of *tonoi, harmoniai,* and genera.[60] Doni had studied law in France and in Pisa, but his first love was classical literature. Although he served as one of the secretaries to Cardinal Francesco Barberini, brother of Pope Urban VIII, he spent much of his time in research on Greek music.

Like Mei and Galilei, Doni knew that no single theoretical system represented musical practice from the time of Plato to early Christian times. The best one could do was to try to understand the individual authors, most of whom were post-classical. He agreed with Mei and Salinas that Ptolemy was the most systematic and lucid expositor of the system of *tonoi* and octave species. He defined *tonos* (his Italian word is *tuono*) as "a system or a singing that is higher or lower in pitch, as when we speak of singing higher or lower while proceeding by the same species or

---

[57]Orlando di Lasso, *Prophetiae Sibyllarum ... chromatico more singulari confectae* (Munich: Nicolaus Heinrich, 1600); ed. in *Prophetiae Sibyllarum*, ed. Reinhold Schlötterer, Sämtliche Werke, neue Reihe, vol. 21 (Kassel: Bärenreiter, 1990).

[58]Luca Marenzio, *Il nono libro de madrigali a 5 voci* (Venice: Gardano, 1599); ed. in Iain Fenlon, *Music and Patronage in Sixteenth-Century Mantua*, 2 vols., Cambridge Studies in Music (Cambridge: Cambridge University Press, 1980), 2:99–105; reprinted in *Norton Anthology of Western Music*, 4th ed., 1:171–83.

[59]Bologna, Civico Museo Bibliografico Musicale, D 143.

[60]G. B. Doni, *Compendio del Trattato de' generi e de' modi della musica* (Rome: Andrea Fei, 1635).

mutation."[61] By "mutation," he meant a certain arrangement of tones and semitones—in other words, an octave species or mode.

Doni may be credited with solving the age-old riddle of the ancient modes. Drawing from the same surviving Greek sources as modern scholars have studied, he had already come in the 1630s to conclusions similar to theirs.[62] He pursued the problem of the genera with the same scholarly detachment. Rejecting the modernizations of Vicentino and Salinas, he restored the genera to their original state as different ways of dividing the tetrachord into more or less spacious upper intervals and more or less dense lower intervals.

Doni's *Compendio del Trattato* was not really a compendium of the treatise on the modes and genera but a bowdlerization and application to modern music of the systems described there. In the *Compendio*, Doni enhanced the tonal system described by the Greek writers to suit modern purposes. He accepted the octave species that were given the names Dorian, Phrygian, and so on, as the foundation of the composer's vocabulary. These modes, which were originally the byproduct of the transpositions (or *tonoi*) of the basic two-octave system, could now be transposed by means of the same *tonoi* into higher or lower scales. For example, the Dorian mode, the natural scale from E to e, could be transposed by means of the Phrygian *tonos* into a scale $F\sharp$ to $f\sharp$, with an additional sharp on c. The octave species remains the same, but the melody is shifted up a semitone. In this way, Doni preserved the scalar variety of the modes while opening up a resource of unlimited transposition and modulation by means of key-like *tonoi*. This offered a rich palette for musical expression.[63]

Lutes and viols could play this kind of music because their equal temperament yielded whole tones of uniform size and semitones half

---

[61]Doni, "Trattato," f. 132r (bk. 2, ch. 4): "Tuono propriamente significa un sistema o modulatione piu acuta o piu graue come quando diciamo cantare più graue o più acuto; etiandio che si procedi per la medesima specie e mutanza."

[62]See Claude V. Palisca, "Giovanni Battista Doni's Interpretation of the Greek Modal System," *Journal of Musicology* 15 (1997): 3–18. For a collective modern view of the ancient system, see Claude V. Palisca, André Barbera, Jon Solomon, Calvin M. Bower, and Thomas J. Mathiesen, "The Ancient Harmoniai, Tonoi, and Octave Species in Theory and Practice," *Journal of Musicology* 3 (1984): 221–86.

[63]For a fuller treatment of Doni's transpositions, see Palisca, *Humanism*, 330–32.

that size. But this temperament did not satisfy him because no consonance besides the octave and its replicates had the pure tuning of the simple ratios. Moreover, even viols and lutes could not properly play the chromatic and enharmonic genera. This led Doni to develop a family of "panharmonic" instruments that could manage the ancient *tonoi*, modes, and genera in a tuning that preserved the pure consonances.

The most famous of these instruments, the Lyra Barberina, dedicated to Pope Urban VIII, had two faces, three sets of unfretted gut strings on the front and a single set of bronze strings on the back face with fixed frets that divided each whole tone into four enharmonic dieses. He also developed diharmonic and triharmonic harpsichords (capable of two and three *tonoi* respectively) and a diharmonic violin. Doni persuaded several composers to create works using these resources, among them Girolamo Frescobaldi, Domenico Mazzocchi, Pietro Eredia, Gino Capponi, Ottaviano Castelli, Luigi Rossi, and Pietro della Valle, whose oratorio for the feast of the Santissima Purificazione is the most extended work to survive. Doni was profoundly disappointed that he could not interest Claudio Monteverdi in trying his hand at this "erudite music," as it has been called.[64]

Doni may have been aware that musicians were developing a modern set of keys and transposable modes not unlike the Greek system. Some theorists, such as Zarlino and his followers, adopted the twelve-mode system pioneered by Glarean, but the trend was not to increase the number of modes from eight to twelve but rather to diminish their number, eventually down to two, major and minor. Although this trend is evident in Italian musical composition and in manuals on accompanying and organ playing, English, French, and German authors most openly manifest the transition to a system of major and minor keys. The reduction of the modes to two—major and minor—is treated as an accomplished fact in two French manuals on singing and composition.

---

[64]Agostino Ziino, "Pietro della Valle e la 'Musica erudita,' nuovi documenti," *Analecta musicologica* 4 (1967): 97–111. For further information on Doni's project, see Claude V. Palisca, "G. B. Doni, Musicological Activist and His *Lyra Barberina*," in *Modern Musical Scholarship*, ed. Edward Olleson (Stocksfield: Oriel Press, 1980), 180–205; reprinted with prefatory remarks in idem, *Studies*, 467–90. See also Claude V. Palisca, *G. B. Doni's* Lyra Barberina: *Commentary and Iconographical Study; Facsimile Edition with Critical Notes*, Miscellanee saggi convegni, vol. 18 (Bologna: Antiquae musicae italicae studiosi, 1981); also issued as *Quadrivium* 22 (1981).

Jean Rousseau (1644–1699) in his *Méthode claire, certaine et facile pour apprendre à chanter la musique sur les tons transposez comme sur les naturels* of 1683 (and many later editions) distinguished between pieces that are "in the major third" (*en tierce majeure*) and those in the "minor third" (*en tierce mineure*). Some *tons* he calls "natural," others "transposed," and they are either major or minor. Mode 1 (medieval Dorian) is D minor and natural, while Mode 2 (Hypodorian) is G minor and natural. Mode 3 (Phrygian) is A minor and natural, while Mode 4 (Hypophrygian) is E minor and transposed. Mode 5 (Lydian) is C major and natural, while Mode 6 (Hypolydian) is F major and natural. Mode 7 (Mixolydian) is D major and transposed (from *G*), and Mode 8 (Hypomixolydian) is G major and transposed (from *D*). Rousseau also names as transposed modes C minor, F minor, A major, B♭ major, B♭ minor, and F♯ minor.[65]

Rousseau's positioning of some of the modes on finals other than those of plainchant goes back to sixteenth-century polyphonic practice. The original Hypodorian octave scale on *A*, with a final on *D*, is too low for sopranos; consequently, the final was raised a fourth to *G* by means of a B♭. For a similar reason, the Phrygian mode's final was raised from *E* to *A*, but without a B♭ (thereby altering its octave species), while the Hypophrygian became an E-mode with sharps on *F* and *C*. The Lydian on *F* normally had a B♭ but lost it when transposed down a fourth to *C*, becoming the C-major scale; the Hypolydian took its place as an F-mode with a B♭. Mixolydian on *G* was transposed up a fifth by adding sharps on *F* and *C*, turning it into D major, while the Hypomixolydian became the G-mode equivalent to G Major by adding a sharp on *F*.[66] The church modes become all but unrecognizable in Rousseau's scheme, which reflects the practice among organists in France.[67]

---

[65]Jean Rousseau, *Méthode claire, certaine et facile pour apprendre à chanter la musique sur les tons transposez comme sur les naturels* (Paris: by the author, 1683), 78–85; all the transpositions are shown earlier in the treatise on pp. 24–34.

[66]The same arrangement is present in Adriano Banchieri, *L'organo suonarino* (Venice: Ricciardo Amadino, 1605; reprint in Bibliotheca musica bononiensis, II/31, Bologna: Forni, 1969), 41.

[67]The transformation of the modes into keys may be traced in Jean Denis, *Traité de l'accord de l'espinette, avec la comparaison de son clavier à la musique vocale* (Paris: Ballard, 1650; reprint with introduction by Alan Curtis, New York: Da Capo, 1969); and in Guillaume-Gabriel Nivers, *Traité de la composition de musique* (Paris: Ballard, 1667); trans. Albert Cohen as *Treatise on the Composition of Music* (Brooklyn: Institute

French musicians were generally skeptical of the characterizations of the modes. When Antoine Boësset (1586–1643) was criticized for choosing the wrong mode for the text "Me veux-tu voir mourir," he answered: "If I please, I can express any kind of passion in one mode as well as another. It is a mistake to believe the contrary. Accidentals, when applied with skill, make them all equal; I maintain that only the beginning and the end make them different."[68]

By the end of the century, Charles Masson (fl. 1680–1700) in his *Nouveau traité des regles pour la composition de la musique* could state: "to make the path to composition easier, I shall demonstrate only two modes, namely the major mode and the minor mode, since these two modes, positioned sometimes higher and at other times lower, contain all that antiquity has taught and even the eight tones that we sing in church, except for certain irregular ones."[69] Jean-Philippe Rameau (1683–1764) was to build on this two-mode system a theory of harmony and tonality in his *Traité de l'harmonie* of 1722.[70] This influential treatise laid

---

of Mediaeval Music, 1961). For a useful study of this later tonal theory, see Gregory Barnett, "Tonal Organization in Seventeenth-Century Music Theory," in *The Cambridge History of Western Music Theory*, ed. Thomas Christensen (Cambridge: Cambridge University Press, 2002), 407–55.

[68]Quoted from the correspondence of Marin Mersenne in D. P. Walker, "Mersenne's Musical Competition of 1640 and Joan Albert Ban," in *Studies in Musical Science in the Late Renaissance* (London: The Warburg Institute; Leiden: E. J. Brill, 1978), 96, n. 64: "quant il me plaira, j'exprimeray toute sorte de passion aussy bien en un Mode qu'en l'aultre. Et c'est une erreur de croire le contraire, les accidentz, desquels l'on se peut servir avec addresse, les rendant tous esgaulx; et je soustiens qu'il n'ya que le commencement et la fin qui les rend dissemblables."

[69]Charles Masson, *Nouveau traité des regles pour la composition de la musique*, 2d ed. (Paris: Ballard 1699; reprint with an introduction by Imogene Horsley, New York: Da Capo, 1967), 9 (ch. 2): "Mais afin de faciliter les moyens de parvenir plus promptement à la Composition, je ne montrerai que deux Modes, sçavoir le Mode majeur, & le Mode mineur: dautantque ces deux Modes posez quelquefois plus haut & quelquefois plus bas, renferment tout ce que l'Antiquité a enseigné, & même les huit Tons que l'on chante dans l'Eglise, excepté quelques-uns qui se trouvent irreguliers."

[70]Jean-Philippe Rameau, *Traité de l'harmonie réduite à ses principes naturels* (Paris: Jean-Baptiste-Christoph Ballard, 1722; reprint in *Complete Theoretical Writings*, vol. 1, ed. Erwin R. Jacobi, Miscellanea, vol. 3 [n.p.]: American Institute of Musicology, 1967).

the basis for the eighteenth- and nineteenth-century theories of tonal relations and chord progressions.[71]

---

[71]For a history of these developments, particularly in Germany, see Joel Lester, *Between Modes and Keys: German Theory, 1592–1802* (Stuyvesant, NY: Pendragon Press, 1989); idem, *Compositional Theory in the Eighteenth Century* (Cambridge: Harvard University Press, 1992); and idem, "Rameau and Eighteenth-Century Harmonic Theory," in *The Cambridge History of Western Music Theory*, ed. Thomas Christensen (Cambridge: Cambridge University Press, 2002), 753–77.

⊰ VI ⊱

HUMANIST REACTION TO POLYPHONY

AT THE VERY TIME when leading practitioners and theorists claimed that polyphonic music had achieved perfection, critics were assailing it as ineffectual, incomprehensible, and unsuitable for places of worship. Some wanted a return to plainchant; others yearned for a music that could awaken devout thoughts and feelings, stirring congregations to spiritual fervor. These and other viewpoints clashed in the Council of Trent, which was convened by Pope Paul III to meet the challenge of the Protestant Reformation and reform the Roman Catholic Church from within. The Council and its commissions met sporadically from 1545 to 1563 and considered among other issues the Church's use of polyphonic and instrumental music and some of the artful genres that had developed in the Middle Ages and early Renaissance.

The twenty-second session on 17 September 1562 decreed in part:

> Masses should be celebrated either simply by the spoken voice or with chant, all pronounced clearly and distinctly so that they gently reach the ears and hearts of the hearers. What is customarily performed with musical rhythms and instruments should contain nothing secular mixed in but only the divine praises of hymnody.[1]

This decree reflects the irritation of the ecclesiastical authorities with practices common among church musicians: organists played seemingly interminable preludes, interludes, and improvisations based on dance tunes and popular songs; a large proportion of the Masses were

---

[1]Quoted in Edith Weber, *Le concile de trente et la musique: De la réforme à la contre-réforme* (Paris: Honoré Champion, 1982), 88: "Decretum de observandis et evitandi in celebratione missae: ... verum ita cuncta moderentur, ut missae, sive plana voce sive cantu celebrentur omnia clara voce patureque prolata: in audientum aures et corda placide descendant. Quae vero rithmis musicis atque organis agi solent in iis nihil profanum, sed hymni tantum et divinae laudes intermisceantur ...." Even beyond her discussion of musical matters, Weber provides a useful summary of the twenty-five sessions of the Council, the basic issues, the participants, and the canons and decrees that were formulated and eventually adopted.

composed on musical themes from chansons and madrigals, employing a style partly derived from these models, which they consequently resembled; singers added florid embellishments to their parts in motets and settings of the Mass with such abandon that the words were no longer recognizable.

Among the critics of the current state of church music was Desiderius Erasmus (1469[?]–1536), who had once contemplated dedicating himself to music. He complained that the music performed in Roman Catholic churches prevented worshippers from understanding the words sung:

> There is a sort of music brought into divine worship that hinders people from distinctly understanding a word that is said; nor have the singers any leisure to mind what they sing.... Pray tell, what do they know of Christ who think he is pleased with this noise of voices? Not content with these, we introduce a laborious and theatrical music in the churches, a tumultuous chatter of diverse voices, the likes of which I believe was never heard in either the Greek or Roman theaters. They drown everything out with trumpets, horns, pipes, and harps, with which the human voices compete. Amorous and shameful songs to which harlots and mimes dance are heard. People flock to a church to soothe their ears as if it were a theater. For this purpose organ builders are maintained at high salaries, herds of boys spend their whole lives learning such barkings, all the while studying nothing of value.[2]

---

[2]Desiderius Erasmus, *In Novum Testamentum annotationes* (Basle: Froben, 1535; facsimile ed. in Anne Reeve and M. A. Screech, *Erasmus' Annotations on the New Testament: Acts–Romans–I and II Corinthians, Facsimile Edition of the Final Latin Text Published by Froben in Basle, 1535, with All Earlier Variants*, Studies in the History of Christian Thought, vol. 42, Leiden: Brill, 1990), 507–8 ("In epistolam ad Corinthios I, cap. 14"): "Vt omittam interim huiusmodi musices genus inductum esse in cultum diuinum, ut ne liceat quidem ullam uocem liquido percipere. Nec ijs qui cantillant ocium est attendendi qui canant.... Obsecro quid sentiunt de Christo, qui credunt illum huiusmodi uocum strepitu delectari. Nec his contenti, operosam quandam ac theatricam musicam, in sacras aedes induximus, tumultuosum diuersarum uocum garritum, qualem non opinor in Graecorum aut Romanorum theatris unquam auditum fuisse. Omnia tubis, lituis, fistulis, ac sambucis perstrepunt, cumque his certant hominum uoces. Audiuntur amatoriae foedaeque cantilenae, ad quas scorta mimique saltitant. In sacram aedem uelut in theatrum concurritur, ad deliniendas aures. Et in hunc usum, magnis salarijs aluntur organorum opifices, puerorum greges, quorum omnis aetas in perdiscendis huiusmodi gannitibus consumitur, nihil interim bonae rei discentium." On Erasmus as a musician, see J.-C. Margolin, *Erasme et la musique* (Paris: Vrin, 1965).

Henricus Cornelius Agrippa (1486–1535) of Nettesheim, the German student of occult philosophy who succeeded Erasmus as historian to Margaret of Austria in Brabant (now Belgium), condemned even more vociferously the music he heard in the churches that trained the world's best singers:

> Cathedral music is so licentious that both in the canon of the Mass, where the organ responds with every obscene song, and in the divine office, the holy mysteries and prayers are chanted by a company of wanton musicians, hired with great sums of money, not to edify the understanding, not to elevate the spirit, but for the itch of fornication. They do not sing with human voices but with beastly loud noises, the boys whinnying the descant, while some bellow the tenor, and others bark the counterpoint; others again shout the treble, while others gnash the bass; and they all contrive so, that though a great variety of sounds is heard, neither sentences, nor even words can be understood.[3]

In Italy, Bishop Jacopo Sadoleto (later cardinal and secretary to Pope Leo X) in his *De pueris recte ac liberaliter instituendis* of 1538 asked:

> What correctness or beauty can the music which is now in vogue possess? It has scarcely any real and stable foundation in word or thought. If it should have for its subject a maxim or proverb, it would obscure and hamper the sense and meaning by abruptly cutting and jerking the sounds in the throat, as though music were designed not to soothe and control the spirit, but merely to afford a base pleasure to the ears, mimicking the cries of birds and beasts, which we should be sorry to resemble. This is to turn soul into body, and weaken self-control.[4]

---

[3]Cornelius Agrippa, *De incertitudine et vanitate scientiarum et artium atque excellentia verbi Dei declamatio* (Antwerp: Joan. Grapheus, 1530), f. E10^V (ch. 17, "De musica"): "hodie verò tanta in Ecclesijs Musicae licentia est, vt etiam vna cum Missae ipsius canone, obscoenae quaeque, cantiunculae, interim in organis pares vices habeant, ipsaque diuina officia, sacrae & orationum preces conductis magno aere lasciuis musicis, non ad audientium intelligentiam, non ad spiritus eleuationem: sed ad fornicariam pruriginem: non humanis vocibus, sed beluinis strepitibus cantillant, dum hinniunt discantum pueri, mugiunt al[i]j tenorem, alij latrant contra punctum, alij boant altum, alij frendent bassum, faciuntque vt sonorum plurimum quidem audiatur, verborum & orationis intelligatur nihil, ..." Cf. the sixteenth-century English translation in *Strunk's Source Readings*, 304–8. See also Karl Gustav Fellerer, "Church Music and the Council of Trent," *Musical Quarterly* 39 (1953): 576–94; and Michael H. Keefer, "Agrippa's Dilemma: Hermetic 'Rebirth' and the Ambivalences of *De vanitate* and *De occulta philosophia*," *Renaissance Quarterly* 41 (1988): 614–53.

[4]Jacopo Sadoleto, *De pueris recte ac liberaliter instituendis* (Basle: Thomas Platterus, 1538), 141–42: "... musica, quid habere in se potest recti ac decori? quae aut nulla

These were reactions to the music that Heinrich Glarean in his *Dodeca-chordon* (1547) called the "the perfect art to which nothing can be added and after which only decline can be expected."[5] Glarean was thinking especially of Josquin des Prez (ca. 1440–1521), to whose sacred motets he dedicated most of the analytical and critical commentary in the book. He lamented the innovations of Josquin's successors,[6] but he steadfastly defended the polyphonic idiom that Erasmus and Agrippa deplored.

In the opinion of Gioseffo Zarlino, a generation later, contrapuntal part-music had reached another summit: the work of his teacher Adrian Willaert set a new standard for elegance and logic in musical composition.

> Adrian Willaert, truly one of the rarest intellects ever to practice music, in the guise of a new Pythagoras examined minutely what might be possible and, finding an infinity of errors, began to remove them and to bring music to that honor and dignity that it once boasted and ought reasonably to have. He demonstrated a rational order of composing with elegant manner every kind of piece, of which he gave very clear examples in his compositions.[7]

Willaert, it is true, exemplified in a great variety of genres, both sacred and secular, a highly refined contrapuntal texture. Consonance prevails, though he expressively and constructively exploited various degrees of dissonance, always keeping them under strict control. Willaert carefully adapted the melodies and rhythms of the individual parts and of the

---

uerborum fermè & sententiarum sede suffulta sit: aut si etiam habeat subiectam aliquam sententiam, illius tamen sensum ac notionem concise fractis ac uibratis inter fauces uocibus infuscet & impediat: quasi uerò iccirco reperta musica sit, non quae mulceat temperetque animor, sed quae auribus tantum deseruiat, & imitetur uoluerum ac bestiarum cantus, quarum tamen similes esse nollemus: at hoc est corporeum animum efficere, & minime compotem sui: ..."; trans. in E. T. Campagnac and K. Forbes in *Sadoleto on Education* (London: Oxford University Press, 1916), 116–17.

[5]Glarean, *Dodecachordon*, 241 (bk. 3, ch. 13): "[ars perfecta] cui ut nihil addi potest, ita nihil ei quam Senium tandem expectandum."

[6]Ibid., 239–41.

[7]Zarlino, *Istitutioni* (1558), 2 (Proemio): "Adriano Willaert, veramente vno de più rari intelletti, che habbia la Musica prattica giamai essercitato: il quale a guisa di nuouo Pithagora essaminando minutamente quello, che in essa puote occorrere, & ritrouandoui infiniti errori, ha cominciato a leuargli, & a ridurla verso quell' honore & dignità, che già ella era, & che ragioneuolmente doueria essere; & hà mostrato vn'ordine ragioneuole di componere con elegante maniera ogni musical cantilena, & nelle sue compositioni egli ne hà dato chiarissimo essempio." This statement is retained in the 1573 edition with only minor changes of wording.

whole texture to the accents, rhythms, and sense of the texts. Zarlino's instructions in the third book of his *Istitutioni harmoniche* (1558) aimed to impart this elegant manner. The technical polish and the conscientious setting of text by the likes of Josquin and Willaert, however, were lost on many churchmen, who were looking for music with more immediate appeal to the masses of worshippers. Influenced by experiments in the North, they wanted more public participation in the music of the service—participation that was discouraged by the professional choirs and their sophisticated repertory.

Across the Alps, the followers of Martin Luther had introduced congregational singing as the central music of the service, which was still the Mass, now often performed in the vernacular in the smaller communities. They adapted German texts to Latin plainsong melodies, turning them into "chorales," measured unison chants that could be sung by the people without accompaniment. Later, secular tunes set to religious poetry, as well as newly composed texts and melodies, enlarged the repertory. Arrangements of the chorales for four and five voices soon followed, intended for clergy and trained singers but adhering to the rhythms of the text, which all the voices pronounced together. Many exposed to this simpler and more direct music and to public participation applauded the change from the artful polyphony maintained in the larger churches.

The movement to reform Catholic church music gathered momentum both within and outside the Council of Trent in the middle of the sixteenth century. A leader in this effort, Bernardino Cirillo, the rector of the famous shrine and mecca for pilgrimages, the Santa Casa of Loreto, sought to convince composers to take as their model ancient Greek music, reputed to move people to a variety of emotional states. The music he heard from the professional choirs of his own and other churches, by contrast, left him unaffected. In 1549, he wrote to an influential member of Cardinal Ranuccio Farnese's staff, Ugolino Gualteruzzi, whose father Carlo was Procuratore della Penitenzieria, the supreme church tribunal, to win support for this campaign.[8] Cirillo made a similar

---

[8]For the background of the letter and the prelates mentioned in it, see Claude V. Palisca, "Bernardino Cirillo's Critique of Polyphonic Church Music of 1549: Its Background and Resonance," in *Music in Renaissance Cities and Courts: Studies in Honor of Lewis Lockwood*, ed. Jessie Ann Owens and Anthony M. Cummings (Warren, MI: Harmonie Park Press, 1997), 281–92. An almost complete translation of the letter is

appeal in person to Cardinal Marcello Cervini, who was soon to become pope. In his letter, he expressed dissatisfaction with the state of church music.

> *Kyrie eleison* means "Lord, have mercy upon us." The ancient musician would have expressed this affection of asking the Lord's pardon by using the Mixolydian mode, which would have evoked a feeling of contrition in the heart and soul. And if it had not moved the listener to tears, at least it would have swayed each hardened mind to piety. Thus he would have used similar modes in accordance with the words, and would have made a contrast between Kyrie and Agnus Dei, between Gloria and Credo, Sanctus and Pleni, psalm and motet. Nowadays they sing these things in any way at all, mixing them in an indifferent and uncertain manner.[9]

Unlike previous critics, Cirillo proposed solutions and even identified a contemporary secular polyphonic piece as a model. He urged composers to revive the ancient Greek modes because the church modes were evidently powerless to move people to different affections. Composers should suit the musical genre to the function, as did the ancients, and not base Masses on popular songs. They should curtail the habit of working out their ideas in fugues because these prevented the words from being understood. Cirillo would not have them revive the chromatic and enharmonic genera, however, because these were already abandoned by the ancients. Nor would he ask composers to abandon polyphony altogether, for at least one composer had succeeded in making music in this medium passionately express the words: Jacob Arcadelt (1507[?]–1568) in the four-voice madrigal *Ahime, dov'è 'l bel viso*.[10] Writing largely in a homophonic style and with simple melodic and harmonic

---

in Giovanni Pierluigi da Palestrina, *Pope Marcellus Mass*, ed. Lewis Lockwood, Norton Critical Scores (New York: Norton, 1975), 10–16; reprinted in *Strunk's Source Readings*, 368–72.

[9]*Lettere volgari di diversi nobilissimi huomini et eccellentissimi ingegni, scritte in diuerse materie*, 3 vols. (Venice: [Aldus], 1564), 3:ff. 114r–118v. The quoted passage, on f. 115r, reads: "Kyrie eleison, uuol dire, Dio habbiue misericordia. Il Musico antico haurebbe con quel modo Mixolidio espresso questo affetto di chieder perdono a Dio, che haurebbe pesto, non che contrito il cuore, e l'animo: & mossa se non a pianto almeno ad affetto pietoso ogni mente indurata: & cosi haurebbe adattati simili modi in conformità delle parole suggette: & fatto differenza dal Kyrie all' Agnus Dei, & dalla Gloria al Credo, & dal Santus al Pleni, & da Salmi a Mottetti, hoggi cantano tutte simil cose in genere promiscuo & incerto."

[10]Jacobus Arcadelt, *Il primo libro di madrigali a quatro con nuova gionta impressi* (Venice: Gardano, 1539), ed. in *Opera omnia*, 10 vols., ed. Albert Seay, Corpus mensurabilis musicae, vol. 31 ([n.p.]: American Institute of Musicology, 1965–70), 2:1–3.

means that did not interfere with the projection of the text, Arcadelt poignantly captured the poet's mournful, nostalgic mood with subtle expressive touches. This made Cirillo hopeful that composers could realize his ideal of a powerfully moving sacred music.

The critics of polyphony as well as some of the leaders in the Council of Trent had in common a humanist education and an admiration of classical culture. They judged modern music from the perspective of ancient philosophy and aesthetics, not as professional musicians or gifted amateurs, and they considered decadent the very music that Glarean and Zarlino signaled as marking a golden age. The humanists were imbued with faith in the power of the word. If the words could not be heard and understood, the message was lost. But they were not afraid of emotion, as was the medieval church.[11] While words carried the thought, music could move people to feel its force.

---

[11]See further discussion of this matter in chapters 10 and 11.

≈ VII ≈

THEORIES OF MONODY AND DRAMATIC MUSIC

E TEND TO ATTRIBUTE musical change to composers: they create the scores performers transmute into living sound. But for
the momentous shift in musical practice and style around 1600,
most of the credit must go to those musicians who were primarily performers. Inspired by the writings of the humanists and musical amateurs, they experimented with new forms, styles, and genres, communicating with the public more directly than the professional composers,
who were mainly trained and employed in religious institutions. In close
touch with those they entertained, performers responded to pleas for a
simpler and more stirring music. They engaged this public through solo
renditions—often embellished—of polyphonic music and pioneered a
new kind of song that came to be called monody.

Although the composers best remembered from the last decades of
the sixteenth century—Giovanni Pierluigi da Palestrina, Orlando di
Lasso, Cipriano de Rore, Giaches de Wert, Andrea and Giovanni
Gabrieli, William Byrd, Hans Leo Hassler, Cristóbal de Morales, Philippe
de Monte—began as performers and often continued to perform or con-
duct for patrons and employers, they distinguished themselves and were
sought out primarily as composers. Their music, whether sacred or
secular, followed the standards that evolved in polyphonic church music.
They sometimes bent these standards to suit secular texts and functions,
but if they experimented with new techniques within the polyphonic
contrapuntal medium, they still felt generally constrained to remain
within it.

By contrast, amateur composers and composers who spent most of
their time as performers, whether in church or courtly circles, felt greater
liberty to try new paths. The leaders of the new monodic movement
were performers who composed primarily to fill their own need for a
repertory their polyphonic brethren failed to supply: the lutenist Vincenzo Galilei, the singers Giulio Caccini and Jacopo Peri, and aristocratic

107

amateurs such as Jacopo Corsi, Emilio de' Cavalieri, and Sigismondo d'India.

Giovanni Bardi, another amateur composer and also a poet, literary critic, and writer, led the informal academy in Florence in the 1570s and 80s known as the Camerata, which helped spread the ideas of the humanists. According to a letter Bardi's son Pietro wrote to Giovanni Battista Doni in 1634, his father, who "took great delight in music and was in his day a composer of some reputation, always had about him the most celebrated men of the city, learned in this profession, and inviting them to his house, he formed a sort of delightful and continual academy ... passing their time not only in pursuit of music, but also in discussing and receiving instruction in poetry, astrology, and other sciences...."[1] In the later 1570s, letters from Girolamo Mei, a Florentine classicist residing in Rome, were regularly on the agenda. They brought reports of his research concerning ancient Greek music and critical views of modern polyphonic music. Vincenzo Galilei, to whom most of the letters were addressed, interpreted their technical content and instructed the group in music theory. The conversations inspired Galilei and Caccini to experiment with new kinds of solo vocal music, which they sang to the circle.

Jacopo Corsi (1561–1602), too, hosted a salon in Florence in the 1590s in which music was rehearsed and discussed, a topic it had in common with such other Florentine academies as the Alterati and the Accademia Fiorentina.[2] In Ferrara, Antonio Goretti (ca. 1570–1649), another amateur and owner of a large musical library and collection of instruments, held musical gatherings, and these provided the occasions on which Giovanni Maria Artusi heard Claudio Monteverdi's madrigals

---

[1]Pietro Bardi to Giovanni Battista Doni, 16 December 1634. Angelo Solerti, *Le origini del melodramma: Testimonianze dei contemporanei* (Turin: Fratelli Bocca, 1903; reprint, Hildesheim: Olms, 1969), 143–44: "gran diletto alla musica, nella quale, in que' tempi, egli era compositore di qualche stima, aveva sempre d'intorno i più celebri uomini della città, eruditi in tal professione, e invitandoli a casa sua, formava quasi una dilettevole e continua accademia, ... trattenendosi non solo nella musica, ma ancora in discorsi e insegnamenti di poesia, d'astrologia, e d'altre scienze, ..."; trans. *Strunk's Source Readings*, 523.

[2]See Claude V. Palisca, "The Alterati of Florence, Pioneers in the Theory of Dramatic Music," in *New Looks at Italian Opera: Essays in Honor of Donald J. Grout,* ed. William W. Austin (Ithaca, NY: Cornell University Press, 1968), 9–38; reprinted in idem, *Studies,* 408–31.

years before they were published. These coteries constituted a counter-culture that hatched many of the new ideals and techniques.

Two composers in particular vied for recognition as the inventor of a "new music": Giulio Caccini and Jacopo Peri. Caccini, a Roman singer employed by the Medici court in Florence, tells in the preface to his collection of solo songs entitled *Le nuove musiche* (1601/2) how he was inspired by Bardi's Camerata to develop his new style of song:

> At the time when the admirable Camerata of the most illustrious Signor Giovanni Bardi, Count of Vernio, was flourishing in Florence, with not only many of the nobility but also the foremost musicians, intellectuals, poets, and philosophers of the city in attendance, I too was present; and I can truly say that I gained more from their learned discussions than from my more than thirty years of counterpoint. For these most knowledgeable gentlemen kept encouraging me, and with the most lucid reasoning convinced me, not to esteem that sort of music which, preventing any clear understanding of the words, shatters both their form and content [*il concetto, & il verso*], now lengthening and now shortening syllables to accommodate the counterpoint (a laceration of the poetry!), but rather to conform to that manner so lauded by Plato and other philosophers (who declared that music is naught but speech, with rhythm and tone coming after, not vice versa) with the aim that it enter into the minds of men and have those wonderful effects admired by the great writers.[3]

---

[3]Giulio Caccini, *Le Nuove musiche* (Florence: I Marescotti, 1602), preface, quoted in Frauke Schmitz, *Giulio Caccini,* Nuove musiche *(1602/1614): Texte und Musik*, Musikwissenschaftliche Studien, vol. 17 (Pfaffenweiler: Centaurus, 1995), 15: "Io veramente ne i tempi che fioriua in Firenze la virtuosissima Camerata dell'Illustrissimo Signor Giouanni Bardi de'Conti di Vernia, oue concorreua non solo gran parte della nobilità, ma ancora i primi musici, & ingegnosi huomini, e Poeti, e Filosofi della Città, hauendola frequentata anch'io, posso dire d'hauere appreso più da i loro dotti ragionari, che in più di trent'anni non ho fatto nel contrapunto, imperò che questi intendentissimi gentilhuomini mi hanno sempre confortato, e con chiarissime ragioni conuinto, à non pregiare quella sorte di musica, che non lasciando bene intendersi le parole, guasta il concetto, & il verso, ora allungando, & ora scorciando le sillabe per accomodarsi al contrappunto, laceramento della Poesìa, ma ad attenermi à quella maniera cotanto lodata da Platone, & altri Filosofi, che affermarono la musica altro non essere, che la fauella, e'l rithmo, & il suono per vltimo, e non per lo contrario, à volere, che ella possa penetrare nell'altrui intelletto, e fare quei mirabili effetti, che ammirano gli Scrittori, ..."; trans. Caccini, *Le Nuove musiche* (ed. and trans. Hitchcock), 44. For a somewhat contrasting translation, see *Strunk's Source Readings*, 608–17.

In the dedication prefaced to his setting of the poet Ottavio Rinuccini's *Euridice*, dated 20 December 1600, Caccini claimed that he was the first to develop this new style,[4] but his claim was disputed by Cavalieri and Peri.[5]

Jacopo Peri's setting of *Euridice* was not published until 1601, with a dedicatory letter dated 6 February 1600 presenting it to Maria de' Medici, Queen of France and Navarre, at whose wedding in Florence it had been staged on 6 October 1600. Ignoring Caccini's claims, Peri acknowledges in the preface following his dedicatory letter that Cavalieri was the first to use a new style of solo singing in the theater. He also claims to have collaborated as early as 1594 with Rinuccini and the amateur composer and patron Jacopo Corsi to produce their musical pastorals, of which *Dafne*, performed in 1598, was the first. Peri speaks of the classical models that inspired him:

> Whence, seeing that it was a question of dramatic poetry and that, therefore, one should imitate in song a person speaking (and without a doubt, no one ever spoke singing), I judged that the ancient Greeks and Romans (who, according to the opinion of many, sang their tragedies throughout on the stage) used a harmony which, going beyond that of ordinary speech, fell so short of the melody of song that it assumed an intermediate form.[6]

---

[4]Giulio Caccini, "Dedication to *Euridice*," in *Strunk's Source Readings*, 605–7.

[5]Dismissing Caccini's claims of priority, Cavalieri says in a letter of 20 January 1601 from Rome that he has just received the printed score. See Claude V. Palisca, "Musical Asides in Cavalieri's Correspondence," *Musical Quarterly* 49 (1963): 339–55, reprinted with the Italian text of quoted extracts in idem, *Studies*, 389–407. The rivalry between Caccini and Peri and their competing settings of *Euridice* are complicated matters that cannot be explored here. For a fuller treatment, see Claude V. Palisca, "The First Performance of *Euridice*," in *Twenty-Fifth Anniversary Festschrift (1937–62)*, ed. Albert Mell (New York: Queens College of the City University of New York, 1964), 1–23; reprinted with a new introduction in idem, *Studies*, 432–51. See also Tim Carter, *Jacopo Peri (1561–1633): His Life and Works*, 2 vols. (New York: Garland, 1989).

[6]Jacopo Peri, *Le musiche sopra l'Euridice* (Florence: G. Marescotti, 1600), preface, quoted in Solerti, *Origini del melodramma*, 45–46: "Onde, veduto che si trattava di poesia dramatica e che però si doveva imitar' col canto chi parla (e senza dubbio non si parlò mai cantando), stimai che gli antichi Greci e Romani (i quali, secondo l'opinione di molti, cantavano su le scene le tragedie intere) usassero un'armonia, che avanzando quella del parlare ordinario, scendesse tanto dalla melodia de cantare che pigliasse forma di cosa mezzana"; trans. *Strunk's Source Readings*, 659–60. For a more detailed study, see Claude V. Palisca, "Peri and the Theory of Recitative," *Studies in Music* 15 (1981): 51–61; reprinted in idem, *Studies*, 452–66.

Although Peri may not have participated in the Camerata's discussions, he would have learned from Galilei that Mei had found evidence of the Greek tragedies being performed with continuous music. Peri probably also owed to Mei the concept of a species of recitation intermediate between song and speech, about which Mei had written to Galilei in his long letter of 8 May 1572. Mei explained in the letter the distinction made by the ancient theorist Aristoxenus between the "diastematic" or intervallic motion of the voice used in singing and the "continuous" motion used in speech.[7] Peri makes a pointed reference to this distinction when he describes the declamation he sought in dramatic music:

> ... that type of voice assigned to singing by the ancients which they called "diastematic" (as it were, sustained and suspended) could at times speed up and take an intermediate path between the suspended and slow movements of song and the fluent, rapid ones of speech ..., approaching that other [species] of speech, which they called "continuous,"...[8]

The view that the Greek tragedies were sung received further reinforcement in the various prefaces of Alessandro Guidotti/Cavalieri, Rinuccini, and Caccini. Writing on behalf of Cavalieri in the dedication of his *Rappresentatione di anima, et di corpo* (1600), Alessandro Guidotti states that Cavalieri adopted "a style similar to that which, it is said, the ancient Greeks and Romans in their stages and theaters used to move spectators to various affections."[9] Rinuccini, in dedicating the edition of his *L'Euridice* to Maria de' Medici, begins:

---

[7]Palisca, *Mei*, 116; trans. Palisca, *Florentine Camerata*, 74. The passage considered by Mei is Aristoxenus *Harmonic Elements* 8–9 (da Rios 13–14); trans. Barker, *Greek Musical Writings*, 2:132.

[8]Peri, *L'Euridice*, preface, quoted in Solerti, *Origini del melodramma*, 46: "... quella sorte di voce, che dagli antichi al cantare fu assegnata, la quale essi chiamavano diastematica (quasi trattenuta e sospesa), potesse in parte affrettarsi, e prender temperato corso tra i movimenti del canto sospesi e lenti, e quegli della favella spediti e veloci, ... avvicinandosi all' altra del ragionare, la quale continuata appellavano: ..."; trans. *Strunk's Source Readings*, 660. See also Palisca, *Humanism*, 427–33.

[9]Guidotti, Letter of dedication to Cardinal Aldobrandini, dated 3 September 1600, in Emilio de' Cavalieri, *Rappresentatione di anima, et di corpo* (Rome: Nicolò Muti, 1600): "fatte à somiglianza di quello stile, co'l quale si dice, che gli antichi Greci, e Romani nelle scene, e teatri loro soleano à diuersi affetti muouere gli spettatori." Also quoted in Solerti, *Origini del melodramma*, 1–2.

It has been the opinion of many, most Christian Queen, that the ancient Greeks and Romans sang their entire tragedies on the stage. But such a noble manner of reciting was neither ever revived nor that I know of until now attempted by anyone, and this I believed was a defect of modern music—by far inferior to the ancient.[10]

In dedicating the score of his *Euridice* to Bardi, Caccini also claimed to cultivate an antique style:

This is likewise the manner which Your Lordship, in the years when Your Lordship's *camerata* was flourishing in Florence, discussing it in company with many other noble virtuosi, declared to be that used by the ancient Greeks when introducing song into the presentations of their tragedies and other fables.[11]

Bardi, too, addressed the matter in his discourse on ancient and modern music. He did not commit himself concerning the singing of the tragedy, but he did express his disdain of counterpoint, which he called "an enemy of music" (*musica nemica*), and urged Caccini to make the verse comprehensible, "not letting yourself be led astray by counterpoint like a poor swimmer who lets himself be carried away by the current, not reaching the other side of the river as he intended."[12] In a discourse on performing tragedy that can be attributed to Bardi, the author does not consider whether the actors, as well as the chorus, sang.[13]

---

[10]Ottavio Rinuccini, *L'Euridice* (Florence: Cosimo Giunti, 1600), dedication (4 October 1600), quoted in Solerti, *Origini del melodramma*, 40: "È stata opinione di molti, Cristianissima Regina, che gli antichi Greci e Romani cantassero sulle scene le tragedie intere; ma sì nobil maniera di recitare nonchè rinnovata, ma nè pur, che io sappia, fin qui era stata tentata da alcuno, e ciò mi credev'io per difetto della musica moderna, di gran lunga all'antica inferiore."

[11]Giulio Caccini, *L'Euridice composta in mvsica in stile rappresentatiuo* (Florence: G. Marescotti, 1600), dedication, quoted in Solerti, *Origini del melodramma*, 50: "E questa è quella maniera altresì, la quale ne gli anni, che fioriva la Camerata sua in Firenze, discorrendo ella, diceva, insieme con molti altri nobili virtuosi, essere stata usata dagli antichi Greci nel rappresentare le loro tragedie e altre favole, adoperando il canto"; trans. *Strunk's Source Readings*, 606.

[12]Bardi, "Discorso mandato a Giulio Caccini," 114–15: "non lasciando trauiarui dal contrapunto quasi cattiuo n[a]tatore che dalla corrente trasportar si lasci, ne arriui oltre al fiume, la oue egli proposto s'haueua, ..."

[13]Giovanni Bardi (?), "[Discorso come si debba recitar Tragedia]," in Claude V. Palisca, *The Florentine Camerata: Documentary Studies and Translations*, Music Theory Translation Series (New Haven, CT: Yale University Press, 1989), 140–51; see the introduction, p. 137.

Contrary to the assertions of Peri and Rinuccini—that many believed the ancient Greeks and Romans sang their entire tragedies on the stage—, most literary historians and critics of their day did not hold such an opinion. The prevailing view held that the choruses were sung but the actors' parts were not. In particular, Piero Vettori, Mei's teacher, whom Mei advised on musical matters during the preparation of Vettori's commentaries on Aristotle's *Poetics*, was skeptical that any roles besides the chorus were sung.[14] Nevertheless, there was support for the idea outside Bardi's Florentine circle. Gian-Vincenzo Gravina (1664–1718) devotes two chapters to this question in his treatise *Della tragedia*, written at the end of the seventeenth century; he is convinced that the entire tragedies were sung and cites Lodovico Castelvetro, Giason de Nores, and Girolamo Mercuriale[15] as supporting the view.[16] To these may be added Francesco Patrizi.

Mei treated this question in the fourth book of his *De modis musicis*, which he sent to Florence in 1573 with the understanding that Vettori would let his friends and associates read it. Detailed notes on Mei's fourth book made by Galilei (or for him) appear in the codex that contains Mei's letters to Galilei and Bardi. The notes include many of the points that Galilei incorporated in his *Dialogo della musica antica, et della moderna* (1581), the most important manifesto of the monodic movement.[17] Mei concluded from his research that in the tragedy, old comedy, and the dithyramb, the chorus had verse, melody, and rhythm, while the other parts had both verse and melody. He found evidence that actors in the tragedies, comedies, and satyr plays were continually accompanied by the aulos.

One of Mei's most convincing pieces of evidence is the Aristotelian *Problems*, Section 19, Problem 48. The text states that the Hypodorian

---

[14]Vettori, *Commentarii in primum librum Aristotelis de arte poetarum*, 18 (commenting on Aristotle *Poetics* [1447b]). This passage is unchanged in the 1573 edition. Vettori completed both editions before receiving Mei's *De modis*, in which Mei argued for the musical performance of the tragedy.

[15]Girolamo Mercuriale, *Artis gymnasticae apvd antiqvos celeberrimae ... libri sex* (Venice: Giunta, 1569), 55 (bk. 3, ch. 7).

[16]Gian-Vincenzo Gravina, *Opere scelte* (Milan: Società tipografica de' classici italiani, 1819), 284.

[17]These notes are transcribed, with references to their places in *De modis*, in Restani, *L'Itinerario di Girolamo Mei*, 166–67.

and Hypophrygian *harmoniai* are best for actors on stage, while others are more suitable for the chorus. Mei emended the names of the *harmoniai* to Dorian and Phrygian, because the "Hypo" modes were not known in Aristotle's time.[18]

Francesco Patrizi likewise adduces Problem 48 in his defense of the singing of tragedy, adding the evidence of Problem 15, which states that the poetry for the actors was not antistrophic because they had to be free to imitate in song the content of their speeches. Patrizi views the music of the tragedy in the context of Greek poetry, which his research had persuaded him was sung in ancient times. This applied to tragedy and comedy, both of which terms contain the root "ode" (ᾠδή), that is, "song": τραγῳδία (*tragodia*), a "goat-song" (so called because of the goat-skins worn by tragic actors) and κωμῳδία (*comodia*), a "revel-song."[19]

Caccini makes a hidden reference to another theory propagated by Mei among the members of the Florentine academies: Greek vocal music always consisted of a single line, not "several airs at the same time," as in polyphony. Caccini wanted the actors' parts—and sometimes the unison choruses too—to be recited without the accompaniment of other voices and supported only lightly by basso continuo players:

> Thus the harmony of the parts reciting in the present *Euridice* is supported above a basso continuo. In this I have indicated the most necessary fourths, sixths, and sevenths, and major and minor thirds, for the rest leaving it to the judgment and art of the player to adapt the inner parts in their places. The notes of the bass I have sometimes tied in order that, in the passing of the many dissonances that occur, the note may not be struck again and the ear offended. In this manner of singing, I have used a certain *sprezzatura* which I deem to have an element of nobility, believing that with it I have approached that much nearer to ordinary speech.[20]

---

[18]Mei's emendations have not found their way into current critical texts of the Aristotelian *Problems*. Mei translated his emended version into Italian in his letter to Galilei of September (?) 1581, ed. in Palisca, *Mei*, 178–79. The letter is almost entirely about the music of the tragedy. For a more detailed study of Mei's views on this subject, see Palisca, *Humanism*, 418–26.

[19]Patrizi, *Della poetica*, 1:331–34 (*La deca istoriale*, bk. 6). For further discussion of Patrizi's views, see Palisca, *Humanism*, 412–17.

[20]Caccini, *L'Euridice*, dedication, quoted in Solerti, *Origini del melodramma*, 51: "Reggesi, adunque, l'armonia delle parti che recitano nella presente *Euridice*, sopra un basso continuato, nel quale ho io segnato le quarte, seste e settime, terze maggiori e minori più necessarie, rimettendo nel rimanente lo adattare le parti di mezzo a' lor luoghi nel giudizio, e nell' arte di chi suona; avendo legato alcune

The accompaniment of a few spare chords did not compete with the voice, and thus the music conveyed the impression of an actor freely declaiming.

Of all Mei's discoveries about ancient Greek music, musicians found it most difficult to accept that the Greeks had no harmony or counterpoint, that when they sang to a lyre, kithara, or aulos, only one melody was heard. Several circumstances had persuaded Mei that all ancient Greek music was monophonic. None of the writings on music known to him spoke of simultaneous consonances besides octaves, and the ancients considered the modern imperfect consonances to be dissonant. But even more than this, Mei was convinced by the power of ancient music to move people to various feelings. In order to do this, the singer or musician would have to vary the pitch and rhythm to suit the words or emotion being expressed. If several "airs" were performed simultaneously, they would present conflicting impressions to the listener, nullifying the effect of particular pitch levels, melodic combinations, durations, and rhythmic patterns.

Other authors before Mei had surmised that much of the music of the ancient Greeks consisted of single-line melodies. Ponthus de Tyard (1521–1605) proposed that there were two classes of composer at that time, the *phonasce*, who set a poem melodiously for a single voice, and the *symphonete*, who laboriously adapted it to several voices. Tyard prefers the first,

> because the purpose of the music seems to be to give such an air to the word that every listener feels moved and lets himself be drawn to the affection of the poet. Whoever knows how to compose suitably a single voice appears to me to achieve his goal, seeing that polyphonic music most often does not convey to the ears but a big noise from which you do not feel any effect.[21]

---

volte le corde del basso, affine che nel trapassare delle molte dissonanze, ch'entro vi sono, non si ripercuota la corda e l'udito ne venga offeso. Nella qual maniera di canto, ho io usata vna certa sprezzatura, che io ho stimato che abbia del nobile, parendomi con essa di essermi appressato quel più alla natural favella"; trans. *Strunk's Source Readings*, 606. Baldassare Castiglione had used the term *sprezzatura* in his *Il Libro del cortegiano* (1528) to describe the confident nonchalance that a courtier should cultivate all the while observing and sometimes deliberately neglecting the rules of good social behavior.

[21]Ponthus de Tyard, *Solitaire second, ou Prose de la musique* (Lyon: Jean de Tournes, 1555), ed. Cathy M. Yandell (Geneva: Droz, 1980), 214: "... car si l'intention de Musique semble estre de donner tel air à la parole que tout escoutant se sente

Although Gioseffo Zarlino defended polyphonic music as a greater achievement, he acknowledged that music for a single voice has a more intense effect on listeners. He asked why the ancients could move listeners to different passions in ways that modern music does not. For one reason, "their songs were not composed of so many parts, nor did they make their pieces for so many voices as we do now, but they performed them in such a way that a musician sang to the accompaniment of a single instrument, whether a pipe, a kithara, or lyre, and in this way gave himself and listeners a welcome pleasure."[22] He found no evidence that the ancients composed in parts: "... I have never found in the writings of any author, either Greek or Latin, even one example from which we could understand how the ancients made many parts sound together; ... it all the more confirms my belief that they never used to make many parts sound together."[23] Zarlino acknowledged that someone singing stanzas of Ariosto, such as those on the death of Zerbino or the lament of his Isabella, moves listeners to compassion and tears, just as happened in ancient times. It is not surprising that modern music rarely has this effect, with such a multitude of parts and instruments

> that at times we do not hear anything but a din of voices mixed with different instrumental sounds, and a singing without any taste or discretion, with such mispronunciations of words that we hear only an uproar and noise. Music performed in this way cannot have any effect worth remembering. But when music is recited with taste and approaches the usage of the ancients, that is, a simple air sung with the playing of a lyra or lute or similar

---

passionné, et se laisse tirer à l'affection du Poëte, celuy qui scet proprement accommoder une voix seule me semble mieux atteindre à sa fin aspirée, vu que la Musique figurée le plus souvent ne rapporte aux oreilles autre chose qu'un grand bruit, duquel vous ne sentez aucune vive efficace."

[22]Zarlino, *Istitutioni*, 62 (bk. 2, ch 4): "ne anco loro cantilene erano composte di tante parti; ne con tante voci faceuano i lor concenti, come hora faciamo: ma le essercitauano di maniera, che al suono di vn solo istrumento, cioè di vn Piffero, o di Cetera, o di Lira, il Musico semplicemente accompagnaua la sua voce, & porgeua in tal modo grato piacere a se & agli ascoltanti."

[23]Zarlino, *Istitutioni*, 307 (bk. 4, ch. 8): "non hauer mai ritrouato appresso di alcuno autore ne Greco, ne Latino pur uno essempio, per il quale si possa comprendere, in qual maniera gli Antichi facessero cantare molte parti insieme; ... più mi confermo nel credere, che mai non vsassero di far cantare molte parti insieme"; trans. *On the Modes*, 32.

instrument to a text that is comic, or tragic, or similar things with long narrations, then we see its effects.[24]

Galilei enthusiastically embraced Mei's theory that only a single vocal line could move people to various affections. Yet he was not convinced that instrumental accompaniments were always in unison with the voice. Galilei cites Plato's complaint that certain singers accompanied themselves in a manner called *proschorda* instead of *symphonon*, that is, with a variety of chords and embellishments instead of with simple harmonies.[25] Galilei proposed as a model for modern music the airs for singing poetry used in the early sixteenth century and popular songs that were known in simple three- and four-part arrangements.[26] The early composers of opera eventually did imitate the air for singing poetry in their prologues and certain other strophic compositions in the dramatic scenes. The most famous of these is "Possente spirto" in Monteverdi's *Orfeo*, which Orpheus sings to Charon as he begs to be ferried to Hades, where Eurydice is held prisoner.[27] Composers also introduced dance-songs, often in strophic form. The recitative style Peri describes in his preface realizes the manner of straightforward chordal background that Galilei thought Plato meant when he spoke of a *symphonon* accompaniment.

Peri's description of the style of recitation intermediate between speech and song that he devised for his *Euridice* realizes the goals of Mei and Galilei without sacrificing harmonic instrumental support. The

---

[24]Zarlino, *Istitutioni*, 75 (bk. 2, ch. 9): "che alle volte non si ode altro che vn strepito de voci mescolate con diuersi suoni, et vn cantare senza alcun giudicio, et senza discrettione, con vn disconcio proferir di parole, che non si ode se non strepito, et romore: onde la Musica in tal modo essercitata non può fare in noi effetto alcuno, che sia degno di memoria. Ma quando la Musica è recitata con giudicio, et più si accosta all' vso de gli antichi, cioè ad vn semplice modo, cantando al suono della Lira, del Leuto, o di altri simili istrumenti alcune materie, che habbiano del Comico, ouer del Tragico, et altre cose simili con lunghe narrationi; allora si vedeno li suoi effetti."

[25]Vincenzo Galilei, "Dubbi intorno a quanto io ho detto dell'uso dell'enharmonio con la solutione di essi," ed. in Rempp, *Kontrapunkttraktate*, 183.

[26]See Claude V. Palisca, "Vincenzo Galilei and Some Links between 'Pseudo-Monody' and Monody," *Musical Quarterly* 46 (1960): 344–60; reprinted with prefatory notes in idem, *Studies*, 346–63.

[27]See Claude V. Palisca, "Aria in Early Opera," in *Festa musicologica: Essays in Honor of George J. Buelow*, ed. Thomas J. Mathiesen and Benito V. Rivera, Festschrift Series, vol. 14 (Stuyvesant, NY: Pendragon Press, 1995), 257–69.

singer gains independence by not having to harmonize each new step of a melody with a chord. Only the syllables that are "intoned" (*intonarsi*) or stressed in the reading of a poem receive a new or repeated harmony. Disregarding the rules of counterpoint, the composer may set other syllables either as dissonances or as consonances. To avoid the impression of "dancing to the movement of the bass" (*ballare al moto del Basso*), the singing voice mimics the "continuous" motion of a speaking voice. The bass moves in time to the "accents that serve us in grief, joy, and in similar states ... now faster, now slower, according to the emotions."[28] In this way, Peri explains, he weans the listener from the constant craving for sweet concordance and a uniform dancelike beat, opening the mind to attend to the text and feeling and to be moved by the singing.

As experience with monody accumulated, finer distinctions emerged. Giovanni Battista Doni, a classicist and historian of Greek music theory as well as an observer of the Italian musical scene, made an enlightened classification of solo song. He, more than anyone, popularized the terms "monody" and "monodic style." He recognized three kinds of monodic style in theatrical music: the narrative (*narrativo*), special recitative (*speciale recitativo*), and expressive (*espressivo*). He excluded from his classification stage music that is choral or songlike (*canzonesco*).

Doni's narrative style refers to the long narrative accounts of messengers. It stays more or less on the same steps with many repeated notes articulated at a fast pace and with a rhythm close to that of speech. Doni cites as an example "Per quel vago boschetto," the messenger's speech recounting the death of Eurydice in Peri's score.[29]

The "special recitative" style derives from the custom of the ancient bards and rhapsodes to recite poetry in song. This style, intermediate between narrative and expressive, is more tuneful (*arioso*) than either and less emotional (*patetico*) than the expressive. It often cadences and is best suited to prologues and heroic poems, poems in blank verse, *ottave rime*, or extended canzoni. As an example of this type of recitative, Doni cites

---

[28]Peri, *L'Euridice*, preface, quoted in Solerti, *Origini del melodramma*, 46: "a quegli accenti che nel dolerci, nel rallegrarci et in somiglianti cose ci seruono, feci muovere il basso al tempo di quegli, or più or meno, secondo gli affetti ..."; trans. *Strunk's Source Readings*, 660.

[29]The example is printed in *Norton Anthology of Western Music*, 4th ed., 1:276–81 (and accompanying recording).

the prologue of Peri's *Euridice*, "Io che d'alti sospiri."[30] This, as well as the prologues of Caccini and Monteverdi, is based on the style of aria used from the beginning of the sixteenth century for singing strophic poetry. The highly ornamented strophic aria Orpheus sings to Charon at the entrance to the underworld in Monteverdi's *Orfeo* also belongs to this category.

Doni gave special emphasis to the "expressive style" as the style truly proper for the stage. The narrative he found too cloying and better replaced by plain speech, while the special recitative was ill suited to dramatic poems.

> In the expressive the object is to express the affections and mimic in some way the natural accents of impassioned speech. This kind has the greatest power on human souls, for when accompanied by vivid acting and a manner of speech proportionately suited to the subject, it wondrously moves to laughter, tears, disdain, and so on. Here is the place for those mutations of mode, of genus [i.e. diatonic, chromatic, enharmonic], and of rhythm that are the richest resources and adornments of music. An example is the lament of Arianna, by now known to everyone, the most beautiful composition yet seen in stage and theater music.

He refers to "Lasciatemi morire," the single surviving fragment from Monteverdi's *Arianna*, performed in the Ducal palace at Mantua in 1608.[31]

Doni would have done away with plain recitative and replaced it with ordinary speech, retaining the expressive recitative. A contemporary of his, the anonymous author of *Il Corago* also doubted the appropriateness of the strophic aria, except for prologues, but considered simple recitative the essence of dramatic music:

---

[30]Ibid., 1:273.

[31]Giovanni Battista Doni, *Annotazioni sopra il Compendio de' generi, e de' modi della musica* (Rome: Andrea Fei, 1640), 61–62: "Nell' Espressiua dunque si fa professione di bene esprimere gli affetti; & in qualche parte quegl'accenti naturali del parlare patetico: e questa è quella ch'hà grandissima forza ne gl'animi humani: a segno che, quando è accompagnata d'vna viuace attione, e d'vn parlare proportionate al sogetto, marauigliosamente commuoue il riso, il pianto, lo sdegno, &c. Qui hanno luogo sopra tutto quelle mutationi di Tuono, di Genere, e di Ritmo, che sono le maggiori ricchezze, e sfoggi della Musica. Essempio ne può dare il lamento d'Arianna; hoggimai noto a tutti, ch'è la più bella compositione che si sia ancor veduta tra le Musiche sceniche, e Teatrali." There are numerous recordings and editions of the lament, among them that in Claudio Monteverdi, *Tutte le opere*, rev. ed. (Vienna: Universal Edition, 1954), 11:161–67.

> From experience we have also learned that the perfection of the recitative style is realized not through the beauty, whimsicality, or majesty of the reiterated air with corresponding ritornellos as much as from the variety and appropriateness of a melody that approaches most closely our common way of speaking, or, better said, of reciting, used by all the most esteemed actors or affecting orators.[32]

The author suggests that the composer have a "worthy and expressive actor" recite the lines and imitate in music the way in which the actor brings out the affections and sense of the poetry.[33]

Monody took different turns in France and England. France had its own humanist movement and a native species of monody. A group of French poets and musicians, like the Florentines, were fascinated by the ancient accounts of music's power over human emotions. They concluded that the path to regaining this power was through the ancient poetic meters, which they set out to imitate. With royal sponsorship, they formed the Académie de Poésie et de Musique in 1570 to pursue this program. One of the leaders, Jean-Antoine de Baïf, wrote French verses in ancient Greek and Latin meters (*vers mesurés à l'antique*), in which syllable quantity rather than stress was the basis of meter and rhythm. The Academy's theorists assigned durations to the vowels and to vowel-consonant combinations to guide composers in their choice of long or short note-values. The resulting music, instead of observing regularly recurring downbeats, consisted of a succession of poetic feet, like a typical line of Greek poetry, that freely mixed groups of two, three, and four beats. For listeners to be affected by this *musique mesurée*, all the voices of a choir or ensemble had to sing the text together in a progression of block harmonies. One famous composition by Claude Le Jeune, *Revecy venir du printans*, was based on a continually repeating pattern: short-short-long, short-long, short-long-long: Re-ve-cy ve-nir du prin-tans

---

[32]*Il Corago o vero alcune osservazioni per metter bene in scena le composizioni drammatiche*, ed. Paolo Fabbri and Angelo Pompilio (Florence: Olschki, 1983), 45: "Ma con l'esperienza anche si è veduto che la perfezione dello stile recitativo si conseguisce non tanto con la vaghezza, bizzaria o maiestà dell'aria ripetuta con i ritornelli a corrispondenza, quanto con quella varietà et acconciamento di modulazione che più s'accosta al nostro commun modo di ragionare, o per dir meglio di recitare che hanno quelli che sono da tutti stimati migliori istrioni o affettuosi dicitori."

[33]Ibid., 61.

RECHANT à 5

Figure 6. Claude Le Jeune, *Revecy venir du printans*[34]

Perhaps this chanson was so popular for the same reason that made the pattern a favorite of the Italian frottola composers in the early sixteenth century: starting with two short upbeats, it suggests a six-beat measure, with alternate measures organized in groups of twos and threes, that is 2 | 3+3 | 2+2+2 | ..., an effect known as hemiola: 5 6 | 1 2 3 4 5 6 | 1 2 3 4. Both Peri and Monteverdi used this rhythmic pattern in their operas for

[34]*Le printemps* (Paris: Ballard, 1603), ed. in Henry Expert, *Les maîtres musiciens de la Renaissance française*, 23 vols. (Paris: Leduc, 1894–1908), 12:11. A complete score and commentary are included in the *Norton Anthology of Western Music*, 4th ed., 1:193–208 (and accompanying recording).

joyful dance airs. The more artful pieces of *musique mesurée* avoided such regularity.

Meanwhile, a new type of song became popular in courtly circles, the *air de cour*. Collections of these airs were sometimes published in four- or five-part arrangements, but usually solo singers performed them with lute accompaniment, reading from a published tablature, as they were arranged in the first printed collection: *Livre d'air de cours miz sur le luth par Adrian Le Roy* (Paris: Le Roy & Ballard, 1571). Baïf was represented among the poets, and the rhythms of *vers mesurés* pervaded some of the airs. The *airs de cour* reflected the society its composers wanted to entertain. As Théodore Gérold put it concisely, "The society for which they worked and on which they depended was largely the precious society .... In this society certain limits may not be crossed: the tender, the sweet, the elegant, the refined, these are the dimensions within which the music dwells."[35]

This type of air found its way into the ballets in the guise of *récits* sung during the scenes. When Jean-Baptiste Lully (1632–1687) eventually developed a French version of the Italian recitative, he adopted the additive metrical patterns that mixed units of two, three, and four beats, giving his recitative a speechlike flow that, like Peri's, avoided the rhythm of dance. Unlike the *récits* of the ballet, the accompaniments of which were usually written out in tablature, the recitatives of Lully, trained in Italy, utilized basso continuo.

A popular category of monody that later dominated the dance-scenes of Lully's operas were airs in the rhythm of dance—*airs de danse*—both sung and played, often accompanying dancing. The sarabandes, gavottes, and courantes tended to be more serious, while minuets, gigues, passepieds, and galliards were lighter in spirit. Scenes of action imported another common type, the *air tendre*, set to an epigrammatic or moralizing text, usually in a dance rhythm treated freely.

---

[35]Théodore Gérold, *L'art du chant en France au XVIIe siècle*, Publications de la Faculté des Lettres de l'Université de Strasbourg (Strasbourg: Faculté des lettres, 1921; reprint in Burt Franklin: Research and Source Works Series: Music History and Reference Series, vol. 3, New York: Burt Franklin, 1973), 102: "La société pour laquelle ils travaillaient et de laquelle ils dépendaient en grande partie était la société précieuse, ... Dans cette société, certaines limites ne doivent pas être dépassées; le tendre, le doux, le galant, le raffiné, voilà les mesures dans lesquelles la musique se tiendra."

Despite the residence of Caccini and the singing members of his family in the French royal court the winters of 1604 and 1605 while Maria de' Medici was queen, his style of monody was rarely imitated in France. The French were both attracted to Italian monody and scornful of it. André Maugars (ca. 1580–ca. 1645) found the recitative style unfamiliar and new when he visited the Oratory of San Marcello in Rome in 1639:

> There is another kind of music that is not used at all in France ... called the *recitative style*.... The voices would begin with a psalm in the form of a motet, and then all the instruments would play a very good symphony. The voices would then sing a story from the Old Testament in the form of a spiritual play.... Each singer represented one person in the story and expressed the force of the words perfectly.... I cannot praise this recitative music enough; you have to hear it on the spot to judge its merits.[36]

Marin Mersenne, the great French *savant* who collected the views of travelers, received from Jean-Jacques Bouchard a typically ambivalent opinion:

> If you want to know my opinion, I'll tell you that for artfulness, technique, and solidity of singing, for the quantity of musicians—principally castrati—Rome surpasses Paris as much as Paris does Vaugirard. But for delicacy and *una certa leggiadria e dilettevole naturalezza* [a certain charm and beguiling naturalness] of the airs, the French greatly surpass the Italians.[37]

In England, the air, or ayre, enjoyed a wide audience from the 1570s through the seventeenth century. The sixteenth-century air was a light

---

[36]André Maugars, *Response faite à un curieux sur le sentiment de la musique d'Italie, escrite à Rome le premier octobre 1639*, quoted in Ernest Thoinan, *Maugars, sa biographie* (Paris: A. Claudin, 1865), 29–30: "il y a encore une autre sorte de Musique, qui n'est point du tout en usage en France.... Cela s'appelle *stile récitatif*.... les voix commençoient par un Psalme en forme de Motet, et puis tous les instrumens faisoient une très doux et très bonne symphonie. Les voix après chantoient une Histoire du Viel Testament, en forme d'une comédie spirituelle.... Chaque chantre représentoit un personnage de l'Histoire et exprimoit parfaitement bien l'énergie des paroles.... Je ne sçaurois louer assez cette Musique Récitative, il faut l'avoir entendue sur les lieux pour bien juger de son mérite."

[37]Letter of Jean-Jacques Bouchard (Rome, 1 January 1635) to Mersenne, in Marin Mersenne, *Correspondance du P. Marin Mersenne, religieux minime*, publiée par Mme Paul Tannery, ed. Cornélis de Waard, 17 vols. (Paris: Presses universitaires de France and CNRS, 1932–88), 5:3: "Que si vous en voulez sçavoir mon jugement, je vous dirai que, pour l'artifice, la science et la fermeté de chanter, pour la quantité de musiciens, principalement de chastrez, Rome surpasse autant Paris, que Paris fait Vaugirard. Mais pour la délicatesse, et *una certa leggiadria, e dilettevole naturalezza* des airs, les François surpassent les Italiens de beaucoup."

and tuneful piece, usually in a dance rhythm, for one or more voices.
Thomas Morley (1557–1602) found it less serious than the madrigal:

> There is also another kind [of music] more light then this [the madrigal]
> which they tearme *Ballette* or dances, and are songs which being song to a
> dittie may likewise be dance. These, and all other kinds of light musicke sav-
> ing the Madrigal are by a generall name called ayres.[38]

Dowland bestowed a more artful and heavier, even melancholic quality on the air, as in his most famous piece, *Flow, my tears*, also known as
the *Lachrymae* pavane, from his *Second Booke of Ayres* (1600).[39] His airs,
which show a trace of Caccini's influence, were usually performed by a
solo voice with lute or viol accompaniment, but unlike Caccini's, they
were published in parts so that more than one voice could sing or instruments could play some of the parts.

Thomas Campion's foreword to his *Two Bookes of Ayres* (1613)
shows the English disdain for the reductive basso continuo:

> These Ayres were for the most part framed at first for one voyce with the
> Lute, or Violl, but vpon occasion, they haue since been filled with more
> parts, which who so please may vse, who like not may leaue. Yet doe wee
> daily obserue, that when any shall sing a Treble to an Instrument, the standers
> by will be offring at an inward part out of their owne nature....[40]

Eventually Italian-style recitative was introduced into masques. Ben
Jonson reported in 1640 that his masque *Lovers made Men* was performed
on 22 February 1617 in London "(after the Italian manner) *Stylo recitativo*, by Master Nicholas Lanier."[41] A musician in William D'Avenant's
Playhouse to be Let (1662) is still apologetic as he justifies the artificiality of
recitative:

---

[38]Thomas Morley, *A Plaine and Easie Introduction to Practicall Musicke* (London:
Peter Short, 1597), 180.

[39]John Dowland, *Second Booke of Ayres* (London: Printed by Thomas Este, the
assigne of Thomas Morley, 1600). Score and commentary in *Norton Anthology of
Western Music*, 4th ed., 1:218–20 (and accompanying recording).

[40]Thomas Campion, *Two Bookes of Ayres* (London: Printed by Tho. Snodham,
for Mathew Lownes, and I. Browne, 1613), quoted in *Collected English Lutenist Partsongs*, 2 vols., ed. David Greer, Musica Britannica, vols. 53–54 (London: Stainer &
Bell, 1987–89), 1:XVIII.

[41]*Ben Jonson*, 11 vols., ed. C. H. Herford and Percy Simpson (Oxford: Clarendon, 1925–52), 7:454.

Recitative music is not compos'd
Of matter so familiar, as may serve
For every low occasion of discourse.
In Tragedy, the language of the Stage
Is rais'd above the common dialect;
Our passions rising with the height of Verse;
And vocal music adds new wings to all
The flights of poetry.[42]

"A brief Discourse of the Italian manner of Singing … written some years since by an English Gentleman who had lived long in Italy, and being returned, taught the same here,"[43] which John Playford (1623–ca. 1687) included for the first time in the fourth edition of *An Introduction to the Skill of Musick* (1664), turns out to be an abridged translation of Caccini's preface to *Le nuove musiche*, with no credit given to Caccini. The sixty years' interval between the original publication and this translation may not correctly measure the time-lag before the English took up some threads of the monodic movement, but it is symptomatic of the resistance to continental music during the Commonwealth period. After the restoration of the monarchy in 1660 with Charles II, English music entered a period of assimilation of French and Italian influences, exemplified by the music of Henry Purcell, who nevertheless strongly preserved a fundamentally English orientation.

In Italy, meanwhile, as the music drama's center of activity shifted from Florence and Mantua to Rome and then to Venice, the concept of the genre changed with the character of the audience, sponsors, authors, composers, and performers. Festive occasions in princely courts, such as weddings and coronations, provided the earliest opportunities for opera. In Florence, the first dramas presented entirely in music grew out of the pastoral play. Ottavio Rinuccini understood that his *L'Euridice*, although meant to be sung in the antique manner of Greek tragedy, was not itself a tragedy.[44] Nevertheless, he gives the honor of singing the prologue to

---

[42]*The Dramatic Works of Sir William D'Avenant*, 5 vols. (Edinburgh: W. Paterson, 1873), 4:23.

[43]The facsimile of the twelfth edition of Playford's treatise (In the Savoy: by the author, 1694), ed. Franklin B. Zimmerman (New York: Da Capo, 1972), contains this "Brief Discourse" on pp. 81–96.

[44]See Barbara Hanning, *Of Poetry and Music's Power: Humanism and the Creation of Opera*, Studies in Musicology, vol. 13 (Ann Arbor, MI: UMI Research Press, 1980), 1–19.

Tragedy, who apologizes for Rinuccini's happy ending. Eurydice, contrary to the legend, comes back to life, a departure from mythology and tradition that the prologue justifies by not wanting to spoil the joy of a happy wedding. Tragedy, returning from antiquity, proclaims: "Behold, the gloomy buskins and the dark rags | I transform, and awaken in the hearts sweeter affections," and in a later strophe she augurs "with a serene countenance | ... | and with happier notes my song | I temper, for the noble heart's sweet delight."[45] On the other hand, Rinuccini's choruses and Peri's setting of them pay homage to ancient drama in their often-reflective function and antistrophic form, as well as to the Greek *kommos* in the device of joining an actor's lament to that of the chorus. Alessandro Striggio, too, employed this device in his libretto for Monteverdi's *Orfeo* but hewed closer to tragedy by arranging his poem in five acts and preserving the legend's sorrowful ending, though still resorting to a *Deus ex machina*—the descent of Apollo—to rescue Orpheus from the Bacchantes, angry at him for rejecting love after losing Eurydice.

Mythology, especially as conveyed in the works of the Roman poet Ovid, furnished the plots and characters favored by the earliest authors of dramatic poems for musical setting. As the anonymous author of *Il Corago* writing in the 1630s or 40s aptly stated, in the known parts of the earth ordinary people do not speak in music, something that "conforms more with the concept that we have of superhuman personages.... Musical speech being more elevated, masterly, sweeter, and nobler than ordinary speech, we instinctively attribute it to personages that have about them more of the sublime and divine."[46] Orpheus and Apollo—both legendary musicians and singers—together with shepherds, and nymphs, did not offend verisimilitude by conversing in song.

The pastoral tradition continued in Rome with Stefano Landi's *La morte d'Orfeo* (1619), Domenico Mazzocchi's *La catena d'Adone* (1626),

---

[45]"Ecco i mesti coturni e i foschi panni | Cangio, e desto ne i cor più dolci affetti"; "... e con sereno aspetto | ... | E su corde più liete il canto mio | Tempro, al nobile cor dolce diletto."

[46]*Il Corago*, 63: "almeno nelle parti più conosciute della terra non si parla in musica ma pianamente dalli uomini ordinarii, più si conforma con il concetto che si ha dei personaggi sopra umani il parlar in musica che con il concetto e manifesta notizia delli uomini dozzinali, perchè essendo il ragionare armonico più alto, più maestrevole, più dolce e nobile dell'ordinario parlare, si attribuisce per un certo connaturale sentimento ai personaggi che hanno più del sublime e divino."

Michelangelo Rossi's *Erminia sul Giordano* (1633, based on Tasso's *Gerusalemme liberata*), Loreto Vittori's *La Galatea* (1639), and Luigi Rossi's *Orfeo*. The latter was performed in 1647 in Paris, where the Barberini family was living in exile, following the death in 1644 of Urban VIII (Maffeo Barberini).

The principal patrons of opera in Rome were the nephews of Pope Urban VIII. A cardinal in the Pope's circle, Giulio Rospigliosi,[47] wrote two new types of libretto texts, *Sant'Alessio* or *La vita humana* (1631), based on the life of a saint, set to music by Stefano Landi; and the comedies *Chi soffre, speri* (1637), set by Virgilio Mazzocchi and Marco Marazzoli, and *Dal male il bene* (1654).

It became customary in Rome to set lyrical moments to flowing, rhythmic pieces that were sometimes labeled "aria," despite the fact that this term was previously limited to settings of strophic texts. Domenico Mazzocchi appended a note to a list of the arias and choruses in the printed score of *La catena d'Adone* (1626) saying that in addition: "There are many other semi-arias scattered throughout the work, which break the tedium of the recitative."[48] If the recitative was tedious, this was partly because Roman composers showed less interest in making it varied and expressive. On the other hand, they often bestowed intense creative attention on ensembles and choruses.

Toward the middle of the century, the hub of operatic production shifted to Venice, a republic with a large patrician and merchant class. Theaters owned by leading families or impresarios leased season-boxes to other families and sold single admissions to the public. The first of these, Teatro S. Cassiano, was leased in 1637 by a traveling opera troupe from Rome. By 1680, seven theaters showed opera simultaneously during the Carnival season (between December 26 and the beginning of Lent in February or March).

Librettists continued to favor classical themes: episodes from Homer, such as Giacomo Badoaro's *Il ritorno d'Ulisse in patria* (1640) and *Ulisse errante* (1644); or Roman history, as in Gian Francesco Busenello's

---

[47]Who in 1667 himself became Pope Clement IX.

[48]Domenico Mazzocchi, *La catena d'Adone* (Venice: A. Vincenti, 1626), [127]; trans. in Stuart Reiner, "Vi sono mol'altre mezz'arie …," in *Studies in Music History: Essays for Oliver Strunk*, ed. Harold Powers (Princeton, NJ: Princeton University Press, 1968; reprint, Westport, CT: Greenwood Press, 1980), 241: "Vi sono molt' altre mezz'Arie sparse per l'Opera, che rompono il tedio del recitatiuo.…"

L'incoronazione di Poppea (1643) and *La prosperità infelice di Giulio Cesare dittatore* (1646) or Francesco Sbarra's *Alessandro vincitor di se stesso* (1651). Catering to a fickle public, librettists cautiously permitted themselves to defy Aristotle's unities of action, time, and place. With Roman statesmen and generals now sometimes holding center stage, authors realized that the operatic convention of speaking in song strained verisimilitude and that improbable or supernatural events were out of place. The Academy of the Incogniti, to which a majority of the authors belonged, took up these issues in its discussions.[49]

The public, less concerned about dramatic principles, delighted in rapid and frequent scene-changes, multiple plots, elaborate scenery, miraculous transformations, and happy endings. Librettists and composers, sometimes reluctantly, catered to popular taste. Giovanni Faustini apologized for dramatically dubious strategies in his *L'Egisto* (1643), set to music by Francesco Cavalli:

> The theaters want machines to arouse wonder and delight, and now and then cosmetics, golds, and purples deceive the eyes and make deformed objects beautiful. If you are a critic, do not detest the madness of my *Egisto*, as an imitation of an action that you have seen walking the boards, transformed from the comic into the musically dramatic, because the authoritative pleas of a person of high rank forced me to insert them in the work to satisfy the bent of him who would produce it.[50]

Composers also dedicated their efforts to satisfy the singers' demand for showy vehicles savored by listeners, writing more and longer, often elaborate, arias, reducing the recitative to a transitional and preparatory

---

[49]For a fuller discussion of this important matter, see Ellen Rosand, *Opera in Seventeenth-Century Venice: The Creation of a Genre* (Berkeley: University of California Press, 1991), 34–65.

[50]Giovanni Faustini, preface to *L'Egisto*, ed. Andrea della Corte, *Drammi per musica dal Rinuccini allo Zeno*, 2 vols., Classici italiani (Turin: Unione Tipografico-Editrice Torinese, 1958), 1:513: "I Teatri vogliono apparati per destar la meraviglia, e il diletto, e talvolta i belletti, gl' ori, e le porpore ingannano gl' occhi, e fanno parere belli li oggetti deformi. Se tu sei Critico non detestare la pazzia del mio Egisto, come imitatione d'un' attione da te veduta altre volte calcare le Scene, trasportata dal Comico nel Drammatico Musicale, perché le preghiere autorevoli di personaggio grande mi ha violentato a inserirla nell' opera, per sodisfare al Genio di chi l'ha da rappresentare." For the opera itself, see Pier Francesco Cavalli, *L'Egisto: Opera in Three Acts and a Prologue*, trans. Geoffrey Dunn, Raymond Leppard, and Karl Robert Marz, performing ed. Raymond Leppard (London: Faber; New York: Schirmer, 1977).

role. Each main character was allotted a number of arias according to the character's rank, which usually reflected the popularity of the singer. Each character's arias expressed a variety of affections and displayed different facets of a singer's talent. A successful aria in a singer's repertory could be transferred to another opera, replacing one expressing a similar sentiment.

The Venetian operas, particularly those of Cavalli and Antonio Cesti, spread to other cities, where princes or wealthy patrons set up permanent public theaters. In Naples, the viceroy established a theater next to his palace in 1652, and two years later a second venue, the Teatro S. Bartolomeo, welcomed the public. Toward the end of the century, Naples began to rival Venice as a creative trend-setter. Meanwhile, the imperial court in Vienna and the Polish royal court in Warsaw saw productions of Venetian-style operas, while in Hamburg German-language operas adopted this model.

Modern listeners, who know seventeenth-century Italian instrumental music better than the vocal music, are sometimes surprised that contemporaries embraced opera as the highest form of musical expression and that composers with a few exceptions pursued it as the principal route to success. Most of the innovations that laid the groundwork for eighteenth-century instrumental music—for example, the symphony, its colorful orchestration, and its arialike slow movements—got their start in the opera house. The opera also expanded the emotional range and the means of expressing it, fundamentally affecting sacred music as well.

⫸ VIII ⫷

MUSIC AND SCIENTIFIC DISCOVERY

T HE CONCERNS of the practicing musician intersected those of the acoustic scientist in the sixteenth and seventeenth centuries at three particular points in a musician's work: when building an instrument, when tuning, and when inquiring into the effect of sounds and music on the hearing and feelings of listeners. As a result, musicians and composers took more than a purely theoretical interest in the science of sound. Likewise, problems arising in the practice of music stimulated some of the earliest investigations and experiments in the mechanics and physics of sound.

Scientists and philosophers for centuries had been asking questions that were significant for music. What is sound and how is it produced? What causes differences of pitch? How are sounds related to numbers? How is sound propagated? Why do some combinations of pitches strike us as consonant? How is consonance related to sympathetic vibration?

In dealing with early science, historians have adopted a broad definition of it that includes at times magic, astrology, and numerology, all of which had strong links with music. Magic or occult science is itself a broad category that hierarchically proceeds from divine intelligence through the stars and planets, angels and demons, down to material things, with occult powers and their communication attributed to all levels.[1] This world of interrelated elements and potencies, of sympathy

---

[1]The distinct realms of science, technology, magic, and religion were not so clearly demarcated as they have tended to be in modern times. On these distinctions, see Robert Mathiesen, "Magic in Slavia Orthodoxa: The Written Tradition," in *Byzantine Magic*, ed. Henry Maguire (Washington, DC: Dumbarton Oaks Research Library and Collection, Harvard University Press, 1995), 155–77 (especially 156–59). On the difficulties of placing the scholarship of the sixteenth and seventeenth centuries in the history of science, see Carlos Ziller Camenietzki, "Baroque Science between the Old and the New World," trans. Paula Findlen and Derrick Allums, in *Athanasius Kircher: The Last Man Who Knew Everything*, ed. Paula Findlen (New York: Routledge, 2004), 311–28. On the relationship between music

and antipathy, consonance and dissonance, had many parallels in music, and music was inevitably interpreted as a means of communicating with the magic realm and in some cases as an imitation of it.

Numerology played an important role both in early science and in music theory, and particular numbers were thought to have divinely ordained force. For the Pythagoreans, the pattern of dots arranged as a pyramid of dots,

which became known as the *tetraktys* of the decad,[2] had unique properties. The ratios of all the intervals recognized by the Pythagoreans as consonances could be formed by using these four numbers: the octave (2:1), fifth (3:2), fourth (4:3), octave-plus-fifth (3:1), and double octave (4:1). The discovery of the relationship between these ratios and the consonances reinforced the Pythagorean belief that number was a universal and divine principle and the means through which the cosmos could be understood.[3] When Plato constructed the World Soul out of number in his *Timaeus*, he was applying Pythagorean principles.[4] Other numbers singled out in the course of time were: 3 for the Christian Trinity; 6 as a perfect number that could also comprise all the ratios necessary to form both the perfect consonances and the imperfect consonances of major

---

and magic, see for example Joscelyn Godwin, ed., *Music, Mysticism and Magic: A Sourcebook* (London: Routledge & Kegan Paul, 1986); and Tomlinson, *Music in Renaissance Magic*.

   [2]A *tetraktys* is a group of four things. Theon of Smyrna (fl. early second century C.E.) identifies eleven *tetraktues* in his *Exposition of Mathematical Matters Useful for Reading Plato*, with the *tetraktys* of the decad as the first. The second *tetraktys* is the set of double and triple multiples (1, 2, 4, 8; and 1, 3, 9, 27), which is used for the creation of the World Soul in Plato's *Timaeus*. See Mathiesen, *Apollo's Lyre*, 424–26.

   [3]For a brief survey of Pythagorean principles, see David Fideler, Introduction to *The Pythagorean Sourcebook and Library*, comp. and trans. Kenneth Sylvan Guthrie, with additional translations by Thomas Taylor and Arthur Fairbanks, Jr. (Grand Rapids, MI: Phanes Press, 1987), 19–54.

   [4]There have been a number of highly detailed studies of the Pythagorean elements in Plato's writings. See, for instance, Francis M. Cornford, *Plato's Cosmology: The* Timaeus *of Plato Translated with a Running Commentary* (London: Routledge & Kegan Paul; New York: Humanities Press, 1937); and Ernest G. McClain, *The Pythagorean Plato: Prelude to the Song Itself* (Stony Brook, NY: Nicolas Hays, 1978).

and minor thirds (5:4 and 6:5);[5] and 9 for the number of Muses and various combinations of the number of planets, the sphere of the zodiac, and the starless sphere. Music was thought by many to be "sounding number," *numerus sonorus.*[6]

Astrology, the study of the influences of the celestial bodies upon human affairs, was bound up with music because the motion of the planets and stars was believed to be regulated by principles of universal harmony. Both Pico della Mirandola and Marsilio Ficino considered music an effective means for gaining the favor of particular planets. Certain modes were thought to be allied with certain planets, and charts that displayed these relationships were included by Bartolomé Ramos de Pareja and Franchino Gaffurio in their treatises.[7]

Philosophers disagreed about the extent to which faith should be placed in magic, numerology, and astrology. In general, the followers of Plato were more inclined to this type of speculation, the followers of Aristotle less so. Those who wanted science to rely on observation, measurement, and experiment excluded supernatural causes or numbers as explanations of phenomena. Nevertheless, explanations based on empirical evidence were not necessarily more correct; mistakes of observation and measurement could lead to false principles. But openness to new methods, theories, and hypotheses, and the constant correction of observations did produce some reliable truths based on stable foundations. The history of this process forms the subject of the present chapter.[8]

---

[5]See pp. 36–37 *supra.*

[6]See, for example in the sixteenth century, Johannes Cochlaeus, *Tetrachordum musices* (Nuremberg: Fridericus Peypus, 1514), f. Aiij[r] (trac. 1, ch. 3); Fogliano, *Musica theorica*, f. 1r (bk. 1, ch. 1); and Nicolaus Wollick, *Enchiridion musices* (Paris: Jean Petit and François Regnault, 1512), f. av[r] (ch. 3).

[7]Ramos de Pareja, *Musica practica*, 61 (tract. 3, ch. 3); Gaffurio, *De harmonia instrumentorum musicorum opus*, f. 94v (bk. 4, chs. 12–13).

[8]The next few pages are partly adapted from my essay, "The Science of Sound and Musical Practice," in *Science and the Arts in the Renaissance*, ed. John W. Shirley and F. David Hoeniger (Washington, DC: The Folger Shakespeare Library; London and Toronto: Associated University Presses, 1985), 59–73.

Legend attributes to Pythagoras the discovery of the ratios of string and pipe lengths that produce certain consonant intervals.[9] Pythagoras himself was probably not so much interested in music as in the harmony of sounds and the rule of proportion. The mathematical doctrine of the Pythagorean cult, however, found its way into musical theory and fixed the theoretical boundary between consonance and dissonance. Boethius transmitted much of this doctrine in his *De institutione musica*, which, as we have seen,[10] is a compendium of Greek music theory based on the second-century Hellenistic Pythagorean mathematician Nicomachus. Boethius applied mathematical reasoning to the selection and ordering of the tonal realm. Numerical proportions determined the pitches, scales, tunings, consonances, gamut, and other relationships and arrangements of tones that are the basis of melodic composition. Pythagorean number theory required that consonant intervals could be represented by only two classes of ratio: the multiple or the superparticular, limited to the numbers from 1 to 4.[11] This allowed for only the five possible intervals embodied in the *tetraktys* of the decad, three of them multiple (the octave, octave-plus-fifth, and double octave) and two superparticular (the fifth and fourth). The tradition stemming from Pythagoras discouraged further investigation of sound, and those most influenced by the tradition as late as the sixteenth century refused to recognize new scientific facts that were at odds with the doctrine.

Myths tend to be more attractive to artists than empirical facts because they are formed in man's own image: Dawn riding a golden chariot explains a sunrise more vividly than a globe revolving on its axis. The myths that evolved from early science sometimes caused art to lose contact with later science.

---

[9]The earliest known version of the legend is the one presented by Nicomachus in the sixth chapter of his *Manual of Harmonics*. See Flora R. Levin, trans. and comm., *The Manual of Harmonics of Nicomachus the Pythagorean* (Grand Rapids, MI: Phanes Press, 1994), 83–97; and idem, *The Harmonics of Nicomachus and the Pythagorean Tradition*, American Classical Studies, no. 1 (University Park, PA: The American Philological Association, 1975).

[10]See pp. 30–31 *supra*.

[11]Multiple ratios are those in which the greater term is an exact integral multiple of the lesser term ($nx:x$, where n is an integer greater than 1); superparticular, those in which the greater term contains the lesser once, plus one integral part of the lesser ($[x +$ one integral part of $x]:x$, where x is an integer greater than 1).

An important achievement of the Renaissance was to bring music theory and practice back in touch with empirical science, as distinct from magic, numerology, and astrology.[12] Aristotle, Aristoxenus, Euclid, Strato, Ptolemy, Nicomachus, and Themistius achieved a high degree of integration between scientific knowledge and musical theory. Boethius summed up aspects of this synthesis, and little was added to the understanding of the mechanics and mathematics of sound before the fourteenth century.[13] Nevertheless, the first advances in the Renaissance came from the recovery of ancient acoustic science.

Our account must begin with that fountainhead of early science, Padua, and specifically with Pietro d'Abano (1250–ca. 1316), who began his commentaries on the Aristotelian *Problems* in Paris and completed them in Padua in 1310.[14] d'Abano was convinced that the *Problems* were a genuine work of Aristotle[15] and strove to elucidate them with the help of some of his other works, particularly *Politics, On the Soul,* and *The Generation of Animals.* The Latin translation accompanying the commentaries was generally assumed to be by Pietro as well, but it has recently been shown to be by Bartolomeo da Messina, active in the court of Manfredi, King of Sicily, who died in 1266.[16]

---

[12]But see n. 1 *supra.*

[13]Although this impression may be subject to modification. For example, A. C. Crombie (*Medieval and Early Modern Science,* 2d ed., 2 vols. [Garden City, NY: Doubleday Anchor Books, 1959], 1:103) has shown that Grosseteste in his commentary on the *Posterior Analytics* 2.4 gave an explanation of the echo that is quite sophisticated.

[14]The date appears in several manuscripts of the work: Venice, Biblioteca Marciana, app. cl. VI/127; Paris, Bibliothèque nationale, lat. 6540; and Cesena, Biblioteca comunale Malatestiana, Plut. 24, destro 2. In the latter, the colophon states that it was begun in Paris and finished in 1310 in Padua. See Sante Ferrari, *I tempi, la vita, le dottrine di Pietro d'Abano: Saggio storico-filosofico,* Atti della università di Genova, vol. 14 (Genoa: R. Istituto Sordomuti, 1900), 98. A similar colophon appears in the first edition, *Expositio problematum Aristotelis: cum textu ejusdem* (Mantua: Paulus de Butzbach, 1475).

[15]See chapter 5, n. 17 *supra.*

[16]A manuscript of Bartolomeo's translation is preserved in Padua, Biblioteca Antoniana, cod. 17, no. 370, dating from the early fourteenth century. For a modern edition of Bartolomeo's translation of section 11 on acoustics, based on the Padua manuscript, collated with Rome, Bibliotheca Apostolica Vaticana, Burghes 37, and Venice, Biblioteca Marciana, app. cl. VI/43 (lat. 2488), see Gerardo

If d'Abano had set out to investigate the physics of sound, he could not have started with a more provocative text than the *Problems*. Although that was not his object, he did undertake in the course of the commentary to explain the mechanics of sound. In relation to Book 11, Problem 1, which deals with the perishability of the sense of hearing, d'Abano makes the observation that in order to produce sound, a body must "vibrate violently and rapidly so that the air is stretched; because of this we see that air, when a rod is suddenly and forcefully moved within it, causes sound."[17] Book 11, Problem 19 gives d'Abano the opportunity to apply this theory to strings. The Aristotelian author observed that a shrill sound is more audible at a distance because it is thinner and thus has greater longitudinal extension. d'Abano expands on this, observing that a string must be thin and tense to produce a sound: "A thin and stretched string that is struck repercusses the air with numerous impulses (*ictus*) before it ceases, so that the jingle (*tinitus*) persists for a long time after the blow, for which reason the medium is filled with the jingle. This does not happen, however, with a thick and loose string."[18] This implies that the thinner and tenser a string, the higher the pitch, but this rule is not explicitly stated. Moreover, d'Abano points out that in the case of a higher pitch, the air breaks up into smaller parts.[19] d'Abano clearly understood the action of the string on the air as causing alternate expansions and contractions of the air, more of them for a higher than a lower pitch, and this is consistent with later findings.

d'Abano clarifies his position and that of the author of the text in his remarks on Book 11, Problem 6. Here, the text explains that sound does not move like a projectile but by means of air impelling air, and it dies not as a projectile falls but when the initial force is spent and air can no longer impel other air. d'Abano sets this rather incidental comment in

---

Marenghi, *Aristotele, Problemi di fonazione e di acustica* (Naples: Libreria scientifica editrice, 1962), 99–117.

[17] d'Abano, *Expositio problematum Aristotelis*, XI, Pr. 1: "... uerberatur vehemens et uelox ut aer fortiter extendatur propter quod videmus aerem subito et fortiter virga in ipso ducta sonum causare...."

[18] Ibid., XI, Pr. 19: "... uidemus enim quod tacta corda subtili et tense repercutit aerem pluribus ictibus antequam cesset unde tinitus diu remanet post tactum quare medium tinitu repletur. In grossa uero corda distensa non euenit illud."

[19] Ibid., XI, Pr. 19: "... in uoce accuta aer mouetur et frangitur in partes minores."

the context of a theory of sound propagation derived from Aristotle's *On the Soul* (Book 2, chapter 8), remarking that the air striking the ear is not the same air set in motion by the sounding body; rather, the air that was first moved is calm by the time the sound arrives at its destination. Moreover, sound is diffused throughout the medium around the vibrating body, while a projectile moves in a single direction. As d'Abano correctly observed, Aristotle had insisted in *On the Soul* that "the speedy is not acute (in pitch) nor the slow grave, but high pitch is caused by speed of motion and low by slowness,"[20] in disagreement with Plato, who believed that high sounds travel faster than lower sounds.

The precise relationship of high to low sounds emerges in Book 19, which is devoted to specific musical problems. Problem 39 asks why we prefer the consonance of the octave for magadizing—the simultaneous singing of boys and men of the same tune an octave apart. The author of the *Problems* answers that the periods of the two sounds agree: "for the second pulse of the air made by *nete* is *hypate* [the note an octave below]."[21] d'Abano, elaborating on an analogy made by the author to poetic meters, compares the combination of a dactyl and anapest, both made up of two breves and a long; and the combination of a tribrach, consisting of three breves, and a spondee comprising two longs. While the first combination joins patterns of equal length, the second joins patterns of unequal length, with the tribrach forming only a fraction of the spondee:

dactyl	—⌣⌣
anapest	⌣⌣—
tribrach	⌣⌣⌣
spondee	— —

This is analogous, d'Abano says, to men's and youths' voices, which produce a poorer consonance—the fifth—than men's and boys' voices, which are an octave apart. In terms of ratios, the poetic and musical examples are not precisely analogous. The temporal ratio of the tribrach to the spondee is 3:4, whereas the ratio of the fifth is 2:3. But d'Abano was probably thinking of the tribrach as equal to one-and-a-half longs,

---

[20]Ibid., XI, Pr. 6: "... dicente uelox non esse accutum neque tardum graue. sed accutum causatur ex uelocitate motus, graue autem ex tarditate."

[21]*Problems* 19.39 (921a): "ἡ γὰρ δευτέρα τῆς νεάτης πληγὴ τοῦ ἀέρος ὑπάτη ἐστίν."

just as the number representing the upper pitch of the fifth (3) is equivalent to one-and-a-half times the number representing the lower pitch (2).

d'Abano faithfully transmitted and explicated a conception of the physical basis of pitch and consonance that laid the foundation for Renaissance advances in the understanding of their acoustical properties. Pitch is seen as originating in cycles or periods of vibration (*tinitus*) of the air caused by plucking a string. A string tuned to the upper note of an octave will move through two such cycles during the time a string tuned an octave lower completes one cycle, at which point the terminations of the two cycles coincide. This relationship holds only for the octave, which is thus the mistress of consonances.

In commenting on Book 19, Problem 35, d'Abano went a step farther than the Aristotelian text in insisting upon the unique position of the octave. He cited the authority of Ptolemy's *Harmonics*: any consonance added to an octave remains a consonance, which is true only of the octave.[22] In d'Abano's remarks on Book 19, Problem 41, he showed that he accepted the consequences of this statement when he included the octave-plus-fourth among the consonances despite its ratio 8:3, which is neither superparticular nor multiple and was therefore excluded by the Pythagoreans and their followers.

d'Abano's commentaries were published in 1475, and other editions appeared in 1482, 1484, 1497, and later. The first work by a musician that could have utilized the printed commentaries was Franchino Gaffurio's *Theoricum opus musice discipline* of 1480.[23] Gaffurio, who was constantly on the lookout for ancient sources, did indeed take advantage of d'Abano's work. He cited Book 19, Problem 21 to support the contention that the interval of the fourth was tolerated in the higher parts of a contrapuntal texture but not when it was the lowest interval. The higher sounds, produced by faster and weaker motion, make a more fleeting impression on the ear than lower notes, he argued, since these are a product of slower and more powerful motion and make a stronger impression.[24]

---

[22]Ptolemy *Harmonics* 1.6. d'Abano must have known Ptolemy's theory through Boethius, *De institutione musica*, bk. 5, chs. 9–10.

[23]Franchino Gaffurio, *Theoricum opus musice discipline* (Naples: Franciscus di Dino Florentinus, 1480; reprint in Musurgiana, vol. 15, ed. Cesarino Ruini, Lucca: Libreria musicale italiana, 1996).

[24]Ibid., ff. [112v–113r] (bk. 5, ch. 8).

In the same book, however, Gaffurio failed to profit by d'Abano's superior explanation of sound and consonance and relied instead upon Boethius's *De institutione musica*, Book 2, chapter 3, which he paraphrased.

> According to Plato, consonance comes about in the hearing in this way: the higher of the two sounds, which is the speedier, precedes the low sound and enters the ear quickly, and the innermost part of the ear, having been struck, bounces the impulse back, as it were, with repeated motion. But now the sound emitted more slowly arrives, not as fast as its first impulse. For this reason, the higher sound, now returning lower, presents itself as similar to the approaching low sound and is blended with it, making one consonance.[25]

Boethius, embroidering on the explanation in Plato's *Timaeus*, tried to account for the speed of the higher sound slowing down in the ear. He seems not to have been totally convinced, however, for he continues by citing the view of Nicomachus—or perhaps he is translating Nicomachus throughout these chapters.[26] Nicomachus, according to Boethius, held that sound consists of not one impulse but many percussions in quick succession. When a string is tense, it produces more frequent and dense pulsations; when it is loose, it produces slow and rare pulsations. It should not be thought that when a string is struck, it yields a moment of sound; rather, as the string continues to vibrate, a series of rapid motions are heard as an uninterrupted tone, and this consists of many vibrations, less frequent for a lower pitch, more frequent for a higher

---

[25]Ibid., f. [21v] (bk. 2, ch. 3): "Sed sit auribus consonantia secundum Platonem hoc modo cum acucior sonus qui uelotior est grauem precesserit in aurem celer ingreditur offensaque extrema eiusdem corporis parte quasi pulsus iterato motu revertitur sed iam segnior nec ita celer ut primo impetu emissus cucurrit quo circa acutior ipse sonus nunc grauior rediens sono primum graui uenienti similis occurrit misceturque ei unam confitiens consonantiam." This explanation is repeated (with a few minor rewordings) in Gaffurio's *Theorica musice*, f. cv^v (bk. 2, ch. 4); trans. *Theory of Music*, 65. The source is Plato *Timaeus* 80a. Boethius's musical treatise, known up to that time through a multitude of manuscript copies, was first published as *De musica libri quinque* in volume 1 of his *Opera*, 2 vols. in 1 (Venice: Johannes et Gregorius de Gregoriis de Forlivio fratres, 1492). It was reissued in 1499 as volume 3 of the *Opera*. For the standard modern edition and translation, see the Bibliography.

[26]Boethius, *De institutione musica*, 221–22 (bk. 1, ch. 31); trans. *Fundamentals of Music*, 48–49.

one. If the percussions of the low pitch are commensurate with the high, consonance results.[27]

In his next book, *Theorica musice* (1492), Gaffurio went to perhaps the most enlightened source then available on the science of sound, the *Paraphrases* of Themistius (ca. 317–388 C.E.) on Aristotle's *On the Soul* in the Latin translation of Ermolao Barbaro.[28] Themistius now became Gaffurio's main source for the theory of sound and hearing. Themistius had insisted, as did d'Abano, that the air struck by the sounding object was not the same as that which reached the ear. He noted, following Aristotle, that the notions of grave and acute were assigned to sounds by analogy with touch, and he elucidated this by saying that the acute voice stabs the air and pungently wounds it, while the grave tone hits bluntly and spreads as it hits. Acute sound quickly moves the sense a lot, grave sound slowly moves it a little.[29] Gaffurio also depended on Themistius to explain the mechanism of hearing. The nature of the ear is akin to that of air, in that the ear is congenitally filled with air that is excited by the air outside and transmits the motion to little sensitized tinders inside a tissue of little breadbaskets (*paniculae*) filled with air. The outside and inside air are continuous, which explains why animals do not hear with their other bodily parts.[30]

With the exception of the citation of Plato by Boethius, all these interpretations of the nature of sound and consonance issued from the Peripatetic tradition. In the late fifteenth and early sixteenth century, they collided head-on with the Pythagorean and Platonic revival. This clash is already evident in Gaffurio, who could not reconcile Themistius's and Ptolemy's empirical tendencies with the strong influence he felt from the side of Ficino and Plato. The split was intensified in Gaffurio's last treatise, *De harmonia musicorum instrumentorum*, finished in 1500 but not pub-

---

[27]Gaffurio, *Theoricum opus*, ff. [18r–19v, 21r–22v] (bk. 2, chs. 1, 3); *Theorica musice*, ff. bvi^v–ci^v and civ^{r–v} (bk. 2, chs. 1 and 4); trans. *Theory of Music*, 49–53 and 65–66.

[28]*Themistii Paraphraseos de anima libri tres, interprete Hermolao Barbaro, nunc recens mendis non oscitanter repurgati, & accurata diligentia typis excusi* (Paris: P. Calvarin, 1535); *In libros Aristoteles De anima paraphrasis; consilio et auctoritate Academiae litterarum regiae borussicae*, ed. Richard Heinze (Berlin: Reimer, 1899).

[29]As Aristotle states in *On the Soul* 2.8. Cf. Themistius, *Paraphrases*, f. 74 (2.30); and Gaffurio, *Theorica musice*, ff. bvi^v–ci^v (bk. 2, ch. 1); trans. *Theory of Music*, 49–53.

[30]Gaffurio, *Theorica musice*, ff. cii^r–ciiij^r (bk. 2, ch. 2); trans. *Theory of Music*, 55; Themistius, *Paraphrases*, 2.28.

lished until 1518,[31] in which he exploited his reading of several newly translated Greek writings by Ptolemy, Bryennius, Bacchius, Aristides Quintilianus, and Bellermann's Anonymous.[32] Although Ptolemy offered solutions to practical problems that should have appealed to Gaffurio as a composer and choirmaster, he could not shed the deeply ingrained Boethian-Pythagorean bias.

Gaffurio's blindness to the incompatibility of the ancient theory of intervals with the current employment of the imperfect consonances is surprising. Ancient theory as transmitted by Boethius accepted the fourth as a consonance but rejected the thirds and sixths. The musical practice of the fifteenth century, on the other hand, required that the fourth be treated in most polyphonic situations as a dissonance and the perfect consonances be mixed and alternated with the so-called imperfect consonances, the thirds (5:4 and 6:5) and sixths (5:3 and 8:5), all the ratios of which were outside the inner sanctum of the first four numbers. The tuning described by Boethius, which is based on the ratios determined by Plato for the basic structure of the World Soul in the *Timaeus*,[33] was ideal for monophonic music and polyphonic music such as organum that treated thirds and sixths as dissonances. But it did not suit more recent polyphonic music, which depended to a considerable degree on the sweeter sounds of the thirds and sixths obtained in other tunings and which treated these intervals as more consonant than the fourth. The mathematician Bartolomé Ramos de Pareja had already proposed in 1482 an alternate tuning for purely practical purposes.[34] In his tuning, the major third had the ratio 5:4 and the minor third 6:5. Gaffurio opposed the tuning as late as 1492 because he knew no theoretical basis or authority for it. In the late 1490s, he discovered that Ptolemy advocated such a tuning. He reported this in his last treatise, *De harmonia musicorum instrumentorum* (1518), but continued to defend the Pythago-

[31]See p. 73 and chapter 2, n. 3 *supra*.

[32]*Anonymi scriptio de musica*, ed. Johann Friedrich Bellermann (Berlin: Förstner, 1841); Dietmar Najock, ed., *Drei anonyme griechische Traktate über die Musik. Eine kommentierte Neuausgabe des Bellermannschen Anonymus*, Göttinger musikwissenschaftliche Arbeiten, vol. 2 (Kassel: Bärenreiter, 1972); idem, ed., *Anonyma de musica scripta Bellermanniana* (Leipzig: B. G. Teubner, 1975).

[33]Plato *Timaeus* 35b–36b.

[34]Ramos de Pareja, *Musica practica*, 4–5 (pt. 1, tract. 1, ch. 2). For a fuller treatment, see Palisca, *Humanism*, 232–34.

rean tuning. Gaffurio's opponents, meanwhile, grasped at this ancient authority and not only confronted him with it but started a groundswell that eventually led to the adoption of Ptolemy's "syntonic" or "intense" diatonic tuning as the ideal system.[35] Giovanni Spataro, a pupil of Ramos, was the main champion of the Ptolemaic tuning,[36] which was later adopted by Lodovico Fogliano and Gioseffo Zarlino in his *Istituti-oni harmoniche*, the most widely read musical textbook of the sixteenth century.[37]

Whereas the Pythagoreans had sanctified the number 4 as the upper limit for the terms of the ratios of consonances, Zarlino regarded the number 6 as equally eligible since it was the first perfect number and legitimized the major and minor thirds and sixths.[38]

Ptolemy's syntonic diatonic represented this expanded repertory of consonances in their purest form and simplest ratios. Adopting this as a new standard, Zarlino maintained that unaccompanied voices always chose these pure forms of the consonances. He posited the *senario* as the foundation of the rules of counterpoint, which permitted much latitude in the use of the consonances formed by the ratios within the first six numbers but severely restricted the use of dissonances, all of which had ratios whose terms exceeded the number 6. Zarlino held tenaciously to this principle, even after it was demonstrated that neither voices nor instruments could hold to the syntonic diatonic tuning without having trouble maintaining a steady pitch.[39]

Zarlino aimed to base his rules on objective facts, such as the ratios of consonances. But the facts he commanded were insufficient, and he was not motivated or inclined to get to the root of the problem. Trained in theology, he had too much respect for authority to question the traditional doctrines, and his confidence in the neo-Platonic ideal of universal harmony prevented him from seeing the contradictions inherent in the world of sound. Meanwhile, the physics of sound had advanced to a point where it could no longer support his premises. The foundation upon which he built his theories was crumbling.

---

[35]See pp. 35–45 *supra*.

[36]See chapter 3, n. 15 *supra*.

[37]See chapters 2, 3, and 5 *supra*.

[38]See pp. 36–37 *supra*.

[39]See pp. 38–41 *supra*.

When physical facts such as the terminations of cycles of vibrations, rather than numbers, are recognized as the basis of consonance, as they appear to be by the author of the *Problems* and d'Abano, there is no precise boundary between consonance and dissonance. The practiced ear is the final judge. Lodovico Fogliano forcefully articulated this position in his *Musica theorica* (1529).[40] His chapters on sound and hearing are an extension of Aristotle's discussion of these matters in *On the Soul* and *Physics*. Fogliano declined to consider music subordinate to mathematics, as it had been classed by most of his predecessors. Insofar as music is sound, it is natural; insofar as it is measured motion, it is mathematical. Sound is generated through the violent breaking up of air, which has any number of causes. When, for example, a solid object is whipped through the air, "air thus torn is very quickly compressed and flows together from every direction, since nature abhors a vacuum. Thus a very rapid condensation of air comes about that resists the striking whip, and this condensation is discharged by exchange with the solid body." Thus, "at least three things concur in the generation of sound, namely that which violently expels the air, the air violently expelled, and the motion or the expulsion."[41] None of these three is itself sound, which is therefore an "accident"—a passive quality derived from the violent motion of the air but commensurate with it, lasting as long as the motion, and potentially moving the sense. Hearing is, similarly, a natural potential, activated by sound through the medium of the air outside and within the ear. Therefore, the sense of hearing is the final judge of consonance and dissonance, and the hearing, preferring the thirds and sixths to the fourth, contradicts reason.

Fogliano applied his empirical methodology to the tuning of the practical musical scale. He replaced the usual mathematical method of dividing the monochord with his, devised "in a new way, almost

---

[40]See chapter 3, n. 11 *supra*.

[41]Fogliano, *Musica theorica*, f. 15r–v (bk. 2, ch. 2): "aer enim sic scissus uelocissime congregatur: & confluit ex omni parte: uacuum abhorrente natura: unde fit uelocissima quaedam aeris condensatio: quae resistit uirgae percutienti: & talis condensatio fungitur uice corporis solidi.... ad generationem soni ad minus tria concurrunt: scilicet: Illud quod uiolenter expellit aerem: & aer uiolenter expulsus: tertium est ipse motus: Siue expulsio...."

according to the sense, and materially."[42] His system permitted a chromatic scale that contained not only pure fifths and fourths, as in Pythagorean tuning, but also pure major thirds and sixths. Whereas the Pythagorean tuning also yielded pure fifths and fourths, its major thirds were slightly too large, 81:64 instead of 80:64 (i.e., 5:4). On the other hand, the syntonic diatonic tuning of Ptolemy did not yield uniformly pure major thirds.[43] In order to find a compromise, the small interval of the syntonic comma, 81:80, would have to be split in half. According to Pythagorean mathematics, this is not possible, as there is no mean proportional between the terms of a superparticular ratio, a circumstance known already to Archytas in the fourth century B.C.E.

Fogliano proposed a geometric solution for the required division, relying upon Euclid's construction of Book 6, proposition 9 (now numbered 13). In Fogliano's figure, AB:BD = 81:80. According to Euclid, if a semicircle is described around line AD and a perpendicular to the circumference is drawn from B, BC is the required geometric mean. Then AB:BC = BC:BD. The string length BC, which cannot be represented by a whole number, will nevertheless sound the desired mean major third against the length 64.

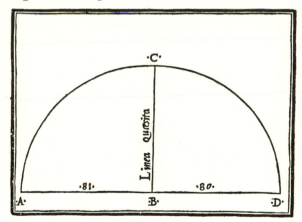

Figure 7. Lodovico Fogliano, *Musica theorica* (1529), f. 36r

---

[42]Ibid., f. 33r (bk. 3, ch. 1): "nouo modo quasi secundum sensum: & materialiter."

[43]See pp. 32–35 *supra*.

Fogliano was not the first to challenge the impossibility of finding a mean proportional between the two terms of a superparticular ratio. Those who preceded him had profited from the revival of interest in the *Elements* of Euclid on the part of humanist mathematicians. The medieval translation of the *Elements* by Campanus had been published in 1482.[44] In 1496, Jacques Lefèvre d'Étaples (ca. 1460–1536) showed how Euclid 6.9 and 6.13 could be applied to find the mean proportional between two string lengths.[45] Heinrich Schreiber (Grammateus) (ca. 1492–1525/26) in 1518 applied the construction to locate a mean-tone between two diatonic steps, for example, the tone between G and A that could serve as both $G\sharp$ and $A\flat$.[46] Erasmus of Höritz (ca. 1465–after 1508) in his manuscript "Musica" of around 1506 showed how the 9:8 tone may be divided by computation and proved the method by Euclidian propositions.[47] The spreading knowledge of Euclid contributed to solving some of the practical problems that surfaced once theorists began to discard some of their prejudices about numbers.[48]

Up to this point, we have not been considering new scientific findings but rather the rediscovery of Greek mathematical and acoustical science and its application to practice. The work of Giovanni Battista Benedetti, however, represents a real advance in scientific knowledge. In two letters of around 1563 addressed to the composer Cipriano de Rore, published in his *Diversarum speculationum mathematicarum & physicarum liber* (1585),[49] Benedetti confronted more realistically and perceptively

---

[44]*Elementa geometriae lat[ine] cum Campani annotationibus* (Venice: Erhardus Ratdolt, 1482).

[45]*Musica libris demonstrata quatuor* (Paris: Joannes Higmanus et Volgangus Hopilius, 1496), ff. gvi^v–gvij^r (bk. 3).

[46]*Ayn new kunstlich Buech* (Nuremberg: Stüchs, 1518).

[47]Rome, Bibliotheca Apostolica Vaticana, Reginensis lat. 1245. See Claude V. Palisca, "The Musica of Erasmus of Höritz," in *Aspects of Medieval and Renaissance Music: A Birthday Offering to Gustave Reese*, ed. Jan LaRue (New York: Norton, 1966), 628–48; reprinted with a prefatory note in Palisca, *Studies*, 146–67.

[48]For a fuller discussion, see Palisca, *Humanism*, 242–44. For a useful survey of the relationship between mathematics and music, see Catherine Nolan, "Music Theory and Mathematics," in *The Cambridge History of Western Music Theory*, ed. Thomas Christensen (Cambridge: Cambridge University Press, 2002), 272–304.

[49]Benedetti, *Diversarum speculationum mathematicarum et physicarum liber*, 277–83. The two letters are reprinted in Josef Reiss, "Jo. Bapt. Benedictus, De intervallis musicis," *Zeitschrift für Musikwissenschaft* 7 (1924–25): 13–20.

than ever before the dilemma of instrumental tuning. In the process, he gave the best account of the mechanics of consonance.[50]

Everyone knows, Benedetti says, that the longer a vibrating string, the more slowly it moves. If a string is divided by a bridge so that two thirds are on one side and one third on the other, and the two sides are plucked, the consonance of the octave will be heard. The larger portion of the string will complete one period of vibration (*intervallum tremoris*) while the shorter completes two. If two fifths of the string are on one side of the bridge and three fifths on the other, the consonance of the fifth will be generated, the longer portion of the string completing two periods of vibration while the lesser portion completes three periods. Benedetti then arrives at the law stating that the product of the numbers representing the string lengths and the periods of vibration in each portion of the string between the moments when the vibrations exactly coincide will be equal. For example, in the case of the fifth, within the period of coincidence, string length 3 will have two periods of vibration, and the product will be 6; string length 2 will have three periods of vibration, and the product will likewise be 6. He proceeds to calculate the products for each of the consonances recognized by Fogliano: octave, 2; fifth, 6; fourth, 12; major sixth, 15; ditone (major third), 20; semiditone (minor third), 30; minor sixth, 40. He notes that these numbers agree among themselves with a "wonderful reasonableness" (*mirabili analogia*). It is not clear whether he saw in this series of numbers anything other than a basis for establishing a hierarchy of consonances.[51] Nor is it

---

[50]For the Latin text and a translation of the passage see Palisca, "Scientific Empiricism," 106–8; reprinted in idem, *Studies*, 215–16.

[51]D. P. Walker, "Galileo Galilei," in *Studies in Musical Science in the Late Renaissance* (London: The Warburg Institute; Leiden: E. J. Brill, 1978), 31, n. 16, contested my claim that Benedetti was establishing here a hierarchy of consonances. That Benedetti was indeed doing so is evident from the paragraph that introduces the demonstration:

Nam, nulli dubium est, quin unisonus sit prima principalis audituque amicissima, nec non magis propria consonantia; et si[c] intelligatur, ut punctus in linea, vel unites in numero, quam immediate sequitur diapason, ei simillima, post hanc vero diapente, caeteraeque. Videamus igitur ordinem concursus	For there is no doubt that the unison is the first, principal, and friendliest to the hearing, and also quite properly a consonance; and it is understood as the point is to a line or unity to number, after which the diapason, most similar to it, directly follows, then the diapente, and so forth. Let us see, then, the order of concur-

evident how he managed to count the vibrations, if he did; he may simply have assumed, like the Aristotelian commentators before him, that they were in inverse proportion to the string lengths, the tension being equal. This is a valid enough assumption, but one that begs for experimental proof.

On the one hand, Benedetti theorized that consonance was produced by the frequent coincidence of the terminations of periods of vibration and that this coincidence was most frequent in the consonances produced by simple ratios. On the other hand, he knew that to base the construction and tuning of instruments on these simple ratios, as others had done, was impractical. There were some serious difficulties with the simple ratios. One is the Pythagorean comma, the difference by which a cycle of twelve fifths exceeds a cycle of seven octaves, a phenomenon discovered in antiquity. A tuning system in which both $D\sharp$ and $E\flat$ could be used in the same piece—and such pieces were being written in the 1560s by Rore among others—required a compromise tuning that tempered the fifths so that a cycle of fifths would equal a cycle of octaves. As we shall see, Benedetti proposed a system of this kind to Rore. Another difficulty, first mathematically demonstrated by Benedetti, occurred when singers intoned pure consonances at all times, as they tended to do and Zarlino claimed they did, causing the pitch to constantly rise and fall. This is a phenomenon painfully familiar to choral conductors.

---

percussionum terminorum, seu undarum aeris, unde sonus generatur.	rence of terminations of percussions or waves of the air through which sound is generated.

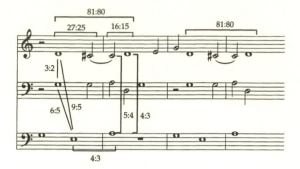

Figure 8. G. B. Benedetti, *Diversarum speculationum*, 280

Benedetti made up an example stating a two-measure musical phrase four times (the first three-and-a-half measures are shown in figure 8): supposing that the "just" tuning of the consonances through simple ratios were maintained through the common tones that link one interval to the next, he calculated that the pitch would fall one syntonic comma (81:80) during each statement. Thus, at the end of figure 8, the pitch will have fallen nearly a half semitone, or more precisely 44 percent of an equal-tempered semitone.

Figure 9. G. B. Benedetti, *Diversarum speculationum*, 279

He showed with another example (figure 9) that even if there were no sharps or flats, certain simple progressions such as the diatonic sequence of chords illustrated here would also lead to a fluctuation of pitch. The pitch in this example would rise in the course of four statements of the pattern nearly a whole semitone. In the first example, the fluctuation is caused by two different sizes of semitones, in the second case it is caused by two different sizes of whole tones.

Needed was a tuning in which all semitones were equal and all whole tones were likewise equal, and this Benedetti proposed to Rore. After making the minor sixth *G* to *Eb* as consonant as possible, Rore was instructed to tune on his harpsichord a series of fifths, each of which was slightly flat, until he reached *G♯*, remaining, however, within a three-octave span by finding the lower perfect octave whenever room was needed to complete the upward spiral. Each note was to be checked against the upper or lower major sixth, which had to be as large as bearable.[52] The resulting tuning was an approximation of equal temperament, not unlike the one proposed by Giovanni Lanfranco (d. 1545) in 1533.[53] In their keyboards *G♯* doubled as *A♭*, and *E♭* similarly functioned as *D♯*. We must assume, further, that Benedetti's starting point, *E♭*, sounded a good tempered fifth against the *G♯* that terminated the cycle.

Benedetti's solution overcame the two main obstacles that had impeded progress in tuning. He eliminated the Pythagorean comma by taking a little of it off each of seven fifths, with the result that as much of the cycle as was used in practice now equaled the parallel cycle of octaves. The fluctuation of pitch he solved by doing away with the unequal whole tones and semitones of the earlier tunings. Of course, having done this, he banished from practical music the simple ratios, about which he had theorized with reference to the coincidence of vibrations of consonance. This did not seem to bother him. Whereas Gaffurio and Zarlino expected art somehow to conform to and follow nature, Benedetti knew that this was impossible: musical practice was not science.[54]

No one resolved the conflicting demands of science and art more clear-headedly than the classicist Girolamo Mei, who had heard lectures on Aristotle's *On the Soul, Concerning the Heavens*, and *The Generation of Animals* in Rome in 1560. It was to Mei that Vincenzo Galilei, father of Galileo, turned in 1572 for advice when he was torn between the ideal of justly tuned consonances and the practical necessity for temperament. Mei responded:

---

[52]Modern tuners use the major third; Benedetti may have preferred the major sixth because its rank number, 15, the lowest of the imperfect consonances, places it before the major third, 20.

[53]*Scintille di musica* (Brescia: Lodovico Britannico, 1533), 132. See J. Murray Barbour, *Tuning and Temperament* (East Lansing: Michigan State College Press, 1953), 45ff. Benedetti probably did not know Lanfranco's treatise, an elementary practical tutor rather than a scientific work such as the treatise of Fogliano, which Benedetti did cite.

[54]See also Palisca, *Humanism*, 257–65.

The science of music goes about diligently investigating and considering all the qualities and properties of the constitutions, systems, and order of musical tones, whether these are simple qualities or comparative, like the consonances, and this for no other purpose than to come to know the truth itself, the perfect goal of all speculation, and as a by-product the false. It then lets art exploit as it sees fit without any limitation those tones about which science has learned the truth.[55]

Galilei paraphrased this passage in his *Dialogo della musica antica, et della moderna* of 1581.[56] It was to become a principle for Galilei to establish securely by experiment the laws of acoustics and to investigate musical practice by observing how the materials of music—the consonances and dissonances and the notes of the scale—were actually applied in composition and performance. For example, the employment of many accidentals in modern music made it necessary to temper the tuning of instruments, and the best method for doing this, in Galilei's opinion, was through the "intense" diatonic of Aristoxenus. "No demonstrable distribution with stable tuning besides this can be found that is simpler and more powerful, whether played or sung."[57] This tense tuning of Aristoxenus is, in effect, equal temperament, and to prove that it was the only tuning equal to the demands of modern music, Galilei composed a piece that could be played by no other means.[58]

---

[55]Mei, letter to Galilei, Rome, 8 May 1572, in Palisca, *Mei*, 103: "la Musica, la scienzia de la quale va diligentemente investigando e considerando tutte le qualità et proprietà de le constituzioni et sistemi et ordini de le voci musicali, si le semplici di ciascuna, come le respettive, tra le quali sono le consonanze e questo non per altro fine che per venire in cognizione de la verità istessa, termine perfetto di ogni speculazione; e per accidente del falso: lasciando poi al' arte servirsi di quelle stesse voci de le quali essa ha conosciuto la verità, ..."

[56]Galilei, *Dialogo*, 105. The interlocutor, Bardi, states: "Vi rispondo à questo, che le scienze hanno diuerso procedere & diuerso fine nell'operare che non hanno le arti. le scienze cercano il vero degli accidenti & proprietà tutte del loro subietto, & insieme le loro cagioni; hauendo per fine la verità della cognitione senza piu: & le arti hanno per fine l'operare, cosa diuersa dall'intendere."

[57]Galilei, *Discorso intorno all'opere di Messer Gioseffo Zarlino*, 113: "... ne altre Distributione dimonstrabile fuor' di questa, puo trouarsi tra corde stabili piu semplice e' piu capace tanto sonata quanto cantata...."

[58]Vincenzo Galilei, "Discorso particolare intorno all'unisono," in Claude V. Palisca, *The Florentine Camerata: Documentary Studies and Translations*, Music Theory Translation Series (New Haven, CT: Yale University Press, 1989), 206.

Apart from the impracticality of the tuning founded on the *senario*, Galilei, like Fogliano before him, questioned the notion of the sonorous number.[59] "Sonorous number," Galilei objected, confused three separate concepts—number, motion, and sound. Numbers are disembodied abstractions describing the sounding body. "A number, having no body, cannot be sonorous."[60] Sensations, on the other hand, were appearances or superficial occurrences.

> The senses apprehend precisely differences in forms, colors, flavors, odors, and sounds. Moreover, they know the heavy from the light, the harsh and hard from the soft and tender, and other superficial occurrences. But the quality and intrinsic virtue of things, with respect to whether they are hot or cold, humid or dry, only the intellect has the faculty of judging, convinced by experiment and not simply by the sense through the medium of the diversity of the forms and colors or other circumstance....[61]

Even more boldly, Galilei questioned the validity of the very numbers that were considered sonorous. To associate particular numbers or ratios with particular consonances was questionable because these numbers varied with the circumstances of the sounding body. 2:1 may not always be the ratio of the octave or 3:2 of the fifth. Galilei was the first to point out that weights suspended from strings must be in the ratio of 4:1, not 2:1, to produce the octave, other factors such as length and thickness being equal. To obtain a fifth, the proportion of weights must be 9:4; a fourth, 16:9.[62] The ratio of string lengths had to be squared and inverted to give the ratio of weights. Moreover, it is mistaken to say that two pipes—one double the length of the other—always yield the octave because, as organ builders know, both the length and diameter must be doubled to get a satisfactory tone; it is the volume of air in the pipes that

---

[59]See chapter 3 *supra*.

[60]Galilei, "Il primo libro della prattica del contrapunto intorno all'uso delle consonanze," 15: "il numero come quello che non ha corpo, non puo essere sonoro."

[61]Galilei, *Discorso intorno all'opere di Messer Gioseffo Zarlino*, 104: "imperoche i sensi conoscano esattamente la diversità delle forme, de colori, de sapori, degl'odori, et de suoni, conoscano inoltre il grave dal leggiero, l'aspro e'l duro dal tenero et molle, et altre si fatti superficiali accidenti: ma la qualità et virtù intrinseca delle cose circa l'essere calde o fredde, o umide o secche; l'intelletto solo ha facultà di giudicarle tali persuaso dall'esperienza, et non semplicemente dal senso mediante la diversità delle forme et de colori, o di altro accidente...."

[62]Ibid., 103–4.

counts, and the best ratio of volumes is 8:1, or the cube of the lengths. Galilei claimed to have discovered these relationships through experiment.[63] He also reported on experiments with strings of various thicknesses and materials. His observations taught him that numbers are significant only when they represent measurements of particular physical characteristics such as string length, tension, or cubic volume. Setting abstract numerical limits on consonance such as the *senario* was useless.

Vincenzo Galilei's investigations, particularly those reported in the *Discorso* of 1589, inspired others in the seventeenth century to look further for answers to the fundamental questions of the physics of sound. A number of scientists of that period had a deep interest in music. Among them were Galileo Galilei (1564–1642), Marin Mersenne (1588–1648), René Descartes (1596–1650), Isaac Beeckman (1588–1637), Johannes Kepler (1571–1630), Isaac Newton (1642–1727), John Wallis (1616–1703), and Christiaan Huygens (1629–1695). All of them had a command of music theory, and some were also amateur musicians. This is not surprising, since music was still considered a branch of mathematics, one of the four disciplines of the quadrivium. Two in particular followed up on Vincenzo Galilei's work, his son Galileo and Marin Mersenne.

Galileo was not only the son of a musician but also a lutenist himself and a brother and father of musicians. In the *Discorsi e dimostrazioni matematiche intorno à due nuove scienze* of 1638, Galileo's interlocutors, Sagredo and Salviati, take up the questions that Zarlino and Vincenzo Galilei had debated. Sagredo asks why he should accept what many learned authors have said—that the octave is contained in the duple ratio, the fifth in the 3:2 ratio, and so on—simply because these are the ratios of the string lengths that produced these consonances. The reason did not impress him as sufficient.

> There are three ways to raise the pitch of a string: first, by shortening it; second, by tightening or stretching it; third, by making it thinner. If we maintain the tension and thickness of the string constant, we obtain the octave by shortening it to one-half, that is, by sounding first the open string and then one-half of it. But if we keep the length and thickness constant and we wish

---

[63]Vincenzo Galilei, "Discorso particolare intorno alla diversità delle forme del Diapason," in Claude V. Palisca, *The Florentine Camerata: Documentary Studies and Translations*, Music Theory Translation Series (New Haven, CT: Yale University Press, 1989), 180–97.

to produce the octave by stretching, it will not suffice to double the weight attached to the string; it must be quadrupled. If the string was first stretched by a weight of one pound, four will be required to raise it to the octave.... Granted these very true observations, I could see no reason why those wise philosophers should have established the duple ratio rather than the quadruple as that of the octave, or why for a fifth they should have chosen the sesquialtera [3:2] rather than the dupla sesquiquarta [9:4].[64]

So far the dialogue rehearses the line of thinking that led Vincenzo to conclude that no specific ratios could define the consonances. But now Galileo announces that he has discovered a fundamental basis for a constant ratio for each interval. The ratios of the frequencies of the vibrations of the sounds are the inverse of those of the string lengths: "... the ratio of a musical interval is not immediately determined either by the length, size, or tension of the strings but rather by the ratio of their frequencies, that is, by the number of vibrations and beats of the waves of the air that strike the eardrum and cause it to vibrate with the same frequency."[65] This had been suggested by Benedetti and Beeckman,[66] but they offered no experimental proof.

---

[64]Galileo Galilei, *Opere,* Edizione nazionale sotto gli auspicii di Sua Maestà il re d'Italia, 20 vols. in 21 (Florence: G. Barbèra, 1890–1909), 8:143–44: "Tre sono le maniere con le quali noi possiamo inacutire il tuono a una corda: l'una è lo scorciarla; l'altra, il tenderla più, o vogliam dir tirarla; il terzo è l'assottigliarla. Ritenendo la medesima tiratezza e grossezza della corda, se vorremo sentir l'ottava, bisogna scorciarla la metà, cioè toccarla tutta, e poi mezza: ma se, ritenendo la medesima lunghezza e grossezza, vorremo farla montare all'ottava col tirarla più, non basta tirarla il doppio più, ma ci bisogna il quadruplo, sì che se prima era tirata dal peso d'una libbra, converrà attaccarvene quattro per inacutirla all'ottava: ... Stante queste verissime esperienze, non mi pareva scorger ragione alcuna per la quale avesser i sagaci filosofi a stabilir, la forma dell'ottava esser più la dupla che la quadrupla, e della quinta più la sesquialtera che la dupla sesquiquarta"; my translation. For an alternate translation, see Galileo Galilei, *Two New Sciences, Including Centers of Gravity and Force of Percussion,* trans. with introduction and notes by Stillman Drake (Madison: University of Wisconsin Press, 1974), 101–2.

[65]Galilei, *Opere,* 8:146: "Ma sequitando il primo proposto, dico che non è la ragion prossima ed immediata delle forme de gl'intervalli musici la lunghezza delle corde, non la tensione, non la grossezza, ma sì bene la proporzione de i numeri delle vibrazioni e percosse dell'onde dell'aria che vanno a ferire il timpano del nostro orecchio, il quale esso ancora sotto le medesime misure di tempi vien fatto tremare." See also Drake, *Two New Sciences,* 104.

[66]Concerning Beeckman's theories, see H. Floris Cohen, *Quantifying Music* (Dordrecht: D. Reidel Publishing Company, 1984).

Galileo submits two experiences to support the contention that the ratio of the frequencies of the octave and fifth are as 1:2 and 2:3. He placed a goblet of water in a larger container filled with water almost to the rim of the goblet. When he rubbed his wet finger around the rim of the goblet, he obtained a clear and consistent pitch but occasionally a note an octave higher. In the water around the goblet he noticed ripples dividing into two equal halves when he heard the octave.[67]

The other observation he made by chance. While scraping a brass plate with a sharp iron chisel to remove some spots, he heard the plate emit a whistling sound. The faster he scraped, the higher the sound. When hearing the whistle, he felt the plate tremble and later noticed a row of fine streaks, parallel and equidistant, on its surface. When he compared the pitches to those of a spinet, he found that the ratio of the number of streaks for a given space was 2:3 when the interval between pitches was a fifth.[68] No one has been able to repeat these two experiences, and this has led one scholar to call them "thought-experiments."[69]

Galileo also pursued Benedetti's explanation of the effect of different consonances on the hearing. Benedetti had suggested that the more frequently the cycles of vibration of two pitches concluded together, the better the consonance. Galileo attributes the pleasing effect of consonance to the fact that the pulses delivered by the two pitches of the consonance are commensurable in number; thus, the eardrum is not constantly bent in different directions but receives pulses delivered simultaneously at regular intervals of time: every two pulses of the higher note for the octave, every three for the fifth, and so on. He adds, however, that we are not necessarily more pleased by the most frequent coincidence of pulses, as in the octave. For example, the fifth produces "a tickling of the eardrum in

---

[67]Galilei, *Opere*, 8:142–43; Drake, *Two New Sciences*, 100.

[68]Ibid., 8:145; Drake, *Two New Sciences*, 102–3.

[69]Walker, "Galileo Galilei," 30. Thomas B. Settle repeated the experiment with the water goblet and photographed the patterns of wavelets, but they were not sufficiently regular to be counted, nor could he confirm any proportionate division when higher notes were emitted, rather a tendency for the ripples to disappear. See his essay, "La rete degli esperimenti Galileiani," in *Galileo e la scienza sperimentale*, ed. Milla Baldo Ceolin (Padua: Dipartimento di Fisica "Galileo Galilei," 1995), 11–62.

which softness is touched with sprightliness, like the combination of a gentle kiss and a bite."[70]

With this observation, Galileo moved in the same direction Descartes had persuaded Mersenne to take, that is, to stop thinking that simplicity of ratios and pleasingness to the ear went hand in hand. In a letter of 13 January 1631 to Mersenne, Descartes proposed:

> Concerning the sweetness of consonances, there are two things to be distinguished, that is, what makes them simpler and more concordant and what makes them more pleasing.

> As for what renders them more pleasing, this depends on the places where they are employed, and there are places where even the diminished fifths and other dissonances are more pleasing than the consonances, so it is not possible to determine absolutely that one consonance is more pleasing than another. One may say, surely, that the thirds and sixths are generally more pleasing than the fourth, that in cheerful compositions the major thirds and sixths are more pleasing than the minor, and the contrary in sad compositions, etc., since there are more opportunities to use them pleasingly....

> So we can say absolutely that the fourth is more concordant than the major third, even though ordinarily it is not more pleasing, in the same way that senna (*la casse*) is sweeter than olives, but not more pleasing to our taste.[71]

In France and the Netherlands, Descartes, Beeckman, and Mersenne took up some of the problems Vincenzo Galilei had addressed. Mersenne remarked in *La verité des sciences* (1625) on the importance of Galilei's discoveries, which, he noted, finally refuted the false opinion of

---

[70]Galilei, *Opere*, 8:149: "fa una titillazione ed un solletico tale sopra la cartilagine del timpano, che temperando la dolcezza con uno spruzzo d'acrimonia, par che insieme soavemente baci e morda"; Drake, *Two New Sciences*, 107.

[71]Mersenne, *Correspondance*, 3:24–25: "Touchant la douceur des consonances, il y a deus choses à distinguer, à sçavoir ce qui les rend plus simples et *accordantes*, et ce qui les rend plus *agréables* à l'oreille.

"Or, pour ce qui les rend plus *agréables*, cela depend des lieus où elles sont employees, et il se trouve des lieus où mesme les fausses quintes et autres dissonances sont plus agreables que les consonances, de sorte qu'on ne sçauroit determiner absolument qu'une consonance soit plus agreable que l'autre. On peut bien dire toutefois que, pour l'ordinaire, les tierces et les sextes sont plus agreables que la quarte, que dans les chans gays les tierces et sextes majeures sont plus agreables que les mineurs, et le contrarire dans les tristes, etc., pour ce qu'il se trouve plus d'occasions où elles y peuvent estre employees agreablement.

"... en sorte qu'on peut dire absolument que la quarte est plus accordante que la tierce majeur, encore la casse est bien plus douce que les olives, mais non pas si agreable à nostre goust."

those who believed Pythagoras had given the correct ratios for the con-sonances when weights were suspended from strings.[72] In his *Harmonie universelle* (1636), he concurred with Galilei that other variables, such as thickness of strings, also affected the pitch-relations. Mersenne refined Galilei's observations of the ratios of intervals under different condi-tions. He summed up his detailed observations of the behavior of strings in a table, which he called "Harmonic Tablature for the Deaf" because with its help, even a deaf person could tune any interval by mea-suring the necessary quantities.[73]

Tablature harmonique pour les sourds.

Les 8 sons, ou notes de l'Octaue.	Les 7 degrez de l'Octaue.	Table I. La tension des chordes proportionnées selon la raison doublée des interualles.				Table II. La grosseur des chordes proportionnée selon la raison simple des interualles.	Table III. La longueur des chordes proportionnées selon la raison simple des interualles.				Table IV. La Tension des chordes proportionnées selon la raison simple des interualles.			
		liures.	onces.	gros.	grains.	parties de ligne	dixiesmes.	pieds.	poulces.	lignes.	liures.	onces.	gros.	grains.
1 VT	ton mi.	1	0	0	0	10		4	0	0	2	0	0	0
2 RE	ton mai.	1	4	15	54	9		3	7	2⅓	1	11	11	58
3 MI	sem.mai.	1	10	9	0	8		3	2	4⅔	1	9	9	43
4 FA	ton mai.	1	14	3	32	7½		3	0	0	1	8	0	0
5 SOL	ton mi.	2	6	4	0	6²		2	8	0	1	5	5	24
6 RE	ton mai.	2	14	3	32	6		2	4	9½	1	3	3	14
7 MI	semi.maj.	3	11	12	18	5½		2	1	7½	1	1	1	5
8 FA		4	4	0	0	5		2	0	0	1	0	0	0

Figure 10. Marin Mersenne, *Harmonie universelle, Livre troisiesme des instrumens à chordes,* 125 (Proposition VII): "Tablature harmonique pour les sourds"

Mersenne showed that to raise the pitch of a string by an octave, any one of three things could be done. First, the tension could be roughly

---

[72]Marin Mersenne, *La verité des sciences contre les sceptiques ou Pyrrhoniens* (Paris: Beauchesne et ses fils, 1932), 203 (bk. 1).

[73]Marin Mersenne, *Harmonie universelle, Livre troisiesme des instrumens à chordes,* 125 (Proposition VII).

quadrupled (equivalent to quadrupling the weight hanging from a string, for example, from 1 pound to 4 pounds, 4 ounces). Second, the thickness (Mersenne apparently meant diameter) of the higher string could be reduced by half, that is, 5/10 against 10/10 of a line (a line is approximately 2.12 millimeters or one-twelfth of an inch). Elsewhere, he showed that the cross-sectional area of the higher string would be the square root of that of the octave below.[74] Third, the length of the string could be reduced from four to two feet to raise the pitch an octave.

Mersenne also confirmed Galilei's assertion that the ratio of cubic volume of organ pipes should vary as 8:1 for the octave. In a table exhibiting the relationship of pipe length and cubic volume for various intervals,[75] Mersenne shows that for an octave, the ratio of lengths is 2:1 but of volumes 8:1; for the fifth, 3:2 and 17:8; and for the major third, 5:4 and 125:64. He gives the corresponding ratios for eighteen intervals from the octave down to the comma.

Mersenne's most important original contribution was to discover the phenomenon now known as harmonics or partials of a fundamental pitch. In 1623, he reported hearing a string emit several tones at once but could not identify the pitches.[76] After further investigation, he identified the component sounds as the natural or fundamental pitch of the string, the upper octave, twelfth, fifteenth, seventeenth, and twentieth.[77] This would be equivalent to a series such as *C c g c' e' a'*. He discussed the phenomenon with his scientific friends, but none of the reasons they proposed satisfied him. He rejected the suggestion that the string may be vibrating in parts as well as in its entirety.

---

[74]Galileo, having noticed that the material out of which a string is made—such as brass, gold, or gut—also affects the pitch, preferred to think of weight rather than size. Thus, to produce an octave, the string had to be four times lighter. Galilei, *Opere*, 8:146; Drake, *Two New Sciences*, 103–4.

[75]Mersenne, *Harmonie universelle, Livre sixiesme des orgues*, 335 (Proposition XIV): "Tablature de la longueur, & de la solidité des tuyaux."

[76]Marin Mersenne, *Quaestiones celeberrimae in Genesim, cum accurata textus explicatione; in hoc volumine athei et deistae impugnantur et expugnantur, et Vulgata editio ab haereticorum calumniis vindicatur, Graecorum et Hebraeorum musica instauratur* (Paris: S. Cramoisy, 1623), col. 1560 (ch. 4, quaest. 57, Art. 3).

[77]Mersenne, *Harmonie universelle, Livre quatriesme des instrumens à chordes*, 208–11 (Proposition IX).

The solution was found through another phenomenon Mersenne studied but could not adequately analyze or explain, that of sympathetic vibration of strings not tuned in unison. Girolamo Fracastoro (1483–1553) in his *De sympathia et antipathia rerum* (1546) explained why a string tuned in unison to a nearby sounding string responded by emitting the same pitch. When two strings of equal length stretched to the same tension are tuned to the same pitch, and one is plucked, the other resounds because the compression caused in the air by the plucked string is communicated to the untouched string. When the plucked string returns to its original position, the air is rarefied, and this allows the second string to return to its position. But if the strings are not tuned to the same pitch, the untouched string does not return, because the condensation-rarefaction cycle to which it responds takes a shorter or longer time.[78] After citing Fracastoro, Mersenne reported on his own experiments with strings tuned to the fifth, octave, twelfth, and seventeenth, finding that they caused each other to vibrate in sympathy.[79] He did not, however, correctly identify the pitches that emanated from the sympathetic strings. He thought, for example, that a plucked string made a string tuned to the lower octave resound at the lower octave, when it actually replied in unison to the higher string, vibrating in halves. He could not bring himself to acknowledge this partial vibration.

The problem was resolved through the work of a group of English scholars. In 1673, William Noble of Merton College and Thomas Pigot of Wadham College, both in Oxford, showed that when strings tuned at the octave, twelfth, and seventeenth below a plucked string vibrated in response, they produced unisons with the sounding string by vibrating in parts—in halves, thirds, and fifths. This was demonstrated by placing paper riders on the sympathetic strings at the points where, if the string were stopped, unisons would be produced: the paper riders remained in place. These points were later called "nodes." Riders put elsewhere on the string would fly off.

---

[78]Girolamo Fracastoro, "De sympathia et antipathia rerum liber unus," in *Opera omnia in unum proxime post illius mortem collecta*, 2d ed. (Venice: Iuntas, 1574), 66–67 (chap. 11).

[79]Marin Mersenne, *Harmonicorum libri in quibus agitur de sonorum natura, causis, et effectibus* …, 2 parts (Paris: Guillaume Baudry, 1636), 65–67 (bk. 4, props. XXVII–XXIX).

John Wallis applied this finding to the study of the vibration of a single string. He observed that multiple sounds occurred only when the nodes were not disturbed by plucking at these points, showing that the string was not only vibrating as a whole but dividing into a number of parts at the same time.[80] In the eighteenth century, Jean-Philippe Rameau was delighted to learn (rather belatedly through Joseph Sauveur[81]) of the phenomenon of harmonics because it proved to him that a chord such as *C-E-G-c* was found in nature, supporting his theory that a succession of such harmonies was the source of all melody and harmony.[82]

Considerable progress was made in the seventeenth century on other problems concerning musical sounds.[83] Robert Hooke and Christiaan Huygens ingeniously constructed wheels with teeth striking metal bars when turned at different speeds, thereby producing different pitches. By counting the number of strikes per unit of time, it was possible to arrive at the cycles per second of a given pitch. Others, studying the action of organ pipes, calculated the length of sound waves of different pitches. The results, for the time being, were approximate, but they would soon be refined.

With Girolamo Fracastoro, Vincenzo Galilei, and Giovanni Battista Benedetti, the study of sound turned from numerology to physical science. Numerical ratios and arithmetical operations remained important,

---

[80]John Wallis, "[Of the Trembling of Consonant Strings]: Dr. Wallis's Letter to the Publisher Concerning a New Musical Discovery," *Philosophical Transactions* 12 (April 1677): 839–42.

[81]Joseph Sauveur, "Système général des intervalles des sons," in *Histoire de l'académie royale des sciences*, Année 1701; *Mémoires*, 2d ed. (Paris: Charles Etienne Hocherau, 1719), 349–56 (sect. 9, "Des sons harmoniques"). For a readily accessible version, see Joseph Sauveur, *Collected Writings on Musical Acoustics (Paris, 1700–1713)*, ed. Rudolf Rasch, Facsimile Editions, Tuning and Temperament Library, no. 2 (Utrecht: Diapason Press, 1984).

[82]Jean-Philippe Rameau, *Nouveau systeme de musique théorique* (Paris: Jean-Baptiste-Christoph Ballard, 1726). Rameau had originally defended this theory by the first six divisions of the string in *Traité de l'harmonie* (1722). See chapter 5, n. 70.

[83]For a survey of vibration theory in this century, see Sigalia Dostrovsky, "Early Vibration Theory: Physics and Music in the Seventeenth Century," *Archive for History of Exact Sciences* 14 (1975): 169–218; and John T. Cannon and Sigalia Dostrovsky, *The Evolution of Dynamics: Vibration Theory from 1687 to 1742* (New York: Springer-Verlag, 1981).

but they were applied to ascertain material relationships among observable phenomena and eventually to establish laws governing the acoustical realm. Galileo, Mersenne, Beeckman, Huygens, and others contributed to this young science in the seventeenth century.[84]

Meanwhile, music theory became for awhile a purely empirical discipline, independent of both physics and metaphysics. Seventeenth-century music theory, when it sought grounds for its speculations outside of music, turned—quite properly perhaps—away from acoustics towards rhetoric and logic. Sixteenth- and seventeenth-century science revealed the inadequacy of theories based on Pythagorean and neo-Platonic number systems and in this way encouraged musicians to look elsewhere or within their art itself for theoretical foundations.

---

[84]For additional detail, see Palisca, "Scientific Empiricism," 91–137; reprinted in idem, *Studies*, 200–235. See also Green and Butler, "From Acoustics to *Tonpsychologie*," 246–56.

❧ IX ❧

ANCIENT AND MODERN:
STYLES AND GENRES

WHILE SCIENTISTS and music theorists debated the limits of consonance, composers ventured beyond its domain into dissonance to express the emotional texts favored in the second half of the sixteenth century. Cipriano de Rore, Giaches de Wert, Luca Marenzio, Luzzasco Luzzaschi, and Claudio Monteverdi, to name the most famous, knew and respected the rules of counterpoint; they also understood the expressive value of breaking them.[1] They defied them not to be iconoclastic but to wrest from the harmonic surprises the forceful expression demanded by the poetic texts they set in their polyphonic madrigals.

The musical crisis brewing in the composition of madrigals erupted in 1600 in an open debate. A disciple of Gioseffo Zarlino, Giovanni Maria Artusi, challenged the modern licenses; the composers Claudio Monteverdi and his brother Giulio Cesare defended them as necessary to modern composition. Monteverdi labeled the new manner the *seconda pratica*, or second practice, to distinguish it from the *prima pratica*, the approved way of writing according to contrapuntal usage of Zarlino.[2]

Artusi's dialogue, *L'Artusi ouero Delle imperfettioni della moderna musica* (1600),[3] attacked two of Monteverdi's madrigals for their dissonances and other contrapuntal lapses. The two madrigals, *Anima mia, perdona* from Monteverdi's Fourth Book of 1603 and *Cruda Amarilli* from the Fifth Book of 1605, neither yet published, had just been performed in a

---

[1]On this subject, see J. Peter Burkholder, "Rule-Breaking as a Rhetorical Sign," in *Festa musicologica: Essays in Honor of George J. Buelow*, ed. Thomas J. Mathiesen and Benito V. Rivera (Stuyvesant, NY: Pendragon Press, 1995), 369–89.

[2]See chapters 1 and 4 *supra*.

[3]See chapter 3, nn. 53–54 *supra*.

private salon.[4] Artusi did not name the composer, and he omitted the text from the short printed musical excerpts, intending that the two interlocutors, Luca, an Austrian musical amateur, and Vario, a learned musician from Arezzo, should discuss the offending extracts as pure, anonymous counterpoint, abstract webs of musical lines.

Luca expresses fascination with the new techniques, while Vario is quick to criticize errors in dissonance usage, faulty melodic and harmonic motion, and failure to observe modal unity. Luca tentatively defends the composer, noting that free use of dissonance is already accepted in improvised music and in the embellishments that singers add to written parts. For him, certain dissonances that pass by quickly as in florid figurations of instrumental music have a certain charm. Vario replies that since the ear is easily fooled, reason should be the judge in such matters as consonance and dissonance because these categories are defined by number ratios.[5]

Monteverdi was irritated enough by the criticism to reply in a short preface to the Fifth Book of Madrigals (1605). It merits a full quotation.

Studious Readers:

Be not surprised that I am giving these madrigals to the press without first replying to the objections that Artusi made against some very minute portions of them. Being in the service of his Serene Highness of Mantua, I am not master of the time I would require. Nevertheless, I wrote a reply to let it be known that I do not do things by chance, and as soon as it is rewritten it will see the light under the title, *Seconda pratica overo perfettione della moderna musica*. Some will wonder at this, not believing that there is any other practice than that taught by Zerlino [*sic*]. But let them be assured concerning consonances and dissonances that there is another way of considering them different from the determined one, a way that defends the modern manner of composition with the assent of the reason and the senses. I wanted to say this both so that the expression *seconda pratica* would not be appropriated by others and so that men of intellect might meanwhile consider other second thoughts concerning harmony. And have faith that the modern composer builds on foundations of truth.

Live happily.[6]

---

[4]Monteverdi, *Tutte le opere*, 4:26–30; 5:1–4 (reprinted in *Norton Anthology of Western Music*, 4th ed., 1:283–88 [and accompanying recording]). See pp. 108–9 *supra*.

[5]Artusi, *L'Artusi*, Ragionamento 2, ff. 39r–44r; trans. Litchfield, "Artusi," 280–315. Cf. the translation in *Strunk's Source Readings*, 526–34.

[6]*Il quinto libro de' madrigali a cinque voci* (Venice: Ricciardo Amadino, 1605), as quoted in Claudio Monteverdi, *Lettere, dediche, e prefazioni*, ed. Domenico De' Paoli,

Neither Artusi's interlocutors nor the composer said a word about the real reason for the new techniques—to express the words. This issue was first confronted by a member of an unidentified academy who calls himself simply by his whimsical nickname L'Ottuso Academico (The Obtuse Academician). Two of his letters to Artusi are quoted in the *Seconda parte dell'Artusi* (1603), which abandons the device of dialogue and turns instead to a consideration of L'Ottuso's defense of Monteverdi, who is called simply "Sign[or] Etc." L'Ottuso gets right to the heart of the matter: the new devices have an expressive purpose.

> The purpose of this new movement of the parts is to discover through its novelty new harmonies and new affections, and this without departing in any way from good reason, even if it leaves behind somehow the ancient traditions of some excellent composers.[7]

New affections represented in the text require new melodic and harmonic combinations, both consonant and dissonant, to express them. L'Ottuso cites precedents: madrigals of Rore, Wert, and Marenzio that took liberties similar to Monteverdi's for the sake of the text. L'Ottuso displays an understanding of the truly important departures in the two madrigals, dissonances that cannot be justified as embellishments but were chosen for their sharpness and harshness to emphasize the text.

Contributi di musicologia (Rome: De Santis, 1973), 391–92: "Studiosi Lettori[.] Non vi meravigliate ch'io dia alle stampe questi Madrigali senza prima rispondere alle oppositioni, che fece l'Artusi contro alcune minime particelle d'essi, perché sen d'io al servigio di questa Serenissima Altezza di Mantoa non son patrone di quel tempo che tal'hora mi bisognarebbe: hò nondimeno scritta la risposta per far conoscer ch'io non faccio le mie cose a caso, e tosto che sia rescritta uscirà in luce portando in fronte il nome di SECONDA PRATICA overo PERFETTIONE DELLA MODERNA MUSICA del che forse alcuni s'ammireranno non credendo che vi sia altra pratica, che l'insegnata dal Zerlino; ma siano sicuri, che intorno alle consonanze, e dissonanze vi è anco un'altra consideratione differente dalla determinata, la qual con quietanza della ragione, e del senso diffende il moderno comporre, e questo ho voluto dirvi si perché questa voce SECONDA PRATICA tal'hora non fosse occupata da altri, si perché anco gli ingegnosi possino fra tanto considerare altre seconde cose intorno al armonia, e credere che il moderno Compositore fabrica sopra li fondamenti della verità. Vivete felici."

[7]Giovanni Maria Artusi, *Seconda parte dell'Artusi ouero delle imperfettioni della moderna musica, nella quale si tratta de' molti abusi introdotti da i moderni scrittori, et compositori* (Venice: Giacomo Vincenti, 1603), 6: "Essendo questa modulatione noua, per ritrouare con la nouità sua noui concenti, & noui affetti, ne discostandosi in niuna parte dalla ragione, se bene s'allontana in vn certo modo dalle antiche tradittioni d'alcuni eccellenti Musici." The same quotation, but with "trouare" instead of "ritrouare" appears on p. 5.

These included the intervals of the second and seventh introduced without the usual preparation, prolongation of such intervals beyond the normal point of resolution, or the reiteration of the dissonant note on the main beat in a suspension.

Artusi denies that there can be any new *concenti* because the number of consonances is limited, outside which there are only unacceptable non-harmonic combinations. He insists on the rules that are based on nature, demonstration, and the models of excellent composers.[8]

Monteverdi never published his expanded defense, but his brother Giulio Cesare wrote a set of glosses on Claudio's 1605 preface and included it in a compilation of the latter's *Scherzi musicali* (1607).[9] This commentary launched the slogans that were to echo through the seventeenth century. Borrowing Plato's definition of song as made up of text, melody (or harmony, as Giulio Cesare understood Ficino's Latin translation), and rhythm and his admonition that the melody and rhythm should follow the text and not the reverse,[10] Giulio Cesare proclaims that while in the first practice "harmony is the mistress of the text," Monteverdi aims "toward the perfection of song, a mode in which harmony turns from mistress to servant of the text, and the text becomes

---

[8]For further discussion of this famous controversy, see Claude V. Palisca, "The Artusi-Monteverdi Controversy," in *The Monteverdi Companion*, ed. Denis Arnold and Nigel Fortune (London: Faber and Faber, 1968), 133–66; reprinted with introduction in Palisca, *Studies*, 54–87. See also Massimo Ossi, *Divining the Oracle: Monteverdi's* Seconda Prattica (Chicago: University of Chicago Press, 2003), 27–57 (chapter 1: "The Public Debate, I: *Prima* and *Seconda Prattica*"); Tim Carter, "Artusi, Monteverdi, and the Poetics of Modern Music," in *Musical Humanism and Its Legacy: Essays in Honor of Claude V. Palisca*, ed. Nancy Kovaleff Baker and Barbara Russano Hanning, Festschrift Series, vol. 11 (Stuyvesant, NY: Pendragon Press, 1992), 171–94.

[9]Giulio Cesare Monteverdi, "Dichiaratione della Lettera stampata nel Quinto libro de suoi madrigali," in Claudio Monteverdi, *Scherzi musicali a tre voci, raccoldi da Giulio Cesare Monteverde suo fratello* (Venice: Ricciardo Amadino, 1607); trans. in *Strunk's Source Readings*, 536–44.

[10]See pp. 3–4 and n. 6 *supra*. Reading from Ficino's translation, Giulio Cesare quotes Plato as saying: "Melodiam ex tribus constare, oratione, harmonia, Rithmo … quandoquidem Rithmus & Harmonia orationem sequuntur non ipsa oratio Rithmum & Harmoniam sequitur."

mistress of the harmony, the principle on which the second practice, or the modern usage is founded."[11]

As clarified by his brother, Monteverdi's program to reform modern music was focused on musical practice. Though inspired by a Greek philosopher, he did not aim to revive Greek music. Nor did he want to devise a new theory of music. By theory, he meant *musica theorica*, the fundamental and mathematical science of music as taught in the first two parts of Zarlino's *Istitutioni harmoniche* (1558). Monteverdi did not feel qualified to rewrite this theory; he would leave that to such learned men as Zarlino (by now deceased) or Ercole Bottrigari.[12] He wanted to describe the practice of music, *musica practica*, the art of combining voices and instruments in a composition that expresses a text, a topic on which he would have had much to say. It is a pity that he was never inclined to write more about it. But many others did.

Practice, indeed, now became the dominant subject of musical theorizing. There were numerous counterpoint manuals based on Zarlino, some of which liberalized the rules, such as Artusi's *Seconda parte dell'arte del contraponto* (1589). Others simplified or translated them, such as Orazio Tigrini in *Il compendio della musica* (1588), Seth Calvisius in ΜΕΛΟΠΟΙΙΑ *sive melodiae condendae ratio, quam vulgo musicam poeticam vocant* (1592), Thomas Morley in *A Plaine and Easie Introduction to*

---

[11]Giulio Cesare Monteverdi, "Dichiaratione": "... (in tal genere di cantilena come questa sua) versar intorno alla perfettione del la Melodia, nel qual modo l'armonia considerata, di padrona diuenta serua al oratione, & l'oratione padrona del armonia, al qual pensamento tende la seconda prattica, ouero l'uso moderno, per tal fondamento ...." Giulio Cesare used the feminine gender because "padrona" and "oratione" are both feminine nouns; therefore, I use the English "mistress" in a sense parallel to "master." I have used the word "song" rather than "melody" to translate Ficino's *melodia* because Plato's word, *melos*, conveys that meaning. In this context, Plato's and Ficino's term *harmonia* meant melody, but Giulio Cesare mistook *harmonia* to mean polyphonic harmony. See pp. 3–4 and n. 6 *supra*.

[12]On Bottrigari, see Maria Rika Maniates, "Bottrigari versus Sigonio: On Vicentino and His Ancient Music Adapted to Modern Practice," in *Musical Humanism and Its Legacy: Essays in Honor of Claude V. Palisca*, ed. Nancy Kovaleff Baker and Barbara Russano Hanning, Festschrift Series, vol. 11 (Stuyvesant, NY: Pendragon Press, 1992), 79–107; and idem, "The Cavalier Ercole Bottrigari and His Brickbats: Prolegomena to the Defense of Don Nicola Vicentino against Messer Gandolfo Sigonio," in *Music Theory and the Exploration of the Past*, ed. Christopher Hatch and David W. Bernstein (Chicago: University of Chicago Press, 1993), 137–88.

Practicall Musicke, Set Downe in Forme of a Dialogue (1597), and Pietro Cerone in *El melopeo y maestro* (1613).[13]

Vincenzo Galilei initiated an effort to allow greater latitude in counterpoint for text-expression in his manuscript treatise on the practice of counterpoint in two books, the first on the use of consonance, the second on the use of dissonance (1589–91).[14] Lodovico Zacconi (1555–1627) published two enormous volumes thirty years apart under the title *Prattica di musica* (1592 and 1622), in which he is as much concerned with improvised music as with the written form.[15] Adriano Banchieri (1568–1634) issued a series of treatises on practical music, the most important of which are *L'organo suonarino* (1605) and *Cartella overo regole utilissime à quelli che desiderano imparare il canto figurato* (1601, with revised editions of 1610 and 1614), in which he takes cognizance of the changes in compositional and performance practices.[16] Joachim Burmeister in his *Musica poetica* (1606) urges young composers to imitate the sensitivity to text displayed in the motets of Orlando di Lasso.[17] Marco Scacchi (ca. 1600–1662) left an epistolary treatise on sacred composition in the older and newer styles and published a defense of the newer styles in his *Breve discorso sopra la musica moderna* (1649).[18] Scacchi's pupil Angelo Berardi (ca.

---

[13]Giovanni Maria Artusi, *Seconda parte dell'arte del contraponto. Nella quale si tratta dell' utile et uso delle dissonanze. Divisa in due libri* (Venice: Giacomo Vincenti, 1589); Seth Calvisius, *ΜΕΛΟΠΟΙΙΑ sive melodiae condendae ratio, quam vulgo musicam poeticam vocant, ex veris fundamentis extructa et explicata* (Erfurt: Georg Baumann, 1592); Orazio Tigrini, *Il compendio della musica nel quale brevemente si tratta dell'arte del contrapunto, diviso in quattro libri* (Venice: Ricciardo Amadino, 1588); see also chapter 4, n. 22, and chapter 7, n. 38 *supra*. For brief descriptions of these and other treatises, with bibliographies of editions and commentaries, see David Damschroder and David Russell Williams, *Music Theory from Zarlino to Schenker, A Bibliography and Guide*, Harmonologia, no. 5 (Stuyvesant, NY: Pendragon Press, 1990).

[14]For Galilei's counterpoint treatises, see Rempp, *Kontrapunkttraktate*, 7–162.

[15]Lodovico Zacconi, *Prattica di musica utile et necessaria si al compositore per comporre i canti suoi regolatamente, si anco al cantore per assicurarsi in tutte le cose cantabili. Divisa in quattro libri* (Venice: Girolamo Polo, 1592); idem, *Prattica di musica seconda parte. Divisa, e distinta in quattro libri* (Venice: Allesandro Vincenti, 1622).

[16]Adriano Banchieri, *Cartella overo regole utilissime à quelli che desiderano imparare il canto figurato* (Venice: Giacomo Vincenti, 1601); for *L'organo suonarino*, see chapter 5, n. 66 *supra*.

[17]See chapter 4, n. 5 *supra* and chapter 11 *infra*.

[18]Marco Scacchi, "Epistola ad Excellentissimum Dn. CS. Wernerum," ed. Erich Katz in *Die musikalischen Stilbegriffe des 17. Jahrhunderts* (Charlottenburg:

1636–1694) treated methods of traditional counterpoint as well as modern applications in his *Ragionamenti musicali* (1681) and *Documenti armonici* (1687).[19] Likewise written under Scacchi's influence, Christoph Bernhard's manuscript treatise, "Tractatus compositionis augmentatus" (ca. 1660) deals with a variety of styles practiced in the mid-century.[20]

Practice occupied the center of musical studies from around 1600 partly because the performer claimed a greater role in the creation of music. The preferred style of music shifted from the polyphony of four or more voices to music for one or two voices with accompaniment. Consequently, one of the major challenges faced by a musician was learning to accompany in an effective manner. The rise of the violin and winds as solo instruments also placed a premium on the accompanist's skill, and a large proportion of the manuals in practical musicianship written in the seventeenth century gave priority to developing the skill. Musicians needed this instruction because composers adopted a shorthand method of indicating the chordal harmonies that would support the solo melodies, leaving the realization of the skeletal score to the accompanist.

A number of the composers who pioneered the method were themselves solo singers: Giulio Caccini, Jacopo Peri, and Sigismondo d'India; or violinists: Biagio Marini, Arcangelo Corelli, and Heinrich Biber. They employed a bass line with chords that harmonized the melodic line, with

---

Wilhelm Flagel, 1926), 83–89; idem, *Breve discorso sopra la musica moderna* (Warsaw: Pietro Elert, 1649), ed. Claude V. Palisca, "Marco Scacchi's Defense of Modern Music (1649)," in *Words and Music: The Scholar's View, A Medley of Problems and Solutions Compiled in Honor of A. Tillman Merritt*, ed. Laurence Berman (Cambridge: Department of Music, Harvard University, 1972), 189–235; reprinted and expanded with a prefatory note, Italian text of Scacchi's treatise, and English trans. in Palisca, *Studies*, 88–145.

[19] Angelo Berardi, *Ragionamenti musicali* (Bologna: Giacomo Monti, 1681); idem, *Documenti armonici ... nelli quali con varii discorsi, regole, et essempii si demostrano gli studii artefiziosi della musica, oltre il modo di usare le ligature, e d'intendere il valore di ciascheduna figura* (Bologna: Giacomo Monti, 1687).

[20] The treatise, together with two others, was published by Joseph Müller-Blattau under the misleading title *Die Kompositionslehre Heinrich Schützens in der Fassung seines Schülers Christoph Bernhard* (Leipzig: Breitkopf & Härtel, 1926; 2d ed., Kassel: Bärenreiter, 1963; 3d ed., Kassel: Bärenreiter, 1999). Müller-Blattau's title is misleading because Bernhard was not a pupil but a colleague of Schütz, and the treatise does not represent his older colleague's teachings. Further discussion of this treatise follows later in this chapter and in chapter 11 *infra*.

occasional dissonances to emphasize cadences or to make smoother transitions between chords. From the bass and solo lines, an experienced player of keyboard or plucked instruments could improvise a sufficient accompaniment. At first, a few numerals or sharps and flats over the bass line indicated the principal intervals that the accompanist needed to include, the rest being assumed. The accompanist improvised the chordal background that literally filled in the pitch space between this bass and the (usually) higher solo parts. This method of notation was particularly useful in early opera, in which singers were only lightly and unobtrusively accompanied. As composers began to introduce more dissonances, they indicated more consistently and carefully the intervals from the bass that the accompanist was obliged to play in the chords. This resulted in a "figured bass," in which numerals, sharps, and flats appeared over every bass note that was not expected to carry the third and fifth natural to the key.

Manuals on accompanying began to appear almost immediately. Already in 1607, Agostino Agazzari (ca. 1580–1642) dwelt on some of the subtleties of this art, dividing the functions of accompanying instruments between filling in the harmony and providing ornamental figurations.[21] Although musicians were still expected to learn counterpoint, usually in the older style, much of their training was directed at knowing the chords that suited particular melodic and bass motions. Lorenzo Penna (1613–1693) treated the subject of thoroughbass in great detail in his primer, *Li primi albori musicali per li principianti della musica figurata* of 1672. The following year, Matthew Locke (ca. 1621–1677) issued a guide devoted to thoroughbass: *Melothesia: or Certain General Rules for Playing upon a Continued-Bass* (1673), and the classic work in the field appeared early in the next century: Francesco Gasparini's (1661–1727) *L'armonico pratico al cimbalo* (1708).[22]

---

[21]Agostino Agazzari, *Del sonare sopra'l basso con tutti li stromenti e dell'uso loro nel conserto* (Siena: Domenico Falcini, 1607).

[22]Lorenzo Penna, *Li primi albori musicali per li principianti della musica figurata; distinti in tre libri* ... (Bologna: Giacomo Monti, 1672); Matthew Locke, *Melothesia: or Certain General Rules for Playing upon a Continued-Bass* ... (London: J. Carr, 1673); and Francesco Gasparini, *L'armonico pratico al cimbalo* ... (Venice: Antonio Bortoli, 1708); trans. Frank S. Stillings as *The Practical Harmonist at the Harpsichord*, ed. David L. Burrows, Music Theory Translation Series (New Haven, CT: Yale School of Music, 1963).

Monteverdi understood that while the foundations of theory were relatively stable, practice was changing. He identified a first practice, faithful to the accepted rules of counterpoint, and a second practice that took liberties to serve the text. A consciousness of the passing of older styles, the revival of still older ones, and innovation has characterized Western musical culture. Composers of the fourteenth century boasted of their *ars nova*. Johannes Tinctoris dismissed the music of the generations before Guillaume Dufay's as unworthy of an attentive hearing. Hermann Finck stated in his *Practica musica* (1556) that "the older composers [*veteres*] were students of proportions and signs, obscure and intricate, while the moderns [*recentiores*] give greater euphony to their works and are diligent in applying music to words, making the two agree suitably, and the music expresses the sense and individual affections appropriately."[23]

Monteverdi's immediate contemporary Lodovico Zacconi identified older and newer styles in his *Prattica di musica*, but from a singer's rather than a composer's point of view. "The ancients," as he called those from the first decades of the sixteenth century, "derived their musical effects from fugues and other obligations, which were disposed always in one and the same style."

> But then with time through the work of Adriano Vuilarth and Ciprian Rore, who were the old, so intelligent and learned in this profession, new and beautiful effects began to be discovered (if, to be sure, their works were not at first recognized or esteemed). So the moderns, having learned from the style of our elders, now compose music with effects that are very dissimilar from those of the ancients. For, besides inventions, beauties have been discovered which then had not yet been found. If they had been discovered, they were not recognized, because their [the ancients'] aim tended only toward obligations, fugues, and stringency. They took pleasure in carrying a whim to its ultimate conclusion, without regard for graciousness and sweetness.[24]

---

[23]Finck, *Practica musica*, ff. Ssi^{r-v} (bk. 5): "... ueteres in proportionibus et signis argutis ac intricatis, studiosi fuerunt: Ita recentiores Euphoniae suauitati magis operam dant, ac praecipue in textu applicando, diligentes curiosique sunt, ut ille notis apposite quadret, ac hae uicissim orationis sensum singulosque affectus, quam proprijssime exprimat."

[24]Zacconi, *Prattica di musica*, f. 7v (bk. 1, ch. 10): "... gl' antichi cauauano gl' effetti Musicali suoi per via di fughe, & altre osseruationi, che si disponeuano sempre a vn medemo stile, ... Ma poi col tempo per opera d'Adriano Vuilarth, & di Ciprian Rore, che furono quei Vecchi nella professione si intelligenti, & dotti, s'incominciò a ritrouarsi altri nuoui, & vaghi affetti: (se bene l'opere loro non

Zacconi missed in this older music the accents and graceful manners that singers of his day added to written music. The older singers were content to read their parts without errors, whereas modern singers take pride in their embellishments and accents. Unlike Monteverdi, Zacconi cared less about conveying the message of the text than about bringing sensuous pleasure to listeners and showing off a musician's prowess.

When in mid-century Marco Scacchi surveyed the musical landscape in his *Breve discorso*, he no longer saw the older practice as old fashioned, to be set aside and replaced by a newer style, but as a viable alternative. If in the past there was only one practice and one style, now a composer could choose between the first and second practice and among three styles.

> Ancient music consists in one practice only and almost in one and the same style of employing consonances and dissonances. But the modern consists of two practices and three styles, that is, the church, chamber, and theater styles. The practices are: the first, which is *ut Harmonia sit Domina Orationis*, and the second, which is *ut Oratio sit Domina Harmoniae*. Each of these three styles contains very great variations, novelties, and inventions of extraordinary dimension.[25]

In a letter of around 1648 to Christoph Werner, a young composer, Scacchi had emphasized the importance of respecting the character and compositional standards of each of the styles while seizing the opportunities for variety of expression that they offered.[26] His letter concentrated on church music. Now he elaborated on the styles of secular

---

furono cosi da principio conosciute, & stimate;) talche hauendo imparato i moderni dallo stile de nostri vecchi compongano hora Musiche con effetti assai dissimili da gl' antichi: perche oltra l'inuentioni, si sono ritouate vaghezze, che a quel tempo, non erano scoperte, & se pur erano qualche poco scoperte non erano conosciute: perche la mira loro non tendeua in altro, che ne gl' oblighi, nelle fughe, & nelle osseruationi: pigliandosi piacere di condurre v[n] capriccio sin al fine, non hauendo rispetto piu che tanto alle vaghezze, & dolcezze."

[25]Scacchi, *Breve discorso*, ff. C3v–C4r, in Palisca, *Studies*, 110–11: "La musica antica consiste in una prattica sola, e quasi in un medesimo stile, di adoperare le consonanze, e dissonanze; Ma la Moderna consiste in due pratiche, et in tre stili, cioè, stili di Chiesa, di Camera, e' di Teatro; le prattiche sono: la prima è, Ut Harmonia sit Domina orationis; la seconda, ut Oratio sit Domina harmoniae; et og'uno di questi tre stili portano in se grandissime variazioni, novità, et invenzioni di non ordinaria considerazione." Scacchi borrowed the Latin phrases from his own previous book, *Cribrum musicum ad triticum Syfferticum* (Venice: A. Vincenti, 1643), in which he attacked an opponent of the new styles.

[26]Scacchi, "Epistola ad Excellentissimum Dn. CS. Wernerum," 83–89.

music. The resources that modern music offered, according to Scacchi, may be summed up in a table (table 5).

Stylus ecclesiasticus (Church style)	*Stylus cubicularis* (Chamber style)	*Stylus scenicus seu theatralis* (Stage or theater style)
1. 4 to 8 voices, no organ	1. Madrigals without instruments	1. Recitative style without gestures
2. Polychoral with organ	2. Madrigals with basso continuo	2. Recitative style with gestures
3. With instruments	3. Compositions for voices and written instrumental parts	
4. Motets in modern mixed style (including a hybrid recitative style)		

Table 5. Marco Scacchi's Classification of Styles

Scacchi's classification shows that the older polyphonic medium of unaccompanied counterpoint for four or more voices could coexist in the church style with the newer media of one or more choirs, accompanied by an organ or other instruments, as well as with music for fewer voices—motets in modern style. These motets, for one or more solo voices, normally accompanied by a basso continuo but sometimes including written instrumental parts for violins or winds, could combine the lyrical, florid manner of Caccini or, later, that of the operatic aria with the speechlike manner of the early operas of Peri, Marco da Gagliano, and Monteverdi.

For the private entertainments—"chamber music"—for which polyphonic madrigals were written in the sixteenth century, there are now diverse possibilities. Madrigals without instruments continue to be written for either amateurs or trained singers in the older polyphonic style. These could now be accompanied by a basso continuo with chordal realizations by keyboard or plucked instruments. Once the basso continuo is available, a composer may choose to lighten the texture within a composition for four or more voices, down to a duet or trio, or simply write for one or two solo voices with thoroughbass accompaniment. Or a composer may choose to abandon the polyphonic, contrapuntal standards altogether and select a medium of voices and instruments that adopts the aria and recitative styles of opera.

Under "stage or theater styles," Scacchi distinguishes between music intended for actor-singers in a theater and for singers who perform without acting out their parts. The latter category is obviously the oratorio and dramatic cantata, in which the theatrical genres of aria, recitative, and ensembles join in a chamber performance.

Scacchi is not only dealing with two practices and three styles—church, chamber, and theater—but also with distinctive genres such as the polychoral motet, concerted motet (for voices and instruments), a cappella madrigal, continuo madrigal, cantata, serenata, oratorio, and opera. Each of these genres utilizes the resources of the two practices in a different way and in different combinations. Scacchi had no word for "genre," but the concept is present in his writing, as it was in some earlier treatises.

Pietro Pontio deserves credit for recognizing at an early stage the importance of genre, although he too lacks a word for it. In his *Ragionamento di musica* (1588), he speaks of the "manner" (*modo*) or "style" (*stile*) suitable for various types of composition. He describes the way to compose a motet:

> The manner or style (as we wish to call it) for making a motet is grave and tranquil. The parts, especially the bass, move with gravity, and the composer should maintain such ordering of the parts from beginning to end. Likewise the individual subject should be grave, even if nowadays some composers make motets and other sacred works in which this is not true. In these they sometimes put the parts together with quick, even very quick motion, ... so that their works almost seem madrigals or canzoni.[27]

Hettore, the preceptor in the dialogue, explains that sometimes all the parts move together with relatively long notes, as Josquin des Prez set them in the Credo at the text "Et incarnatus est de Spiritu Sancto." But two or three parts may more typically proceed in slower motion, while a fourth or perhaps a fifth part have quicker but never very fast notes, as might happen in a madrigal.

Pontio's instructions imply a distinction between style and genre. For example, the severe style (*stile grave*) may be applied to either a Mass or

---

[27]Pontio, *Ragionamento*, 154 (Rag. 4): "Il Modo, ò stile, che dir vogliamo, volendo far vn Motetto, è graue, & quieto; doue si vede le parti mouersi con grauità, & in particolar la parte Bassa; & il compositore deue seruare tal ordine con le parti dal principio fin' all'vltimo; & parimente le inuentioni debbono esser graui; ancora c'hoggi dì in alcuni compositori frà suoi Motetti, & cose ecclesiastiche non seruano tal ordine; ma talmente pongono le parti insieme con moto veloce, & velocissimo, che paiono Madrigali, e Canzoni." The section on styles trans. in *Strunk's Source Readings*, 472–78.

motet: "the style, that is to say, the manner, of Masses conforms with that of the motet, meaning, that is, the movement of the parts, but the way the parts are arranged is different."[28] The style may be the same, but diverse genres demand different procedures. Other genres Pontio considers are Psalms, Magnificats, hymns, madrigals, and ricercari. Pietro Cerone borrowed much of Pontio's section on style, amplifying it, giving new examples, and adding remarks on genres that Pontio neglected, such as the frottola, canzonetta, and strambotto.[29]

Monteverdi in the preface to his Eighth Book of Madrigals, *Madrigali guerrieri, et amorosi* (1638), showed a concern for genre and even used the term, though in a special sense. He recognized three principal passions or affections—anger, temperance, and humility—and associated three genres (*genera*) of the human voice with these, namely excited (*concitato*), soft (*molle*), and moderate or restrained (*temperato*). Of the three, the excited affection had not yet, in his opinion, found a proper voice in music. He discovered that through the rapidly reiterated pulse of the Greek pyrrhic meter, he could achieve the expression of anger. This led him, he says, to devise a new genre of madrigal, the *madrigale guerriero*, which is illustrated in a number of the madrigals of the collection. The *molle* genus of affection and voice is presumably represented especially in the *madrigali amorosi* of that collection.[30]

In the same preface, Monteverdi considered the classification of secular musical styles and the methods of performance. He divided the music used in princely courts into three manners (*modi*): theatre, chamber, and dance; and the method or medium of performance (*maniere di sonare*) into oratorical, harmonic, and rhythmic, which he did not define. But we may assume that by "oratorical," he meant the solo voice; by "harmonic," vocal and instrumental polyphony; and by "rhythmic," dance. All three methods are represented in the madrigals of the Eighth Book.

---

[28]Ibid., 155 (Rag. 4): "Lo stile, ouer modo, come vogliamo dire, di Messe è conforme à quello del Motetto, intendendo però il far mouimento con le parti; ma quanto all'ordine, esso è diuerso; …"

[29]Cerone, *El melopeo*, 685–95 (bk. 12, chs. 12–19).

[30]For an analysis of Monteverdi's categories of affections, voices, and madrigals, see Barbara Russano Hanning, "Monteverdi's Three Genera: A Study in Terminology," in *Musical Humanism and Its Legacy*, ed. Nancy Kovaleff Baker and Barbara Russano Hanning, Festschrift Series, vol. 11 (Stuyvesant, NY: Pendragon Press, 1992), 145–70.

Monteverdi's categories, vague though they are, echoed in subsequent efforts to classify styles and genres.[31]

The scheme that Athanasius Kircher conceived in his *Musurgia universalis* (1650) had lasting influence. Although a Jesuit priest, he directed his attention equally toward sacred and secular music. His main categories related to two principal venues, church and theater, but he did not organize his system around these institutions. He treated style mainly and not always consistently in two chapters located in widely separated books: "Concerning Musical Style" and "Concerning the Varied Technique of Harmonic Styles."[32]

Kircher called his categories *styli melothetici*—perhaps best translated as "musical styles." Ecclesiastical style (*stylus ecclesiasticus*) can be strict (*ligatus*), that is, based on Gregorian chant and rigorously following the rules of counterpoint. A specific type of such strict composition is the canonic style (*stylus canonicus*)—composition by means of fugue or canon. The ecclesiastical style can also be free (*solutus*), that is, not tied to plainchant or other borrowed subjects and less limited by the necessity of holding to a mode or to the scruples of counterpoint, indulging in artifice and flights of harmonic imagination, as in the motet style (*stylus motecticus*). His characterization of the motet style betrays the influence of Pontio: "a harmonic progress that is severe, full of majesty, blooming with variety, not bound to a subject."[33]

Not limited to either sacred or secular uses are the categories of madrigal, melismatic, and symphonic styles (*stylus madrigalescus, melismaticus*, and *symphoniacus*). The madrigal style effectively treats both spiritual and amorous subjects. It is the style most popular in Italy—cheerful, sprightly, full of grace and sweetness, indulging in diminutions, and avoiding slow motion unless the words require it. The melismatic style is tuneful, harmonically repetitious, and apt for rhythmic poetry, as in the villanella. The symphonic style covers ensemble instrumental music. A special type of instrumental music is the fantastic style (*stylus phantasticus*), not bound to any subject, "intended to display talent and to teach

---

[31]Ossi, *Divining the Oracle*, provides an incisive study of Monteverdi's use of genre. See especially chapter 6, "The *Genere Concitato*."

[32]Kircher, *Musurgia universalis*, 1:309–13 (bk. 5, ch. 17): "De stylis melotheticis"; and 1:581–92 (bk. 7, part 3, ch. 5): "De vario stylorum harmonicorum artificio."

[33]Kircher, *Musurgia universalis*, 1:585 (bk. 7, ch. 5): "processus harmonicus, grauis, maiestate plenus, summa varietate floridus, nullo subiecto adstrictus."

how to exercise remote harmonic relations and ingenious musical periods and fugues."[34] Subdivisions of this style are fantasias, ricercatas, toc-
catas, and sonatas.

The richest category is the threefold *stylus theatralis*: (1) the dramatic or
recitative style in which one or two persons converse accompanied by a
bass; (2) the choral or polyphonic, used particularly in interludes or
intermedi; and (3) and the festive, dance, or ballet style (*stylus festivus,
hyporchematicus sive saltatorius*), which contains many species favored by
the French and Germans, commonly called chansons, allemandes,
courantes, galliards, passamezzos, doubles, and sarabandes.

Kircher clearly had a broad conception of the term *stylus*. It included
religious and theatrical concepts that were situational and sociological,
generally determining style rather than designating distinctive musical
characters. Other categories, such as "strict ecclesiastical" (*ecclesiasticus ligatus*), pertain more to constructive strategies than style in the sense of
manner. A movement from a Mass in strict canon may not differ stylis-
tically from a freely composed motet if style is defined as a characteristic
collection of traits of melody, counterpoint, use of consonance and dissonance, rhythm, and so on. At other times, Kircher seems to be dealing
with genres, such as the motet, madrigal, toccata, or dance piece. Nevertheless, he demonstrates an extraordinary sensitivity to musical usages
appropriate to particular functions, genres, and media. His classification
of styles, combined with that of Scacchi, served as the foundation for
Johann Mattheson's in the eighteenth century.[35]

Scacchi's line of attack on styles and genres was revived in Germany by
Christoph Bernhard (1628–1692) in a treatise of around 1660 left in
manuscript, "Tractatus compositionis augmentatus."[36] A native of
Danzig, Bernhard probably knew Scacchi's writings through Christoph
Werner, choirmaster of St. Catherine's, to whom Scacchi had addressed
an epistolary treatise. Bernhard adopted Monteverdi's distinction

---

[34]Ibid.: "… ad ostentandum ingenium, & abditam harmoniæ rationem, inge-
niosumque harmonicarum clausularum, fugarumque contextum docendum insti-
tutus, …"

[35]Johann Mattheson, *Der vollkommene Capellmeister* (Hamburg: Christian Herold,
1739; reprint in Documenta musicologica, I/5, Kassel: Bärenreiter, 1954), 68–93
(part 1, ch. 10).

[36]Müller-Blattau, *Kompositionslehre*, 40–131; trans. Walter Hilse in "The Treatises
of Christoph Bernhard," *The Music Forum* 3 (1973): 31–196.

between the first and second practices, broadening their scope to denote "antique style" (*stylus antiquus*) and "modern style" (*stylus modernus*). Bernhard wrote in German but borrowed many Latin and Italian phrases because the German language lacked technical musical terms. In the antique style, he included the a cappella church style; under the modern style, he distinguished the "common" style, in which the text and harmony are on equal terms, from the theatrical style (*stylus comicus* or *theatralis*, also called *recitativus* or *oratorius*), in which the text is "the absolute mistress" (*domina absolutissima*) of the harmony. He understood the modern style to include music with sacred texts.

Bernhard's older colleague in Dresden, the composer Heinrich Schütz (1585–1672) left some of his own thoughts on style in his prefatory letter to *Geistliche Chormusik* (1648). He observes that the Italian *concertato* style of composition on a basso continuo ("dem über den Bassum continuum concertirende Stylus Compositionis, aus Italia") was well liked in Germany and had many followers. Nevertheless, he considered it essential for a composer to master the "style without basso continuo" through serious study of counterpoint, thus acquiring the requisites for ordered composition, such as "the disposition of the modes, simple, mixed, and inverse fugues, double counterpoint, the differences of style in musical art, vocal part writing, the connection of subjects, etc."[37] In his own work, Schütz took for granted the coexistence of the antique and modern styles, publishing throughout his life works in both idioms, a bifurcated path that was to persist into the eighteenth century.[38]

Never before the Baroque period did style and genre so vitally guide and inspire composition. The new styles did not displace the old. Monteverdi could write a Mass in the old style while writing motets in the new concerted solo idiom. The aria in the first decades of the century preserved the character it had in the previous century; it required that the text be strophic and that the music of stanzas after the first vary that of the first, sometimes with vocal flourishes. The solo madrigal retained some

---

[37]Heinrich Schütz, "Günstiger Leser," in *Musicalia ad chorum sacrum, das ist: Geistliche Chormusik ... erster Theil*, op. 11 (Dresden: Johann Klemmens, 1648): "Dispositiones Modorum; Fugæ Simplices, mixtæ, inversæ; Contrapunctum duplex: Differentia Styli in arte Musicâ diversi: Modulatio Vocum: Connexio subiectorum, &c."

[38]See Christoph Wolff, *Der stile antico in der Musik Johann Sebastian Bachs: Studien zu Bachs Spätwerk* (Wiesbaden: Steiner, 1968).

of the traits of its polyphonic predecessor, allowing repetition of a single line of a poem and its music but not a complete stanza: it was "through-composed," with florid vocal passages embellishing important syllables and ends of lines. The new recitative, by contrast, shunned word repetition and ornamentation, except in France. The secular cantata, which replaced the madrigal as the favorite genre of vocal chamber music, combined the tradition of the strophic aria with the new recitative. Monteverdi's *Orfeo* (1607) was a potpourri of old and new styles and genres: the early sixteenth-century aria for singing verses in the Prologue and in Orpheus's plea—"Possente spirto"—for Eurydice's freedom; recitative; the polyphonic madrigal in some of the choruses, choral recitative in others; the solo madrigal; the *concertato* madrigal; the canzonet; and the dance-song with instrumental refrains. Many other examples could illustrate the interaction of old and new as well as the exchange of the new for the old.

By the last decades of the seventeenth century, many of the new genres had matured and stabilized. When, around 1670, a composer chose to write a church sonata for two violins and continuo, certain assumptions ensued: there would be four movements, probably in the order slow-fast-slow-fast; the first fast movement would be fugal, the last fast movement a dance; the first slow movement would be introductory, the second slow movement would emulate a duet-aria in an opera or cantata. On the other hand, choosing to compose a chamber sonata for the same medium meant that the first movement would probably be in the style of a French overture and the other movements would be primarily binary dance pieces. A concerto gave a soloist an opportunity to display facile technique and to improvise cadenzas, formally introduced by a passage for the full orchestra and interrupted or joined by the orchestra for short interludes. In order to succeed, a composer or musician had to know, if not observe, the conventions and be at home in these and many other such idioms.

Scacchi's observation—that the older music had only one style, while his contemporaries enjoyed a plurality of styles—was a simplification, but it had a lot of truth in it. In the time of Josquin des Prez, a chanson was hardly distinguishable from a motet except by its text, a motet differed little from a movement of a Mass or from a ricercare for an instrumental ensemble. Vocal and instrumental music and the genres grew apart in the second half of the sixteenth century, as Pietro Pontio keenly observed. This was particularly true of the instrumental genres, each of which developed a treasured individuality: toccata, canzona, ricercare, tiento, fantasia, variations, and the various dance types, such as passa-mezzo, pavane, and galliard. The differentiation reached its height in the seventeenth century. The variety of style and genre that emerged assured the longevity that Baroque music enjoys.

⚜ X ⚜

THEORIES OF THE AFFECTIONS AND IMITATION

BEGINNING AROUND the middle of the sixteenth century, composers increasingly bent their creative efforts towards moving the affections. Nicola Vicentino was an early champion of this goal. In setting secular poetry, he wrote in his *L'Antica musica ridotta alla moderna prattica* (1555): "the composer's sole obligation is to animate the words and, with harmony, to represent their passions—now harsh, now sweet, now cheerful, now sad—in accordance with their subject matter."[1] In the 1530s and 1540s, Jacob Arcadelt and Adrian Willaert had already demonstrated this skill in their madrigals. When Francesco dalla Viola, himself a composer, published *Musica nova* (1559), Willaert's collection of secular madrigals and sacred motets composed mostly in the 1540s, he praised the composer's ability to "make the soul feel, at his bidding, every affection that he proposes to move."[2]

Although no one questions the importance of the affections in the music of the Baroque period, scholars have paid comparatively little attention to their role in sixteenth-century music and thought.[3] Yet this is when the vogue of the affections began. The wave of interest had

---

[1]Vicentino, *L'Antica musica*, f. 48r (bk. 3, ch. 15): "... il Compositore potrà uscire fuore dell'ordine del Modo, & intrerà in un' altro, perche non haurà obligo di rispondere al tono, di nissun Choro, ma sarà solamente obligato à dar l'anima, à quelle parole, & con l'Armonia di mostrare le sue passioni, quando aspre, & quando dolci, & quando allegre, & quando meste, & secondo il loro suggietto; ...", trans. *Ancient Music*, 150. The context of the remark is a comparison of the necessity of keeping to a chosen mode in certain sacred pieces and the freedom to wander from it in secular music.

[2]Francesco dalla Viola, Letter of dedication to Alfonso II d'Este, 15 September 1558, in Adrian Willaert, *Musica nova* (Venice: Antonio Gardane, 1559): "che ad ogni sua richiesta fa sentir nell'animo tutti gli affetti, che si propone di muouere...."

[3]Interest in the affections was promulgated by the monumental study of Wilhelm Dilthey, *Weltanschauung und Analyse des Menschen seit der Renaissance und Reformation* (Leipzig: B. G. Teubner, 1914).

complex causes, with the revival of classical rhetorical theory as a primary one. Circumstances created a demand for stirring oratory, from persuasive advocacy in civil affairs to rousing sermons in Reformation and Counter-Reformation churches. Humanism had made readily available ancient models and instruction in oratory that stressed moving the passions.

Although it cannot be said that a single or consistent theory of the affections, an *Affektenlehre*, emerged in the sixteenth or seventeenth centuries,[4] a substantial body of theory concerning the affections existed prior to the time of René Descartes, Marin Mersenne, and Athanasius Kircher, to which they added in their own writings. A number of Italian and Spanish authors made significant contributions to this theory and its relation to the sense of hearing and music. An acute awareness of the affections in Italy in the second half of the sixteenth century prepared the way for a shift in musical style toward more intense expression, which manifested itself in the madrigals of the *seconda pratica* and in monodies of Giulio Caccini, Jacopo Peri, and Claudio Monteverdi.[5]

It became common in the sixteenth century, and remains so today, to think of music as a language of the emotions, yet people did not always believe that the affections were worth communicating. Early Christian and medieval theologians and philosophers deplored the passions as afflictions to be extinguished, not aroused or communicated, and they could buttress this conviction with the authority of Plato, Cicero, and other ancient authors. Cicero, an author widely read in the Renaissance, emphatically denied the passions a place in a healthy mind. Taking a stand consistent with the Stoic philosophers, he called them "disorders" (*perturbationes*) and a principal source of distress (*aegritudo*). Among them he named envy, jealousy, compassion, anxiety, mourning, sadness, grief, fear, shame, rapture, anger, hatred, lust, and longing.[6] Cicero based his position on the belief, widely shared at the time, that the soul was divided into rational and irrational parts; the irrational, where the

---

[4]See George J. Buelow, "Johann Mattheson and the Invention of the *Affekten-lehre*," in *New Mattheson Studies*, ed. George J. Buelow and Hans Joachim Marx (Cambridge: Cambridge University Press, 1983), 393–407.

[5]See chapter 7 *supra*.

[6]Marcus Tullius Cicero *Tusculan Disputations* 4.7–8.

passions arose, should be ruled by the rational part. The last thing one should wish to do is arouse the passions through music.

If Renaissance humanists generally admired Cicero, especially his prose style and his grammatical works, the genial acceptance of the passions by Aristotle and the Epicurean philosophers was more appealing to some of them than the strict discipline of the Stoic philosophers. Lorenzo Valla (1407–1457) choreographed his dialogues in *De voluptate ac vero bono* (1512) around three major philosophical schools personified by well-known living humanists as speakers: a Stoic (Leonardo Bruni), an Epicurean (Antonio Beccadelli known as Panormita), and a Christian (Niccolò Niccoli). Although Valla allowed each to hold his own, he subtly promoted the Epicurean ideal of pleasure—*voluptas*—as the highest good.[7]

While the Stoics elevated the virtues, such as prudence, justice, temperance, and fortitude, Valla raised to equal heights the human emotions and passions. An affection was seen as a movement toward something good for a person and away from something injurious. The attainment of a good thing brings pleasure. Thus, the desire for pleasure manifests the urge for self-preservation and procreation. Through the passions, we fully partake of nature and life.

The Latin *passio* translates the Greek πάθος (*pathos*), a suffering, an emotion, or a passive state, something a person feels as a passive subject. *Passio* in Christian literature most often applies to the suffering of Christ, for which worshippers feel *compassio*, "sympathy." πάθος is distinct from ἦθος (*ethos*), moral character, which in Plato's view could be influenced by music; so, for example, the Dorian and Phrygian modes were conducive to good moral character, the Lydian was not.[8] The Latin *affectio* or, more rarely, *affectus*, a state of mind or feeling, are nouns derived from the verb *afficio*, to "affect," to put someone in a certain state. In English,

---

[7]Lorenzo Valla, *De voluptate ac vero bono* (Paris: Josse Badius, 1512). In an earlier version published under the title *De vero falsoque bono* (Cologne: Quentell, 1509), Maffeo Vegio was the Epicurean, Catone Sacco the Stoic, and A. Raudense the Christian. For a translation of the later final version, see Lorenzo Valla, *On Pleasure, De voluptate*, trans. A. Kent Hieatt and Maristella de Panizza Lorch, with an introduction by Maristella de Panizza Lorch (New York: Albaris Books, 1977). See also Lorch's own study, *A Defense of Life: Lorenzo Valla's Theory of Pleasure* (Munich: Wilhem Fink, 1985).

[8]Plato *Republic* 3.10 (398e). See p. 76 *supra*.

"affection" has generally been preferred to "passion" as the term for a permanent or semi-steady state of the mind or feeling because "affection" implies the result of some action rather than suffering. Both terms, however, signify a persistent sentiment, subject to change only by some active force, as distinct from a transitory feeling.[9]

Those who defended the passions looked to Aristotle, for he recognized their importance to oratory, music, and poetry. The passions could sway judges in a trial, and in his *Rhetoric*, Aristotle taught how to arouse and move the passions through oratory. He defined and treated fifteen affections, among them anger, mildness, love, hatred, fear, confidence, shame, pity, indignation, envy, and emulation. In the *Politics*, he observed how the passions could be moved and purged through music, and in the *Poetics* through tragedy.[10] Among the later rhetoricians, Cicero and Quintilian considered a smaller number of affections and were less concerned with their definition than with their usefulness to oratory.

An eloquent defender of the passions in the Renaissance was the Aristotelian Juan Luis Vives (1492–1540). Born in Valencia in or around 1492 of Jewish parents who had converted to Catholicism, he spent most of his life in self-exile in Bruges, partly in fear of the Inquisition, which had executed his father. In his *De anima et vita*, published in 1538 two years before he died, the entire third book is devoted to the passions. According to Vives, the soul, in men as in animals, possesses the faculties of imagination to receive impressions of the senses, of memory to retain these, of fantasy to perfect them, and finally, of judgment to assess whether a sensed object is congenial or injurious. It is this judgment that arouses the affections.

> The critical cognition of the injurious and of the beneficial generates in us a desire for the useful and an aversion and alienation from the injurious, as well as movements of the soul that incline us toward a present or future good and away from what may harm us. These movements are called affections or disorders.[11]

---

[9]"Affection" and "passion" are preferable in English to "áffect," which is merely an anglicized form of the German *Affekt* but also carries modern psychological connotations.

[10]Aristotle *Rhetoric* 2.2–11 (1378a–1388b); *Politics* 8 (1337a–1342b); *Poetics* (1447a–1450b). See also pp. 58–59 *supra*.

[11]Juan Luis Vives, *De anima et vita libri tres* (Basle: Winter, 1538), bk. 1, ch. 10 ("De cognitione interiore"), ed. and trans. Mario Sancipriano, Università di Parma,

The movement that responds to a present good is joy, which turns to love when confirmed. The response to a future good is desire. The movement responding to evil is anger, which turns to hate when confirmed. Present evil leads to sadness, future evil to fear or courage. Where there is no movement as in tranquillity and equanimity, there is no passion.

In twenty-three chapters, Vives describes in detail individual affections and gradations of them.[12] The operations of the soul depend on the senses and the body, specifically on very thin and clear spirits that evaporate from the blood in the heart and flow to the brain. On the way, the blood mixes with other humors secreted by the pituitary gland (phlegm), the liver (yellow bile or choler), and the spleen (black bile). Distillations of these four humors make up the spirits.[13] A healthy person enjoys a balance of the humors, hence an even temperament. Excess of blood in the spirits provokes a sanguine temperament, of yellow bile a choleric one, of phlegm a phlegmatic temperament, and of black bile a melancholic one (see table 6 on the following page).

This doctrine of the spirits, humors, and temperaments is not far removed from the doctrine of Galen (129–ca. 200 C.E.), a Greek physician who practiced in Rome and whose writings, revived and translated in the fifteenth century, became the foundation of Renaissance medical science. Adhering to the traditions of Greek medicine, Galen believed that each of the three fundamental members of the body—the liver, the heart, and the brain—refines and is dominated by a particular spirit (*pneuma*). The physical spirit (*pneuma physicon*), associated with the liver, controls nutrition, growth, and reproduction. The vital spirit (*pneuma zotikon*), mixed in the heart with inhaled air, conveys heat and life through the arteries. Distilled in the brain, this becomes the animal or psychical spirit (*pneuma psychicon*), which controls the feelings and

---

Istituto di scienze religiose, Pensatori religiosi, vol. 9 (Padua: Gregoriana, 1974), 174: "Ex cognitione censuraque noxij et benefici, appetitus nascitur congruentis, fuga autem damni et aversio; tum motus animi de bono præsenti, ac malo, deque eisdem venturis aut iam appetentibus; qui affectus dicuntur, seu perturbationes, …" See also Carlos G. Noreña, *Juan Luis Vives and the Emotions* (Carbondale: Southern Illinois University Press, 1989), 45; and Vives, *De anima et vita*, 180–215 (bk. 1, ch. 12 ["Quid sit anima"]).

[12]Ibid., 472–721 (bk. 3, chs. 2–24).

[13]Noreña, *Juan Luis Vives*, 110.

pleasures and activates the body and the senses by means of canals in the nerves.[14]

The spirits are produced in the organs through the power of the four qualities: warm, cold, moist, and dry; these, Aristotle theorized, animate living bodies. Heat in the veins alters food to produce blood. When nutriment is not in proper proportion, other humors result: yellow bile or choler from disproportionate heat combined with dry conditions, phlegm from insufficient heat and wetness, black bile from cold and dryness. The qualities derive their powers from the four elements: warmth from fire, dryness from air, wetness from water, and cold from earth (see table 6). This theory, Galen states, was not his alone but depended on Hippocrates (ca. 460–ca. 377 B.C.E.), Plato, Aristotle, and many others.[15]

Elements	Qualities	Organs	Humors	Temperaments
Fire	Heat	Heart	Blood	Sanguinous
Air	Dryness	Liver	Yellow bile	Choleric
Water	Humidity	Brain	Phlegm	Phlegmatic
Earth	Cold	Spleen	Black bile	Melancholic

Table 6. Interrelationships among the Elements, Qualities, Organs, Humors, and Temperaments

Galen's theories reached most sixteenth- and seventeenth-century readers through intermediaries. One of the favorite transmitters was the thirteenth-century encyclopedist Bartholomaeus Anglicus. His *De proprietatibus rerum* was widely read, often in translation.[16] Batman's English

---

[14]Galen, *On the Passions and Errors of the Soul*, trans. Paul W. Harkins, with an introduction by Walther Riese (Columbus: Ohio State University, Press, 1963), 15–16.

[15]Galen, *On the Natural Faculties*, trans. Arthur J. Brock, Loeb Classical Library (Cambridge: Harvard University Press, 1916), 166–219 (bk. 2, chs. 8–9). For a fuller consideration of Galen, see Guido Majno, *The Healing Hand: Man and Wound in the Ancient World* (Cambridge: Harvard University Press, 1975), especially chapter 10, "Galen—and into the Night."

[16]Bartholomaeus Anglicus, *On the Properties of Soul and Body, De proprietatibus rerum libri iii et iv*, edited from Bibliothèque nationale, lat. 16098 by R. James Long, Toronto Medieval Latin Texts, no. 9 (Toronto: Centre for Medieval Studies, Pontifical Institute of Mediaeval Studies, 1979). According to the Introduction (pp. 1–

translation, for example, was published in 1582 and reprinted many times.[17]

Bartholomaeus regarded the soul as threefold: vegetable, which enables life but no feeling, as in plants; sensible, which endows life and feeling but not reason, as in animals; and rational, which sustains life, feeling, and reason, as in humans. He elaborated on the generation and composition of the spirits. A spirit is a thin and airy substance that excites the powers of the body to accomplish their actions. Heat boils the blood in the liver to yield this thin vapor, which, refined by the veins of the liver, becomes the *natural spirit*. It spreads to other parts through the pulsation of the arteries, supplying life and pulse, sense and voluntary motion through the nerves and muscles. The heart further purifies this vapor, producing the *vital spirit*, which too spreads to all parts of the body through the arteries and veins. Still more subtle is the *animal spirit*, generated in the anterior ventricle of the brain, partly disseminated through the sense organs and partly remaining in the same ventricle for the operation of common sense and imagination.[18]

Animal spirit plays an important part in hearing. In a chapter dedicated to this sense, Bartholomaeus argues that at least four things are necessary to hearing: an efficient cause, a suitable organ, a medium to convey the sound, and a mind intent on hearing it. The efficient cause is the animal faculty of hearing (*virtus animalis audibilis*). The organ is a certain rock-hard or cartilaginous bone (the *os petrosum*) in the ear that is concave, dry, twisted, and hard. It is concave so that it might contain spirit and air; twisted so that a sudden strong blow would not hurt the audible spirit but rather permit it to arrive smoothly and delight the hearing; hard and dry so that the air may strike it strongly. The medium is the beaten air (*aer percussus*), which enters the orifice and strikes the hard bone that is the first instrument of hearing. Finally, a focused mind is necessary because if its attention is extended to a plurality of things, it is less capable of engaging completely in the action of the hearing faculty.

Hearing comes about when two nerves issuing from the interior part of the brain carry the animal spirit to the *ossa petrosa*, to which the exterior

---

2), there were eighteen printed editions of the Latin text and translations into six vernacular languages.

[17] *Batman vppon Bartholome, his booke De proprietatibus rerum* (London: Thomas East, 1582).

[18] Bartholomaeus Anglicus, *On the Properties of Soul and Body*, 54–56 (bk. 3, ch. 22).

air communicates the form of a sound. The animal spirit, altered according to the properties of the beaten air, returns to the chamber of the phantasy and presents its changed form to the mind.[19]

If the ear contains animal spirit, which is thus in immediate contact with the exterior air, sounds can influence the animal spirit and the mind more directly than the objects of the senses of sight, taste, smell, or touch are able to do. Thus, music has a privileged entry into the soul, making it an ideal link to the body.

Marsilio Ficino was among those who seized upon this juncture. Although he did not recognize the common threefold division of the spirits into natural, vital, and animal, he understood the spirit as a vapor of the blood that is pure, subtle, hot, and clear. "Formed from the subtler blood by the heat of the heart, it flies to the brain, and there the soul assiduously employs it for the exercise of both the interior and exterior senses."[20] Song, composed of mental images as well as sounds, finds its way from the fantasy of the singer to that of the hearer through the junction of the external air and the spirit, moving the hearer to the emotion expressed by the singer and communicating as well the meanings conveyed by the words.[21] Sounds, moreover, arising from the movement of air, are able to transmit movement; the other senses cannot do this. By comparison, sight delivers static images, while taste, smell, and touch have no intellectual content.

> Musical sound by the movement of the air moves the body: by purified air it excites the aerial spirit which is the bond of body and soul: by emotion it affects the senses and at the same time the soul: by meaning it works on the

---

[19]The above is a paraphrase of the first part of Bartholomaeus's book 3, chapter 18 on the hearing. The rest of the chapter deals with afflictions and injuries to the organ of hearing. It is important to note here the relationship between these theories of hearing and early acoustic theory. See pp. 135–40 *supra*.

[20]Marsilio Ficino, "De vita libri tres," in *Opera omnia*, 2 vols. (Basle: Henricpetrina, 1576; reprint, Turin: Erasmo, 1959), 1:496 (bk. 1, ch. 2): "Atque ab ipso cordis calore, ex subtiliori sanguine procreatus uolat ad cerebrum, ibique animus ipso ad sensus tam interiores, quàm exteriores exercendos assiduè utitur"; trans. Walker, *Spiritual and Demonic Magic*, 3.

[21]Echoes of Ficino's ideas and interpretations of Plato abound in Zarlino's *Istitutioni* (1558), for example, in bk. 1, ch. 4. On the other hand, Zarlino's account of how music moves the passions in bk. 2, chs. 7–8 is eclectic and depends as well on Galen, Aristotle, Horace, and Augustine. For a different view, see Sabine Ehrmann, "Marsilio Ficino und sein Einfluß auf die Musiktheorie," *Archiv für Musikwissenschaft* 18 (1991): 234–49, especially 244–45.

mind: finally, by the very movement of the subtle air it penetrates strongly: by its contemperation it flows smoothly: by the conformity of its quality it floods us with a wonderful pleasure: by its nature, both spiritual and material, it at once seizes and claims as its own, man in his entirety.[22]

Gioseffo Zarlino, the most widely read music theorist of the mid-sixteenth century, exemplifies the impact of the doctrine of the qualities, humors, and affections upon musical thought. Chapter 8 in Book 2 of his *Istitutioni harmoniche* (1558) bears the title: "How melody and rhythm can move the soul, disposing it to various affections, and induce in a human being various behaviors."

> It is not a great wonder that some deem it strange that harmony and rhythm (*numero*) should have the power to dispose and induce various passions in the soul because these are undoubtedly extrinsic things that have little to do with human nature. But, truly, it is only too evident that they do, for the passions are located in the sensitive corporeal and organic appetite as its true subject. Each of these passions consists of a certain proportion of hot, cold, humid, and dry according to a certain material distribution. When one of these passions is active, one of the named qualities prevails. Thus humid heat predominates in anger, inciting its arousal; cold dryness predominates in fear, constraining the spirits. The same happens in the other passions, which are generated by the dominance of one of the named qualities.[23]

---

[22]Ficino, "Commentarium in Timaeum," in *Opera omnia*, [2]:1453 (ch. 29): "Concentus autem per aeream naturam in motu positam mouet corpus: per purificatum aerem concitat spiritum aereum animæ corporisqúe nodum: per affectum, afficit sensum simul & animum: per significationem, agit in mentem: denique per ipsum, subtilis aeris motum penetrat uehementer: per contemperationem lambit suauiter; per conformèm qualitatem mira quadam uoluptate perfundit: per naturam tàm spiritalem, quàm materialem, totum simul rapit & sibi uendicat hominem"; trans. Walker, *Spiritual and Demonic Magic*, 9.

[23]Zarlino, *Istitutioni* (1558), 73 (bk. 2, ch. 8): "In qual modo la Melodia, & il Numero possino muouer l'animo, disponendolo a varij affetti; & indur nell' huomo varij costumi. Cap. 8. Non sarebbe gran marauiglia, se ad alcuno paresse strano, che l'Harmonia, & il Numero hauessero possanza di dispor l'animo, & indurlo in diuerse passioni; essendo senza alcun dubbio cose estrinseche, le quali nulla, o poco fanno alla natura dell'huomo: Ma in vero è cosa pur troppo manifesta, che l'hanno: percioche essendo le passioni dell'animo poste nell'appetito sensitiuo corporeo, & organico, come nel suo vero soggetto; ciascuna di esse consiste in vna certa proportione di calido & frigido; & di humido & secco, secondo vna certa dispositione materiale; di maniera che quando queste paßioni sono fatte, sempre soprabonda vna delle nominate qualità in qualunque di esse. Onde si come nell'Ira predomina il calido humido, cagione dell'incitamento de essa; cosi predomina nel Timore il frigido secco, il quale induce il ristrengimento de i spi-

Neither Ficino nor Zarlino described how the movements of the air produced the affections. Girolamo Mei, the learned classical philologist who was also the author of treatises on Tuscan prose and poetry, took a step in this direction when he analyzed in the 1540s the effect of pitch accent in Tuscan prose. He attributed the emotional effect of speech on a listener partly to the height or lowness of the reciting voice's pitch.

> Since in speech we hear prominently and principally the voice's height and lowness—differences befitting it, originating in diverse qualities of movement—the sense organ, when struck, must hear them according to those qualities from which they arise and must represent images altogether resembling these to the faculty that is their natural judge. Height of pitch, being generated by the force and speed of motion (as musicians clearly demonstrate . . .), of necessity must have the power to express and make felt only qualities of affection similar and corresponding to the nature of that [motion] and entirely different from low pitch, whose mother, as it were, is slowness and sluggishness. Consequently, as much as one of these is heard to surpass the other, that much more will the quality of one be represented than the quality of the other. When we hear the two as equivalent, a median or temperate disposition will appear, because every resemblance, stirring almost naturally passions similar to itself, always moves in the subject born to receive them affections that correspond in proportion to its potential.[24]

Mei's statements parallel Pietro Bembo's observations that words possess qualities of low and high pitch, roughness and smoothness,

---

riti. Il simile intrauiene etiandio nelle altre passioni, che dalla soprabondanza della nominate qualità si generano."

[24]Mei, "Della compositura delle parole," Florence, Biblioteca nazionale centrale, Magliabechianus VI/34, ff. 61v–62r: "Poiche adunque nel' parlar si senton' manifestamente e principalmente l'acutezza e grauità della uoce, sue proprie differenze, le quali hanno per la quasi fonte diuersa qualità di mouimento, di necessità, fà di mestiere che il sensorio, che percosso le dee sentire secondo la uirtù, onde esse hanno origine, quando egli le sente, ne rappresenti alla potenzia, che naturalmente n'è giudice, concetto tutto simigliante. L'acutezza adunque essendo (come apertamente dimostrono i musici, e' come poco sopra incidentemente s'è detto) generata dalla potenza e velocita del mouimento, necessariamente non può hauer' uirtù senon' d'exprimere e' far' apparir' qualità d'effetto simile e' respondente alla natura di quello, e' interamente diuersa dalla grauità, la cui quasi madre è la lentezza e tardità di lui, e perciò conseguentemente quanto più l'una di queste due uien' soperchiando l'altra nell'udirsi tanto maggiormente è necessario che ui si rappresenti più la uirtù dell'una, che dell'altra; e che la doue le si senton' del pari si apparisca mezzana e temperata disposizione conciosiache ciascuna simiglianza, quasi destando naturalmente passioni simili a se, muoua nell'obietto nato al riceuergli proporzionatamente alla sua uirtù sempre affetti simiglianti."

lightness and heaviness, which permit them to express both meaning and feeling.[25] Mei concentrates on pitch: when high, it expresses excitement and liveliness; when low, sleepiness and depression; when intermediate, calm and steadfastness. There is a natural relationship between pitch and emotional state, related to the amount of heat in the speaker's soul.

The speed of delivery and the rhythms formed by the acute and grave accents of speech, Mei theorized, have a similar effect on the affections. When the soul heats up, its movements accelerate, and these are reflected in the pitch movements of the voice.[26] Some years later, in a letter of 8 May 1572 to Vincenzo Galilei, Mei applied his theory more directly to music. It is clear, he said, that:

> affections are moved in the souls of others by representing, as if before them, whether as objects or recollections, those affections that have been previously aroused by these images. Now this cannot be brought about by the voice except with its qualities of low, high, or intermediate pitch, which nature provided for this effect and which is a proper and natural sign of that [affection] one wants to arouse in the listener.[27]

Galilei popularized Mei's ideas in his *Dialogo della musica antica, et della moderna* (1581). He pointed out that there are differences among the natures of high, intermediate, and low pitch and of fast and slow motion; mixing them up simultaneously as was done in polyphony canceled out their power to move the affections.[28] Echoing Mei, Galilei complained that the music of his own day had no other goal than to

---

[25]Pietro Bembo, *Prose ... della volgar lingua* (Venice: G. Tacuino, 1525).

[26]The application of Mei's theory in Tuscan poetry is explained by Hanning, *Of Poetry and Music's Power,* 32–34.

[27]Mei, letter to Vincenzo Galilei, 8 May 1572, trans. in Palisca, *Florentine Camerata,* 58, from idem, *Mei,* 92: "... le affezzioni si muovono negli animi altrui rapresentandosi loro quasi innanzi ò per obbjetto, o per memoria que' tali affetti che da queste tali apparenze sono fatte lor apparire. Or questo con la voce altramente far non si puo che con quelle qualità di lei, sia ella, ò grave, ò acuta, ò mezzana che da la natura l'è stata appropriata per questo effetto, e che è nota propria e naturale di quello che altri vuol commuovere nel uditore."

[28]Galilei, *Dialogo,* 81; trans. *Dialogue,* 200–203.

please the hearing, whereas the ancient music aimed "to lead others by its means into the same affection as one felt oneself."[29]

A younger admirer and associate of Mei in the Florentine Accademia degli Alterati and Accademia Fiorentina, Lorenzo Giacomini de' Tebalducci Malespini pursued the psycho-physiological theory of musical expression to a deeper level in two academic discourses of 1586–1587 that were later published. The Alterati had devoted one of their sessions—on 28 February 1572—to the question "whether the movement of the affections is outside the art of rhetoric" and the next five sessions to the passions in oratory. The subject of the affections even reached the Florentine stage in 1574 with a carnival masque entitled *Gli affetti*.[30]

It would be difficult to find a better statement of music's position among the liberal arts and the means of moving the affections than Julio del Bene's speech as he opened his year as Regent of the Accademia degli Alterati on 16 February 1575. We study the liberal arts, he said,

> so that we may through grammar argue well and correctly, since we do not possess this by nature; through rhetoric persuade and lead people's wills wherever we choose; through music learn to be ordered and well composed in our soul and to move the affections no less than is done with rhetoric, and to delight and relax us after the strains that we experience daily in human operations; and finally through poetry so that we may describe and demonstrate by imitating people's actions almost the idea of virtue and the virtue of excellent persons; and through verse, which is thought to be the speech of the gods, express ideas and imitate the affections and customs of others, and to delight and benefit one another by means of this most pleasing and beautiful art.[31]

---

[29]Ibid., 89: "per essere non altro il fine di questa [d'hoggi] che il diletto dell' vdito, & di quella [antica] il condurre altrui per quel mezzo nella medesima affettione di se stesso"; trans. *Dialogue*, 224.

[30]Palisca, "Alterati of Florence," 23; reprinted in idem, *Studies*, 419.

[31]Julio del Bene, "Del convivio delli Alterati," Florence, Biblioteca nazionale centrale, Magliabechianus IX/137, ff. 17v–19r, quoted in Palisca, "Alterati of Florence," 14, n. 8; reprinted in idem, *Studies*, 413, n. 15: "à fine che noi possiamo, per la gramatica bene et correttamente ragionare, non havendo noi questo da natura, per la retorica persuadere, et tirare la volunta delli huomini dove ci pare, et per la musica imparare ad essere ordinati et composti bene nel animo nostro, et a movere gli affetti non meno che si faccia la retorica et per delettarsi et sollevarci dalle fatiche che nelle operatione humane ogni giorno supportiamo. et finalmente della poesia accio che possiamo descrivere et dimostrare col imitare lationi delli huomini quasi lidea delle virtu et de virtu de gli eccelenti huomini, et id il verso, nel quale é opinione che sia il parlare delli dei exprimere inoltre concetti et

The Alterati returned to the topic of the affections in March 1584, when Giacomini argued that poetry was better at moving the passions, rhetoric at persuading. Giacomini treated the affections in music as well as in poetry and drama in a discourse of 1586, "De la purgatione de la tragedia,"[32] a lengthy commentary on a cryptic passage in Aristotle's *Poetics*, the meaning of which was much debated at this time. In defining tragedy, Aristotle had written: "Tragedy is an imitation of an action ... through pity and fear affecting the proper catharsis, or purgation of these emotions."[33] Some thought he meant that an affection such as fear could be purged by representing the opposite, driving out the fear by representing a courageous deed. Giacomini argued that Aristotle wanted to compare the effect of tragedy to cathartic medications that are homeopathic, such as rhubarb, aloe, and black hellebore, which were administered to purge humors that were similar in nature to the cure: the choleric, phlegmatic, and melancholic respectively.[34] In his view, a tragedy represents fear to drive out fear and wrath to rid us of anger.

Of the ancient musical modes and instruments, the Phrygian and Mixolydian and the aulos best effected purgation because they actively moved the affections, while the Dorian tended rather to calm the listener.[35] Music in the first two modes contracted the soul and relieved it of the spirits that rise to the seat of the fantasy in the anterior part of the brain when a person is excited or saddened. The contraction explains the cries of lamentation,

> expelled by Nature through a natural instinct to remove the bad disposition that afflicts the sensitive part of the soul, constraining it and weighting it down, and especially the heart, which, full of spirits and heat, suffers most. Therefore the heart moves to shake off its pain and expand and liberate itself

---

imitare gli affetti et i costumi altrui, e delettare et giovare l'uno laltro per questa cosi piacevole et bella arte."

[32]Giacomini, *Orationi e discorsi*, 29–52. On Giacomini, see also p. 25 *supra*.

[33]Aristotle *Poetics* (1449b): "ἔστιν οὖν τραγῳδία μίμησις πράξεως ... δι᾽ ἐλέου καὶ φόβου περαίνουσα τὴν τῶν τοιούτων παθημάτων κάθαρσιν."

[34]Giacomini refers the reader to Galen and to Alexander Aphrodisias's commentary in his Problem 58.

[35]Giacomini was apparently a musical amateur and had a command of Greek. He left in manuscript a respectable translation of the pseudo-Aristotelian *Problems*, section 19 on music. His amanuensis was Giorgio Bartoli, who copied, perhaps for Giacomini, the only existing exemplar of Mei's letters to Vincenzo Galilei and Giovanni Bardi: Rome, Bibliotheca Apostolica Vaticana, Regina lat. 2021.

of anguish. The lungs and other organs of the voice are set in motion and emit shrieks and groans if not impeded by the intellect. In this way, the soul burdened by sorrow lightens itself and gives birth to sad conceits and liberates the passionateness that was in it. Having delivered itself of these, the soul remains free and unburdened. So, even if it wants to cry some more, it cannot, because the vapors that filled the head and are the substance of tears have been consumed. They remain scarce until the mind returns to its earlier disposition because of some internal alteration of the vapors, or through some active qualities, sad imaginings, or an external incident.[36]

These changes in the soul may be brought about not only by real-life experiences but also by imitations of them presented to the eyes and ears: "happy or painful objects reaching the soul through the sight or hearing alter or move it in such a manner that the soul, surprised and almost enchanted by the delight of the imitation and other delights that poetry contains, not stopping to contemplate the reality of the thing, feels internally those affections that it is accustomed to feel for real things."[37] But the author must feel the emotion deeply to be able to embody it in the imitation. "True affection makes us find and express images capable of moving others' souls through the force of sympathy. Focused imagination places the poet in an affection and results in his operating not in make-believe and coldly but almost from the heart."[38]

---

[36]Giacomini, *Orationi e discorsi*, 39–40: "Da la medesima cagione derivano le voci lamenteuoli per naturale instinto senza nostro accorgimento da la Natura procacciate; per rimuouere cioè la mala dispositione, che affligge ristringendo & aggrauando la parte sensitiua, e 'l cuore principalmente, che come pieno di spiriti, e di calore, piu patisce. onde per scuotere il dolore, e per allargarsi, e liberarsi dal affanno, si muoue, e muouesi il polmone, e gli altri organi de la voce, e fansi strida, e gemiti, se dal intelletto non sono impediti. Per queste vie l'anima grauida di mestizia si sgraua, e partorisce i dolorosi concetti, e gli appassionamenti, che erano in lei, i quali partoriti, resta libera, e scarica, si che quando il bramasse, piu non potrebbe piagnere, essendo consumati quei vapori materia del piano, che riempieuano il capo, fino a che o per altra interna alterazione di vapori, o da qualità attiue, o per trista imaginatione o per accidente esterno non ritorna a la primiera disposizione."

[37]Giacomini, "Del furor poetico," in *Orationi e discorsi*, 63: "gli oggetti lieti o dolorosi per mezzo de la vista o del vdito arriuando al anima, in tal maniera l'alterano, e commuouono, che soprapresa e quasi incantata dal diletto del imitatione, e da gli altri diletti; che seco porta la poesia, non curando discorrere intorno a la verità de le cose, in se sente quelli affetti, che sentir suole per le cose vere."

[38]Ibid., 67: "il vero affetto fa trouare & esprimere concetti atti a commouere per la virtù de la simpathia gli animi altrui, così la fissa imaginazione constituirà il

Science in the seventeenth century established a foundation for modern physics, planetary astronomy, mechanics, and acoustics, among other fields. But understanding of the psychology and physiology of the affections did not advance much beyond the theories just described. The originality of Descartes's *Passions de l'âme* (1649), apart from its adaptation of traditional theory to the newly discovered circulation of the blood, resided more in fanciful and dialectical analyses than in new observations, experiments, or interpretation of the facts. Nevertheless, Descartes abandoned the tripartite division of the soul and the traditional physiology of the four elements, humors, and temperaments while retaining the animal spirits. By contrast, Athanasius Kircher based the hundred or so pages of his *Musurgia universalis* (1650) dedicated to the passions in music on the familiar doctrine of the divided soul, the humors, temperaments, and spirits.

Although Descartes, residing in Holland since 1629, had probably completed his *Passions de l'âme* by 1646, it was not published until late 1649 in Amsterdam and Paris. Kircher, who wrote his book in Rome and finished it in 1647,[39] did not have the opportunity to study Descartes on the passions and is not known to have corresponded with him. The two authors conceived their works independently, though they had in common not only a deep engagement with the passions but also the conviction that moving the affections was a primary goal for music. Descartes began his *Musicae compendium* (1618) with the words "Renatus Cartesius' Compendium of music, whose object is sound, whose end is to delight and move in us various affections ...."[40] Kircher similarly declared that harmony naturally affects human beings and moves them to a variety of passions, devoting many pages to this subject.[41] Kircher in Rome, Mersenne in Paris, and Descartes in Holland—distant from each other geographically as well as philosophically, each went his separate way in studying the affections.

---

poeta in affetto, e farà che operi non fingendo e con freddezza ma quasi di cuore."

[39]According to a letter to Giovanni Battista Doni in A. M. Bandini, *Commentariorum*, 214, cited in Scharlau, *Athanasius Kircher*, 40.

[40]René Descartes, *Musicae compendium* (Utrecht: Gisbertus à Zijll & Theodorus ab Ackersdijck, 1650), 5: "Compendium musicae Renati Cartesii huius objectum est sonus finis ut delectet, variosque in nobis moveat affectus ...."

[41]Kircher, *Musurgia universalis*, 1:544–55 (bk. 7, especially Erothemae 6–8).

Kircher, with his unlimited curiosity, asked some fundamental questions. What characteristics in music are responsible for moving the affections? How do these relate to observable changes in the body of the performer and listener? What affections is music capable of moving and by what means? By what process is an affection communicated through the hearing to human feeling? What different affections do diverse genres of music move? Is it possible to define a musical vocabulary of the passions? Why do people respond differently to the same music?

Kircher begins his treatment of the affections with a summary of traditional humoral theory.[42] The vapors from the four humors mix in various proportions according to the objects of the imagination. If the object is full of indignation or jealousy, the spirits and the vapors from the gall bladder, mobilized by the imaginative force, acquire the temperament of warmth and dryness and drive the soul into affections of anger, fury, and rage. An object that is agreeable and full of love causes sanguinous vapors from the liver to become warm and humid; agitated by soft and harmonious movements, they sweetly and tenderly move the soul to taste joy, hope, confidence, love, and cheer. If the object is terrifying, sad, and tragic, the vapors rising from the receptacle of black bile endow the animal spirit with a cold and dry temperament, subjecting the soul to melancholy, sorrow, pain, lamentation, and similar affections. A delicate, smooth, and moderate object, neither sad nor joyous, causes the vapors to become cold and humid, and the animal spirits impel the soul to passions of cheerfulness, calm, confidence, and noble love.

Kircher's explanation of how music can initiate this process or flow from it depends on his essentially Pythagorean and neo-Platonic conception of a common architecture of harmonic numbers shared by the soul and music.[43] Consonance pleases because its ratios agree with the innate harmonic structure of the soul. If the sounding motion of the air is proportionate, it affects the hearing and soul felicitously; if disproportionate, unfavorably. Both the outer and inner air are in constant motion, the outer depending on the sound, the inner on the individual temperament. Particular temperaments are receptive to certain frequencies, but the outer air's tremors can alter the motions of the inner air.

---

[42]Ibid., 1:551–52 (bk. 7, Erothema 7).

[43]This is detailed in ibid., 1:564–68 (bk. 7, part 2, ch. 1 ["De musurgia patheticae ... ratione"]).

The active harmonic agent for Kircher is the ascending or descending melodic interval. An interval affects the soul in different manners if it is small or large, and this is particularly true of the tone and semitone and their location within a scale. The sound-bearing exterior air stirs the air within the ear and communicates to the animal spirit the proportions of the exterior sounds.

> Height and lowness of pitch, tension and relaxation, rapidity and slowness, softness and hardness by their proportion and temperament alter the spirit and this in turn alters the soul. When sound is high pitched (tense), the spirit will be similar to the higher fire and cholera; if low pitched (relaxed), it will resemble the lower earthy humor; if intermediate, it will cause moderate affections....[44]

> Granted that a musical tone is a movement that communicates to the air a motion exactly proportionate, that the air is in a continuum with the animal spirit, which itself is in perpetual motion, it follows that at the same time as the soul (in which harmony is innate and congenital ...) is excited by the song and the fantasy by the object represented by the words, the air excites a natural humor altogether equivalent and proportional to the object and to the sonorous movements. As to the vapor, it rises and mixes with the animal spirit already excited by the sonorous numbers of the air that is continuous with it. Finally, by its movement the spirit impels the soul to affections proportionate to the numbers and to the words....

> Therefore the sonorous number, as it sets the interior air in motion, impresses on it the harmonic movements, then animates the imagination. The latter, in turn, communicates these impulses to the humors, and the humors, mixed with the vaporous spirit—the interior air—, finally move the person to what they convey. It is in this manner and none other that harmony moves the passions.[45]

---

[44]Ibid., 1:566 (bk. 7, part 2, ch. 1): "Acumen itaque & grauitas, intensio & remissio, celeritas & tarditas sonori motus, quas mollities & durities consequuntur, qua proportione & temperamento spiritum alterant, hoc eodem & animam alterabunt. qui si intensior fuerit & acutior, acutiores & igni seu cholerae similes; si remissior, remissiores & terreo humori similes; si medium tenuerit, medias affectiones efficiet."

[45]Ibid., 1:552 (bk. 7, Erothema 7): "Nam cum sonus harmonicus motus quidam fit aerem ea prorsus proportione qua ipse constat, incitans; aer autem spiritui animali, qui in perpetuò similiter motu est, continuus sit, fit vt simul, ac anima (cui harmonia naturaliter, vt in metaphysica nostra musica dicetur, insita est eidemque congenita) harmonia, phantasia verò obiecto, quod verba praesentant, fuerit concitata, aer concitet naturalem humorem obiecto, & harmonicis motibus prorsus similem, & proportionatum, vapor verò inde eleuatus spiritui animali iam ad harmoniae, aerisque continui harmonici numeros concitato commistus; animam

Marin Mersenne was more interested in the physical properties of musical sounds than in music's effect on the passions, a subject he approached with circumspection. He recognized that animals use their voices to express their feeling, tending toward high pitch in sadness and anger, low when they are melancholy. In humans, pitch indicates mostly the size of the vocal organs; the quality of the voice and the pace of speech are surer signs of the affection. The bilious speak quickly and brusquely, while the melancholic speak slowly and the sanguine at a moderate pace.[46] Mersenne was more interested in how song could express the affections through "accentual music" (*la musique accentuelle*). This is accomplished through "the art of the harmonic orator, who must know all the steps, rhythms, movements, and accents suited to excite listeners to any desired feeling."[47] In speech, meaning is conveyed through words, passion through accent and inflection.

Each passion and affection has its own accents. For the sake of brevity, Mersenne reduces the passions to three: anger, joy, and sorrow. In angry speech, for example, the voice may rise a whole tone, third, fourth, or fifth, leaning on the last syllables of a word, while in a sad affection it often descends a semitone.[48] Rhythmics applied in the practice

---

tandem agitatione sua ad affectus numeris, & verbis proportionatos compellet: latent enim in singulis rebus proportiones quaedam, quarum concursu omnes rerum exoticae operationes perficiuntur, vtique in admirabili rerum consensu dissensuque; quam sympathiam, & antipathiam Graeci vocant, ita maximè in harmonico negotio elucescunt.

"Numerus igitur harmonicus primò aerem cùm intrinsecum concitat, eique harmonicos motus imprimit; deinde phantasiam impellit, haec impulsa humores concitat, homores vaporosi spiritui siue aeri intrinseco misti, tandem hominem ad id inclinat, quod referunt, atque hoc pacto harmonia, non alio passiones mouet."

[46]Mersenne, *Harmonie universelle, Livre premier de la voix*, 8–10 (Prop. VII).

[47]Mersenne, *Harmonie universelle, Livre sixiesme de l'art de bien chanter, Partie III, De la musique accentuelle*, 365: "l'Art de l'Orateur Harmonique, qui doit connoistre tous les degrez, les temps, les mouemens, & les accents propres pour exciter ses auditeurs à tout ce qu'il veut ...." For other analogies Mersenne makes to oratory, see David Allen Duncan, "Persuading the Affections: Rhetorical Theory and Mersenne's Advice to Harmonic Orators," in *French Musical Thought, 1600–1800*, ed. Georgia Cowart, Studies in Music, vol. 105 (Ann Arbor, Mich.: UMI Research Press, 1989), 149–76.

[48]Mersenne, *Harmonie universelle, Livre sixiesme de l'art de bien chanter, Partie III, De la musique accentuelle*, 373 (Prop. XVI).

of drums, trumpets, dances, ballets, songs, and poems gives delight to listeners and spectators and excites them to various passions.[49]

Descartes at the outset boasted of being the first to treat the passions and consequently felt compelled to start afresh because the little the ancients wrote about them was incredible.[50] Descartes may have staked out too broad a claim, and his own credibility was vulnerable. This was not an area of study in which he could apply mathematics and geometry, through which he reached truthful accounts in the physical sciences. We may forgive him for ignoring Bartholomaeus Anglicus. He evidently had read some of the writings of Vives,[51] but his notorious aversion to the theories of others would have discouraged any close consultation. A highly original product of pure meditation and introspection, the treatise on the passions is an important, systematic, insightful analysis of the subject.

Descartes highlighted some distinctions that were only implied in previous treatises. As opposed to the Aristotelians, he emphasized that the body, not the soul, is the source of life, since the soul remains after death (Art. 6). The passions exist in the body as movements of "a certain very thin air or wind called animal spirits"[52] that travel in the nerves, tiny tubelike filaments, conveying the impressions of the senses and controlling the body's muscular movements (Art. 7). As opposed to these bodily functions, the soul, though capable also of voluntary actions, experiences passively the movements of the spirits as affections or perceptions (Art. 27). The soul has little control over the actions and representations that cause the passions, which persist as long as their cause remains present. The will cannot stop them but only resist some of their effects, such as denying an urge to violence aroused by hate (Art. 46).

Descartes proposed the novel theory that while only the thin animal spirits can enter the brain's minute pores, through which they reach the nerves, the denser components of the blood flow speedily everywhere

---

[49]Ibid., 374 (Prop. XVII).

[50]René Descartes, *Passions de l'âme*, introduction and notes by Geneviève Rodis-Lewis, Bibliothèque des textes philosophiques (Paris: J. Vrin, 1955), 65 (part 1, article 1).

[51]See Noreña, *Juan Luis Vives*, 161, 167–68. *De anima et vita libri tres* was published in Basle in 1538 and among the reprints was one of 1563 in Utrecht.

[52]Descartes, *Passions*, 71: "… un certain air ou vent tres-subtil, qu'on nomme les esprits animaux."

else (Art. 10). In another fanciful departure, Descartes identified the pineal gland, an unpaired organ in the middle of the brain, as the communication center to which all the nerves lead and from which the animal spirits are distributed to the appropriate parts of the body (Art. 35). The one reference to an artistic application, which points indirectly to music, is the idea that we can take pleasure in feeling moved by passions—even sadness and hate—when we see them represented in the theater because in that context they do not threaten our bodies while barely tickling the soul (Arts. 94, 147, 187).

The vogue of the passions swept England in the late sixteenth and early seventeenth century. In 1516, Thomas More (1478–1535) in his *Utopia* had already praised the ideal music of the Utopians for its capacity to "affect, penetrate, and inflame the souls of listeners, according to whether the text is happy, soothing, agitated, mournful, or angry...."[53] Timothie Bright, Thomas Wright, William Fenner, and Thomas Hobbes,[54] among others, published treatises dedicated to the passions. For Roger North in 1728, moving the affections while delighting the sense of hearing was still a goal of music: "Musick hath 2 ends, first to pleas the sence, & that is done by the pure Dulcor of Harmony, which is found chiefly in ye elder musick, of wch much hath bin sayd, & more is to come, & secondly to move ye affections or excite passion."[55]

The Italians, though they theorized less about the passions than the French or English, intuitively found the means to move them through music. Most of the musical examples Kircher presents in score to illustrate the affections are by Italians of previous generations, such as

---

[53]Thomas More, *Utopia*, ed. E. Surtz, S. J. and J. H. Hexter (New Haven, CT: Yale University Press, 1965), 236: "... seu deprecantis oratio sit seu laeta, placabilis, turbida, lugubris, irata, ita rei sensum quendam melodiae forma repraesentat, ut animos auditorum mirum in modum adficiat, penetrat, incendat."

[54]Timothie Bright, *A Treatise of Melancholy ... with Diuerse Philosophicall Discourses Touching Actions and Affections of Soule, Spirit and Body* (London: John Windet, 1586); Thomas Wright, *The Passions of the Minde* (London: V. S. or W. B., 1601); William Fenner, *A Treatise of the Affections, or, The Soules Pulse* (London: Printed by E. G. for I. Rothwell, 1641); and Thomas Hobbes, *Humane Nature, or, The Fundamental Elements of Policie: Being a Discoverie of the Faculties, Acts, and Passions of the Soul of Man, from their Original Causes* (London: T. Newcomb for Fra: Bowman of Oxon, 1650).

[55]Roger North, *Musical Grammarian* (c. 1728), ed. Hilda Andrews (London: Oxford University Press, 1925), 15, quoted in Paul Henry Lang, *Music in Western Civilization* (New York: Norton, 1941), 436.

Palestrina and Gesualdo, or by composers in his Roman circle, including Johann Hieronymus Kapsberger (ca. 1580–1651), Antonio Maria Abbatini (ca. 1609–ca. 1677), Giovanni Troiano (fl. 1571–1622), Gino Angelo Capponi (ca. 1607–1688), and Giacomo Carissimi (1605–1674).[56] An anonymous Italian author writing about dramatic music somewhat before Kircher advises the inexperienced composer to make note of the best passages and imitate how master composers have expressed various affections:

> It will be of great help to those who lack great inventiveness, to better assure their success, if they put in score the most beautiful passages of musical actions already done . . . and set down the passages in which master musicians in this genre have well expressed, for example, the affection of sorrow, for many of them have beautifully and diversely composed on this affection, as also on the affections of disdain, vengeance, love, languor, and others.[57]

Preoccupation with the passions peaked in Germany, where the ubiquity of the affections in every artistic domain in the mid-seventeenth century is strikingly illustrated by Lohenstein's play *Agrippina*, first published in Breslau in 1665, in which one critic has found mentioned 110 different terms for affections.[58] The title page of the choral-instrumental collection *Theatrum affectuum humanorum* (1717) shows ten figures representing *odium* (hate), *desperatio* (desperation), *tristitia* (sorrow), *timor* (fear), *puca* (*pudor?* shame), *ira* (anger), *gaudium* (joy), *spes* (hope), *audacia* (courage), and *amor* (love). In the middle stands *virtus in medio* (virtue in

---

[56]Kircher, *Musurgia universalis*, 1:586–620 (bk. 7, part 2, chs. 5–6). Kircher tended to choose music by composers he knew in Rome or whose music was available there.

[57]*Il Corago*, 81: "Sarà di grand'aiuto a questo per che non avesse grand'inventiva e per maggior sicurezza di far bene, avere spartiti i passi più belli dell'azioni armoniche già fatte sotto certi capi verbigrazia di affetti, come dire sotto l'affetto del dolore porre i passi con che i musici perfetti in questo genere hanno espresso bene questo affetto perchè molti e variamente e vagamente vi hanno composto: così sotto l'affetto dello sdegno e vendetta, dell'amore e languore e altri ...."

[58]Reinhart Meyer-Kalkus, *Wollust und Grausamkeit: Affektenlehre und Affektdarstellung in Lohensteins Dramatik am Beispiel von 'Agrippina'* (Göttingen: Vandenhoeck & Ruprecht, 1986).

the middle), proclaiming the moral that we should seek moderation, a happy medium among the competing affections (figure 11).[59]

Figure 11. Franz Lang, *Theatrum affectuum humanorum*, title-page

Despite all the theorizing by Mersenne, Descartes, Bernard Lamy,[60] and others, the passions remained largely foreign to French music in the seventeenth century. Mersenne missed in French music the accent of the passions that he heard in the Italian:

[59]Franz Lang, *Theatrum affectuum humanorum, sive, Considerationes morales ad scenam accommodatae: et in oratorio almae sodalitatis majoris B.V. Mariae ab angelo salutatae matris propitiae* (Munich: Mathias Riedl, 1717).

[60]Bernard Lamy, *L'art de bien parler* (Paris: Pralard, 1676). See William G. Waite, "Bernard Lamy, Rhetorician of the Passions," in *Studies in Eighteenth-Century Music: A Tribute to Karl Geiringer on His Seventieth Birthday*, ed. H. C. Robbins Landon in collaboration with Roger E. Chapman (London: George Allen and Unwin, 1970), 388–96.

They [the Italians] observe many things in their recitatives that are missing in ours because they represent as much as they can the passions and affections of the soul and of the mind, for example, anger, fury, scorn, rage, fainting of the heart, and many others, with a violence so strange that one would think that they were touched by the same affections as they represent in singing. Our French singers instead content themselves with pleasing the ear, using a perpetual sweetness in their songs that deprive them of vigor.[61]

The prevailing rationalism and neo-classicism of French poets, dramatists, and literary critics throttled emotional expression. The cult of the clear and distinct idea, moderation, decorum, and the golden mean dominated the creative and performing arts. The idea of art as imitation, stemming partly from Aristotle's *Poetics*, appealed to the literary minded, who ingeniously made it fit music.[62]

French critics gave a special twist to Aristotle's idea that art imitates reality. Jean-Laurent Lecerf de la Viéville (1674–1707), who defended French opera against a partisan of Italian opera, proposed that music imitated nature indirectly. The composer of an opera imitated the poetry of the librettist, which in turn imitated nature directly.

Wherein lies the beauty of music in the operas? It is in successfully rendering the poetry of these operas: a painting that truly speaks. That is, as if to retouch it, give it its final colors. Now how can music *repaint* poetry, how will they serve each other unless they are linked with utmost precision, unless they merge in perfect harmony?[63]

---

[61]Mersenne, *Harmonie universelle, Livre sixiesme de l'art de bien chanter, Seconde Partie, De l'art d'embellir la voix, les recits, les airs, ov les chants*, 356 (prop. 6): "Quant aux Italiens, ils obseruent plusieurs choses dans leurs recits, dont les nostres sont priuez, parce qu'ils representent tant qu'ils peuuent les passions & les affections de l'ame & de l'esprit, par exemple, la cholere, la fureur, le dépit, la rage, les defaillances de coeur, & plusieurs autres passions, auec vne violence si estrange, que l'on iugeroit quasi qu'ils sont touchez des mesmes affections qu'ils representent en chantant; au lieu que nos François se contentent de flatter l'oreille, & qu'ils vsent d'vne douceur perpetuelle dans leurs chants; ce qui en empesche l'energie."

[62]Mersenne asserts that music is an imitation or representation, just as are poetry, tragedy, and painting (*Harmonie universelle, Livre second des chants*, 93 [prop. 2]).

[63]Jean-Laurent Lecerf de la Viéville, *Comparaison de la musique italienne et la musique françoise* (Brussels: Foppens, 1704; reprint of 1706 ed. in three parts, Geneva: Minkoff, 1972), 1:169: "Maintenant quelle est la beauté de la Musique des Opera? C'est d'achever de rendre la Poésie de ces Opera, une peinture vraiment parlante. C'est, pour ainsi dire, de la retoucher, de lui donner les dernieres couleurs. Or comment la Musique *repeindra-t-elle* la Poësie, comment s'entreserviront-elles; à moins qu'on ne les lie avec une extrême justesse, a moins qu'elles ne se mêlenet

Instrumental music was another matter. The seventeenth-century French public expected instrumental music, aside from dance music, to reflect nature. Jean le Rond d'Alembert (1717–1783), who edited the famous *Encyclopédie* with Diderot, voiced this attitude in his preliminary essay: "All music that paints nothing is just noise…. It should give no more pleasure than a series of harmonious and sonorous words devoid of order or connection."[64] But the only things in nature that instrumental music could imitate directly were natural sounds, and they could not form the basis of serious compositions. Nevertheless, Lully complied by inserting in his *tragédies lyriques* symphonies of winds, storms, battles, and even sleep. In the next century, Jean-Baptiste Dubos (1670–1742) and Charles Batteux[65] (1713–1780) continued to believe that music, like painting, sculpture, and literature, could stand under Aristotle's umbrella as an imitative art, but they did not naively believe that the principal subjects of imitation should be natural sounds. Batteux likened that to landscape painting; sentiments and passions were nobler subjects. Instead of saying that music should move the passions, they thought in terms of imitations that would arouse not real passions but harmless imitations of them. Later in the eighteenth century, Michel-Paul Guy de Chabanon (1729/30–1792), a classicist and amateur musician, concluded that music does not imitate anything. He insisted that a listener could enjoy music without recognizing any imitation or representation, but simply for itself.[66] The idea of music as imitation had at last run its course in France.

---

ensemble par l'accord le plus parfait?" For a fuller treatment of theories of musical imitation, see Georgia Cowart, *The Origins of Modern Musical Criticism: French and Italian Music, 1600–1750*, Studies in Musicology, vol. 38 (Ann Arbor, MI: UMI Research Press, 1981).

[64]Jean Le Rond d'Alembert, "Discours preliminaire," in *Encyclopédie, ou dictionnaire raisonné des sciences, des arts et des metiers*, 28 vols. (Paris: Brisson, 1751–72), 1:xij: "Toute Musique qui ne peint rien n'est que du bruit; … elle ne feroit guere plus de plaisir qu'une suite de mots harmonieux & sonores dénués d'ordre & de liaison."

[65]Jean-Baptiste Dubos, *Refléxions critiques sur la poësie et sur la peinture* (Paris: Jean Mariette, 1719); Charles Batteux, *Les beaux arts réduits à un même principe* (Paris: Durand, 1743; reprint of 1747 ed., New York: Johnson Reprint, 1970).

[66]Michel-Paul Guy de Chabanon, *Observations sur la musique et principalement sur la metaphysique de l'art* (Paris: Pissot, 1779; reprint, Geneva: Slatkine, 1969). See John Neubauer, *The Emancipation of Music from Language: Departure from Mimesis in Eighteenth-Century Aesthetics* (New Haven, CT: Yale University Press, 1986), 169ff.

⋽ XI ⋤

Music and Rhetoric

ROWING SENSITIVITY to meanings and sentiments in texts led musicians to look to poetry and oratory as models of communication. Poetry moves listeners and readers through images, rhythm, and sound, as well as through the sense of its verses. Oratory draws from an arsenal of devices and ornaments to move an audience while persuading it through logical arguments. A composer can fashion images with melody, harmony, and rhythm, as a poet does with words and their sound and rhythm, but conveying literal meaning is largely beyond music's power. Like a poet or orator, a composer invents ideas and elaborates or develops them in keeping with a logic and syntax peculiar to music, sets a slow or fast pace, and divides the communication into periods with shorter or longer resting points, weaker or fuller stops. Grammar and rhetoric can therefore apply to music as well as to poetry and oratory.

Rhetoric, most broadly defined, is the art of communicating by means of words. Renaissance scholars, however, had a less comprehensive view of rhetoric, distinguishing it from its sister disciplines in the trivium, grammar and dialectic. Grammar taught the principles of constructing sentences, punctuation, and the classification and use of such elements as nouns, verbs, adjectives, and adverbs. Dialectic concerned rules of logic and proofs. Rhetoric was the art of persuading and moving readers and listeners to believe and feel as the author or orator intended.

To move and persuade, rhetoric uses tropes and figures, such as reversing the normal word order; repetition; replacing an ordinary word with an evocative one, as in a metaphor; saying one thing and implying another, as in irony; or embellishing discourse with ornate turns of expression. Rhetoric also teaches an orator to shape a speech by resorting to certain introductory strategies at the beginning, elaborative and argumentative tactics in the middle, and summarizing or concluding techniques at the end.

203

Composers of music have usually operated in a way similar to writers and speakers but have not always considered rhetoric, grammar, and dialectics as models for their working methods. In a word-dominated culture such as that of the sixteenth and seventeenth centuries, the disciplines of the trivium inevitably influenced how people thought about the creation of music, but music theorists did not always acknowledge their debts to these disciplines. Gioseffo Zarlino, for example, rarely makes a point of them; nevertheless, grammatical, dialectical, and rhetorical principles pervade his *Istitutioni harmoniche*, the very title of which may have been inspired by Marcus Fabius Quintilian's *Institutio oratoria*.[1]

Early writers on music had already discovered that grammatical theory provided a vocabulary and set of procedures for explaining the organization of music. In the eleventh century, Guido of Arezzo, followed a century later by his commentator Johannes, recognized several levels of closure in plainchant, which the Latin rhetoricians called *distinctiones*: comma, colon, and period. These were marks of punctuation in prose; setting the prose to music converted them into species of cadence, the comma in prose demanding a weak ending in melody, a colon a fairly strong one, and a period a conclusive one. To designate functions within a piece of early polyphony in the twelfth and thirteenth centuries, music theorists again borrowed grammatical terminology. In prose, for example, a *punctus* referred to a final punctuation mark but also to a section of a composition; it signified this as well in early polyphony. Similarly, *clausula*, literally a close, came to mean the phrase, whether verbal or musical, that preceded a cadence.[2]

Beyond these syntactic categories, musicians did not recognize until much later how they could apply rhetoric's means for persuading and stirring the emotions. Classical rhetoric was divided into five parts: *inventio*, *dispositio*, *elocutio* (sometimes called *elaboratio* or *decoratio*), *memoria*, and *pronuntiatio*. Different historical periods saw various "parts" of rhetoric applied to music. The sixteenth century greatly valued the first, *inventio*, which in oratory was the discovery of arguments in favor of a cause. Zarlino's concern with the kinds of "subjects" (*soggetti*) on which a com-

---

[1]Martha Feldman in *City Culture and the Madrigal at Venice* (Berkeley: University of California Press, 1995), 171–93, argues convincingly that Zarlino's *Istitutioni* is a Ciceronian work. The parallel paths of musical composition and literature in the sixteenth century were discussed in chapter 4.

[2]See pp. 54 and 64–68 *supra*.

poser could base his composition reflects this emphasis on invention.[3] In the eighteenth century, Johann David Heinichen (1683–1729) expansively developed this aspect, showing how a composer of opera could stimulate creativity by studying the antecedents, concomitants, and consequences of a dramatic situation or text, as an advocate or prosecutor might search for evidence.[4] In rhetoric, these were among the *loci*, or "places" where ideas could be found. Johann Mattheson (1681–1764) did not limit himself to dramatic music but showed how the consideration of *loci* could stimulate invention even in purely instrumental music. He listed as *loci topici* such technical procedures as notation, instrumentation, and solo-tutti textures.[5]

Dispositio, the distribution of the arguments or material discovered through *inventio*, naturally fit the techniques employed by sixteenth-century composers in developing their subjects through fugue, imitation, and other kinds of repetition and variation. In the eighteenth century, the construction of themes, phrases, and periods, and the manipulation of motives in melody naturally invited comparisons to the rhetoric of "disposition."

Elocutio, which may be translated as "eloquence" or "style," occupied a central place in the late sixteenth and throughout the seventeenth century. This part of rhetoric taught how to ornament an oration with figures of speech, a principal means for moving the affections. Joachim Burmeister around 1600 and Christoph Bernhard a few generations later

---

[3]Zarlino, *Istitutioni* (1558), 171–72 (bk. 3, ch. 26: "Quel che si ricerca in ogni compositione, & prima del Soggetto"). For an examination of the relationship between rhetoric and music during the Renaissance, see Blake M. Wilson, "*Ut oratoria musica* in the Writings of Renaissance Music Theorists," in *Festa musicologica: Essays in Honor of George J. Buelow*, ed. Thomas J. Mathiesen and Benito V. Rivera, Festschrift Series, vol. 14 (Stuyvesant, NY: Pendragon Press, 1995), 341–68.

[4]Heinichen's analysis appears in his introduction to *Der General-Bass in der Composition* (Dresden: by the author, 1728). The introduction is translated in George J. Buelow, *Thorough-Bass Accompaniment According to Johann David Heinichen*, rev. ed. (Ann Arbor, MI; UMI Research Press, 1986; reprint, Lincoln: University of Nebraska Press, 1992), 307–80 (appendix B).

[5]Mattheson, *Der vollkommene Capellmeister*, 121–32 (pt. 2, ch. 4: "Von der Erfindung"). The most complete study of the relationship between music and rhetoric during this period is Dietrich Bartel, *Musica poetica: Musical-Rhetorical Figures in German Baroque Music* (Lincoln: University of Nebraska Press, 1997); on the *loci topici*, see especially pp. 77–80.

built their teaching of music composition around systems of figures modeled on those of rhetoric.

Memoria, or memory, preoccupied the orator, who needed a firm grasp of words and subject matter. Performers of music had to develop memory of melodies, texts, intervallic relationships, and rhythmic patterns. During the Middle Ages, suggestive markings such as neumes and a variety of symbols, not to mention schemes such as the Guidonian hand and solmization, aided the memory in recalling music that was only partially notated, if at all. As notation became more explicit, memory ceased to be an object of much concern to the theorist.

Pronuntiatio (delivery or performance) received little attention as a rhetorical category in music, perhaps because its agents, voice and gesture, were already an everyday concern of the musician. Like a poem, play, or oration, music remains silent in the mind or on parchment or paper unless performed. Nearly every writer on music speaks unselfconsciously about performance. Yet there are moments in history when the art of performance takes center stage. The years around 1600 were such a time. Monody is more than just a way of singing a piece. It is song that asserts a new attitude toward performance: the singer becomes a protagonist and projects a text through music. This is especially true of dramatic recitative, which is neither fully song nor pure speech. Like the orator's *pronuntiatio*, it is a delivery that narrates, persuades, and moves. It is a fulfillment of the rhetorical process.[6]

It is a paradox that in Italy, where musical rhetoric was practiced most successfully in the sixteenth and seventeenth centuries, musicians and composers rarely spoke of it. Of course, classical rhetoric was not a component of the training of a singer or composer in Italy as it was of a would-be notary, secretary, lawyer, or political leader. Musicians learned their craft by practice rather than by reading books of theory. In Germany, on the other hand, theorists keenly cultivated and developed the idea of a musical rhetoric, and choirboys, particularly after the Reformation, attended Latin schools attached to their churches in which the curriculum included a thorough study of rhetoric. By the time musical composition was attempted, the vocabulary and concepts of rhetoric, already

---

[6]The relation of this aspect of rhetoric to musical performance is explored by Don Harrán in "Toward a Rhetorical Code of Early Music Performance," *Journal of Musicology* 14 (1997): 19–42. On monody, see chapter 7 *supra*.

ingrained, could be called upon to illuminate unfamiliar procedures and serve as mnemonic aids for advanced and elegant composition.[7]

Although Italian theorists did not systematically invoke rhetoric, a number of them showed awareness of the parallels between oratory and music, especially after becoming acquainted with the rhetorical treatises of Cicero and Quintilian. The first-century Roman Quintilian acknowledged the value of music in an orator's training in his *Institutio oratoria,* printed in 1470 in Rome, one of the first printed books to include a discussion of music. Known previously only in incomplete copies, the treatise was first restored in its entirety by Poggio Bracciolini (1380–1459) on the basis of a manuscript he discovered in St. Gall in 1416 while attending the Council of Constance. Both the discovery and the first and subsequent printings stirred interest in classical rhetoric. By 1500 there were at least eighteen editions, with another 130 or more by 1600.[8] In Book I, chapter 11, Quintilian likened oratory to music in its power to move people to various passions and showed how the orator must learn to modulate the pitch of his voice to suit the affections, imitating the inflections of melody. Cicero in his *De oratore,* restored in 1421 and printed in 1470 in Venice, likewise taught orators to control their pitch and rhythm. The means by which musicians gave pleasure to the ears with their verse and melody—that is, through the rhythm of words and the modulation of the voice, for musicians were also poets in the old days—, he suggested, could be transferred from poetry to rhetoric.[9]

Johannes Tinctoris, who read widely in classical literature, compared in 1477 the use of dissonances in counterpoint to figures of speech. The

---

[7]See Bartel, *Musica poetica,* 59–76.

[8]Brian Vickers, "Figures of Rhetoric/Figures of Music?" *Rhetorica* 2 (1984): 1–44. See also James Jerome Murphy, *Renaissance Rhetoric: A Short-Title Catalogue of Works on Rhetorical Theory from the Beginning of Printing to A.D. 1700, with Special Attention to the Holdings of the Bodleian Library, Oxford: With a Select Basic Bibliography of Secondary Works on Renaissance Rhetoric* (New York: Garland, 1981).

[9]Cicero *De oratore* 3.174. *Cicero in Twenty-Eight Volumes,* vol. 4, *De oratore, Book III; De fato; Paradoxa Stoicorum; De partitione oratoria,* trans. Horace Rackham, Loeb Classical Library (Cambridge: Harvard University Press, 1968), 138: "Namque haec duo musici, qui erant quondam eidem poetae, machinati ad voluptatem sunt, versum atque cantum, ut et verborum numero et vocum modo delectatione vincerent aurium satietatem. Haec igitur duo, vocis dico moderatione et verborum conclusionem, quoad orationis severitas pati possit, a poetica ad eloquentiam traducenda duxerunt."

introduction of short dissonances, such as those allowed in his rules of counterpoint, he said, "are permitted by musicians just as logical [i.e. rhetorical] figures were by grammarians for reasons of ornament and necessity. A melody is ornamented when it ascends or descends from one consonance to another by acceptable means and syncopations that at times cannot be made without dissonances."[10] As we shall see, Christoph Bernhard was to build a theory of the use of dissonance paralleling the rhetorical figures.

Angelo Poliziano (1454–1494) seems to be thinking of the rhetoric of *pronuntiatio* when he describes the voice of a young reciter of an epic poem:

> A voice neither quasi reading, nor quasi singing, in which, however, as you sense both, you distinguish neither, varied according as the place demands— whether uplifting, depressing, striving, slow, excited—always correct, always clear, always sweet. The gesturing is not indifferent, not sluggish, though not affected or annoying.[11]

Nicola Vicentino, too, has the performer in mind when he counsels certain nuances that cannot be written down:

> The measure should change according to the words, now slower and now faster .... The experience of the orator can be instructive, if you observe the technique he follows in his oration. For he speaks now loud and now soft, now slow and now fast, thus greatly moving his listeners. This technique of changing the measure has a powerful effect on the soul.[12]

---

[10]Tinctoris, "Liber de arte contrapuncti," 2:140 (bk. 2, ch. 31): "Verumtamen modis aliquando praedictis discordantiae parvae a musicis, sicut figurae rationabiles a grammaticis ornatus necessitatisve causa assumi permittuntur. Ornatur enim cantus, quando fit ascensus vel descensus ab una concordantia ad aliam per media compatibilia et per syncopas quae interdum sine discordantiis fieri non possunt."

[11]Angelo Poliziano, letter to Pico della Mirandola, "Epistolae, XII, 2," in *Omnia opera* (Venice: Aldus, 1498), quoted in F. Alberto Gallo, "Pronuntiatio: Ricerche sulla storia di un termine retorico-musicale," *Acta musicologica* 35 (1963): 42: "Vox ipsa nec quasi legentis, nec quasi canentis, se in qua tamen utrumque sentires, neutrum discerneres, uarie tamen prout locus posceret, aut aequalis, aut inflexa, nunc distincta, nunc perpetua, nunc sublata, nun deducta, nunc remissa, nunc contenta, nunc lenta, nunc incitata, semper emendata, semper clara, semper dulcis. Gestus non ociosus, non somniculosus, se nec uultuosus tamen ac molestus."

[12]Vicentino, *L'Antica musica*, f. 94v (bk. 4, ch. 42): "... il moto della misura si dè muouere, secondo le parole, più tardo, & più presto .... la esperienza, dell'Oratore l'insegna, che si uede il modo che tiene nell'Oratione, che hora dice forte, & hora piano, & più tardo, & più presto, e con questo muoue assai gl'oditori, &

Giulio Caccini in the preface to his second collection of monodies of 1614 drew a comparison between the figures of rhetoric and specific vocal embellishments, "such as tremolos, running passages, and similar ornaments that may be introduced now and then in every affection."[13] Although a composer could mark the places where they should be introduced and sometimes wrote them out, the performer usually inserted and improvised them. In the process of *pronuntiatio*, the singer thus contributed to the *elocutio*, the elaboration of melody by means of figures.

In the Artusi-Monteverdi controversy, the unidentified academician who calls himself L'Ottuso compares an unprepared dissonance to a metaphor. Like a more vivid word assumed for the expected one, a dissonance taking the place of a consonance awakens an emotional reaction.[14]

These are among the few links between rhetoric and music indulged by Italian writers of this period. In Germany, on the other hand, rhetorical technique developed into a pedagogical strategy of prime importance. Gallus Dressler in his *Praecepta musicae poeticae* (1563–1564) taught that a musical composition, like an oration, consisted of an *exordium* or opening introduction, a *medium* or middle, and a *finis* or conclusion.[15]

Joachim Burmeister laid the foundation for a rhetorical method of teaching musical composition in three treatises published between 1599 and 1606. Rhetoric came naturally to Burmeister, who earned a Master's degree in law from the University of Rostock. From 1593, he taught classics in the town school of Rostock and served as Cantor of its principal church, St. Marien. He had previously held positions as musical director in two churches, but now his main occupation was teaching Latin grammar and eventually also Greek. He had studied at the Lüneburg

---

questo modo di muouere la misura, fà effetto assai nell'animo, ...";trans. *Ancient Music*, 301. Zarlino makes a similar remark in *Sopplimenti musicali*, 317–19 (bk. 8, ch. 11), responding to Galilei's urging in his *Dialogo della musica antica, et della moderna* that composers should take as a model the way in which comic and tragic actors imitate the manner of speaking of various types of characters. See chapter 4 *supra* (especially p. 64).

[13]Giulio Caccini, *Nuove musiche e nuova maniera di scriverle* (Florence: Pigoni, 1614), preface, quoted in Schmitz, *Giulio Caccini*, 44: "... alle figure, e à i colori rettorici assimiglierei, i passaggi, i trilli, e gli altri simili ornamenti, che sparsamente in ogni affetto si possono tal'ora introdurre."

[14]Artusi, *Seconda parte dell'Artusi*, 16. See chapter 9 *supra*.

[15]See p. 50 and chapter 4, n. 4 *supra*.

Latin school, which for two years included three hours a week of dialectic and two of rhetoric, based on the teachings of Philipp Melanchthon (1497–1560), the famous Lutheran reformer and biblical commentator. In addition to this, he was obliged to read and analyze Cicero's orations and to compose imitations of them. He applied in his treatises the analytical and pedagogical techniques learned in these classes.[16]

Burmeister's first treatise, *Hypomnematum musicae poeticae ... synopsis* of 1599, is a compendium of an earlier treatise, now lost. It contains notes on topics further developed in his second published work, *Musica autoschediastike* (1601), and put into more definitive form in *Musica poetica* (1606).[17] Burmeister taught composition through analysis and emulation of exemplary works by composers of previous generations, predominantly by Orlando di Lasso (1530/32–1594), André Pevernage (1543–1591), and Clemens non Papa (ca. 1510–1555/56). He believed that it was not sufficient to master the use of consonances and dissonances in counterpoint; rather, the composer had to learn to embellish simple and correct writing with artful devices, which Burmeister regarded as analogous to the figures of rhetoric. Music is akin to oratory:

> For just as the art of oratory derives its power not from a simple collection of simple words, or from a proper yet rather plain construction of periods, or from their meticulous yet bare and uniform connection, but rather from those elements where there is an underlying grace and elegance due to ornament and to weighty words of wit, and where periods are rounded with emphatic words—so also, this art of music, surpassing the bare combination of pure consonances, offers to the senses a work composed of a mixture of perfect and imperfect consonances and of dissonances. This cannot but touch one's heart.[18]

---

[16]The most detailed study of Burmeister's life is Martin Ruhnke, *Joachim Burmeister: Ein Beitrag zur Musiklehre um 1600* (Kassel: Bärenreiter, 1955).

[17]Joachim Burmeister, *Hypomnematum musicae poeticae ... synopsis* (Rostock: S. Myliander, 1599); idem, *Musica αὐτοσχεδιαστικὴ quae per aliquot accessiones in gratiam philomusorum ... in unum corpusculum concrevit* (Rostock: C. Reusner, 1601). For *Musica poetica*, see chapter 4, n. 5 *supra*.

[18]Burmeister, *Musica autoschediastike*, ff. A2v–3r: "Perinde enim ut ars oratoria vim suam, qua pollet, non in simplici verborum simplicium collectione; periodorum debita circuitione, et quidem plana; in illarum connexione exquisita, nuda, et sibi semper aequabili, situm habet; sed in iis, quibus ex ornatu subest lepos et elegantia, ex ponderosis verbis argutiae, et quarum periodis sunt circumscripti verborum emphaticorum ambitus. Ita et haec ars praeter nudam consonantiarum

Burmeister continues by citing Lasso's motet *Deus qui sedes super thronum*, in which "through the care of the master composer ... the conglomerate is transformed from simplicity to a certain majesty of gesture and ornament." Demosthenes and Cicero could not "have more exquisitely presented to the eyes, relayed to the ears, and instilled in the heart the heaviness and sorrow of labor as Orlando did in this harmonic work of art."[19]

Lasso had been cited around forty years earlier for his ability to make a text come alive in his music by the humanist Samuel Quickelberg in a preface to the sumptuous manuscript that preserves Lasso's *Penitential Psalms*:

> [Lasso] expressed these psalms so appropriately, in accommodating, according to necessity, the thoughts and words with lamenting and plaintive tones, in expressing the force of the individual affections, in placing the object almost alive before the eyes, that one is at a loss to say whether the sweetness of the affections more greatly enhanced the lamenting tones or the lamenting tones brought greater ornament to the sweetness of the affections.[20]

Burmeister divides the ornaments available to a composer, akin to those called tropes and figures in rhetoric, into two classes: ornaments of

---

merarum connexionem, contextum ex consonantiarum perfectarum et imperfectarum, tum et dissonantiarum permixtione compositum sensui offert, qui non possit aliter quin pectus tangat"; trans. *Musical Poetics*, 232–33 (appendix A2). For a slightly different translation, see Claude V. Palisca, "*Ut oratoria musica*: The Rhetorical Basis of Musical Mannerism," in *The Meaning of Mannerism*, ed. Franklin W. Robinson and Stephen G. Nichols, Jr. (Hanover, NH: University Press of New England, 1972), 40; reprinted with a prefatory note in idem, *Studies*, 288.

[19]Burmeister, *Musica autoschediastike*, f. A3r: "sed industria artificis notitiam habentis concordantias utrasque cum dissonantiis ita permiscendi, ut a simplicitate ad quandam gestus et ornatus maiestatem sit dimota syntaxis. Non mehercle Apelles exactissima artis suae peritia, non Demosthenes, non Cicero, persuadendi, flectendi, movendi, eloquendique artificio laboris pondus et lamentationem magis composite ad oculos poneret, ad aures deferret, in cor ingereret, quam harmonico hoc artificio Orlandus fecit"; trans. *Musical Poetics*, 234–35.

[20]Wolfgang Boetticher, *Orlando di Lasso und seine Zeit, 1532–1594: Repertoire-Untersuchungen zur Musik der Spätrenaissance*, 2 vols., Quellenkataloge zur Musikgeschichte, vol. 27 (Kassel: Bärenreiter, 1958; reprint, Wilhelmshaven: Florian Noetzel, Heinrichshofen, 1999), 1:250: "... hos psalmos qui[n]q[ue] potissimum vocibus componendos, qui quidem adeo opposite lamentabili ac qu[a]erula voce, ubi opus fuit, ad res et verba accommodando, singulorum affectuum vim exprimendo, rem quasi actam ante oculos ponendo, expressit, ut ignorari possit: suavitasne affectuum, lamentabilis voces, an lamentabiles voces, suavitate affectuum plus decorarint." The manuscript is preserved in the Bayerische Staatsbibliothek as Mus. Ms. A (*olim* Cim 207).

melody, that is, those affecting individual voices; and ornaments of harmony, which apply to an ensemble of voice-parts. Some figures belong to both categories.[21] A passage containing a figure is delimited by cadences, that is, it starts after a cadence and ends with one. Burmeister calls such a passage, phrase, or period an "affection" (*affectio*). "A melody is an affection consisting of an intervallic sequence of pitches, devised or made to produce musical movement that will evoke affections in a man who is not altogether unmusical."[22] Burmeister's purpose in dividing a composition into affections is to observe the means by which each period affects the listener so that a young composer may study and emulate each technique and acquire a vocabulary of devices.[23]

Although Burmeister fails to point this out, not all the figures he enumerates were used for expressive reasons. Composers resorted to some of them for purely musical or constructive purposes or for the sake of variety of sound and texture. It is possible to write an affection or period without figures, that is, a succession of consonant chords making up the statement of a musical phrase. While such a period may be correct, Burmeister would not consider it praiseworthy or worthy of imitation. Figures are essential, whether for beauty and elegance or effect.

The figures Burmeister classifies as melodic are six: *parembole, palillogia, climax, parrhesia, hyperbole,* and *hypobole.* Some of these have corresponding figures, synonymously named, in verbal rhetoric.[24] *Parembole* refers to a voice in a fugal passage that does not participate in the fugue but is merely filler to achieve full harmony.[25] The verbal *parembole* is an insertion or interpolation of a parenthetical remark within a sentence. *Palillogia* is a repetition at the same pitch of a fragment of melody in several successive phrases, making it a subtler kind of repetition than its literary counterpart, which describes the repetition of a name or word. *Climax* is such a

---

[21]Burmeister, *Musical Poetics,* 156–57 (ch. 12).

[22]Ibid., 56–57 (ch. 4): "Melodia est pro intervallorum ratione sonorum se invicem subsequentium affectio, ad modulamen, affectus in homine non plane amuso creans, parata, vel facta."

[23]Ibid., pp. 200–203 (ch. 15).

[24]The following definitions of the verbal figures are based on Rivera's notes in *Musical Poetics,* 176–83 (ch. 12).

[25]See Rivera's translation and appendix for transcriptions of Burmeister's musical examples and of passages from the works of Lasso and others mentioned in *Musica poetica* and Burmeister's previous treatises.

repetition at lower or higher levels of pitch, similar to the device now called a sequence. Literary *climax* or *gradatio* is a graduated progression from one word and idea to another, as "subordinate matters beget negligence, negligence recklessness, and recklessness ruins men."[26] Although Burmeister considers *parrhesia* a melodic figure, it involves more than a single voice because it consists of inserting a relatively long note that is dissonant between notes that are consonant with the other parts. In an oration, a *parrhesia* is a bold statement that in everyday speaking would be considered offensive. *Hyperbole* and *hypobole* are opposites, the first referring to a melody's crossing the upper boundary of a mode, the latter transgressing the lower boundary. *Pathopoeia* consists of an alteration of a natural step of a mode by lowering or raising it a half-step, as by an accidental flat or sharp, for the sake of arousing an affection, most often of sorrow or pain. In rhetoric, *pathopoeia* denotes exclamations, pleas, or prayers.

Of these melodic figures, some are more likely than others to fulfill an expressive function. *Parrhesia*, because it introduces a dissonance that is noticeable to the ear, often underscores tension in the text. *Hyperbole* and *hypobole* can respond to mention of highness or lowness in the text. *Parembole, palillogia,* and *climax* may serve as images, but they are useful devices for accompanying and developing the melodic material of a piece, irrespective of the words.

The ornaments or figures of harmony are departures from note-against-note consonant writing. Burmeister names several types of contrapuntal imitation or fugue.[27] All but one have no counterparts in literature. *Fuga realis* is a point of imitation in which one voice announces a subject and the other voices take it up in turn, usually at the fifth above or the fourth below. *Metalepsis* is a double fugue, that is, a fugue with two subjects; *hypallage*, a fugue in which the answer is in contrary motion to the subject. *Apocope*, which in rhetoric refers to cutting off the end of a

---

[26]The definition and example are from Lucas Lossius, *Erotemata dialecticae et rhetoricae Philippi Melanchthonis et praeceptionum Erasmi Roterodami* (Frankfurt: P. Brub, 1552), 196, quoted in *Musical Poetics*, 181, n. 42.

[27]The term *fuga* (fugue) in the sixteenth century could mean a composition in "canon," in which each voice, following the previous voice after an interval of time, sings the same melody at the unison or other pitch interval. More often, *fuga* simply means melodic imitation, and it is in this sense that Burmeister employs the term.

word, is a fugue that is interrupted before being completed in all the voices.

Noëma marks a change of texture from imitative or free counterpoint to note-against-note writing, in which all the parts declaim the text together. It is often used for dramatic effect or to call attention to an important statement or a plea such as "Exaudi Domine vocem meam." In rhetoric, *noëma* is a resort to a commonplace. Burmeister names several figures related to *noëma*: *analepsis*, a reiteration of a *noëma* (in rhetoric, *analepsis* or *epanalepsis* is the repetition of a word that begins a verse at the end); *mimesis*, duplication or imitation of a *noëma* at a higher or lower register; and *anadiplosis*, a double *mimesis* (in rhetoric, *anadiplosis* is the repetition of a word that closes a verse to begin another).

Perhaps the most essential figure for the musical representation of a text is *hypotyposis*. In rhetoric, this figure places almost before the eyes an event or object described, while in music, it evokes the image of such an object through harmony, rhythm, melody, and texture.[28]

In the course of his treatise, Burmeister defines and illustrates more than twenty figures.[29] Nevertheless, as Heinz Brandes, Brian Vickers,[30] and others have pointed out, the figures of Burmeister and other musical writers are not truly comparable with those of verbal rhetoric because most literary figures—apart from a few formal techniques, such as inversion of word-order—are tied up with the meanings of the words being manipulated, while pitches and rhythmic units and their combinations bear no literal semantic signifier. Of course, Burmeister could not have been so naive as to believe that the musical figures to which he gave the traditional names were identical or even obviously parallel to their verbal models. Throughout his treatise, where he could find a classical Greek or Latin term or one he could coin out of these languages that described a musical technique, he preferred such a term to the Latin commonly used. For example, he wrote "antiphonum" instead of "contrapunctus" for polyphony or counterpoint and "syntaxis" for the method of combining melodic lines commonly called counterpoint. Rather than invent an

---

[28]Burmeister, *Musical Poetics*, 158–77 (ch. 12).

[29]For a useful synopsis, see Burmeister, *Musical Poetics*, xxxviii–xlv. See also Bartel, *Musica poetica*, 93–99.

[30]Heinz Brandes, *Studien zur musikalischen Figurenlehre im 16. Jahrhundert* (Berlin: Triltsch & Huther, 1935); Brian Vickers, *In Defence of Rhetoric* (Oxford: Clarendon, 1988), 341–74 (ch. 7: "Rhetoric and the Sister Arts"). See also n. 8 *supra*.

entirely original terminology for the musical techniques he identified, he sought terms in rhetoric already familiar to students that would recall musical procedures resembling—sometimes only remotely—those similarly named in literature. By giving them names, Burmeister could elicit from students and readers images of distinctive devices that previously lacked conventional labels and often were not even recognized as compositional strategies.

Burmeister capped his treatment of musical rhetoric with an analysis of Lasso's motet *In me transierunt*.[31] This analysis is important not only because it shows the pervasiveness in Lasso's music of the figures Burmeister identifies but also because it is a rare early specimen of a multifaceted step-by-step technical analysis of an entire piece of music for the purpose of teaching composition. Rather than repeating here Burmeister's exegesis of this piece, which he chose because it is loaded with figurative writing, we may observe the dynamic interaction between grammar or rhetoric and music in a setting by Lasso for five voices of a secular Latin poem by the Neapolitan humanist and philosopher Giovanni Pontano (1426–1503), *Cum rides mihi*.[32]

Burmeister, perhaps because of his position as an ecclesiastical musician, confined his repertory of examples to sacred music and singled out Lasso's motets as most worthy of emulation for their rhetorical gestures. *Cum rides mihi*, sometimes classified as a motet, is clearly secular. The text and a translation of Pontano's verses follow:

---

[31]*Sacrae cantiones quinque vocum* (Nuremberg: J. Montanus & U. Neuber, 1562), ed. in Orlando di Lasso, *Sämtliche Werke*, ed. Franz X. Haberl and A. Sandberger, 21 vols. (Leipzig: Breitkopf & Härtel, 1894–1926), 9:49–52. The motet is transcribed into modern score and the analysis discussed in Palisca, "*Ut oratoria musica*," 37–65; reprinted in idem, *Studies*, 282–309.

[32]*Moduli*, for 4 to 9 voices (Paris: Le Roy & Ballard, 1577), ed. in Orlando di Lasso, *Sämtliche Werke, Neue Reihe*, ed. S. Hermelink, W. Boetticher, etc. (Kassel: Bärenreiter, 1956–), 1:23–31.

Cum rides mihi, basium negasti,	When you laugh at me, you have denied me a kiss.
cum ploras mihi, basium dedisti,	When you cry for me, you have granted me a kiss.
una in tristitia libens benigna es,	In sorrow you are at once willing and obliging.
una in laetitia volens severa es.	In joy you are at once desirous and stern.
Data est de lachrymis mihi voluptas, de risu dolor, o miselli amantes.	Pleasure is given to me by tears, pain by laughter. O wretched lovers,
Sperate simul omnia et timete.	together hope and fear everything.

The poem itself is highly figurative, with parallel clauses (*isocolon*), similar beginnings (*anaphora*) and endings (*homoioteleuton*) in the first and second and in the third and fourth lines, *antitheses* in every line, a return to the thoughts of the first four lines in the fifth and sixth (*epanodos* or *regressio*), and an *apostrophe* to all lovers at the end.

Lasso's setting reflects the rhetorical structure and figures of the poem and in addition employs musical means to evoke the feeling of each hemistich. A possible analysis of the grammatical, rhetorical, and text-expressive aspects of the first four lines of this song is presented in the following paragraphs.

Figure 12. Orlando di Lasso, *Cum rides mihi*, mm. 1–3

Figure 12 (cont'd). Orlando di Lasso, *Cum rides mihi*, mm. 4–9

The syllable "ri" of "rides" receives a melodic flourish suggesting laughter (*hypotyposis*) that dominates the opening subject of this fugue, from which one voice (the Tenor) departs (*anaphora*) by omitting the opening leap of an ascending fourth. This *exordium* ends in m. 9 with a strong formal cadence, where all the voices unite in a fully voiced chord on *G*, the central tonality. The ascending fourth, which appears in the Bassus at the cadence, was characterized by Vincenzo Galilei in his *Dialogo della musica antica, et della moderna* as happy and excited.[33]

---

[33]Galilei, *Dialogo*, 76; trans. *Dialogue*, 185.

Figure 13. Orlando di Lasso, *Cum rides mihi,* mm. 10–12

In figure 13, the voices sing almost note-against-note in the declamatory style Burmeister called *noëma.* The accidental notes B♭, and C♯, neither in the mode of the piece (Mode 7, or Mixolydian) introduce a plaintive semitone motion (*pathopoeia*). The passage ends with an uncertain cadence in which the lowest sounding note of the harmony rises a fifth (moving from the *d* in the Bassus to the *a* in the Tenor), a motion Galilei characterized as sad.[34]

Figure 14. Orlando di Lasso, *Cum rides mihi,* mm. 13–15

---

[34]Ibid.

Figure 14 (cont'd). Orlando di Lasso, *Cum rides mihi*, mm. 16–21

The hemistich in figure 14 parallels "cum rides mihi," the opening line, and constitutes a literary *isocolon*. By once again using the same succession *fuga-noëma* as he used at the beginning, Lasso indicates that he recognizes the figure. All five voices now participate in the fugue, which is therefore a *fuga realis*. The melody for "cum ploras" exploits the semitone *Bb-A* as well as the semitones *C–B* and *F–E* (again *pathopoeia*). Most of the entries follow a minim rest (a half note rest in the transcription), which produces the effect of a sigh (*hypotyposis*). The passage concludes with a device Burmeister did not name but which later analysts called *stretto*, with the voices entering in close, overlapping imitation.[35] An

[35]Meinrad Spiess in *Tractatus musicus compositorio-practicus* (Augsburg: Johan Jacob Lotter Erben, 1745), 134, describes this technique: "In den Fugen ... wird die

otherwise strong cadence (m. 21) in which the Bassus moves down a tone and the Quintus up a semitone—the major sixth going to the octave—is weakened and made doleful by the descending semitone of the Superius.

Figure 15. Orlando di Lasso, *Cum rides mihi*, mm. 22–25

The passage in figure 15 parallels the declamatory section on "basium negasti" (mm. 10–12), except that the Superius and Quintus exchange

gröste *Force* mit vollstimmiger *Constringit-Repetit*-und *Imitirung* des *Thematis, Subjecti,* & c. gebraucht zu Ende der Composition." The passage is quoted in Gregory G. Butler, "Fugue and Rhetoric," *Journal of Music Theory* 21 (1977): 97. Butler relates the device to the rhetorical *constrictio,* a compressed drawing together of the main points at the end of a presentation of arguments (the *confirmatio*) in an oration, immediately before the peroration. On Spiess, see also Bartel, *Musica poetica,* 144–48.

parts and both the Superius and Bassus are given generally ascending lines to suggest the positive sense of "granted" (*dedisti*) as opposed to the descending direction of the first line's "denied" (*negasti*). To close Pontano's first couplet, the passage culminates in m. 25 with the strongest cadence thus far, formed with an octave between the Bassus and Superius on the fifth degree of the mode and reached by the Bassus falling a fifth, a movement characterized by Galilei as joyful.[36]

Figure 16. Orlando di Lasso, *Cum rides mihi*, mm. 25–30

---

[36]Galilei, *Dialogo*, 76; trans. *Dialogue*, 185.

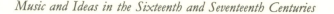

Figure 16 (cont'd). Orlando di Lasso, *Cum rides mihi*, mm. 31–37

Since no comma interrupts this line, it is set as a unit (figure 16). The Tenor intrudes offbeat in m. 25 with a new subject, overlapping the cadence ending the preceding line, perhaps naively suggesting the "one" (*una*) of the text (*hypotyposis*). This period is freely fugal with two subjects (*metalepsis*). For a sorrowful effect at "tristitia," Lasso altered the *B* to *B♭* in m. 27 (*pathopoeia*) and introduced a deliberate cross- or false-relation (*F-B*) between the Tenor and Bassus in mm. 27–28, a device repeated prominently at "libens benigna" in mm. 32–33 (between the b' in the Superius and the f' in the Tenor) and 35–36 (between the e" in the Superius and the b♭' in the Cantus). Burmeister did not give a name to this device, prohibited by Zarlino,[37] who called it a non-harmonic rela-

---

[37]Zarlino, *Istituzioni* (1558), 179–81, 195–99 (bk. 3, chs. 30 and 42).

tion. The last repetition of "libens benigna" brings all the parts together in a "plagal" cadence.

In figure 17, the Bassus enters alone on "una" (paralleling the Tenor's earlier *hypotyposis*). Lasso split this line into two parts because of its contrary affections. "Una in laetitia" receives two subjects, each beginning with two measures of sprightly movement (*hypotyposis*), for a double fugue (*metalepsis*). Because there is no comma, Lasso carefully elided the two halves of the line through the evaded cadence[38] at m. 45. The rigor of "volens severa" is portrayed with a succession (*pleonasmus*) of syncopations, suspensions (termed *syncope* or *syneresis* by Burmeister), and harsh progressions of the major sixth to the fifth.[39] This type of progression is noted as an expressive license by Galilei—because the major sixth should always resolve to the octave[40]—but not by Burmeister. In keeping with the lover's complaint, Lasso chose a plagal cadence to bring the first *pars* of the composition to a close.

Without analyzing closely the *secunda pars*, it is worth pointing out that the last line, "sperate simul omnia et timete," contains a musical antithesis similar to that of the fourth line, shifting from a homorhythmic section in joyful sprightly tempo with some graceful runs on "sperate" (hope) to a foreboding slow progression on "timete" (fear), the latter conveyed by a chain of syncopations and suspensions, which pile up at the end (*pleonasmus*) to prepare the final cadence.

---

[38]Burmeister did not give a name to this important device, which was compared to a rhetorical figure by Francis Bacon: "Is not the Trope of Musicke, to auoyde or slyde from the close or Cadence, common with the Trope of Rhetoricke of deceyuing expectation?" *The Tvvoo Bookes Of the Proficiencie and Aduancement of Learning diuine and humane* (London: Henrie Tomes, 1605), ff. 21v–22r. Descartes (*Musicae compendium*, 55) also saw in such an evasion a rhetorical figure: "... sed etiam in medio cantilenae, huius cadentiae fuga non parvam affert delectationem, cum scilicet vna pars velle videtur quiescere, alia autem vlterius procedit. Atque hoc est genus figurae in Musica, quales sunt figurae Rhetoricae in oratione; ... [... in the midst of a vocal composition, the evasion of such a cadence (ending on an octave or fifth preceded by a suspension) gives no little pleasure, as when a part seems to want to rest, while another proceeds onward. This is a kind of figure in music like the figures of rhetoric in oratory ...]."

[39]In mm. 46–47, the intervals between the Bassus and the Cantus; in mm. 48–49, the intervals between the Bassus and the Tenor.

[40]Vincenzo Galilei, *Fronimo dialogo* (Venice: G. Scotto, 1568), 13.

Figure 17. Orlando di Lasso, *Cum rides mihi*, mm. 37–45

Figure 17 (cont'd). Orlando di Lasso, *Cum rides mihi*, mm. 46–52

Lasso treated this text as would an orator, measuring carefully his phrases, punctuation, and pauses, altering his manner of expression with each phrase to sway the listener to the sentiments he aimed to arouse, emphasizing words that are charged with feeling and meaning. This is a triumph of the union of grammar, rhetoric, poetry, and music, the new quartet of arts, a new quadrivium.

Burmeister's method for analyzing a piece of vocal polyphony admirably suits the manneristic approach to composition common in madrigals and motets of the last half of the sixteenth century. It is one of the ironies of history that as soon as a practice matures and becomes sufficiently stable to support a theory, the theory loses its relevance as a guide to composition because of changing taste. Although polyphonic motets and madrigals continued to be written after 1606, younger composers were turning to composition for solo voices with basso continuo, to which only few of the artifices described by Burmeister's figures are applicable.

Nevertheless, German music theorists continued to name new figures as well as redefining some of the terms Burmeister introduced.[41] For example, Johannes Nucius (ca. 1556–1620) in his *Musices poeticæ siue De compositione cantûs* (1613) proposes *complexio*, in which the end of a polyphonic piece repeats the beginning, as in Lasso's motet *Domine Dominus noster*.[42] As a literary example, he offers Vergil's line (*Eclogue* 7), "Ambo florentes aetatibus, Arcades ambo" (Both young, Arcadians both). Nucius seems intent on pinning terms to familiar procedures rather than offering young composers creative options and paths to artful invention, as Burmeister had tried to do. Nucius's definition of the musical *homoioteleuton* is particularly insensitive to literary usage, in which it refers to rhymes or similar line-endings; Nucius associates the figure with a simultaneous rest in all the parts.[43]

By contrast, the cosmopolitan German Athanasius Kircher, residing in Rome and receiving reports from fellow Jesuits all over the world, was more closely in touch with the newer monodic styles and saw the relevance of rhetorical figures to current compositional practice.[44] He admired Carissimi, for example, for his ability to move the affections, and he dwells on this power of rhetoric. Although not all the figures he names are necessarily expressive,[45] he states his position forcefully:

---

[41]Hans-Heinrich Unger in *Die Beziehungen zwischen Musik und Rhetoric im 16.–18. Jahrhundert* (Würzburg: K. Triltsch, 1941), 151–54, lists 163 figures, either musical or potentially musical, proposed by various German authors. For a thorough study of German sources and definitions and translations of the musical-rhetorical figures, see also Bartel, *Musica poetica*, passim.

[42]Lasso, *Sämtliche Werke*, 17:39–42. The first six measures are repeated with the same text at the end.

[43]On Nucius, see Bartel, *Musica poetica*, 99–103.

[44]See Eugenio Lo Sardo, "Kircher's Rome," in *Athanasius Kircher: The Last Man Who Knew Everything*, ed. Paula Findlen (New York: Routledge, 2004), 51–62; and Bartel, *Musica poetica*, 106–11.

[45]For a listing see Scharlau, *Athanasius Kircher*, p. 243, n. 3.

Just as rhetoric through various arguments and reasons as through the complex of various figures and tropes now delights, now saddens, now provokes anger, pity, indignation, revenge, vehement passion and other affections, and, in sum, inclines the consenting listener completely to whatever commotion the orator intends, so music through the construction of a variety of musical periods excites the soul to diverse states.[46]

The three principal general affections moved in this way, he continues, are joy, piety, and compassion, all of which have many subcategories, such as love, desire, modesty, and religious devotion. Like his compatriots, Kircher succumbs to the temptation to name some of the graphic patterns that the monodists took over from the polyphonic composers, such as ascending lines (*anabasis*) when the text mentions upward movement, descending effects (*catabasis*) for the opposite, and circular melodic patterns (*kyklosis* or *circulatio*) for ideas of turning and returning.[47]

The German author who most successfully made the transition to a musical rhetoric suited to seventeenth-century styles is Christoph Bernhard, a composer who worked closely with Heinrich Schütz in Dresden, though his repertory of figures was primarily derived from his knowledge of Italian music gained during his sojourns in Rome, which brought him into contact with the music of Carissimi, Luigi Rossi, and their contemporaries. He left three treatises, "Von der Singe-Kunst oder Manier," "Tractatus compositionis augmentatus" (written in German despite its Latin title), and "Ausführlicher Bericht vom Gebrauche der Con- und Dissonantien." Though not published until recently, Bernhard's treatises enjoyed a limited readership in the seventeenth and eighteenth centuries through manuscript copies.[48]

---

[46]Kircher, *Musurgia universalis*, 2:142 (bk. 8, § 2): "Sicuti Rhetorica varijs argumentis & rationibus veluti per figurarum troporumque varium contextum animum nunc delectat, nunc contristat, nunc ad iracundiam, iam ad commiserationem, modò ad indignationem, vindictam, impetus vehementes, aliosque affectus prouocat, & denique peracta mentis commotione tandem ad id, quod Orator intendit, consentiendum Auditorem inclinat. Ita & Musica pro vario periodorum contextu tonorumque diuersa dispositione, variè animum agitat...."

[47]Ibid., 2:145 (bk. 8, ch. 8, § 8).

[48]See chapter 9, n. 20 and pp. 175–76 *supra*. All the treatises are translated with a preface and notes by Walter Hilse in "Treatises of Christoph Bernhard," 1–196. For a further examination of Bernhard's theory, see Hellmut Federhofer,

Bernhard observed in the music of his time a proliferation of figures, brought on partly by the recitative style:

> In our times, the art of music has reached such a high level, it may well be compared to a *rhetorica* on account of the great quantity of figures, especially lately in the increasingly embellished *stylus recitativus.*[49]

Unlike Burmeister, Nucius, and others, Bernhard did not draw his terminology from classical rhetoric but rather invented most of the descriptive Latin names for his *figurae melopoeticae.*[50] Some, he says, call them *licentiae*—licenses. Like many of the tropes and figures of rhetoric, most of Bernhard's figures are in fact licenses, exceptions to the normal rules of good writing. As Quintilian remarked: "every figure of this kind would be an error, if it were accidental and not deliberate."[51] Bernhard defines *figura* as "a way of employing dissonances that renders them not only inoffensive but altogether agreeable, displaying the art of the composer."[52]

A highly original feature of Bernhard's treatise on composition is his reduction of passages from their figurative, embellished form to a primitive contrapuntal framework that follows the rules of the *stile antico* or *stile grave.* This process of reduction to a correct skeletal counterpoint has attracted the attention of followers of Heinrich Schenker's analytical method, which depends very much on reducing complex music to a hypothetical simple "background" level of "voice leading."[53]

"Christoph Bernhards Figurenlehre und die Dissonanz," *Die Musikforschung* 42 (1989): 110–27.

[49]Müller-Blattau, *Kompositionslehre*, 147 ("Ausführliche Bericht," ch. 13): "Biß daß auff unsere Zeiten die *Musica* so hoch kommen, daß wegen Menge der *Figuren*, absonderlich aber in dem neu erfundenen und bisher immer mehr ausgezierten *Stylo recitativo*, sie wohl einer *Rhetorica* zu vergleichen."

[50]Ibid., 42–43 ("Tractatus compositionis," ch. 3, § 9).

[51]Quintilian *Institutio oratoria* 9.3: "Esset enim omne schema vitium, si non peteretur, sed accideret."

[52]Müller-Blattau, *Kompositionslehre*, 63 ("Tractatus compositionis," ch. 16): "*Figuram* nenne ich eine gewiße Art die *Dissonantzen* zu gebrauchen, daß dieselben nicht allein nicht wiederlich, sondern vielmehr annehmlich werden, und des *Componisten* Kunst an den Tag legen."

[53]This mainly accounts for the dedication of most of the third volume of the movement's journal, *Music Forum*, to a translation of Bernhard's three treatises. See chapter 9, n. 36.

Bernhard divides the figures into those serving the *stylus gravis*, the "severe" or strict style of conventional a capella sacred polyphony, and those used in the *stylus luxurians* (flamboyant style), which in turn is divided into *communis* and *theatralis*. The figures of the severe style may be described briefly in modern terms as: *transitus*, a dissonant passing note; *quasi-transitus*, an accented dissonant passing note; *syncopatio*, a dissonant suspension; and *quasi-syncopatio*, a suspension in which the dissonant note is repeated either on or just before the beat. Except for the last, all these are allowed by the rules of sixteenth-century counterpoint.[54]

The licenses of the *stylus luxurians*, more noticeable because impermissible in strict counterpoint, started to creep into the late madrigals of the *seconda pratica*. They are most at home in monodic vocal music with thoroughbass accompaniment, where a dissonance may grate against the chord demanded by the basso continuo, as distinct from dissonant intervals between two parts in strict counterpoint. It is to Bernhard's credit that he recognized most of the "non-harmonic tones" now canonized in modern textbooks of common-practice harmony.

Many of the figures of the *stylus luxurians communis* may be compactly described in modern terms: *superjectio*, an upper escape-note or *échappé* that rises a step before leaping down to a consonance; *anticipatio*, a dissonant anticipation of a consonant note; *subsumptio*, a lower escape-note or *échappé*; *variatio*, a pattern of runs and turns embellishing the notes of a melody; *multiplicatio*, a repetition of the dissonant note in a figure; *prolongatio*, extending the duration of a dissonant note; *syncopatio catachrestica*, an irregular resolution of a suspension; *passus duriusculus*, half-step motion; *saltus duriusculus*, a dissonant leap, such as by an augmented fourth; *mutatio modi*, a change of mode or modulation; *inchoatio imperfecta*, beginning a composition on other than a perfect consonance; *longinqua distantia*, leaving a wide pitch-space between voices; *consonantiae impropriae*, perfect, augmented, and diminished fourths, diminished and augmented fifths, diminished seventh, and augmented second; *quaesitio notae*, approaching a consonance by a leap to a dissonant note immediately below or, rarely, above; and *cadentiae duriusculae*, cadences that contain unusual dissonances.[55]

---

[54]Müller-Blattau, *Kompositionslehre*, 63–70 ("Tractatus compositionis," chs. 16–20).

[55]Ibid., 71–82 ("Tractatus compositionis," chs. 21–34).

The *stylus luxurians theatralis* (flamboyant theatrical style) comprehends the boldest dissonance usages, those applied in the recitative style (*stylus recitativus* or *oratorius*). Whereas in the severe style, "harmony is the mistress of the text" and in the *luxurians communis* style "both the text and the harmony are mistress," in the theatrical style "the text is the absolute mistress of the harmony."[56] This gives the theatrical style the greatest freedom to transgress the norms of dissonance usage. From the earliest examples of Jacopo Peri, the recitative style allowed the free introduction of dissonances to imitate speech and to heighten emotional expression.[57]

Bernhard gives Latin names as well to the devices that evolved in theatrical recitative: *extensio*, lingering on a dissonant note over numerous beats, as when several syllables are sung on a dissonance that could be interpreted, for example, as a *transitus*; *ellipsis*, omission of the consonance that would normally resolve a dissonance; *mora*, resolution of a suspended dissonance by rising instead of descending a step; *abruptio*, interrupting by a rest the resolution of a dissonance; *transitus inversus*, an accented passing dissonance, usually prolonged through *multiplicatio*; and *heterolepsis*, a leap to a dissonance in an imagined neighboring voice part.[58]

Bernhard's successors added little to the repertory of dissonant figures before Johann David Heinichen systematized the theory of nonharmonic tones.[59] German authors continued, however, to add to the nomenclature of figures in general and to speculate about the relationship of music to rhetoric. In the eighteenth century, the general trend was

---

[56]Ibid., 83 ("Tractatus compositionis," ch. 35): "Und wiel in diesem *Genere* [*Stylo theatrali*] die *Oratio Harmoniae Domina absolutissima*, so wie in *Stylo gravi Harmonia Orationis Domina* und in *luxuriante communi* sowohl *Oratio* als *Harmonia Domina* ist, also rühret daher diese *General* Regel, daß man die Rede aufs natürlichste *exprimiren* solle." These formulations, deriving from Giulio Cesare Monteverdi, are obvious paraphrases of those in Scacchi's *Cribrum musicum* (1643) and *Breve discorso sopra la musica moderna* (1649). See chapter 9 *supra*. A native of Danzig, Bernhard probably knew Scacchi's writings through Christoph Werner, choirmaster of St. Catherine, with whom he probably studied.

[57]See chapter 7 *supra*.

[58]Müller-Blattau, *Kompositionslehre*, 83–89 ("Tractatus compositionis," chs. 36–41).

[59]Heinichen, *General-Bass in der Composition*; and Buelow, *Thorough-Bass Accompaniment According to J. D. Heinichen*.

toward a rhetorical description of musical form, leaving the expressive functions, which tended toward broader gestures, to the new field of aesthetics.[60]

---

[60]For figures such as Wolfgang Caspar Printz (1641–1717), Johann Georg Ahle (1651–1706), Tomáš Baltazar Janovka (1669–1741), Mauritius Johann Vogt (1669–1730), Johann Gottfried Walther (1684–1748), Johann Mattheson (1681–1764), Meinrad Spiess (1683–1761), Johann Adolf Scheibe (1708–1776), and Johann Nikolaus Forkel (1748–1818), see Bartel, *Musica poetica*, 119–64. On the relationship between rhetoric and music in the eighteenth century, see Leonard G. Ratner, *Classic Music: Expression, Form, and Style* (New York: Schirmer Books, 1980); Kofi Agawu, *Playing with Signs: A Semiotic Interpretation of Classic Music* (Princeton, NJ: Princeton University Press, 1991); and Wye J. Allanbrook, "Theorizing the Comic Surface," in *Music in the Mirror: Reflections on the History of Music Theory and Literature for the 21st Century*, ed. Andreas Giger and Thomas J. Mathiesen, Publications of the Center for the History of Music Theory and Literature, vol. 3 (Lincoln: University of Nebraska Press, 2002), 195–216.

❧ APPENDIX ❧

Principal Treatises Cited (arranged in approximate chronological order by date of composition or publication)[1]

d. 347 B.C.E.	Plato. See Ficino (1491) and (1532) *infra.*
d. 322 B.C.E.	Aristotle. See d'Abano (1475) *infra.*
ca. 300 B.C.E.	Euclid. See 1482 *infra.*
1st century B.C.E.	Cicero. *De oratore, De re publica, De legibus, Tusculanae disputationes*
1st–2d century C.E.	Nicomachus of Gerasa. *Manuale Harmonices*
129–ca. 200 (?)	Galen. *De naturalibus facultatibus, De animae passionibus.*
3d–4th century	Aristides Quintilianus. *De musica.*
ca. 317–388	Themistius. See 1535 *infra.*
ca. 430	Macrobius. *In somnium Scipionis.*
6th century	Boethius. *De institutione arithmetica libri duo; De institutione musica libri quinque.*
9th century	*Alia musica* (ed. Chailley).
ca. 900	*Musica et scolica enchiriadis* (ed. Schmid).
10th century (?)	*Anonymi scriptio de musica* (ed. Bellermann, Najock).
ca. 1026	Guido of Arezzo. *Micrologus.*
d. after 1078	Psellus, Michael. See 1532 *infra.*
ca. 1100	Johannes Affligemensis. *De musica cum tonario.*

---

[1]For full bibliographic listings of these and all other primary sources, including modern editions and translations, see Biblkiography: Primary Sources, p. 243 *ff.*

ca. 1240	Bartholomaeus Anglicus. *De proprietatibus rerum libri iii et iv.* See also 1582 *infra.*
ca. 1270	Aegidius de Zamora, Johannes. *Ars musica.*
ca. 1310	Odington, Walter. *Summa de speculatione musicae.*
betw. 1431 and 1448	Ugolino of Orvieto. *Declaratio musicae disciplinae.*
betw. 1458 and 1464	Gallicus, Johannes. *Ritus canendi.*
1475	d'Abano, Pietro. *Expositio problematum Aristotelis: cum textu ejusdem.*
1477	Tinctoris, Johannes. "Liber de arte contrapuncti."
1480	Gaffurio, Franchino. *Theoricum opus musice discipline.*
1482	Euclid. *Elementa geometriae lat[ine] cum Campani annotationibus.* Ramos de Pareja, Bartolomé. *Musica practica.*
1490	Adam of Fulda. "Musica."
1491	Plato. *Opera.* Trans. Marsilio Ficino.
1492	Gaffurio, Franchino. *Theorica musice.*
1496	d'Étaples, Jacques Lefèvre. *Musica libris demonstrata quatuor.* Gaffurio, Franchino. *Practica musice.*
1498	Albertus Magnus. *Summa de creaturis.* Valla, Giorgio. Ἐπιτομὴ λογικῆς.
d. 1499	Ficino, Marsilio. *Opera omnia.* 2 vols.
1501	Valla, Giorgio. *De expetendis et fugiendis rebus opus.*
ca. 1506	Erasmus of Höritz. "Musica."
1507	Valgulio, Carlo. *Prooemium in Musicam Plutarchi ad Titum Pyrrhinum.*
1509	Valla, Lorenzo. *De vero falsoque bono.*

1512	Valla, Lorenzo. *De voluptate ac vero bono.*
	Wollick, Nicolaus. *Enchiridion musices.*
1514	Cochlaeus, Johannes. *Tetrachordum musices.*
1518	Gaffurio, Franchino. *De harmonia musicorum instrumentorum opus.*
	Schreiber, Heinrich. *Ayn new kunstlich Buech.*
1521	Spataro, Giovanni. *Errori de Franchino Gafurio da Lodi.*
1525	Aron, Pietro. *Trattato della natura et cognitione di tutti gli tuoni di canto figurato.*
	Bembo, Pietro. *Prose … della volgar lingua.*
1529	Fogliano, Lodovico. *De musica theorica.*
1530	Agrippa, Cornelius. *De incertitudine et vanitate scientiarum et artium atque excellentia verbi Dei declamatio.*
	Valgulio, Carlo. "Plutarchi Chaeronei philosophi clarissimi, Musica. Carlo Valgulio Brixiano interprete."
1532	Plato. *Omnia opera.* Trans. Marsilio Ficino.
	Psellus, Michael. *Opus dilucidum in quatuor mathematicas disciplinas.*
1533	Lanfranco, Giovanni. *Scintille di musica.*
	Listenius, Nicolaus. *Rudimenta musicae.*
	Sadoleto, Jacopo. *De liberis recte instituendis liber.*
1535	Erasmus, Desiderius. *In Novum Testamentum annotationes.*
	Themistius. *Paraphraseos de anima libri tres, interprete Hermolao Barbaro, nunc recens mendis non oscitanter repurgati, & accurata diligentia typis excusi.*
1537	Listenius, Nicolaus. *Musica.*
1538	Sadoleto, Jacopo. *De pueris recte ac liberaliter instituendis.*
	Vives, Juan Luis. *De anima et vita libri tres.*

1540	del Lago, Giovanni. *Breve introduttione di musica misurata.*
1547	Glarean, Heinrich. *ΔΩΔΕΚΑΧΟΡΔΟΝ* [Dodecachordon].
1540s	Mei, Girolamo. "Della compositura delle parole."
1552	Lossius, Lucas. *Erotemata dialecticae et rhetoricae Philippi Melanchthonis et praeceptionum Erasmi Roterodami.*
1555	Bermudo, Juan. *Declaración de instrumentos musicales.*
	Tyard, Ponthus de. *Solitaire second, ou Prose de la musique.*
	Vicentino, Nicola. *L'Antica musica ridotta alla moderna prattica.*
1556	Finck, Hermann. *Practica musica, exempla variorum signorum, proportionum et canonum, iudicium de tonis, ac quaedam de arte suaviter et artificiose cantandi continens.*
1558	Zarlino, Gioseffo. *Le Istitutioni harmoniche.*
1560	Vettori, Piero. *Commentarii in primum librum Aristotelis de arte poetarum.*
1562	Trissino, Giovanni Giorgio. *La quinta e la sesta divisione della poetica.*
1563–64	Dressler, Gallus. *Præcepta musicæ poëticæ.*
1567	Barbaro, Daniele. *I dieci libri dell'architettura di M. Vitruvio tradotti e commentati.*
1568	Galilei, Vincenzo. *Fronimo dialogo.*
1569	Mercuriale, Girolamo. *Artis gymnasticae apvd antiqvos celeberrimae ... libri sex.*
1573	Mei, Girolamo. "De modis." Rome, Bibliotheca Apostolica Vaticana, lat. 5323.
1574	Fracastoro, Girolamo. *Opera omnia in unum proxime post illius mortem collecta.*

1577	Salinas, Francisco de. *De Musica libri Septem, in quibus eius doctrinae veritas tam quae ad Harmoniam, quam quae ad Rhythmum pertinet, iuxta sensus ac rationis iudicium ostenditur, et demonstratur.*
1578	Bardi, Giovanni. "Discorso mandato a Giulio Caccini detto romano sopra la musica e 'l cantar bene."
1581	Galilei, Vincenzo. *Dialogo della musica antica, et della moderna.*
1582 (?)	Bardi (?), Giovanni. "[Discorso come si debba recitar Tragedia]."
1582	Batman. *Batman vppon Bartholome, his booke De proprietatibus rerum.* See also ca. 1240 *supra*.
1585	Benedetti, Giovanni Battista. *Diversarum speculationum mathematicarum et physicarum liber.*
1586	Bright, Timothie. *A Treatise of Melancholy ... with Diuerse Philosophicall Discourses Touching Actions and Affections of Soule, Spirit and Body.* Patrizi, Francesco. *Della Poetica, La deca disputata.*
1588	Pontio, Pietro. *Ragionamento di musica.* Tigrini, Orazio. *Il compendio della musica nel quale brevemente si tratta dell'arte del contrapunto, diviso in quatro libri.*
1588	Zarlino, Gioseffo. *Sopplimenti musicali.*
1589	Artusi, Giovanni Maria. *Seconda parte dell'arte del contraponto. Nella quale si tratta dell' utile et uso delle dissonanze. Divisa in due libri.* Galilei, Vincenzo. *Discorso intorno all'opere di Messer Gioseffo Zarlino da Chioggia, et altri importanti particolari attenenti alla musica.*

betw. 1588 and 1591	Galilei, Vincenzo. "Discorso particolare intorno all'unisono."
	——. "Discorso particolare intorno alla diversità delle forme del Diapason."
	——. "Discorso di Vincentio Galilei intorno all'uso delle dissonanze."
	——. "Il primo libro della prattica del contrapunto intorno all'uso delle consonanze."
1590–91	Galilei, Vincenzo. "Discorso di Vincentio Galilei intorno all'uso dell'enharmonio, et di chi fusse autore del cromatico."
	——. "Dubbi intorno a quanto io ho detto all'uso dell'enharmonio, con la solutione di essi."
1592	Calvisius, Seth. ΜΕΛΟΠΟΙΙΑ *sive melodiae condendae ratio, quam vulgo musicam poeticam vocant, ex veris fundamentis extructa et explicata.*
	Zacconi, Lodovico. *Prattica di musica utile et necessaria si al compositore per comporre i canti suoi regolatamente, si anco al cantore per assicurarsi in tutte le cose cantabili. Divisa in quattro libri.*
1594	Benelli, Alemanno [Ercole Bottrigari]. *Il Desiderio overo de' concerti di varii strumenti musicali.*
1597	Giacomini, Lorenzo. *Orationi e discorsi.*
	Morley, Thomas. *A Plaine and Easie Introduction to Practicall Musicke.*
1599	Burmeister, Joachim. *Hypomnematum musicae poeticae … synopsis.*
1600	Artusi, Giovanni Maria. *L'Artusi ouero delle imperfettioni della moderna mvsica.*
1601	Banchieri, Adriano. *Cartella overo regole utilissime à quelli che desiderano imparare il canto figurato.*
1601	Burmeister, Joachim. *Musica αὐτοσχεδιαστικὴ quae per aliquot accessiones in gratiam philomusorum … in unum corpusculum concrevit.*

	Wright, Thomas. *The Passions of the Minde.*
1603	Artusi, Giovanni Maria. *Seconda parte dell'Artusi ouero delle imperfettioni della moderna musica, nella quale si tratta de' molti abusi introdotti da i moderni scrittori, et compositori.*
1605	Bacon, Francis. *The Tvvoo Bookes Of the Proficiencie and Aduancement of Learning diuine and humane.*
	Banchieri, Adriano. *L'organo suonarino.*
1606	Burmeister, Joachim. *Musica poetica: Definitionibus et divisionibus breviter delineata, quibus in singulis capitibus sunt hypomnemata praeceptionum instar sunoptik«w addita.*
1607	Agazzari, Agostino. *Del sonare sopra'l basso con tutti li stromenti e dell'uso loro nel conserto.*
1613	Cerone, Pietro. *El melopeo y maestro: Tractado de música theorica y pratica.*
1619	Kepler, Johannes. *Harmonices mundi libri V.*
1622	Zacconi, Lodovico. *Prattica di musica seconda parte. Divisa, e distinta in quattro libri.*
1623	Galilei, Galileo. *Il Saggiatore.*
	Mersenne, Marin. *Quaestiones celeberrimae in Genesim, cum accurata textus explicatione; in hoc volumine athei et deistae impugnantur et expugnantur, et Vulgata editio ab haereticorum calumniis vindicatur, Graecorum et Hebraeorum musica instauratur.*
1625	Mersenne, Marin. *La verité des sciences contre les sceptiques ou Pyrrhoniens.*
1630s (early)	Doni, Giovanni Battista. "Trattato de' generi e de' modi della musica." Bologna, Civico Museo Bibliografico Musicale, D 143.
1635	Doni, Giovanni Battista. *Compendio del Trattato de' generi e de' modi della musica.*

1636	Mersenne, Marin. *Harmonicorum libri in quibus agitur de sonorum natura, causis, et effectibus* .... 2 parts.
1636–37	Mersenne, Marin. *Harmonie universelle.* 8 parts.
1638	Galilei, Galileo. *Discorsi e dimostrazioni matematiche intorno à due nuove scienze.*
1640	Doni, Giovanni Battista. *Annotazioni sopra il Compendio de' generi, e de' modi della musica.*
1641	Fenner, William. *A Treatise of the Affections, or, The Soules Pulse.*
ca. 1648	Scacchi, Marco. "Epistola ad Excellentissimum Dn. CS. Wernerum."
1649	Descartes, René. *Passions de l'âme.* Scacchi, Marco. *Breve discorso sopra la musica moderna.*
1650	Denis, Jean. *Traité de l'accord de l'espinette, avec la comparaison de son clavier à la musique vocale.* Descartes, René. *Musicae compendium.* Hobbes, Thomas. *Humane Nature, or, The Fundamental Elements of Policie: Being a Discoverie of the Faculties, Acts, and Passions of the Soul of Man, from their Original Causes.* Kircher, Athanasius. *Musurgia universalis sive ars magna consoni et dissoni in X libros digesta.* 2 vols.
ca. 1660	Hilse, Walter. "The Treatises of Christoph Bernhard." Müller-Blattau, Joseph. *Die Kompositionslehre Heinrich Schützens in der Fassung seines Schülers Christoph Bernhard.*
1667	Nivers, Guillaume-Gabriel. *Traité de la composition de musique.*
1672	Penna, Lorenzo. *Li primi albori musicali per li principianti della musica figurata; distinti in tre libri* ....

1673	Locke, Matthew. *Melothesia: or Certain General Rules for Playing upon a Continued-Bass ....*
1676	Lamy, Bernard. *L'art de bien parler.*
1677	Wallis, John. "[Of the Trembling of Consonant Strings]: Dr. Wallis's Letter to the Publisher Concerning a New Musical Discovery."
1681	Berardi, Angelo. *Ragionamenti musicali.*
1683	Rousseau, Jean. *Méthode claire, certaine et facile pour apprendre à chanter la musique sur les tons transposez comme sur les naturels.*
1687	Berardi, Angelo. *Documenti armonici ... nelli quali con varii discorsi, regole, et essempii si demostrano gli studii artefiosi della musica, oltre il modo di usare le ligature, e d'intendere il valore di ciascheduna figura.*
1694	Playford, John. *An Introduction to the Skill of Musick.* 12th ed.
1697	Werckmeister, Andreas. *Hypomnemata musica oder Musicalisches Memorial.*
1699	Masson, Charles. *Nouveau traité des regles pour la composition de la musique.*
1704	Lecerf de la Viéville, Jean-Laurent. *Comparaison de la musique italienne et la musique françoise.*
1708	Gasparini, Francesco. *L'armonico pratico al cimbalo ....*
1717	Lang, Franz. *Theatrum affectuum humanorum, sive, Considerationes morales ad scenam accommodatae: et in oratorio almae sodalitatis majoris B.V. Mariae ab angelo salutatae matris propitiae.*
1719	Dubos, Jean-Baptiste. *Refléxions critiques sur la poësie et sur la peinture.*
	Sauveur, Joseph. "Système général des intervalles des sons."
1722	Rameau, Jean-Philippe. *Traité de l'harmonie réduite à ses principes naturels.*

1726	Rameau, Jean-Philippe. *Nouveau systeme de musique théorique.*
1728	Heinichen, Johann David. *Der General-Bass in der Composition.*
ca. 1728	North, Roger. *Musical Grammarian.*
1739	Mattheson, Johann. *Der vollkommene Capellmeister.*
1743	Batteux, Charles. *Les beaux arts réduits à un même principe.*
1745	Spiess, Meinrad. *Tractatus musicus compositorio-practicus.*
1751–72	d'Alembert, Jean Le Rond, and Denis Diderot, eds. *Encyclopédie, ou dictionnaire raisonné des sciences, des arts et des metiers.* 28 vols.
1779	Chabanon, Michel-Paul Guy de. *Observations sur la musique et principalement sur la metaphysique de l'art.*

❧ BIBLIOGRAPHY ☙

Primary Sources (including editions and translations)

Adam of Fulda. "Musica." In *Scriptores ecclesiastici de musica sacra potissimum*, 3 vols., ed. Martin Gerbert, 3:329–81. St. Blaise: Typis San-Blasianis, 1784; reprint, Hildesheim: Olms, 1963.

Aegidius de Zamora, Johannes. *Ars musica.* Ed. Michel Robert-Tissot. Corpus scriptorum de musica, vol. 20. [Rome]: American Institute of Musicology, 1974.

Agazzari, Agostino. *Del sonare sopra'l basso con tutti li stromenti e dell'uso loro nel conserto.* Siena: Domenico Falcini, 1607.

Agrippa, Cornelius. *De incertitudine et vanitate scientiarum et artium atque excellentia verbi Dei declamatio.* Antwerp: Joan. Grapheus, 1530.

Albertus Magnus. *Summa de creaturis.* Venice: Simon de Luero, impensis Andree Toresani de Asula, 1498.

Allen, Michael J. B., ed. and trans. *Marsilio Ficino and the Phaedran Charioteer.* Publications of the Center for Medieval and Renaissance Studies, UCLA, vol. 14. Berkeley: University of California Press, 1981.

Arcadelt, Jacobus. *Opera omnia.* 10 vols. Ed. Albert Seay. Corpus mensurabilis musicae, vol. 31. [n.p.]: American Institute of Musicology, 1965–70.

Aristides Quintilianus. *On Music in Three Books.* Translated with introduction and annotations by Thomas J. Mathiesen. Music Theory Translation Series. New Haven, CT: Yale University Press, 1983.

Aristotle. See d'Abano, Pietro; Marenghi, Gerardo; Themistius; Valla, Giorgio; and Vettori, Piero *infra.*

Aron, Pietro. *Trattato della natura et cognitione di tutti gli tuoni di canto figurato.* Venice: Bernardino de Vitali, 1525; reprint in Bibliotheca musica bononiensis, II/9, Bologna: Forni, 1971.

Artusi, Giovanni Maria. *L'Artusi ouero delle imperfettioni della moderna mvsica.* Venice: Giacomo Vincenti, 1600.

243

———. *Seconda parte dell'arte del contraponto. Nella quale si tratta dell' utile et uso delle dissonanze. Divisa in due libri.* Venice: Giacomo Vincenti, 1589.

———. *Seconda parte dell'Artusi ouero delle imperfettioni della moderna musica, nella quale si tratta de' molti abusi introdotti da i moderni scrittori, et compositori.* Venice: Giacomo Vincenti, 1603.

———. See also Litchfield, Malcolm *infra.*

Bacon, Francis. *The Tvvoo Bookes Of the Proficiencie and Aduancement of Learning diuine and humane.* London: Henrie Tomes, 1605.

Banchieri, Adriano. *Cartella overo regole utilissime à quelli che desiderano imparare il canto figurato.* Venice: Gaicomo Vincenti, 1601.

———. *L'organo suonarino.* Venice: Ricciardo Amadino, 1605; reprint in Bibliotheca musica bononiensis, II/31, Bologna: Forni, 1969.

Barbaro, Daniele. *I dieci libri dell'architettura di M. Vitruvio tradotti e commentati.* Venice: Francesco de' Franceschi Senese e Giovanni Chrieger Alemanno, 1567.

Bardi (?), Giovanni. "[Discorso come si debba recitar Tragedia]." In Claude V. Palisca, *The Florentine Camerata: Documentary Studies and Translations,* 140–51. Music Theory Translation Series. New Haven, CT: Yale University Press, 1989.

Bardi, Giovanni. "Discorso mandato a Giulio Caccini detto romano sopra la musica e 'l cantar bene." In Claude V. Palisca, *The Florentine Camerata: Documentary Studies and Translations,* 90–131. Music Theory Translation Series. New Haven, CT: Yale University Press, 1989.

Bartholomaeus Anglicus. *On the Properties of Soul and Body, De proprietatibus rerum libri iii et iv.* Edited from Bibliothèque nationale MS. latin 16098 by R. James Long. Toronto Medieval Latin Texts, no. 9. Toronto: Centre for Medieval Studies, Pontifical Institute of Mediaeval Studies, 1979.

Batman. *Batman vppon Bartholome, his booke De proprietatibus rerum.* London: Thomas East, 1582.

Batteux, Charles. *Les beaux arts réduits à un même principe.* Paris: Durand, 1743; reprint of 1747 ed., New York: Johnson Reprint, 1970.

Bellermann, Johann Friedrich, ed. *Anonymi scriptio de musica.* Berlin: Förstner, 1841.
        See also Najock, Dietmar *infra.*

Bembo, Pietro. *Prose ... della volgar lingua.* Venice: G. Tacuino, 1525.

Benedetti, Giovanni Battista. *Diversarum speculationum mathematicarum et physicarum liber.* Turin: Haeredes Nicolai Bevilaquae, 1585.

Benelli, Alemanno [Ercole Bottrigari]. *Il Desiderio overo de' concerti di varii strumenti musicali.* Venice: R. Amadino, 1594; reprint in Bibliotheca musica bononiensis, II/28, Bologna: Forni, 1969.

Berardi, Angelo. *Documenti armonici … nelli quali con varii discorsi, regole, et essempii si demostrano gli studii artefíciosi della musica, oltre il modo di usare le ligature, e d'intendere il valore di ciascheduna figura.* Bologna: Giacomo Monti, 1687.

———. *Ragionamenti musicali.* Bologna: Giacomo Monti, 1681.

Bermudo, Juan. *Declaración de instrumentos musicales.* Ossuna: Juan de Léon, 1555.

Bernhard, Christoph. See Hilse, Walter; and Müller-Blattau, Joseph *infra.*

Boethius, A. M. S. *De institutione arithmetica libri duo: De institutione musica libri quinque. Accedit geometria quae fertur Boetii. E libris manu scriptis.* Edidit Godofredus Friedlein, Leipzig: B. G. Teubner, 1867.

———. *Fundamentals of Music.* Translated with introduction and annotations by Calvin M. Bower. Music Theory Translation Series. New Haven, CT: Yale University Press, 1989.

———. *Hec sunt opera Boetii que in hoc volumine continentur ….* 2 vols. in 1. Venice: Johannes et Gregorius de Gregoriis de Forlivio fratres, 1492.

———. *Hec sunt opera Boetii que in hoc volumine continentur ….* 3 vols. in 1. Venice: Johannes et Gregorius de Gregoriis de Forlivio fratres, 1499.

Bottrigari, Ercole. *Il desiderio; or, Concerning the Playing together of Various Musical Instruments.* Translated by Carol MacClintock. Musicological Studies and Documents, no. 9. [Rome]: American Institute of Musicology, 1962.

Bright, Timothie. *A Treatise of Melancholy … with Diuerse Philosophicall Discourses Touching Actions and Affections of Soule, Spirit and Body.* London: John Windet, 1586.

Burmeister, Joachim. *Hypomnematum musicae poeticae … synopsis.* Rostock: S. Myliander, 1599.

———. *Musica αὐτοσχεδιαστικὴ quae per aliquot accessiones in gratiam philomusorum … in unum corpusculum concrevit.* Rostock: C. Reusner, 1601.

————. *Musica poetica: Definitionibus et divisionibus breviter delineata, quibus in singulis capitibus sunt hypomnemata praeceptionum instar sunoptik«w addita.* Rostock: S. Myliander, 1606.

————. *Musical Poetics.* Translated with introduction and annotations by Benito V. Rivera. Music Theory Translation Series. New Haven, CT: Yale University Press, 1993.

Caccini, Giulio. *L'Euridice composta in mvsica in stile rappresentatiuo.* Florence: G. Marescotti, 1600.

————. *Le Nuove musiche.* Florence: I Marescotti, 1602.
Ed. and trans. H. Wiley Hitchcock. Madison, WI: A-R Editions, 1970. See also Schmitz, Frauke *infra.*

————. *Nuove musiche e nuova maniera di scriverle.* Florence: Pigoni, 1614.
See also Schmitz, Frauke *infra.*

Calvisius, Seth. *ΜΕΛΟΠΟΙΑ sive melodiae condendae ratio, quam vulgo musicam poeticam vocant, ex veris fundamentis extructa et explicata.* Erfurt: Georg Baumann, 1592.

Campion, Thomas. *Two Bookes of Ayres.* London: Printed by Tho. Snodham, for Mathew Lownes, and I. Browne, 1613.

Cavalieri, Emilio de'. *Rappresentatione di anima, et di corpo.* Rome: Nicolò Muti, 1600.

Cavalli, Pier Francesco. *L'Egisto: Opera in Three Acts and a Prologue.* Translated by Geoffrey Dunn, Raymond Leppard, and Karl Robert Marz. Performing edition by Raymond Leppard. London: Faber; New York: Schirmer, 1977.

Cerone, Pietro. *El melopeo y maestro: Tractado de música theorica y pratica.* Naples: Juan Bautista Gargano y Lucrecio Nucci, 1613.

Chabanon, Michel-Paul Guy de. *Observations sur la musique et principalement sur la metaphysique de l'art.* Paris: Pissot, 1779; reprint, Geneva: Slatkine, 1969.

Chailley, Jacques, ed. *Alia musica (Traité de musique du IXe siècle): Edition critique commentée avec une introduction sur l'origine de la nomenclature modale pseudo-grecque au Moyen-Age.* Paris: Centre de documentation universitaire et Société d'édition d'enseignement supérieur réunis, 1965.

Cicero. *Cicero in Twenty-Eight Volumes.* Vol. 4, *De oratore, Book III; De fato; Paradoxa Stoicorum; De partitione oratoria.* Translated by Horace Rackham. Loeb Classical Library. Cambridge: Harvard University Press, l968.

———. *Cicero in Twenty-Eight Volumes.* Vol. 16, *De re publica, De legibus.* Translated by Clinton Walker Keyes. Loeb Classical Library. Cambridge: Harvard University Press, 1928.

Cochlaeus, Johannes. *Tetrachordum musices.* Nuremberg: Fridericus Peypus, 1514.

d'Abano, Pietro. *Expositio problematum Aristotelis: cum textu ejusdem.* Mantua: Paulus de Butzbach, 1475.

d'Alembert, Jean Le Rond, and Denis Diderot, eds. *Encyclopédie, ou dictionnaire raisonné des sciences, des arts et des metiers.* 28 vols. Paris: Brisson, 1751–72.

D'Avenant, William. *The Dramatic Works of Sir William D'Avenant.* 5 vols. Edinburgh: W. Paterson, 1873.

d'Étaples, Jacques Lefèvre. *Musica libris demonstrata quatuor.* Paris: Joannes Higmanus et Volgangus Hopilius, 1496.

da Vinci, Leonardo. See MacCurdy, Edward *infra.*

del Lago, Giovanni. *Breve introduttione di musica misurata.* Venice: Ottaviano Scotto, 1540; reprint in Bibliotheca musica bononiensis, II/17, Bologna: Forni, 1969.

Denis, Jean. *Traité de l'accord de l'espinette, avec la comparaison de son clavier à la musique vocale.* Paris: Ballard, 1650; reprint with introduction by Alan Curtis, New York: Da Capo, 1969.

Descartes, René. *Musicae compendium.* Utrecht: Gisbertus à Zijll & Theodorus ab Ackersdijck, 1650.

———. *Passions de l'âme.* Introduction and notes by Geneviève Rodis-Lewis. Bibliothèque des textes philosophiques. Paris: J. Vrin, 1955.

Doni, Giovanni Battista. *Annotazioni sopra il Compendio de' generi, e de' modi della musica.* Rome: Andrea Fei, 1640.

———. *Compendio del Trattato de' generi e de' modi della musica.* Rome: Andrea Fei, 1635.

———. "Trattato de' generi e de' modi della musica." Bologna, Civico Museo Bibliografico Musicale, D 143.

Dowland, John. *Second Booke of Ayres.* London: Printed by Thomas Este, the assigne of Thomas Morley, 1600.

Dressler, Gallus. *Præcepta musicæ poëticæ.* Edited and translated by O. Trachier and S. Chevalier. Centre d'Études Supérieures de la Renaissance, Collection "Épitome musical." Paris–Tours: Minerve, 2001. See also Engelke *infra.*

Dubos, Jean-Baptiste. *Refléxions critiques sur la poësie et sur la peinture*. Paris: Jean Mariette, 1719.

Engelke, Bernhard. "Gallus Dressler, Praecepta musicae poëticae." *Geschichtsblätter für Stadt und Land Magdeburg* 49/50 (1914-1915): 213-50.

Erasmus of Höritz. "Musica." Rome, Bibliotheca Apostolica Vaticana, Reginensis lat. 1245.

Erasmus, Desiderius. *In Novum Testamentum annotationes*. Basle: Froben, 1535.

Euclid. *Elementa geometriae lat[ine] cum Campani annotationibus*. Venice: Erhardus Ratdolt, 1482.

Fenner, William. *A Treatise of the Affections, or, The Soules Pulse*. London: Printed by E. G. for I. Rothwell, 1641.

Ficino, Marsilio. *Opera omnia*. 2 vols. Basle: Henricpetrina, 1576; reprint, Turin: Erasmo, 1959.

———. See also Allen, Michael J. B. *supra*.

Finck, Hermann. *Practica musica, exempla variorum signorum, proportionum et canonum, iudicium de tonis, ac quaedam de arte suaviter et artificiose cantandi continens*. Wittenberg: haeredes Georgii Rhaw, 1556.

Fogliano, Lodovico. *De musica theorica*. Venice: Io. Antonius et Fratres de Sabio, 1529; reprint in Bibliotheca musica bononiensis, II/13, Bologna: Forni, 1970.

Fracastoro, Girolamo. *Opera omnia in unum proxime post illius mortem collecta*. 2d ed. Venice: Iuntas, 1574.

Gaffurio, Franchino. *De harmonia musicorum instrumentorum opus*. Milan: Gotardus Pontanus, 1518; reprint, Bologna: Forni, 1972; New York: Broude Bros., [1979].

———. *Practica musice*. Milan: Ioannes Petrus de Lomatio, 1496; reprint, New York: Broude Bros., 1979.

———. *Theorica musice*. Milan: Ioannes Petrus de Lomatio, 1492; reprint, New York: Broude Bros., 1967.

———. *Theoricum opus musice discipline*. Naples: Franciscus di Dino Florentinus, 1480; reprint in Musurgiana, vol. 15, ed. Cesarino Ruini, Lucca: Libreria musicale italiana, 1996.

———. *The Theory of Music*. Translated with introduction and annotations by Walter Kurt Kreyszig. Music Theory Translation Series. New Haven, CT: Yale University Press, 1993.

Galen. *On the Natural Faculties.* Translated by Arthur J. Brock. Loeb Classical Library. Cambridge: Harvard University Press, 1916.

———. *On the Passions and Errors of the Soul.* Translated by Paul W. Harkins, with an introduction by Walther Riese. Columbus: Ohio State University, Press, 1963.

Galilei, Galileo. *Le opere di Galileo Galilei.* Edizione nazionale sotto gli auspicii di Sua Maestà il re d'Italia. 20 vols. in 21. Ed. Antonio Favaro et al. Florence: Barbèra, 1890-1909.

———. *Il Saggiatore.* Rome: G. Mascardi, 1623.

———. *Two New Sciences, Including Centers of Gravity and Force of Percussion.* Translated with introduction and notes by Stillman Drake. Madison: University of Wisconsin Press, 1974.

Galilei, Vincenzo. *Dialogo della musica antica, et della moderna.* Florence: G. Marescotti, 1581.

———. *Dialogue on Ancient and Modern Music.* Translated with introduction and annotations by Claude V. Palisca. Music Theory Translation Series. New Haven, CT: Yale University Press, 2003.

———. "Discorso di Vincentio Galilei intorno all'uso dell'enharmonio, et di chi fusse autore del cromatico." In *Die Kontrapunkttraktate Vincenzo Galileis*, ed. Frieder Rempp, 163–80. Cologne: A. Volk, 1980.

———. "Discorso di Vincentio Galilei intorno all'uso delle dissonanze." In *Die Kontrapunkttraktate Vincenzo Galileis*, ed. Frieder Rempp, 77–162. Cologne: A. Volk, 1980.

———. *Discorso intorno all'opere di Messer Gioseffo Zarlino da Chioggia, et altri importanti particolari attenenti alla musica.* Florence: G. Marescotti, 1589; reprint in Collezione di trattati e musiche antiche edite in facsimile, Milan: Bollettino bibliografico musicale, 1933.

———. "Discorso particolare intorno all'unisono." In Claude V. Palisca, *The Florentine Camerata: Documentary Studies and Translations*, 198–207. Music Theory Translation Series. New Haven, CT: Yale University Press, 1989.

———. "Discorso particolare intorno alla diversità delle forme del Diapason." In Claude V. Palisca, *The Florentine Camerata: Documentary Studies and Translations*, 180–97. Music Theory Translation Series. New Haven, CT: Yale University Press, 1989.

———. "Dubbi intorno a quanto io ho detto all'uso dell'enharmonio, con la solutione di essi." In *Die Kontrapunkttraktate Vincenzo Galileis*, ed. Frieder Rempp, 181–84. Cologne: A. Volk, 1980.

——. *Fronimo dialogo.* Venice: G. Scotto, 1568.

——. "Il primo libro della prattica del contrapunto intorno all'uso delle consonanze." In *Die Kontrapunkttraktate Vincenzo Galileis,* ed. Frieder Rempp, 7–77. Cologne: A. Volk, 1980.

Gallicus, Johannes. *Ritus canendi.* Ed. Albert Seay. Critical Texts, no. 13. Colorado Springs: Colorado College Music Press, 1981.

Gasparini, Francesco. *L'armonico pratico al cimbalo* …. Venice: Antonio Bortoli, 1708.

——. *The Practical Harmonist at the Harpsichord.* Translated by Frank S. Stillings. Ed. David L. Burrows. Music Theory Translation Series. New Haven, CT: Yale School of Music, 1963.

Giacomini, Lorenzo. *Orationi e discorsi.* Florence: Sermartelli, 1597.

Glarean, Heinrich. *ΔΩΔΕΚΑΧΟΡΔΟΝ* [Dodecachordon]. Basle: Henrichus Petri, 1547; reprint, New York: Broude Bros., 1967.

Gravina, Gian-Vincenzo. *Opere scelte.* Milan: Società tipografica de' classici italiani, 1819.

Guido of Arezzo. *Guidonis Aretini Micrologus.* Ed. Jos. Smits van Waesberghe. Corpus scriptorum de musica, vol. 4. [Rome]: American Institute of Musicology, 1955.
See also Hucbald, Guido, and John *infra.*

Heinichen, Johann David. *Der General-Bass in der Composition.* Dresden: by the author, 1728.

Hilse, Walter. "The Treatises of Christoph Bernhard." *The Music Forum* 3 (1973): 31–196.

Hobbes, Thomas. *Humane Nature, or, The Fundamental Elements of Policie: Being a Discoverie of the Faculties, Acts, and Passions of the Soul of Man, from their Original Causes.* London: T. Newcomb for Fra: Bowman of Oxon, 1650.

Hucbald, Guido, and John On Music: Three Medieval Treatises. Translated by Warren Babb. Ed. and annotated by Claude V. Palisca. Music Theory Translation Series. New Haven, CT: Yale University Press, 1978.

Johannes Affligemensis. *De musica cum tonario.* Ed. Jos. Smits van Waesberghe. Corpus scriptorum de musica, vol. 1. [Rome]: American Institute of Musicology, 1950.
See also Hucbald, Guido, and John *supra.*

Jonson, Ben. *Ben Jonson.* 11 vols. Ed. C. H. Herford and Percy Simpson. Oxford: Clarendon, 1925–52.

Josquin Desprez. *Werken.* Ed. A. Smijers et al. 5 vols. in 55 parts. Amsterdam: Alsbach 1921–69.

Kepler, Johannes. *Harmonices mundi libri V.* Linz: Godefredus Tampachius, 1619.

Kircher, Athanasius. *Musurgia universalis sive ars magna consoni et dissoni in X libros digesta.* 2 vols. Rome: Corbelletti [vol. 1] and Grignani [vol. 2], 1650.

Lamy, Bernard. *L'art de bien parler.* Paris: Pralard, 1676.

Lanfranco, Giovanni. *Scintille di musica.* Brescia: Lodovico Britannico, 1533.

Lang, Franz. *Theatrum affectuum humanorum, sive, Considerationes morales ad scenam accommodatae: et in oratorio almae sodalitatis majoris B.V. Mariae ab angelo salutatae matris propitiae.* Munich: Mathias Riedl, 1717.

Lasso, Orlando di. *Moduli.* Paris: Le Roy & Ballard, 1577.

———. *Moduli.* Ed. Wolfgang Boetticher. Sämtliche Werke, neue Reihe, vol. 1. Kassel: Bärenreiter, 1956.

———. *Prophetiae Sibyllarum.* Ed. Reinhold Schlötterer. Sämtliche Werke, neue Reihe, vol. 21. Kassel: Bärenreiter, 1990.

———. *Sacrae cantiones quinque vocum.* Nuremberg: J. Montanus & U. Neuber, 1562.

———. *Sämtliche Werke.* Ed. Franz X. Haberl and A. Sandberger. 21 vols. Leipzig: Breitkopf & Härtel, 1894–1926.

Lecerf de la Viéville, Jean-Laurent. *Comparaison de la musique italienne et la musique françoise.* Brussels: Foppens, 1704; reprint of 1706 ed. in three parts, Geneva: Minkoff, 1972.

Lettere volgari di diversi nobilissimi huomini et eccellentissimi ingegni, scritte in diuerse materie. 3 vols. Venice: [Aldus], 1564.

Listenius, Nicolaus. *Musica.* Wittenberg: Georg Rhau, 1537.

———. *Rudimenta musicae.* Wittenberg: Georg Rhau, 1533.

Litchfield, Malcolm. "Giovanni Maria Artusi's *L'Artusi overo delle imprefettioni della moderna musica* (1600): A Translation and Commentary." M.A. thesis, Brigham Young University, 1987.

Locke, Matthew. *Melothesia: or Certain General Rules for Playing upon a Continued-Bass* .... London: J. Carr, 1673.

Lossius, Lucas. *Erotemata dialecticae et rhetoricae Philippi Melanchthonis et praeceptionum Erasmi Roterodami.* Frankfurt: P. Brub, 1552.

MacCurdy, Edward. *The Notebooks of Leonardo da Vinci.* 2 vols. New York: Reynal & Hitchcock, 1938.

Macrobius. *Commentary on the Dream of Scipio.* Translated with introduction and notes by William Harris Stahl. Records of Western Civilization. New York: Columbia University Press, 1952.

Marenghi, Gerardo. *Aristotele, Problemi di fonazione e di acustica.* Naples: Libreria scientifica editrice, 1962.

Masson, Charles. *Nouveau traité des regles pour la composition de la musique.* 2d ed. Paris: Ballard 1699; reprint with an introduction by Imogene Horsley, New York: Da Capo, 1967.

Mattheson, Johann. *Der vollkommene Capellmeister.* Hamburg: Christian Herold, 1739.

Mazzocchi, Domenico. *La catena d'Adone.* Venice: A. Vincenti, 1626.

Mei, Girolamo. "De modis." Rome, Bibliotheca Apostolica Vaticana, lat. 5323.

———. *De modis.* Ed. Eisuke Tsugami. Tokyo: Keiso Shobo, 1991.

———. "Della compositura delle parole." Florence, Biblioteca nazionale centrale, Magliabechianus VI/34.

Mercuriale, Girolamo. *Artis gymnasticae apvd antiqvos celeberrimae … libri sex.* Venice: Giunta, 1569.

Mersenne, Marin. *Correspondance du P. Marin Mersenne, religieux minime.* Publiée par Mme Paul Tannery. Ed. Cornélis de Waard. 17 vols. Paris: Presses universitaires de France and CNRS, 1932–88.

———. *Harmonicorum libri in quibus agitur de sonorum natura, causis, et effectibus ….* 2 parts. Paris: Guillaume Baudry, 1636.

———. *Harmonie universelle.* 8 parts. Paris: Cramoisy, 1636–37.

———. *Quaestiones celeberrimae in Genesim, cum accurata textus explicatione; in hoc volumine athei et deistae impugnantur et expugnantur, et Vulgata editio ab haereticorum calumniis vindicatur, Graecorum et Hebraeorum musica instauratur.* Paris: S. Cramoisy, 1623.

———. *La verité des sciences contre les sceptiques ou Pyrrhoniens.* Paris: Beauchesne et ses fils, 1932.

Missae tredecim quatuor vocum a praestantissimis artificribis compositae. Nuremberg: H. Grapheus, 1539.

Monteverdi, Claudio. *Lettere, dediche, e prefazioni.* Ed. Domenico De' Paoli. Contributi di musicologia. Rome: De Santis, 1973.

——. *Il quinto libro de' madrigali a cinque voci.* Venice: Ricciardo Amadino, 1605.

Monteverdi, Giulio Cesare. "Dichiaratione della Lettera stampata nel Quinto libro de suoi madrigali." In Claudio Monteverdi, *Scherzi musicali a tre voci, raccolti da Giulio Cesare Monteverde suo fratello.* Venice: Ricciardo Amadino, 1607.

More, Thomas. *Utopia.* Ed. E. Surtz, S. J. and J. H. Hexter. New Haven, CT: Yale University Press, 1965.

Morley, Thomas. *A Plaine and Easie Introduction to Practicall Musicke.* London: Peter Short, 1597.

Müller-Blattau, Joseph. *Die Kompositionslehre Heinrich Schützens in der Fassung seines Schülers Christoph Bernhard.* Leipzig: Breitkopf & Härtel, 1926; 2d ed., Kassel: Bärenreiter, 1963; 3d ed., Kassel: Bärenreiter, 1999.

Musica Enchiriadis and Scolica Enchiriadis. Translated with introduction and annotations by Raymond Erickson. Music Theory Translation Series. New Haven, CT: Yale University Press, 1995.

Musica et scolica enchiriadis una cum aliquibus tractatulis adiunctis. Ed. Hans Schmid. Bayerische Akademie der Wissenschaften, Veröffentlichungen der Musikhistorischen Kommission, vol. 3. Munich: Bayerische Akademie der Wissenschaften; C. H. Beck, 1981.

Najock, Dietmar, ed. *Anonyma de musica scripta Bellermanniana.* Leipzig : B. G. Teubner, 1975.
See also Bellermann, Friedrich *supra.*

——, ed. *Drei anonyme griechische Traktate über die Musik. Eine kommentierte Neuausgabe des Bellermannschen Anonymus.* Göttinger musikwissenschaftliche Arbeiten, vol. 2. Kassel: Bärenreiter, 1972.
See also Bellermann, Friedrich *supra.*

Nicomachus of Gerasa. *The Manual of Harmonics of Nicomachus the Pythagorean.* Translated with commentary by Flora R. Levin. Grand Rapids, MI: Phanes Press, 1994.

Nivers, Guillaume-Gabriel. *Traité de la composition de musique.* Paris: Ballard, 1667.

——. *Treatise on the Composition of Music.* Translated by Albert Cohen. Brooklyn: Institute of Medieaval Music, 1961.

North, Roger. *Musical Grammarian* (c. 1728). Ed. Hilda Andrews. London: Oxford University Press, 1925.

Odington, Walter. *Summa de speculatione musicae.* Ed. Frederick F. Hammond. Corpus scriptorum de musica, vol. 14. [Rome]: American Institute of Musicology, 1970.

Palestrina, Giovanni Pierluigi da. *Pope Marcellus Mass.* ed. Lewis Lockwood. Norton Critical Scores. New York: Norton, 1975.

Patrizi, Francesco. *Della Poetica, La deca disputata.* Ferrara: V. Baldini, 1586.

———. *Della poetica.* 3 vols. Ed. Danilo Aguzzi Barbagli. Florence: Palazzo Strozzi, 1969–71.

Penna, Lorenzo. *Li primi albori musicali per li principianti della musica figurata; distinti in tre libri* .... Bologna: Giacomo Monti, 1672.

Peri, Jacopo. *Le musiche sopra l'Euridice.* Florence: G. Marescotti, 1600.

Plato. *Omnia opera.* Trans. Marsilio Ficino. Basle: H. Frobenius et N. Eplacopius, 1532.

———. *Opera.* Trans. Marsilio Ficino. Venice: Bernardinus de Choris de Cremona et Simon de Luero, impensis Andree Toresani de Asula, 13 August 1491.

Playford, John. *An Introduction to the Skill of Musick.* 12th ed. In the Savoy: by the author, 1694; reprint, ed. Franklin B. Zimmerman, New York: Da Capo, 1972.

Pontio, Pietro. *Ragionamento di musica.* Parma: Erasmo Viotto, 1588; reprint in Documenta musicologica, I/XVI, Kassel: Bärenreiter, 1959.

Psellus, Michael. *Opus dilucidum in quatuor mathematicas disciplinas.* Venice: S. Sabio, 1532.

Ptolemy, Claudius. *Harmonics.* Translation and commentary by Jon Solomon. Mnemosyne supplementa, no. 203. Leiden: Brill, 2000.

Rameau, Jean-Philippe. *Nouveau systeme de musique théorique.* Paris: Jean-Baptiste-Christoph Ballard, 1726.

———. *Traité de l'harmonie réduite à ses principes naturels.* Paris: Jean-Baptiste-Christoph Ballard, 1722.

———. *Traité de l'harmonie réduite à ses principes naturels.* Paris: Jean-Baptiste-Christoph Ballard, 1722; reprint in *Complete Theoretical Writings,* vol. 1, ed. Erwin R. Jacobi, Miscellanea, vol. 3 [n.p.]: American Institute of Musicology, 1967.

Ramos de Pareja, Bartolomé. *Musica practica.* Bologna: Baltasar de Hiriberia, 1482.

———. *Musica practica*. Ed. Johannes Wolf. Publikationen der internationalen Musikgesellschaft, Beihefte, vol. 2. Leipzig: Breitkopf und Härtel, 1901.

Rinuccini, Ottavio. *L'Euridice*. Florence: Cosimo Giunti, 1600.

Rore, Cipriano de. *Opera omnia*. 8 vols. Foreword by Bernhard Meier. Corpus mensurabilis musicae, vol. 14 [n.p.]: American Institute of Musicology, 1956–97.

Rousseau, Jean. *Méthode claire, certaine et facile pour apprendre à chanter la musique sur les tons transposez comme sur les naturels*. Paris: by the author, 1683.

Sadoleto, Jacopo. *De liberis recte instituendis liber*. Venice: Io. Antonius et fratres de Sabio, sumptu et requisitione D. Melchioris Sessae, 1533.

———. *De pueris recte ac liberaliter instituendis*. Basle: Thomas Platterus, 1538.

Salinas, Francisco de. *De Musica libri Septem, in quibus eius doctrinae veritas tam quae ad Harmoniam, quam quae ad Rhythmum pertinet, iuxta sensus ac rationis iudicium ostenditur, et demonstratur*. Salamanca: Mathias Gastius, 1577.

Salutati, Coluccio. *De laboribus Herculis*. Ed. B. L. Ullman. Zurich: Thesaurus mundi, 1951.

Sauveur, Joseph. *Collected Writings on Musical Acoustics (Paris, 1700–1713)*. Ed. Rudolf Rasch. Facsimile Editions, Tuning and Temperament Library, no. 2. Utrecht: Diapason Press, 1984.

———. "Système général des intervalles des sons." In *Histoire de l'académie royale des sciences*, Année 1701; *Mémoires*, 2d ed., 349–56. Paris: Charles Etienne Hocherau, 1719.

Scacchi, Marco. *Breve discorso sopra la musica moderna*. Warsaw: Pietro Elert, 1649.

———. "Epistola ad Excellentissimum Dn. CS. Wernerum." In *Die musikalischen Stilbegriffe des 17. Jahrhunderts*, ed. Erich Katz, 83–89. Charlottenburg: Wilhelm Flagel, 1926.

Schmitz, Frauke. *Giulio Caccini, Nuove musiche (1602/1614): Texte und Musik*. Musikwissenschaftliche Studien, vol. 17. Pfaffenweiler: Centaurus, 1995.

Schreiber, Heinrich. *Ayn new kunstlich Buech*. Nuremberg: Stüchs, 1518.

Schütz, Heinrich. "Günstiger Leser." In *Musicalia ad chorum sacrum, das ist: Geistliche Chormusik ... erster Theil*, op. 11. Dresden: Johann Klemmens, 1648.

Spataro, Giovanni. *Errori de Franchino Gafurio da Lodi*. Bologna: Benedetto di Ettore Faelli, 12 January 1521.

Spiess, Meinrad. *Tractatus musicus compositorio-practicus*. Augsburg: Johan Jacob Lotter Erben, 1745.

Themistius. *In libros Aristoteles De anima paraphrasis; consilio et auctoritate Academiae litterarum regiae borussicae*. Ed. Richard Heinze. Berlin: Reimer, 1899.

——. *Paraphraseos de anima libri tres, interprete Hermolao Barbaro, nunc recens mendis non oscitanter repurgati, & accurata diligentia typis excusi*. Paris: P. Calvarin, 1535.

Tigrini, Orazio. *Il compendio della musica nel quale brevemente si tratta dell'arte del contrapunto, diviso in quatro libri*. Venice: Ricciardo Amadino, 1588.

Tinctoris, Johannes. *The Art of Counterpoint*. Translated by Albert Seay. Musicological Studies and Documents, no. 5. [Rome]: American Institute of Musicology, 1961.

——. "Liber de arte contrapuncti." In *Opera theoretica*, 3 vols. in 2, ed. Albert Seay, 2:11–157. Corpus scriptorum de musica, vol. 22. [Rome]: American Institute of Musicology, 1975-78.

Tiraboschi, Girolamo. *Biblioteca modenese*. 6 vols. Modena: Società tipografica, 1781–86.

Trissino, Giovanni Giorgio. *La quinta e la sesta divisione della poetica*. Venice: Andrea Arrivabene, 1562; reprint in Poetiken des Cinquecento, vol. 25, Munich: Fink, 1969.

——. "La quinta e la sesta divisione della poetica [ca. 1549]." In *Trattati di poetica e retorica del cinquecento*, ed. Bernard Weinberg, 2:7–90. 3 vols. Bari: G. Laterza e Figli, 1970–74.

Tyard, Ponthus de. *Solitaire second, ou Prose de la musique*. Lyon: Jean de Tournes, 1555.

——. *Solitaire second*. Ed. Cathy M. Yandell. Textes littéraires français. Geneva: Droz, 1980.

Ugolino of Orvieto. *Declaratio musicae disciplinae*. 3 vols. Ed. Albert Seay. Corpus scriptorum de musica, vol. 7. [Rome]: American Institute of Musicology, 1959–62.

Valgulio, Carlo. "Plutarchi Chaeronei philosophi clarissimi, Musica. Carlo Valgulio Brixiano interprete." In *Plutarchi Caeronei, philosophi, historicique clarissimi opuscula (quae quidem extant) omnia*, ff. 25v–32v. Basle: And. Cratandrus, 1530.

———. "The Proem on Plutarch's *Musica* to Titus Pyrrhinus." In Claude V. Palisca, *The Florentine Camerata: Documentary Studies and Translations*, 13–44. Music Theory Translation Series. New Haven, CT: Yale University Press, 1989.

———. *Prooemium in Musicam Plutarchi ad Titum Pyrrhinum*. Brescia: Angelus Britannicus, 1507.

Valla, Giorgio. *De expetendis et fugiendis rebus opus*. Venice: Aldus Romanus, 1501.

———. Ἐπιτομὴ λογικῆς. *G. Valla Placentino Interprete. Hoc in volumine hec continentur: Nicephori [Blemmidae] logica. G. Valla libellus de argumentis. Euclidis quartus decimus elementorum. Hypsiclis interpretatio eiusdem libri euclidis. Nicephorus [Gregoras] de astrolabo. Proclus de astrolabo. Aristarchi samii de magnitudinibus distantiis solis lune. Timeus de mundo. Cleonidis musica. Eusebii pamphili de quibudam theologicis ambiguitatibus. Cleomedes de mundo. Athenagore philosophi de resurrectione. Aristotelis de celo. Aristotelis magna ethica. Aristotelis ars poetica. Rhazes de pestilentia. Galenus de inequali distemperantia. Galenus de bono corporis habitu. Galenus de confirmatione corporis humani. Galenus de presagitura. Galenus de presagio. Galeni introductorium. Galenus de succidaneis. Alexander aphrodiseus de causis febrium. Pselus de victu humano.* Venice : Simon Bevilaqua, 1498.

Valla, Lorenzo. *De vero falsoque bono*. Cologne: Quentell, 1509.

———. *De voluptate ac vero bono*. Paris: Josse Badius, 1512.

———. *On Pleasure, De voluptate*. Translated by A. Kent Hieatt and Maristella de Panizza Lorch, with an introduction by Maristella de Panizza Lorch. New York: Albaris Books, 1977.

Varchi, Benedetto. *L'Hercolano*. Florence: Giunti, 1570.

Vettori, Piero. *Commentarii in primum librum Aristotelis de arte poetarum*. Florence: Haeredes B. Iuntae, 1560; 2d ed., Florence: officina Iuntarum, Bernardi filiorum, 1573.

Vicentino, Nicola. *Ancient Music Adapted to Modern Practice*. Translated with introduction and annotations by Maria Rika Maniates. Music Theory Translation Series. New Haven, CT: Yale University Press, 1996.

———. *L'Antica musica ridotta alla moderna prattica*. Rome: Antonio Barre, 1555; reprint in Documenta musicologica, I/17, Kassel: Bärenreiter, 1959.

——. *Opera omnia.* Ed. Henry W. Kaufmann. Corpus mensurabilis musicae, vol. 26. [n.p.]: American Institute of Musicology, 1963.

Vives, Juan Luis. *De anima et vita libri tres.* Basle: Winter, 1538.

——. *De anima et vita.* Ed. and translated by Mario Sancipriano. Università di Parma, Istituto di scienze religiose, Pensatori religiosi, vol. 9. Padua: Gregoriana, 1974.

Wallis, John. "[Of the Trembling of Consonant Strings]: Dr. Wallis's Letter to the Publisher Concerning a New Musical Discovery." *Philosophical Transactions* 12 (April 1677): 839–42.

Werckmeister, Andreas. *Hypomnemata musica oder Musicalisches Memorial.* Quedlinburg: T. P. Calvisius, 1697.

Willaert, Adrian. *Musica nova.* Venice: Antonio Gardane, 1559.

Wollick, Nicolaus. *Enchiridion musices.* Paris: Jean Petit and François Regnault, 1512.

Wright, Thomas. *The Passions of the Minde.* London: V. S. or W. B., 1601.

Zacconi, Lodovico. *Prattica di musica utile et necessaria si al compositore per comporre i canti suoi regolatamente, si anco al cantore per assicurarsi in tutte le cose cantabili. Divisa in quattro libri.* Venice: Girolamo Polo, 1592.

——. *Prattica di musica seconda parte. Divisa, e distinta in quattro libri.* Venice: Allesandro Vincenti, 1622.

Zarlino, Gioseffo. *The Art of Counterpoint: Part Three of* Le istitutioni harmoniche, *1558.* Translated by Guy Marco and Claude V. Palisca. Music Theory Translation Series. New Haven, CT: Yale University Press, 1968; reprint, New York: Norton, 1976; reprint, New York: Da Capo, 1983.

——. *Le Istitutioni harmoniche.* Venice, 1558.

——. *On the Modes.* Translated by Vered Cohen, with an introduction by Claude V. Palisca. Music Theory Translation Series. New Haven, CT: Yale University Press, 1983.

——. *Sopplimenti musicali.* Venice: Francesco de' Franceschi Sanese, 1588.

Secondary Sources

Agawu, Kofi. *Playing with Signs: A Semiotic Interpretation of Classic Music.* Princeton, NJ: Princeton University Press, 1991.

Allanbrook, Wye J. "Theorizing the Comic Surface." In *Music in the Mirror: Reflections on the History of Music Theory and Literature for the 21st Century,* ed. Andreas Giger and Thomas J. Mathiesen, 195–216.

Publications of the Center for the History of Music Theory and Literature, vol. 3. Lincoln: University of Nebraska Press, 2002.

Barbour, J. Murray. *Tuning and Temperament.* East Lansing: Michigan State College Press, 1953.

Barker, Andrew. *Greek Musical Writings.* Vol. 2, *Harmonic and Acoustic Theory.* Cambridge: Cambridge University Press, 1989.

Barnett, Gregory. "Tonal Organization in Seventeenth-Century Music Theory." In *The Cambridge History of Western Music Theory,* ed. Thomas Christensen, 407–55. Cambridge: Cambridge University Press, 2002.

Bartel, Dietrich. *Musica poetica: Musical-Rhetorical Figures in German Baroque Music.* Lincoln: University of Nebraska Press, 1997.

Bayreuther, Rainer. "Johannes Keplers musiktheoretisches Denken." *Musiktheorie* 19 (2004): 3–20.

Bloom, Harold. *The Anxiety of Influence: A Theory of Poetry.* New York: Oxford University Press, 1973.

Boccadoro, Brenno. "Éléments de grammaire mélancolique." *Acta musicologica* 76 (2004): 25–65.

———. *Ethos e varietas: Trasformazione qualitativa e metabole nella teoria armonica dell'antichità greca.* Historiae musicae cultores, vol. 93. Florence: Olschki, 2002.

Boetticher, Wolfgang. *Orlando di Lasso und seine Zeit, 1532–1594: Repertoire-Untersuchungen zur Musik der Spätrenaissance.* 2 vols. Quellenkataloge zur Musikgeschichte, vol. 27. Kassel: Bärenreiter, 1958; reprint, Wilhelmshaven: Florian Noetzel, Heinrichshofen, 1999.

Brandes, Heinz. *Studien zur musikalischen Figurenlehre im 16. Jahrhundert.* Berlin: Triltsch & Huther, 1935.

Brown, Howard Mayer. "Emulation, Competition, and Homage: Imitation and Theories of Imitation in the Renaissance." *Journal of the American Musicological Society* 35 (1982): 1–48.

Buelow, George J. "Johann Mattheson and the Invention of the *Affektenlehre.*" In *New Mattheson Studies,* ed. George J. Buelow and Hans Joachim Marx, 393–407. Cambridge: Cambridge University Press, 1983.

———. *Thorough-Bass Accompaniment According to Johann David Heinichen.* Rev. ed. Ann Arbor, MI; UMI Research Press, 1986; reprint, Lincoln: University of Nebraska Press, 1992.

Burkholder, J. Peter. "Rule-Breaking as a Rhetorical Sign." In *Festa musicologica: Essays in Honor of George J. Buelow*, ed. Thomas J. Mathiesen and Benito V. Rivera, 369–89. Stuyvesant, NY: Pendragon Press, 1995.

Butler, Gregory G. "Fugue and Rhetoric," *Journal of Music Theory* 21 (1977): 49–109.

Camenietzki, Carlos Ziller. "Baroque Science between the Old and the New World." Trans. Paula Findlen and Derrick Allums. In *Athanasius Kircher: The Last Man Who Kenw Everything*, ed. Paula Findlen, 311–28. New York: Routledge, 2004.

Campagnac, E. T., and K. Forbes. *Sadoleto on Education*. London: Oxford University Press, 1916.

Cannon, John T., and Sigalia Dostrovsky. *The Evolution of Dynamics: Vibration Theory from 1687 to 1742*. New York: Springer-Verlag, 1981.

Carapetyan, Armen. "The Concept of *Imitazione della natura* in the Sixteenth Century." *Journal of Renaissance and Baroque Music* (= *Musica disciplina*) 1 (1946): 47–67.

Carter, Tim. "Artusi, Monteverdi, and the Poetics of Modern Music." In *Musical Humanism and Its Legacy: Essays in Honor of Claude V. Palisca*, ed. Nancy Kovaleff Baker and Barbara Russano Hanning, 171–94. Festschrift Series, vol. 11. Stuyvesant, NY: Pendragon Press, 1992.

———. *Jacopo Peri (1561–1633); His Life and Works*. 2 vols. New York: Garland, 1989.

Chadwick, Henry. *Boethius: The Consolations of Music, Logic, Theology, and Philosophy*. Oxford: Clarendon Press, 1981.

Cohen, David E. "Notes, Scales, and Modes in the Earlier Middle Ages." In *The Cambridge History of Western Music Theory*, ed. Thomas Christensen, 307–63. Cambridge: Cambridge University Press, 2002.

Cohen, H. Floris. *Quantifying Music*. Dordrecht: D. Reidel Publishing Company, 1984.

Cornford, Francis M. *Plato's Cosmology: The Timaeus of Plato Translated with a Running Commentary*. London: Routledge & Kegan Paul; New York: Humanities Press, 1937.

Cowart, Georgia. *The Origins of Modern Musical Criticism: French and Italian Music, 1600–1750*. Studies in Musicology, vol. 38. Ann Arbor, MI: UMI Research Press, 1981.

Crombie, A. C. *Medieval and Early Modern Science.* 2 vols. 2d ed. Garden City, NY: Doubleday Anchor Books, 1959.

Damschroder, David, and David Russell Williams. *Music Theory from Zarlino to Schenker, A Bibliography and Guide.* Harmonologia, no. 5. Stuyvesant, NY: Pendragon Press, 1990.

della Corte, Andrea. *Drammi per musica dal Rinuccini allo Zeno.* 2 vols. Classici italiani. Turin: Unione Tipografico-Editrice Torinese, 1958.

Dilthey, Wilhelm. *Weltanschauung und Analyse des Menschen seit der Renaissance und Reformation.* Leipzig: B. G. Teubner, 1914.

Dostrovsky, Sigalia. "Early Vibration Theory: Physics and Music in the Seventeenth Century." *Archive for History of Exact Sciences* 14 (1975): 169–218

Duncan, David Allen. "Persuading the Affections: Rhetorical Theory and Mersenne's Advice to Harmonic Orators." In *French Musical Thought, 1600-1800,* ed. Georgia Cowart, 149–76. Studies in Music, vol. 105. Ann Arbor, Mich.: UMI Research Press, 1989.

Ehrmann, Sabine. "Marsilio Ficino und sein Einfluß auf die Musiktheorie." *Archiv für Musikwissenschaft* 18 (1991): 234–49.

Einstein, Alfred. *The Golden Age of the Madrigal.* New York: Schirmer, [1942].

Expert, Henry. *Les maîtres musiciens de la Renaissance française.* 23 vols. Paris: Leduc, 1894–1908.

Fabbri, Paolo, and Angelo Pompilio, eds. *Il Corago o vero alcune osservazioni per metter bene in scena le composizioni drammatiche.* Florence: Olschki, 1983.

Federhofer, Hellmut. "Christoph Bernhards Figurenlehre und die Dissonanz." *Die Musikforschung* 42 (1989): 110–27.

Feldman, Martha. *City Culture and the Madrigal at Venice.* Berkeley: University of California Press, 1995.

Fellerer, Karl Gustav. "Church Music and the Council of Trent." *Musical Quarterly* 39 (1953): 576–94.

Fenlon, Iain. *Music and Patronage in Sixteenth-Century Mantua.* 2 vols. Cambridge Studies in Music. Cambridge: Cambridge University Press, 1980.

Ferrari, Sante. *I tempi, la vita, le dottrine di Pietro d'Abano: Saggio storico-filosofico.* Atti della università di Genova, vol. 14. Genoa: R. Istituto Sordomuti, 1900.

Fideler, David. Introduction to *The Pythagorean Sourcebook and Library*. Comp. and trans. Kenneth Sylvan Guthrie, with additional translations by Thomas Taylor and Arthur Fairbanks, Jr. Grand Rapids, MI: Phanes Press, 1987.

Findlen, Paula, ed. *Athanasius Kircher: The Last Man Who Knew Everything*. New York: Routledge, 2004.

Fuller, Sarah. "Defending the *Dodecachordon*: Ideological Currents in Glarean's Modal Theory." *Journal of the American Musicological Society* 49 (1996): 191–224.

Gallo, F. Alberto. "Pronuntiatio: Ricerche sulla storia di un termine retorico-musicale," *Acta musicologica* 35 (1963): 38–46 and 172–74.

Gérold, Théodore. *L'art du chant en France au XVIIe siècle*. Publications de la Faculté des Lettres de l'Université de Strasbourg. Strasbourg: Faculté des lettres, 1921; reprint in Burt Franklin: Research and Source Works Series: Music History and Reference Series, vol. 3, New York: Burt Franklin, 1973.

Gingerich, Owen. *The Book Nobody Read: Chasing the Revolutions of Nicolaus Copernicus*. New York: Walker, 2004.

Godwin, Joscelyn. *Athanasius Kircher: A Renaissance Man and the Quest for Lost Knowledge*. London: Thames and Hudson, 1979.

———, ed. *Music, Mysticism and Magic: A Sourcebook*. London: Routledge & Kegan Paul, 1986.

Gouk, Penelope. "The Role of Harmonics in the Scientific Revolution." In *The Cambridge History of Western Music Theory*, ed. Thomas Christensen, 223–45. Cambridge: Cambridge University Press, 2002.

Green, Burdette, and David Butler. "From Acoustics to *Tonpsychologie*." In *The Cambridge History of Western Music Theory*, ed. Thomas Christensen, 246–71. Cambridge: Cambridge University Press, 2002.

Greer, David, ed. *Collected English Lutenist Partsongs*. 2 vols. Musica Britannica, vols. 53–54. London: Stainer & Bell, 1987–89.

Hanning, Barbara Russano. "Monteverdi's Three Genera: A Study in Terminology." In *Musical Humanism and Its Legacy*, ed. Nancy Kovaleff Baker and Barbara Russano Hanning, 145–70. Festschirft Series, vol. 11. Stuyvesant, NY: Pendragon Press, 1992.

———. *Of Poetry and Music's Power: Humanism and the Creation of Opera*. Studies in Musicology, vol. 13. Ann Arbor, MI: UMI Research Press, 1980.

Harrán, Don. "The Theorist Giovanni del Lago: A New View of the Man and His Writings." *Musica Disciplina* 27 (1973): 107–51.

———. "Toward a Rhetorical Code of Early Music Performance." *Journal of Musicology* 14 (1997): 19–42.

Judd, Cristle Collins. *Reading Renaissance Music Theory: Hearing with the Eyes*. Cambridge Studies in Music Theory and Analysis. Cambridge: Cambridge University Press, 2000.

———. "Renaissance Modal Theory." In *The Cambridge History of Western Music Theory*, ed. Thomas Christensen, 364–406. Cambridge: Cambridge University Press, 2002.

Keefer, Michael H. "Agrippa's Dilemma: Hermetic 'Rebirth' and the Ambivalences of *De vanitate* and *De occulta philosophia*." *Renaissance Quarterly* 41 (1988): 614–53.

Koestler, Arthur. *The Sleepwalkers: A History of Man's Changing Vision of the Universe*. London: Hutchinson, 1959.

Kristeller, Paul O. "The Modern System of the Arts: A Study in the History of Aesthetics (I)." *Journal of the History of Ideas* 12 (1951): 506.

Lang, Paul Henry. *Music in Western Civilization*. New York: Norton, 1941.

Lester, Joel. *Between Modes and Keys: German Theory, 1592–1802*. Stuyvesant, NY: Pendragon Press, 1989.

———. *Compositional Theory in the Eighteenth Century*. Cambridge: Harvard University Press, 1992.

———. "Rameau and Eighteenth-Century Harmonic Theory." In *The Cambridge History of Western Music Theory*, ed. Thomas Christensen, 753–77. Cambridge: Cambridge University Press, 2002.

Levin, Flora R. *The Harmonics of Nicomachus and the Pythagorean Tradition*. American Classical Studies, no. 1. University Park, PA: The American Philological Association, 1975.

Lindley, Mark. *Lutes, Viols and Temperaments*. Cambridge: Cambridge University Press, 1984.

Lo Sardo, Eugenio. "Kircher's Rome." In *Athanasius Kircher: The Last Man Who Kenw Everything*, ed. Paula Findlen, 51–62. New York: Routledge, 2004.

Lockwood, Lewis. "On 'Parody' as a Term and Concept." In *Aspects of Medieval and Renaissance Music: A Birthday Offering to Gustave Reese*, ed. Jan LaRue, 560–75. New York: Norton, 1966.

————. "A View of the Early Sixteenth-Century Parody Mass." In *Queen's College Department of Music Twenty-Fifth Anniversary Festschrift (1937-1962)*, ed. Albert Mell, 53-77. New York: Queen's College Press, 1964.

Lorch, Maristella de Panizza. *A Defense of Life: Lorenzo Valla's Theory of Pleasure*. Munich: Wilhem Fink, 1985.

Lowinsky, Edward E. "Humanism in the Music of the Renaissance." In *Proceedings of the Southeastern Institute of Medieval and Renaissance Studies, Summer, 1978*, ed. Frank Tirro, 87–220. Medieval and Renaissance Studies, vol. 9. Durham, NC: Duke University Press, 1982.

————. *Music in the Culture of the Renaissance and Other Essays*. 2 vols. Ed. Bonnie J. Blackburn. Chicago: University of Chicago Press, 1989.

Majno, Guido. *The Healing Hand: Man and Wound in the Ancient World*. Cambridge: Harvard University Press, 1975.

Maniates, Maria Rika. "Bottrigari versus Sigonio: On Vicentino and his Ancient Music Adapted to Modern Practice." In *Musical Humanism and Its Legacy: Essays in Honor of Claude V. Palisca*, ed. Nancy Kovaleff Baker and Barbara Russano Hanning, 79–107. Festschrift Series, vol. 11. Stuyvesant, NY: Pendragon Press, 1992.

————. "The Cavalier Ercole Bottrigari and His Brickbats: Prolegomena to the Defense of Don Nicola Vicentino against Messer Gandolfo Sigonio." In *Music Theory and the Exploration of the Past*, ed. Christopher Hatch and David W. Bernstein, 137–88. Chicago: University of Chicago Press, 1993.

Margolin, J.-C. *Erasme et la musique*. Paris: Vrin, 1965.

Mathiesen, Robert. "Magic in Slavia Orthodoxa: The Written Tradition." In *Byzantine Magic*, ed. Henry Maguire, 155–77. Washington, DC: Dumbarton Oaks Research Library and Collection, Harvard University Press, 1995.

Mathiesen, Thomas J. *Ancient Greek Music Theory: A Catalogue raisonné of Manuscripts*. Répertoire International des Sources Musicales, BXI. Munich: Henle, 1988.

————. *Apollo's Lyre: Greek Music and Music Theory in Antiquity and the Middle Ages*. Publications of the Center for the History of Music Theory and Literature, vol. 2. Lincoln: University of Nebraska Press, 1999.

————. "Mimesis." In *The New Grove Dictionary of Music and Musicians*, 2d ed., 29 vols., ed. Stanley Sadie, 16:709. London: Macmillan, 2001.

McClain, Ernest G. *The Pythagorean Plato: Prelude to the Song Itself.* Stony Brook, NY: Nicolas Hays, 1978.

Meier, Bernhard. *The Modes of Classical Vocal Polyphony: Described according to the sources, with revisions by the author.* Translated by Ellen S. Beebe. New York: Broude Bros., 1988.

———. *Die Tonarten des klassischen Vokalpolyphonie.* Utrecht: Oosthoek: Scheltema & Holkema, 1974.

Meyer-Kalkus, Reinhart. *Wollust und Grausamkeit: Affektenlehre und Affektdarstellung in Lohensteins Dramatik am Beispiel von 'Agrippina'.* Göttingen: Vandenhoeck & Ruprecht, 1986.

Murphy, James Jerome. *Renaissance Rhetoric: A Short-Title Catalogue of Works on Rhetorical Theory from the Beginning of Printing to A.D. 1700, with Special Attention to the Holdings of the Bodleian Library, Oxford: with a Select Basic Bibliography of Secondary Works on Renaissance Rhetoric.* New York: Garland, 1981.

Neubauer, John. *The Emancipation of Music from Language: Departure from Mimesis in Eighteenth-Century Aesthetics.* New Haven, CT: Yale University Press, 1986.

Nolan, Catherine. "Music Theory and Mathematics." In *The Cambridge History of Western Music Theory,* ed. Thomas Christensen, 272–304. Cambridge: Cambridge University Press, 2002.

Noreña, Carlos G. *Juan Luis Vives and the Emotions.* Carbondale: Southern Illinois University Press, 1989.

Ossi, Massimo. *Divining the Oracle: Monteverdi's Seconda Prattica.* Chicago: University of Chicago Press, 2003.

Owens, Jessie Ann. "Mode in the Madrigals of Cipriano de Rore." In *Altro Polo: Essays on Italian Music in the Cinquecento,* ed. Richard Charteris, 1–16. Sydney: Frederick May Foundation for Italian Studies, 1990.

Palisca, Claude V. "The Alterati of Florence, Pioneers in the Theory of Dramatic Music." In *New Looks at Italian Opera: Essays in Honor of Donald J. Grout,* ed. William W. Austin, 9–38. Ithaca, NY: Cornell University Press, 1968.

———. "Aria in Early Opera." In *Festa musicologica: Essays in Honor of George J. Buelow,* ed. Thomas J. Mathiesen and Benito V. Rivera, 257–69. Festschrift Series, vol. 14. Stuyvesant, NY: Pendragon Press, 1995.

——. "The Artusi-Monteverdi Controversy." In *The Monteverdi Companion*, ed. Denis Arnold and Nigel Fortune, 133–66. London: Faber and Faber, 1968.

——. "Bernardino Cirillo's Critique of Polyphonic Church Music of 1549: Its Background and Resonance." In *Music in Renaissance Cities and Courts: Studies in Honor of Lewis Lockwood*, ed. Jessie Ann Owens and Anthony M. Cummings, 281-92. Warren, MI: Harmonie Park Press, 1997.

——. "Boethius in the Renaissance." In *Music Theory and Its Sources: Antiquity and the Middle Ages*, ed. André Barbera, 259–80. Notre Dame, IN: University of Notre Dame Press, 1990.

——. "The First Performance of *Euridice*." In *Twenty-Fifth Anniversary Festschrift (1937–62)*, ed. Albert Mell, 1–23. New York: Queens College of the City University of New York, 1964.

——. "G. B. Doni, Musicological Activist and His *Lyra Barberina*." In *Modern Musical Scholarship*, ed. Edward Olleson, 180-205. Stocksfield: Oriel Press, 1980.

——. *G. B. Doni's* Lyra Barberina: *Commentary and Iconographical Study; Facsimile Edition with Critical Notes*. Miscellanee saggi convegni, vol. 18. Bologna: Antiquae musicae italicae studiosi, 1981; also issued as *Quadrivium* 22 (1981).

——. "Giovanni Battista Doni's Interpretation of the Greek Modal System." *Journal of Musicology* 15 (1997): 3-18.

——. *Girolamo Mei (1519–1594), Letters on Ancient and Modern Music to Vincenzo Galilei and Giovanni Bardi: A Study with Annotated Texts*. 2d ed. Musicological Studies and Documents, no. 3. Stuttgart: Hänssler-Verlag, American Institute of Musicology, 1977.

——. *Humanism in Italian Renaissance Musical Thought*. New Haven, CT: Yale University Press, 1985.

——. "Marco Scacchi's Defense of Modern Music (1649)." In *Words and Music: The Scholar's View, A Medley of Problems and Solutions Compiled in Honor of A. Tillman Merritt*, ed. Laurence Berman, 189–235. Cambridge: Department of Music, Harvard University, 1972.

——. "Mode Ethos in the Renaissance." In *Essays in Musicology: A Tribute to Alvin Johnson*, ed. Lewis Lockwood and Edward Roesner, 126–39. [Philadelphia, PA]: American Musicological Society, 1990.

———. "The Musica of Erasmus of Höritz." In *Aspects of Medieval and Renaissance Music: A Birthday Offering to Gustave Reese*, ed. Jan LaRue, 628–48. New York: Norton, 1966.

———. "Musical Asides in Cavalieri's Correspondence." *Musical Quarterly* 49 (1963): 339–55.

———. "Peri and the Theory of Recitative." *Studies in Music* 15 (1981): 51–61.

———. "The Science of Sound and Musical Practice." In *Science and the Arts in the Renaissance*, ed. John W. Shirley and F. David Hoeniger, 59–73. Washington, DC: The Folger Shakespeare Library; London and Toronto: Associated University Presses, 1985.

———. "Scientific Empiricism in Musical Thought." In *Seventeenth Century Science and the Arts*, ed. H. H. Rhys, 91–137. Princeton, N.J.: Princeton University Press, 1961.

———. *Studies in the History of Italian Music and Music Theory*. Oxford: Clarendon Press, 1994.

———. "*Ut oratoria musica*: The Rhetorical Basis of Musical Mannerism." In *The Meaning of Mannerism*, ed. Franklin W. Robinson and Stephen G. Nichols, Jr., 37–65. Hanover, NH: University Press of New England, 1972.

———. "Vincenzo Galiei and Some Links between 'Pseudo-Monody' and Monody." *Musical Quarterly* 46 (1960): 344–60.

———, ed. *The Norton Anthology of Western Music*. 4th ed. 2 vols. New York: Norton, 2001.

Palisca, Claude V., André Barbera, Jon Solomon, Calvin M. Bower, and Thomas J. Mathiesen. "The Ancient Harmoniai, Tonoi, and Octave Species in Theory and Practice." *Journal of Musicology* 3 (1984): 221–86.

Pöhlmann, Egert. *Denkmäler altgriechischer Musik*. Erlanger Beiträge zur Sprach- und Kunstwissenschaft, vol. 31. Nürnberg: Hans Carl, 1970.

Pöhlmann, Egert, and Martin L. West. *Documents of Ancient Greek Music: The Extant Melodies and Fragments*. Oxford: Clarendon Press, 2001.

Powers, Harold S. "Tonal Types and Modal Categories in Renaissance Polyphony." *Journal of the American Musicological Society* 34 (1981): 428–70

Quereau, Quentin W. "Sixteenth-Century Parody: An Approach to Analysis." *Journal of the American Musicological Society* 31 (Fall 1978): 407-41.

Ratner, Leonard G. *Classic Music: Expression, Form, and Style*. New York: Schirmer Books, 1980.

Reeve, Anne, and M. A. Screech. *Erasmus' Annotations on the New Testament: Acts–Romans–I and II Corinthians, Facsimile Edition of the Final Latin Text Published by Froben in Basle, 1535, with All Earlier Variants*. Studies in the History of Christian Thought, vol. 42. Leiden: Brill, 1990.

Reiner, Stuart. "Vi sono mol'altre mezz'arie ...." In *Studies in Music History: Essays for Oliver Strunk*, ed. Harold Powers, 241–58. Princeton, NJ: Princeton University Press, 1968; reprint, Westport, CT: Greenwood Press, 1980.

Reiss, Josef. "Jo. Bapt. Benedictus, De intervallis musicis." *Zeitschrift für Musikwissenschaft* 7 (1924–25): 13–20.

Rempp, Frieder. *Die Kontrapunkttraktate Vincenzo Galileis*. Cologne: A. Volk, 1980.

Restani, Donatella. *L'Itinerario di Girolamo Mei dalla «poetica» alla musica con un'appendice di testi*. Studi e testi per la storia della musica, vol. 7. Florence: Olschki, 1990.

Rosand, Ellen. *Opera in Seventeenth-Century Venice: The Creation of a Genre*. Berkeley: University of California Press, 1991.

Ruelle, Charles-Emile. "Rapports sur une mission littéraire et philologique en Espagne." *Archives des missions scientifiques et littéraires* III/2 (1875): 497–627.

Ruhnke, Martin. *Joachim Burmeister: Ein Beitrag zur Musiklehre um 1600*. Kassel: Bärenreiter, 1955.

Sachs, Curt. *Rhythm and Tempo: A Study in Music History*. New York: Norton, 1953.

Scharlau, Ulf. *Athanasius Kircher (1601-1680) als Musikschriftsteller: Ein Beitrag zur Musikanschauung des Barock*. Studien zur hessischen Musikgeschichte, vol. 2. Kassel: Bärenreiter, 1969.

Settle, Thomas B. "La rete degli esperimenti Galileiani." In *Galileo e la scienza sperimentale*, ed. Milla Baldo Ceolin, 11–62. Padua: Dipartimento di Fisica "Galileo Galilei," 1995.

Solerti, Angelo. *Le origini del melodramma: Testimonianze dei contemporanei*. Turin: Fratelli Bocca, 1903; reprint, Hildesheim: Olms, 1969.

Strunk's Source Readings in Music History. Rev. ed. Ed. Leo Treitler. New York: Norton, 1998.

Thoinan, Ernest. *Maugars, sa biographie.* Paris: A. Claudin, 1865.

Tomlinson, Gary. *Music in Renaissance Magic: Toward a Historiography of Others.* Chicago: University of Chicago Press, 1993.

Unger, Hans-Heinrich. *Die Beziehungen zwischen Musik und Rhetoric im 16.–18. Jahrhundert.* Würzburg: K. Triltsch, 1941.

Vickers, Brian. "Figures of Rhetoric/Figures of Music?" *Rhetorica* 2 (1984): 1–44.

———. *In Defence of Rhetoric.* Oxford: Clarendon, 1988.

Waite, William G. "Bernard Lamy, Rhetorician of the Passions." In *Studies in Eighteenth Century Music: A Tribute to Karl Geiringer on His Seventieth Birthday,* ed. H. C. Robbins Landon in collaboration with Roger E. Chapman, 388–96. London: George Allen and Unwin, 1970.

Walker, D. P. "The Aims of Baïf's Académie de poésie et de musique." *Journal of Renaissance and Baroque Music (= Musica disciplina)* 1 (1946): 91–100.

———. *Spiritual and Demonic Magic from Ficino to Campanella.* London: The Warburg Institute, 1958.

———. *Studies in Musical Science in the Late Renaissance.* London: The Warburg Institute; Leiden: E. J. Brill, 1978.

Weber, Edith. *Le concile de trente et la musique: De la réforme à la contre-réforme.* Paris: Honoré Champion, 1982.

Weinberg, Bernard. *A History of Literary Criticism in the Italian Renaissance.* 2 vols. Chicago: University of Chicago Press, 1961.

Wiering, Frans. "The Language of the Modes: Studies in the History of Polyphonic Modality." Ph.D. dissertation, University of Amsterdam, 1995.

Wilson, Blake M. "*Ut oratoria musica* in the Writings of Renaissance Music Theorists." In *Festa musicologica: Essays in Honor of George J. Buelow,* ed. Thomas J. Mathiesen and Benito V. Rivera, 341–68. Festschrift Series, vol. 14. Stuyvesant, NY: Pendragon Press, 1995.

Wolff, Christoph. *Der stile antico in der Musik Johann Sebastian Bachs: Studien zu Bachs Spätwerk.* Wiesbaden: Steiner, 1968.

Woodward, William Harrison. *Vittorino da Feltre and Other Humanist Educators.* Cambridge: Cambridge University Press, 1897; reprint in

Renaissance Society of America Reprint texts, no. 5, with a foreword by Eugene F. Rice Jr., Toronto: University of Toronto Press, 1996.

Ziino, Agostino. "Pietro della Valle e la `Musica erudita,' nuovi documenti." *Analecta musicologica* 4 (1967): 97–111.

Page numbers in italics indicate illustrations.

Lydian, 3; Phrygian, 3, 114; system of, 77, 90, 93

harmonic series, 38

harmonics, 34 (n. 17), 38, 61, 157, 159

harmony, 32, 114, 159, 162, 164–65, 168, 179, 198, 203, 214; block, 53, 120; Burmeister's ornaments of, 211–15; celestial, 16, 22; chordal, 53, 118, 148, 167–68; common-practice, 229; cosmic, 25–26; divine, 16, 22–23; full, 212; and mode, 82–84; and motion, 13, 22, 51, 58, 162, 168, 174, 193, 195, 218; of numbers, 10, 14; perfect, 37, 201; simple, 117; and the soul, 17, 26, 187, 195; of sounds, 15, 134; of the spheres, 15, 26; and text, 67, 69, 104–5, 117, 176, 223, 230; textbook, 229; theory of, 28, 97; of Tinctoris, 18; universal, 9, 13–28, 37, 133, 142; Werckmeister's view of, 26–27; of the world, 2, 10. *See also* consonance; dissonance; embellishment; imitation; mean; melody; nature; number; passions; religion; sound; tone

harp, 100

harpsichord, 92, 149; diharmonic and triharmonic, 95

Harrán, Don, 68 (n. 46), 206 (n. 6)

Hassler, Hans Leo, 107

Hatch, Christopher, 165 (n. 12)

hearing: *See* consonance; music; passions; sense; sound

Heinichen, Johann David (1683–1729), 205, 230; *Der General-*

Bass in der Composition, 205 (n. 4), 230 (n. 59)

Heinze, Richard, 140 (n. 28)

Heraclides Ponticus, 77 (and n. 16)

Herford, C. H., 124 (n. 41)

Hermelink, S., 215 (n. 32)

Hexter, J. H., 198 (n. 53)

Hieatt, A. Kent, 181 (n. 7)

Hilse, Walter, 175 (n. 36)

Hippocrates, 184

history: of Greek and modern music, 41; of Greek music, 8, 88; of Greek music theory, 88, 118; intellectual, 1–12; and irony, 225; literary, 113

Hitchcock, H. Wiley, 5 (n. 8), 109 (n. 3)

Hobbes, Thomas, 198; *Humane Nature*, 198 (n. 54)

Hoeniger, F. David, 133 (n. 8)

Hooke, Robert, 159

Horace, 12, 51, 186 (n. 21); *Ars poetica*, 51–52 (nn. 8–10)

horn, 100

Horsley, Imogene, 97 (n. 69)

humanism, 1, 54, 180; and polyphony, 86, 99–105; and revival of modes and genera, 71–98

humanist, 8, 30, 66, 68, 74, 88–89, 105, 107–8, 145, 181, 211; Florentine, 7; French, 120; literary, 32; musical, 32; Neapolitan, 215; Renaissance, 181; Swiss, 7. *See also* genus; instruction; mode

Huygens, Christiaan (1629–1695), 152, 159–60

hymn, 37, 58, 68, 76, 173; Greek, 1, 88

hypate, 137